Metropolitan Governance in the Federalist Americas

Metropolitan Governance in the Federalist Americas

Strategies for Equitable and Integrated Development

Edited by

Peter K. Spink, Peter M. Ward,
and Robert H. Wilson

University of Notre Dame Press

Notre Dame, Indiana

Manufactured in the United States of America

Library of Congress Cataloging-in-Publication Data

Metropolitan governance in the federalist Americas : strategies for equitable
and integrated development / edited by Peter K. Spink, Peter M. Ward, and
Robert H. Wilson.
    p.   cm.
  Includes bibliographical references and index.
  ISBN-13: 978-0-268-04141-0 (pbk. : alk. paper)
  ISBN-10: 0-268-04141-5 (pbk. : alk. paper)
  ISBN-13: 978-0-268-09266-5 (ebook)
  1. Metropolitan government—America.   2. Federal government—America.
3. Comparative government.   I. Spink, Peter.   II. Ward, Peter M., 1951–
III. Wilson, Robert Hines.
  JS1300.M47   2012
  320.8'5097—dc23

                                                                    2012030900

∞ *The paper in this book meets the guidelines for permanence and
durability of the Committee on Production Guidelines for
Book Longevity of the Council on Library Resources.*

CONTENTS

LIST OF TABLES

LIST OF FIGURES

International collaborative research projects can be productive, intellectually stimulating, and rewarding, despite the challenges brought by unique institutional and governmental contexts across countries as well as cultural and disciplinary perspectives. Such projects tend to have long gestation periods. This book takes its point of departure from a question arising in our earlier "companion" volume, *Governance in the Americas: Decentralization, Democracy, and Subnational Government in Brazil, Mexico, and the USA* (University of Notre Dame Press, 2008). In that work, we found that despite substantial, though uneven, progress in the effectiveness of state and local governments resulting from decentralization processes in each of the three countries, governance of the metropolitan areas in these countries had largely been bypassed. Given high rates of urbanization and the emergence of large metropolitan areas, we identified an apparent lacuna in efforts to improve the performance of the public sector. Three members of the *Governance in the Americas* project, Peter K. Spink, Peter M. Ward, and Robert H. Wilson, decided to pursue this question and initiated an assessment of metropolitan governance in all six federalist countries in the Americas, for reasons discussed in chapter 1. This book is the result.

We organized the effort through the institutional framework of our home institutions, the Lyndon Baines Johnson School of Public Affairs and the College of Liberal Arts at the University of Texas at Austin, and the Escola de Administracão de Empresas (EAESP) of the Fundacão Getulio Vargas in São Paulo (FGV/SP). We were joined by additional colleagues, Andrew Sancton (University of Western Ontario), David Myers (Pennsylvania State University), and Pedro Pírez (Centro de Estudios Avanzados, Buenos Aires), each with expertise in metropolitan governance in specific countries. Papers on each of the six countries were originally commissioned for a workshop held at the LBJ School of Public Affairs in April 2005 to explore the viability of and potential for the comparative project. Outside experts Tim Campbell (World Bank) and Alan Gilbert (University College London) provided commentary on the papers and on the proposed project. Sufficient promise was found to justify the elaboration of more formal research questions and a common methodology for the six country case studies that later formed the basis for comparative analysis by lead authors Spink, Ward, and Wilson.

We are grateful to the University of Notre Dame Press for their interest in the new project and for their support in undertaking a companion study to the earlier publication *Governance in the Americas.* Stephen Little at the University of Notre Dame Press joined the enterprise midway, and we wish to acknowledge his support in bringing the project to fruition. In addition, we are very appreciative of the three external reviews of earlier drafts of the manuscript solicited by the Press. These reviews led to a substantially stronger book.

Financial support for the project came from several sources: specifically, the Mike Hogg Professorship for Urban Policy; the Policy Research Institute of the LBJ School of Public Affairs; the C. B. Smith Sr. Centennial Chair in U.S.-Mexican Relations in the College of Liberal Arts at the University of Texas in Austin; and the EAESP/FGV research fund in Brazil. Wilson undertook the final round of revisions to the manuscript during his appointment as a Public Policy Scholar at the Woodrow Wilson International Center for Scholars, Washington, D.C.

We are grateful to many research assistants and graduate students who provided valuable assistance to the project along the way, including Aradhana Dhakal, of Brigham Young University, Brian M. Friedman, Hector Robles Pereiro, and Alejandra Ramírez Cuesta at the LBJ School and Fernando Burgos at FGV.

We also thank Shannon Halley, in Austin, for her expert editorial assistance as well as her preparation of the index; Jonathan Ogren for preparing the numerous figures for the book, and the Office of the President of the University of Texas at Austin for providing a subvention toward the costs of their preparation; and Cheryl McVay and Martha Harrison for providing further editorial and secretarial assistance.

Finally, we are grateful to the large number of scholars for their collective enthusiasm and willingness to debate how policy makers and citizens might best address the challenges of good government and democratic governance in large metropolitan areas in the Americas. Their interest greatly helped us to maintain our own commitment in completing this study.

Peter K. Spink
Peter M. Ward
Robert H. Wilson
June 2011

Chapter 1

The Challenge of Metropolitan
Governance in the Federal Americas

ROBERT H. WILSON, PETER M. WARD,
AND PETER K. SPINK

Night photographs of the earth taken from satellites reveal the extensive urban setting of much of the planet's contemporary population. Although vast expanses are still dark, a mass of pinpricks of light reveals the growing presence of large-scale human settlements. At the beginning of the twentieth century, relatively few pinpricks would have been observed, reflecting the limited adoption of electrification and relatively low levels of urbanization. But the relatively sparse pinpricks of yesteryear on many of the landmasses are now often joined together in larges splashes of light. These are the metropolitan areas of today's world, and their numbers and sizes are ever increasing, soon to house the majority of the world's population (United Nations Habitat 2008). Further, in many places the large splashes are themselves connected by ribbons of light, reflecting the presence of interurban corridors and transit routes. This book examines the effectiveness of the governance systems being constructed to meet the challenges of collective life in these large and complex metropolitan areas, with specific reference to those in the six federalist countries of the Americas: Argentina, Brazil, Canada, Mexico, the United States, and Venezuela.

1

The terms *metropolitan* and *governance* have multiple meanings, both in the academic literature and in the world of practice, and require clarification at the outset. For the purpose of discussion, *metropolitan* refers to large, contiguous, built-up areas, involving one or usually more local governmental jurisdictions, that have come about through processes of increased urbanization and often conurbation and that normally contain upwards of five hundred thousand inhabitants and often well over a million (Gilbert 1996, 1998). This operational definition is, however, but an opener for a broader discussion that we will introduce below, for *metropolitan* as a term has been around for many centuries and has gathered many meanings along the way.

The term *governance,* on the other hand, has a more recent provenance. Unlike *government,* which describes a set of institutional and organizational structures and authority, *governance* describes the process that defines the expectations of participation by different sectors of civil and political society in the decision-making process and in the clarification of roles for performance verification and assessment. This broadening of political life and public action beyond the classical institutional definition of government (Hirst 2000) can be seen as referring to the mechanisms through which different sets of social and institutional actors seek to arrive at "mutually satisfactory and binding decisions by negotiating with each other and cooperating in the implementation of these decisions" (Schmitter 2008, 14). As such, governance provides a more open and elastic framework for investigating the multiple dimensions of the relationship between governments and governed (a fuller discussion of the term *governance* follows below).

The growing relevance of governance in relationship to metropolitan issues (see, for example, Devas 2005; Klink 2008; Rodriguez-Acosta and Rosenbaum 2005; United Cities and Local Governments 2009) has resulted from several concerns that are relevant to this study. First is a concern about the ability of government to efficiently provide better-than-adequate public services in highly complex settings (Lynn, Heinrich, and Hill 2001). Second is a concern with the institutional dynamics of planning for and providing those services in areas where multiple governments are often required to coexist and create interjurisdictional mechanisms for coordination. Third is the concern with the capacity of existing political systems to effectively incorporate citizen preferences and participation in metropolitan-wide affairs. Increasingly, the practical answers to these concerns — how to guarantee service provision, interjurisdictional coordination, and citizen participation — seem to be requiring new forms of association and public action that lie beyond the stricter definitions of government. Finally, there is concern, given the high levels of socioeconomic and tax base disparities in the metropolis, about the extent to which emerging practices of governance effectively address issues of social equity and the question "Whose metropolis is it?" On these issues, we heed the often-forgotten warning given many years ago by Ostrom, Tiebout, and Warren (1961) not to assume that metropolitan arrangements are by definition dysfunctional and "pathological," or, to use some of today's headlines, set on a disaster course. However, we do feel, and this is the principal motivation for this study, that these different "polycentric political systems," to use the same authors' expression, are by no means as functional as they could be, especially in relation to the quality and sufficiency of government services and to guarantees of dignity and equity.

The central question that we set out to examine is: *Are current and emerging initiatives and structures of governance capable of meeting the challenges of collective life in these large and complex metropolitan areas?* In answering this we will also ask:

1. What are the key characteristics of the institutional and organizational forms and the policy issues addressed by these metropolitan initiatives?
2. What factors shape the emergence and dynamics of these metropolitan-based systems?
3. Are the initiatives offering opportunities for democratic governance and creating incentives for citizens to participate and thereby acquiring political legitimacy?

On the basis of the findings for individual countries, our final chapter seeks to answer the research questions. To foreshadow our conclusions, we find that the challenges of collective life are not being well served in existing governance systems. We attempt to explain this outcome and use our findings to identify several "paths forward" to meeting governance challenges in metropolitan areas.

The authors of this book bring different disciplinary perspectives to this project. They have worked together in previous studies in which the multi- and interdisciplinary approaches have, we believe, been adopted to good effect. In addition, in much of our previous work we have sought a comparative framework of analysis — comparing countries, cities, and regional governments to gain insights about common processes and to explain and account for differences (Wilson et al. 2008; Gilbert and Ward [1985] 2008). We are well aware that this approach can raise difficulties, especially in fields where individual disciplines have staked out prior claims for ownership or have developed preferred methods of analysis. Engaging with metropolitan issues cuts across many of these boundaries (from political science, through urban sociology, geography, and planning, to public administration, policy, and area studies), and while we have attempted to be as open as possible to different arguments, we are nevertheless unable to do justice to the literature in all the individual disciplines. Our focus on policy certainly helps to maintain these different lines of communication but can never be perfect.

Equally, in looking at the federalist Americas through case studies of six countries, we firmly position ourselves in the comparativist camp. For reasons that we do not profess to fully understand, in some circles it is becoming "fashionable" to be critical of comparative studies, arguing that such approaches are overly grounded in Western or North American conceptualization and experiences and that they are superficial and insufficiently nuanced in their treatment of complex local realities (see, for example, Kanai 2009; Le Galès 2009; Robinson 2006). In response we would point out that many of the structuralist intellectual challenges to modernization theory and functionalism actually came from social scientists embedded in specific regions (see, for example, Wood and Roberts 2004). Moreover, as scholars we are among the first to recognize and applaud the uniqueness of places and the need to think inductively out of such experience and differences. Here, as in our previous study on decentralization and federalism, we have taken great trouble to avoid any assumption that one country is in some way the root model for all others; our different metropolitan areas are indeed "ordinary cities" (Robinson 2006), and our analytical playing field is a level one. The comparative perspective, we find, allows researchers to explore the counterfactual and the reasons for divergence (and convergence), as well as to broaden analyses and conclusions beyond those of the minutiae of a particular case. In short, we make no apologies for our comparative approach and are somewhat surprised that others should eschew it so. Perhaps it is a matter of fashion; even so, we doubt that comparative studies will ever become passé.

While the federalist Americas are at the center of this study, we recognize that any study of metropolitan governance in a specific region will inevitably address questions that are present elsewhere (Stren and Cameroon 2005) and that even a study that uses the federalist institutional model as a baseline for comparison will also find itself in dialogue with scholars of metropolitan issues in unitary states. We will make connections with these broader and most recent debates in the final chapter, but in this book we hold to our original interest in federal polities for both theoretical and pragmatic reasons. Federalist systems create unique institutional environments in which state and provincial governments often play central roles in the metropolitan question, a topic elaborated below. And while we will also show that in some federalist countries state-local relations mirror those found in national unitary systems, the nature of federal constitutions and practices defines the institutional contexts of state and provincial governments and justifies our limiting of cases to federalist countries. On pragmatic grounds, the large number of metropolitan areas in the federalist countries in the Americas with very significant proportions of each country's population suggest that citizens who live in these large and complex urban centers are probably asking themselves questions about social justice, dignity, and economic inclusion. Attempting to find some answers to these concerns from within the practical possibilities of the region seems at least a good place to start.

What Is a Metropolis?

"A large, contiguous and built-up area, involving one or usually more local jurisdictions, that has come about through processes of increased urbanization and often conurbation, containing normally from upwards of five hundred thousand inhabitants and often well over a million," may seem a very cumbersome way to describe a metropolitan area. Indeed, it could well be asked why anyone should even bother to define *metropolitan,* for since epic visualizations such as Fritz Lang's 1927 film *Metropolis,* everybody seems to know what the term means; it has become part of everyday life. Or so it would seem from the academic literature and government reports on metropolitan questions. Most academics, planners, and political debaters just pick up the term and use it. This may be workable if discussion is taking place within the context and focus of a single-country framework where everybody shares a cultural, historical, and institutional understanding and therefore can assume that each knows what the other means. It is more problematic, however, in situations where meanings can vary considerably. Here, not being clear about how different versions of *metropolitan* are constructed in specific historical, social, and institutional processes can lead not only to invalid conclusions but, even worse, to inadequate propositions and ineffective investment decisions by international agencies, many of which are highly involved in urban issues.

Most planners and academics from the urban and social sciences use the term *metropolitan* to refer to the large splashes of light that we mentioned in the opening paragraph of this chapter, the large urban and interurban sprawls. Geographer Jean Gottman gave the name *Megalopolis* (1961) to the increasingly dense sprawl growing between Boston and Washington, D.C., on the northeastern U.S. seaboard. International agencies, when discussing how Latin America is becoming increasingly urban, will often choose photographs of houses crammed up on top of each other in places like Mexico City or São Paulo that comprise a population of over twenty million inhabitants. Yet beyond these more generic descriptions, the term has had many different and interweaving layers of meaning.

Official statistical agencies are providers of one layer of "metro meanings." Canada has Census Metropolitan Areas; the United States, Metropolitan Statistical Areas; and Mexico, metropolitan and conurbation statistics. Brazil, Argentina, and Caracas, Venezuela, all gather statistics on metropolitan areas. Here, as Frey et al. (2004) point out, the emphasis is not on political or jurisdictional characteristics but on an "economically and socially linked collection of large and small communities." Recently in the United States a new terminology and a broadening of the definition of *metropolitan* has led to the creation of "micropolitan statistical areas," which consist of one or more counties centered on a contiguous urban area with a core area population between ten thousand and fifty thousand people. At a stroke this has increased from 20 to 40 percent the territorial coverage of the U.S. that falls within areas that are economically and socially linked to an urban core. In contrast, less than 2 percent of Brazil's territory is covered by its designated metropolitan regions.

Businesspeople often join planners and technical staff in thinking about the term *metropolitan,* not least since these large contiguous areas are very visible examples of market opportunities. Certainly service providers for large urban conurbations, where supplies have to be shifted and stocked, have good reason to think and plan in larger spatial metropolitan terms, as does the state when public-level services are regionalized on epidemiological or population grounds. In the specific case of the United States, being in a metro area can also, as Frey et al. (2004) argue, bring new incentives for economic development merely through the rebranding of many small counties and towns of former "rural" America as "metro-something." Being metro-something represents another layer of meaning, and one that is not always seen positively, as we will see as we move from country to country.

Curiously, although the term *metropolitan* is widely used in government statistical agencies, only in Brazil is it used to refer to territorial regions in constitutional terms. In the other countries considered here (Argentina, Canada, Mexico, United States, and Venezuela) metropolitan areas may have some laws and institutions of their own and often agencies with *metropolitan* in the title, but they do not form part of the formal federal constitutional architecture.

Further layers of metro meaning in everyday life can be found in newspapers that have a metropolitan section, but here the term can stand for anything from the local affairs of small towns to the midrange issues of large conurbations. *Metropolitan* can carry hints of cultural centrality, indicating where significant events, art galleries, and major museums are to be found and, in the case of New York, also sometimes naming them. Even though London has its Tube, France has given the world its favorite expression for an underground railway, "le Metropolitain" (referred to universally as "le Metro"), which has been adopted in a number of other cities from Mexico City to Washington, D.C. London got its chance to contribute to the widening web of meanings with the creation, by the then home secretary Robert Peel, of the Metropolitan Police Bill of 1829—legislation that still holds today. Washington, D.C., followed suit with the founding of its Metropolitan Police Department in 1861. In marked contrast to the use of this more urban and interjurisdictional notion of *metropolitan* in policing, both the cities of São Paulo and Rio de Janeiro recently created their own municipal and solely intrajurisdictional police force with the title of Guarda Civil Metropolitana (Metropolitan Civil Guard).

If, on the one hand, the lexicon of metro meanings in English basically refers to a technical or descriptive frame of activity, other languages have advanced in other directions that have less to do with descriptors and more to do with power. In early Greek, *metropolis* meant the mother city (*metra*-[womb]-*polis*), a word adapted into Latin to mean the capital of a province. Mainland France remains today Metropolitan France in relation to its overseas territories, and in early Brazil metropolitan authority was an expression used not only in relation to Lisbon but also, more explicitly, in relation to religious authority. The use of *metropolitan* for geographical and hierarchical organization was widespread in the Catholic Church, where the metropolitan bishop would oversee religious activity over a wide area from his seat in (usually) the capital or other significant

European center. Even today, the Curia Metropolitana of São Paulo continues to look out over the surrounding state.

By invoking such multiple and sometimes vague meanings so early in the volume we may be opening a Pandora's box, but our aim in doing so is to make clear at the outset that we are not proposing to order metro meanings in any specific way or even to submit them to a single academic definition. Neither do we wish to suggest that similar processes are present in each of our cases. However, we do wish to suggest that the subtle, and at times not so subtle, interplay between differently situated ways of talking and thinking about the concept of the metropolis may well help to clarify the background to Lefèvre's (1998) observation that in general the top-down institutional reform of metropolitan areas seems to have failed in the principal Western countries and is being replaced by a bottom-up governance approach. Equally we think that a comment by Rodriguez-Acosta and Rosenbaum (2005, 305) in their survey of Buenos Aires, Santiago, Lima, Santa Fé de Bogotá, São Paulo, Mexico City, and San Salvador may provide an important clue to understanding at least part of the inadequacy of metropolitan governance in Latin America: "In virtually no instance has it been possible to overcome the complexities of multiple jurisdictions, high levels of inequality and extensive political conflict, to address these matters through united government action." A similar conclusion has emerged in a recent Inter-American Development Bank study (Rojas, Cuadrado-Roura, and Guell 2008). Thus we begin our country-based study of the different attempts to meet the challenge of metropolitan governance in the federalist Americas with skepticism about the utility of the term *metropolitan* as a simple and problem-free common denominator.

METROPOLITAN GROWTH IN THE AMERICAS

Urbanization Patterns and Metropolitan Growth: From Argentina to Mexico

The dynamics of urbanization in the Americas have varied substantially by subregions (Hardoy 1972), and there is ample evidence to argue that the pre-Colombian period had many large urban centers. Certainly at the time of colonization there were large and complex cities in Cuzco and Tenochititlán (Mexico City). In what is today Latin America, the connections with the Iberian peninsula began to produce new settlements and new dynamics of urban growth. Town plans were drawn up in Lisbon and Madrid, and church architects were sent out to provide the growing centers with the buildings necessary to accommodate the many new souls that were being drawn into the pastoral fold. Given that the economic histories of the regions would take different routes, especially in relation to later industrialization, patterns of urbanization were also different.

While there were several significant-sized centers and emerging metropolitan areas throughout the Americas at the beginning of the twentieth century, urbanization, and specifically metropolitanization, has been largely a product of the past one hundred years. In Latin America these processes have been even more recent. Even though several colonial and postcolonial cities in Latin America and Mexico were large by any standards—both Rio de Janeiro and Buenos Aires contained nearly 700,000 people by the late 1890s, and Mexico City had around 350,000 inhabitants at the end of that century—the more rapid and dramatic phases of Latin American urban growth did not really begin until the 1920s in the Southern Cone and until the 1950s in much of the rest of the region. These early cities were often labeled "primate" (Harris 1971), a reference to the situation in which a single city dominated the urban structure of the country and contained a disproportionately large share of the country's urban population. In this respect Buenos Aires and Santiago were classic examples, with around 43 percent of their total national (urban) populations respectively in 1950, and Mexico City at that time contained around a quarter of Mexico's total urban population. Other cities such as Rio de Janeiro, which held some 19 percent of Brazil's population, were not primate in structure but shared many of their primate sister city attributes (Harris 1971, 179).

Urbanization generally quickened throughout Latin America from the 1950s onwards, with growth rates of between 3 to 5 percent per annum being commonplace. Starting in the Southern Cone countries and regions, rapid urbanization spread through the rest of the southern continent and Mexico by midcentury, arriving somewhat later to the Central American countries. The general trend was growth fueled by migration from provinces to cities and by high natural growth rates among usually young and positively selected migrants with relatively high skills and education levels. Growth was fueled by a new economic model being proposed by the UN Economic Commission for Latin America and the Caribbean (ECLAC/CEPAL) in Santiago, Chile, fostering import-substituting industrialization (ISI) and inward-oriented growth strategies. As the name implies, this industrialization platform was designed to meet the demand from national markets and later also the local regional common markets. ISI generated large numbers of formal sector (but low-paid) jobs, and this, above all else, was what accelerated migration into the cities. Women, too, while less likely to be employed in the formal sector industries, found informal service sector jobs, especially in domestic service, from the 1950s through the 1980s.

In the last two decades of the twentieth century, further changes began to occur. Important shifts in urbanization took place associated with growing concerns over the extremely large absolute city sizes: rising negative externalities allegedly associated with large city size (pollution, transportation, servicing); a slowdown in the capacity of the ISI model to generate growth and to sustain high levels of formal job creation (albeit low-wage); and an emerging social unrest born of rising poverty levels. Financial crises from the 1980s onwards forced governments to undertake structural adjustment programs to reduce public expenditures and to reorient their economies away from the interior markets toward export-oriented growth. At first not all Latin American countries pursued the switch, but those that did — Chile, Brazil, and Mexico — were forced to find ways to cushion or offset the impacts of restructuring. But also by the 1980s winds of democratic change (later referred to as "third-wave democracy"; Hagopian and Mainwaring 2005) were strongly blowing across the region as military regime after military regime succumbed to more plural and competitively elected governmental structures. The demise of overarching centralized decision making vested in authoritarian governments, coupled with the rising influence of elected regional and local governments, strengthened the incentives for cities to pursue their own growth strategies, but now relatively unfettered by the center.

This dramatic political and economic change dovetailed with other emerging shifts, namely the move toward the stimulation of growth of "intermediate"-sized cities to produce for the export market, and a decentralization of power and resources to regional and local governments. Often guided by multilateral organizations such as the International Monetary Fund and the World Bank, decentralization led at times to what was termed a "polarization reversal," in which the promotion of subsidiary centers took place at the cost of the metropolitan trend (Townroe and Keene 1984). However, even with these broader patterns of secondary growth, the large metropolitan areas have persisted. Metropolitan areas can be found throughout the Americas, thirty-four of them have populations of over three million, and six of them belong to the "megacities" category (over ten million population as defined by some authors and in the Megacities Project, www.megacitiesproject.org). In this volume we deliberately do not try to insert our analyses into the megacities literature, even though a number of metropolitan areas across four of the federalist Americas would qualify by the population threshold of more than ten million. This is not because we have any issue with the concept of megacity per se, though the population threshold required to constitute one has generally been rather loosely defined and though authors often appear to adopt a definition that allows them to accommodate the cities in which they have a particular interest. More important is that our study seeks primarily to address questions of governance, organization, and administrative complexity in metropolitan areas across our countries as a whole and not the very specific problems and grassroots innovations related to the extensive scale and size of individual megacities. For this reason also we think it would be misleading to make more detailed reference to this different, though interesting, body of work (Gilbert 1996; Jones and Douglass 2008). Most of the metropolitan areas discussed in this volume would not meet the population criterion of a megacity (no matter where the minimum threshold was drawn: at three, five, or ten million), yet all have much to contribute to our cross-country comparisons.

Although the overall pattern of the last hundred or so years in Latin America is one of increased urbanization, it is important to avoid the assumption of a homogeneous model of urban life (see table 1.1). Many of Latin America's so-called urban inhabitants still live in smaller-sized municipalities and villages where daily life is distinctly rural or rural-urban, with its accompanying social and economic problems, opportunities, cultural patterns, and questions of governance. Drawing attention, as we do, to the metropolitan question does not mean that we see the future of Latin America as one big ribbon of light from the Magellan Straits to the Rio Grande. Indeed, an important challenge for future studies will be to examine how policy makers will respond to new settlements of residential populations not wishing to be absorbed in the large contiguous and highly built-up areas on which we will be focusing.

Urbanization Patterns and Metropolitan Growth: Canada and the United States

While colonial governments throughout the Americas played a key part in early urban affairs, government has generally had a much greater role in shaping the process of twentieth-century urbanization in Canada and the United States than in Latin America (for the case of the United States,

Table 1.1. Urban Population in the Americas

Region/ Country	% Urban Population			
	1975	*1990*	*2005*	*2015*
North America	73.8	75.4	80.7	83.4
Canada	75.6	76.6	80.1	81.2
Mexico	62.8	71.4	76.3	79.3
United States	73.7	75.3	80.8	83.6
Central America	57.1	64.9	70.4	73.5
South America	63.6	74.1	82.1	85.5
Argentina	81	87	91.4	93.2
Brazil	60.8	73.9	84.2	88.2
Venezuela	75.8	84.3	91.9	94.4

Source: United Nations Population Division (2009).

see Elazar 1987). By design Canada has always been primarily an urban nation, even though much of its wealth is built upon agrarian and mineral production. Traditionally internal migration was east to west along the forty-ninth parallel and the St. Lawrence Seaway, forming the initial colonial entrepôt cities—Quebec, Montreal, Halifax, and St. Johns. Later, commercial interests superseded those of the imperial powers and led to the expansion of regional commercial centers tied to extended transportation networks of railroads, which fueled the industrialization and the growth of the major central Canadian cities during the latter part of the nineteenth century—most notably Montréal and Toronto.

The 1940–70s period saw a rapid expansion of population through migration into Canada, mostly into the major cities, including those of the interior, such as Calgary and Edmonton, and the Pacific West (Vancouver), creating four principal urban regions: the "Golden Horseshoe" in southern Ontario, which contains over one-quarter of Canada's total population; Montreal and its hinterland; the Calgary-Edmonton corridor; and the lower mainland and Southern Vancouver Island in British Columbia. Fifty-one percent of Canada's population lived in these four metropolitan regions in 2001.

While initial growth was in the central cities, since the 1940s Canada has suburbanized, with its principal growth rates occurring in new suburban areas and in the periurban hinterland ("exurbia"). Canadian municipalities do not have legal standing in the constitution, and while they do have considerable autonomy their powers and responsibilities are firmly controlled by, and subject to, provincial governments. This pattern of metropolitan growth differs considerably from that of the United States in three respects (Collin and Tomás 2004). First, Canadian provincial governments have sought to reduce the fragmentation of metropolitan areas into separate municipalities. Second, and closely linked, the "home rule" protections of local government boundaries that are widespread in the United States do not exist in Canada. Third, city regions are less polarized in terms of differences in social, ethnic, and economic conditions between the central city area and beyond. Thus urban growth in Canada needs to be seen as a result of, if not an anticipated shaping of possibilities, at least some level of constant debate. Today, including Calgary and Edmonton (both of which have passed the one-million population threshold since 2001), Canada has six metropolitan areas with one million or more inhabitants, the largest being Toronto with just over four million. Despite their lack of legal recognition and strength, Canadian municipalities do enjoy considerable fiscal and financial autonomy, not least because almost 85 percent of revenues are generated locally.

In the United States it was not until the 1920s that more than half the population lived in cities. Indeed only in the latter part of the nineteenth century did urbanization begin in earnest, with industrialization primarily in the Northeast and spreading across the Midwest, reinforced by the expansion of the railroad network, with railheads fostering growth of cities like Chicago. The big cities of that era were New York, Boston, Philadelphia, and Chicago, later joined by large cities arising in the West (San Francisco and Los Angeles). After the Second World War, these cities expanded further, but now different changes were under way that would begin to recast the metropolitan areas of the United States.

The first was rapid suburbanization and flight of the growing middle class to the suburbs, leaving the old city cores with vestige (often poor) populations, industrial decline, and dereliction. Thus a new metropolitan structure began to emerge built around new economic activities leading to job creation, the development of suburban shopping malls, and large new tracts of residential development. The second change was a shift away from the traditional urban areas of the Northeast and Midwest (the "Frostbelt") to high-amenity growth spots in the "Sunbelt" of the South and West (Atlanta, Florida, Texas, and Arizona). As a result, many of the earlier industrial cities have lost population since 1950. Detroit, for example, lost nearly half its population, while cities such as Pittsburgh and Cleveland lost more than 10 percent, and many others are also shrinking, albeit not quite so dramatically, even though the suburban population surrounding these cities has frequently grown. The new-growth cities have been successful in attracting new "footloose" industries that need not locate according to the old transportation-hub and agglomeration rationales but are satisfied with transport by highways and air freight. Scholars have referred to this process as "counterurbanization," since it led to a shift in urbanization from the Northeast toward the South and West, where dramatic growth occurred from the 1960s onwards.

Since the 1990s these trends and patterns have shifted yet again. The historic trends of declining population and increasing racial/ethnic segregation in city centers appear to have been arrested. Many cities are seeking to fill the "doughnut" hole of the old derelict and vacated downtown and to engage in widespread restructuring of the older "first suburbs" by bringing in new "smart" growth, services, and residential opportunities (Puentes and Warren 2006). While these cities invariably continue to grow, today it is the newer, smaller metropolitan areas that are showing a more dramatic spike in their urban growth rates. These cities and even some larger metropolitan areas such as Houston, Dallas, Las Vegas, and Raleigh-Durham are becoming the new "gateway" entry and jumping-off points for immigration into the United States (Rogers 2006, 287).

Common Features of Metropolitan Growth in the Americas

Notwithstanding the variation in metropolitan expansion patterns outlined above, a number of common features associated with metropolitan growth emerge. First, absolute demographic growth and the spatial expansion associated with suburbanization have meant that in most metropolitan areas the original built-up area has expanded beyond its original boundaries into adjacent jurisdictions. As we shall observe throughout the case studies, it is increasingly common for large urban areas of a half million or more to span more than one jurisdiction: more often than not they encompass several municipalities or borough equivalents, and occasionally they embrace several dozen separate jurisdictions spread across two or more states and provinces (as our cases of Mexico City and Buenos Aires amply demonstrate). In some cases, such as those along the U.S.-Mexico and U.S.-Canadian borders, conurbations are even cross-national in configuration.

A second feature common to many of these metropolitan areas is a demographic slowdown—especially in the very large ones that grew rapidly during industrialization in the late nineteenth century and the first half of the twentieth century in the United States and Canada, or in the second half in the case of Latin America. This slowdown is generating profound changes in metropolitan population structures that require new — and spatially differentiated — policy approaches. Governments seek to cope with aging and vestige populations in inner cities of the United States and Canada, while their Latin American counterparts are learning to expand their capacity to absorb young to middle-aged populations and also to anticipate an aging population structure early in the new millennium (Ward 1998b). Only in the smaller metropolitan regions targeted for industrial growth are high growth rates being sustained, but even there the recent economic events of the second half of 2008 must lead to questions about long-term stability.

Third, migration patterns are changing, with metropolitan core areas no longer the target reception area for national migration flows. Indeed, some metropolitan areas have experienced absolute population loss (at least in their inner-city areas) and have high-priority needs for policies to cope with urban redevelopment and rehabilitation in both the inner-city and inner-ring (former suburban) parts of the city. To the extent that there is continuing in-migration to the periphery and periurban areas of metropolitan centers, this is further reshaping the parameters and scale of economic and demographic change. Indeed, the "hot spots" of metropolitan growth today may be not in the built-up area itself, but instead in surrounding periurban and semirural hinterlands (Aguilar and Ward 2003).

Fourth, in a number of ways cities have always been heterogeneous: ethnically, culturally, and socioeconomically, as well as in terms of labor market structure and employment opportunities and varied and complex land use patterns. But to the extent that there is quantum increase in absolute size, and that several formerly discrete and separate centers find themselves linked into a single area, so, too, will heterogeneity increase. Given that they are often dynamic economic centers, metropolitan areas are crucibles of both wealth creation and income inequality and disparities. A fifth change taking place — or, more strictly speaking, common experience — is in the nature of global engagement. Metropolitan areas — especially the larger ones — were once the interlocutors with the external world, even under periods of economic protection and import-substituting industrialization. But under globalization and economic liberalization the role of metropolitan areas has altered markedly: production activities are increasingly moving to smaller urban areas or offshore and the new metropolitan centers are becoming foci for services, irrespective of whether they are "world" or regional cities (Friedmann 1995; Knox and Taylor

1995). Attempts to rank or locate large cities within this global system often neglect the ways in which territorial organization is also being rescaled (Brenner 2003, 2004), and new intermediary dynamics are making the global local interface more complex as a new generation of secondary-city mayors learn the lessons of their big-city predecessors.

The global economic crisis that began in the second half of 2008 is still working its way through metropolitan regions, and, leaving aside the initial and immediate impacts on the financial service industries, the current situation of economic distress and restructuring is one of far more doubts than certainties. However, in the multijurisdictional settings that we describe in the chapters on specific countries, pressures for competitiveness will arise, as will the need to support many people who will find themselves economically vulnerable from one day to the next. Here again the question of governance across regions and jurisdictional boundaries will arise, as Newman (2000) found in Europe.

GOVERNANCE AND INSTITUTIONS

The Democratic Backdrop to Metropolitan Governance

As we have begun to outline, several imperatives drive the search for a new metropolitan governance architecture, including the growth and expansion of urban areas, globalization, decentralization, and a growing need for subnational governments to have the expertise and capacity to manage large urban populations. In addition, and especially in Latin America, democratization and the need for legitimacy oblige us to look anew at how cities are managed and how civil society functions. As democracy has been extended to formerly authoritarian or one-party regimes, new governance institutions have been forged that are predicated upon representational democracy. This has meant experimentation in recasting traditional state-society relations, whether these were patrimonial, corporatist, or dominated by party political machines. It has also raised a need to consider how citizenship and participation can be strengthened in ways that will respond to the emerging civic culture and civil society.

A rich literature about democratic consolidation in Latin America has emerged. Juan Linz and Alfred Stepan argued over a decade ago that five elements are necessary for consolidation: a free and lively civil society; a relatively autonomous and valued political society; a rule of law to ensure guarantees for citizens' freedom and associations; a state bureaucracy;

and an institutionalized economic society (1996, 7). Andreas Schedler (1998), following Samuel Huntington, argues that the minimal criteria for consolidation are two sets of elections, power changing hands, and no threat of a democratic breakdown. In reviewing democratic transitions and consolidations in Latin America, Peter H. Smith (2005, 342) concludes that present-day democracy remains rather shallow (see also Dominguez and Shifter 2003; Mainwaring and Scully 2010; Mainwaring and Scully 2008; Tulchin and Selee 2004). Electoral democracy has taken root, and most countries have met the "two-turnover" test. But this observation addresses consolidation at the national level. At the subnational level, at least in the Latin American countries, checks and balances tend to be few, representative institutions weak and untested, and freedoms and rights restricted—in practice if not in principle (Domínguez and Shifter 2003).

Reform of the state has been the subject of policy discussions around the world, and in the Latin American context democratization has occurred contemporaneously with reform in most countries. The element of reform most relevant to our study of metropolitan governance is decentralization. Despite some conflation of decentralization and democratization in Latin America, it is now well established that these are distinct processes (Montero and Samuels 2004; Gibson 2004; Eaton 2006; Mainwaring and Scully 2010). But both processes—democratization in terms of citizen involvement in metropolitan issues, further discussed in this section, and decentralization, particularly the capacity of local government structures, discussed in the next section—are important to our work.

Alfred Stepan, in *Decentralization and Democracy in Latin America* (Gibson 2004), addresses the territorial basis of party systems and proposes a continuum, from democracy enhancing to democracy constraining, to assess one dimension of change in federalist structures. He calls attention to political competition at the subnational level and the degree to which democracy is enhanced by decentralization (for institutionalization of party systems, see Mainwaring and Scully 2010). Given the large size and regional diversity of most federalist countries, it is likely that some regions will develop more political competition and will more readily overturn traditional oligarchies, even though all regions in the country are subject to the same set of structural reforms. Furthermore, variation across political parties within a country, particularly the ability of the national party to unify subnational political processes, may produce incentives for politicians that either strengthen or undermine the level of regional competition (for Brazil, see Souza 2002). The spatial basis of political processes will be found below to affect and often to impede the emergence of metropolitan initiatives.

A number of Latin American populations, however, have shown a growing disenchantment with their national leaders, and for the past ten to fifteen years a bottom-up resurgence of interest in local government and in a "new federalism" has shifted the locus of power away from central government toward the subnational state and city levels (Lindert 2009; Campbell 2003; Myers and Dietz 2002). Echoing Dahl (1971), along the way the institutional practices of formal representative democracy have become no longer the single means by which political participation takes place; community-based budgeting and control, direct democracy, and consultative councils and forums have broadened the democratic experience (Wilson et al. 2008; Zovatto 2007).

The opportunities for local self-governance in metropolitan areas are a concern of this study, especially in relation to the particular challenges of mobilization and participation faced by the residents of metropolitan areas. As citizens of both a local and possibly a metropolitan entity, leaving aside their identity with state or provincial governments and even national government, how is their experience of citizenship "constructed"? Two subissues arise here: the institutional structures whereby citizens are represented (*representational democracy,* that is, voting and elections of their authorities) and the structures and channels through which citizens participate in city governance (*participatory* or *direct democracy*). The point to ascertain here is whether being a citizen of a "metropolitan" city embedded within a local district or municipality has any special significance in terms of self-identification and whether it is desirable that these two democratic imperatives have some sort of articulation at a metropolitan level in addition to the local (municipal) one. And if "place matters," as geographers argue, does place have multiple significances depending upon the vantage point of municipality, city, or metro area?

We need to know whether very large metropolitan and multijurisdictional areas are innately different when it comes to embracing public participation and personal identification with the city. How do citizens identify with their city? It is not unusual for residents and the native born of metropolitan areas to identify with that city or region—as *chilangos* in the Federal District of Mexico, *porteños* in Buenos Aires, *cariocas* in Rio de Janeiro, *caraqueños* in Caracas, and *Austinites* in Austin, Texas. However, as we show in the case of Guadalajara, which we analyze in detail in the Mexico chapter, residents often have multiple identities—as *tapatios* (from central Jalisco); as residents of Guadalajara (municipal or metropolitan area); and more specifically as *zapopenses* (from the municipality of Zapopan). Submetropolitan identities can be found throughout the regions in our study, and cities and municipalities often cultivate a strong sense of identity that is invoked in city (political) as well as commercial marketing strategies. Different personal identities may act as incentives or disincentives to different levels of participation.

Governance and Legitimacy

The term *governance* has become widely used in scholarly and policy communities in recent decades (Demmers, Jilberto, and Hogenboom 2004; Bevir and Trentmann 2007; Bevir 2010). We feel this term is particularly relevant to our work, since we expect to find in the metropolitan context new forms of collaboration between governments and new relationships between government and the governed. But the term has interesting origins and has been applied in quite different contexts. In international development, the term was applied by the World Bank to its work in Africa in recognition of the importance of the rule of law and other political institutions in economic development (Demmers, Jilberto, and Hogenboom 2004; Mkandawire 2007). African scholars consulted at the time argued that citizens and an array of democratic institutions were vital to the management and development of economies — thus the importance of citizens in establishing policy priorities and in holding government accountable.

Governance has come to be used for multiple purposes, and in all of these a reconceptualization of the state and its relationship to citizens and markets is implied within national contexts as well as in the global arena. One type of focus is on the nature and evolution of civil society and its interactions with the state, particularly in the context of redemocratization (Rosenblum and Post 2002). In the context of governmental reform within nations, neoliberal-inspired downsizing of the state has led to the increasing importance of nonhierarchical processes of governance (Demmers, Jilberto, and Hogenboom 2004; Bevir 2010), sometimes conceptualized as network governance (Sørensen and Torfing 2007). In the global context, the term is being applied in recognition of the existence of multiple centers of power among state actors (i.e., nations) and the presence of a range of nonstate actors, including intergovernmental organizations, nongovernmental organizations and corporations, quasi–state institutions, and transnational communities, in nonhierarchical negotiating space (Wolfish and Smith 2000).

In the public sphere, the broadening of political life and public action (Hirst 2000; Spink and Best 2009) suggests new relationships that contain "formal legal dimensions, such as the protection of human rights, rule of law and free and fair elections (in the democratic context), as well as informal dimensions including political culture, civic engagement, interest group formation, openness of government to citizen input, public spaces, a free press, and political parties" (Wilson et al. 2008, 22). Political scientists refer to governance in the context of a political system, as distinct from political institutions, and argue for its usefulness in comparative studies (see Almond et al. 2007).

In a recent study (Mainwaring and Scully 2010), assessment of democratic governance takes into account whether a set of public policies is effective. That is, the success of governance is determined, in part, through effectiveness of economic development policies to reduce poverty and improve education (See also Tulchin and Brown 2002). This distinction between the quality of democratic practice itself and the effectiveness of government action is consistent with the perspective adopted in this research project. We are concerned with not only how citizens engage in metropolitan issues but whether metropolitan initiatives are improving the lives of citizens. Mainwaring and Scully (2010) conclude that the quality of institutions is important for democratic governance, a particularly salient observation for this volume, since the metropolitan initiatives that we observe almost invariably occur through the construction of new institutions.

But the use of the term *governance,* especially in a normative sense of "good governance," has its critics (Demmers, Jilberto, and Hogenboom 2004; Bevir 2010). Seen as ideologically laden, its imprecise and contested definition undermines its use in scholarly analysis. For example, rationalizing governance beyond the state can undermine democratic practices (Swyngedouw 2005). Or redefining the citizen as consumer in what some believe to be a cultural dimension of the neoliberal governance project changes fundamentally the nature of the relation between state, market, and citizen (Bevir and Trentmann 2007). Unclear definitions and rules about representation and poor accountability procedures may favor power-based interests.

Recognizing the term's potential for mischief or confusion, we nevertheless find it helpful for thinking outside the classical government framework and examining the process of creating new metropolitan institutions—usually the result of collaboration among existing governments and governmental agencies, as discussed below—and the roles citizens and nongovernmental organizations play in these initiatives. Indeed, as we discuss later, it is possible that within the restricted range of our federalist comparisons, with at least two and in one case three levels of government within the federalist pact, the opportunities for more "government" are somewhat limited. The role played by citizens and nongovernmental organizations is likely to be a key element in establishing the political legitimacy of metropolitan initiatives. In traditional democratic theory, citizens elect, either directly or indirectly, their governmental leaders, thereby providing legitimacy. Direct elections allow voters to choose which individual represents them, whereas indirect elections are a process of collective choice (such as proportional representation from candidate lists based upon the percentage of the overall vote polled). Both systems may be in place within the same polity, especially when there is concern that a minority segment of the population would not be represented, as may occur under direct elections. But beyond electoral processes, legitimacy will also be affected by effectiveness of governmental institutions in delivering goods and services to citizens.

Latin America is now almost thirty years into its so-called "third wave of democracy," yet the slow pace at which the quality of life has improved for many residents in the metropolitan areas of the region threatens to undermine the survival of representative democratic institutions, as seen by developments in Venezuela and Bolivia and in the so-called "Brown Zones" (O'Donnell 1993) where the rule of law remains weak. Political legitimacy is also an important consideration in the United States and Canada. In the United States metropolitan governance institutions have not been particularly effective in delivering urban services to the poor, providing security, or planning, leading to the existence of zones where adherence to law is tenuous at best and the institutions of local, state, and national government are viewed as only marginally legitimate. In short, there is a need for new institutions and experiences in metropolitan areas that will provide better and more appropriate governance for the twenty-first century than the often ad hoc arrangements of yesteryear. Delivery of a higher level and quality of goods and services by political institutions will increase satisfaction with the political rules of the game and correspondingly increase the legitimacy of the existing democratic institutions, while failure to do so may lead to the decay of representative democracy.

Institutional Complexity and Subnational Governments

The policy-making systems in federalist structures are often complex, since they incorporate interactions between the central and subnational governments, each with varying degrees of autonomy and responsibility to the other. Federalist models are elastic and can be pushed and pulled in various directions with designs that are quite different one from the other, yet all share this theme of autonomy and co-responsibility (Rosenn 1994; for an overview of the U.S. case, see Bowman 2002). The resulting complexity is accentuated in metropolitan areas as they stretch beyond the geographic boundaries of individual municipal jurisdictions and assume increasing importance as economic centers.

Governance systems for cities take a multitude of forms, both across countries and even within some countries. The growth of cities has historically led to new forms of local government with new powers and functions. In the United States, for example, the consolidation of adjacent local governments was already a feature in the mid–nineteenth century (in Baltimore, Philadelphia, and San Francisco around the 1850s) and at the turn of the century (beginning in 1898) as the boroughs of the Bronx, Brooklyn, Manhattan, Queens, and Staten Island were consolidated into New York City. Similarly, as we observe in Canada, provincial governments have legislated municipal annexation and consolidation to reduce institutional complexity and maximize efficiency. And in Latin America we can observe the process of new governance mechanisms emerging in many capital cities (Myers and Dietz 2002).

This complexity has been reinforced by *decentralization* and *devolution* — whether between the tiers of a metropolitan (city) administration or within individual government agencies. This process has found increasing support among international agencies such as the World Bank (V. Rodríguez 1997; Campbell 2003; Eaton 2004; Ward 2004; United Cities and Local Governments 2009). Decentralization efforts in Latin America are of sufficient duration that assessments of impacts have been conducted (Diaz-Cayeros 2006; Falleti 2005, 2010; Smoke, Gomez, and Peterson 2006; Wilson et al. 2008). Associated with decentralization is the frequent need to recast federalism not only in the vertical decentralization of power to different government levels, but also in the process of horizontal decentralization between the branches and the recognition of the separation of powers that in the United States constitute the "checks and balances" of government (V. Rodríguez 1997). In some cases, too, arguments in favor of *recentralization* have reappeared, as governments react to perceived inefficiencies caused by inability or indifference of local governments to exercise newly acquired authority and responsibility (Wilson et al. 2008).

Eaton (2004) adopts a historical and comparative perspective to examine the design of subnational governments in four Southern Cone countries in Latin America. He reminds us that tensions between national and subnational governments are inherent in governmental systems and that they evolve over time. Similarly, the evolution of local government structures in the United States, discussed above, reflects the new policy challenges arising from urbanization. Thus the contemporary processes of decentralization are not unexpected, and we anticipate that the challenges of metropolitan governance will create tensions leading to new types of institutional design. To foreshadow our findings, in many countries decentralization has not led to robust municipal governments and has instead impeded the progress of metropolitan initiatives. But it also follows from Eaton's analysis that the expanding demands of the economies and populations in metropolitan areas will eventually lead to new designs for subnational governments.

A further contemporary complexity associated with decentralization and devolution is the need to develop more systemic and efficient procedures in the ways the business of administration and government is conducted (for example, reducing "red tape," expediting payments for local services and taxes and the processing of planning applications), all of which are important to ensure greater transparency and accountability to municipal and local government budgeting. These improvements allow for greater efficiency in the provision and cost recovery of urban improvement programs and make the delivery of urban services more sustainable (Ward 1998a). This obliges us to consider issues of devolution, empowerment, and accountability, since city administrators today recognize the political benefits of accounting more openly to those they serve, as well as the benefits of exploring areas of administrative innovation (Wilson and Cramer 1995; Cabrero Mendoza 1995). City and metropolitan authorities have also had to deal with reductions in public expenditure and declining intergovernmental transfers, but at the same time, as the second GOLD report by the United Cities and Local Governments shows, they are being increasingly challenged to provide key services (United Cities and Local Government 2010). In the Latin American context, developing local tax systems remains a work in progress. Certainly in today's economic climate greater fiscal responsibility, including enhanced revenue-raising activities, is and will continue to be required of local governments

(Cabrero Mendoza 1996). Not surprisingly, people are becoming increasingly concerned about how their local taxes are spent.

Directly relevant to this discussion of decentralization is the concept of subsidiarity, which has grown in visibility in part through its adoption as a principle of the European Union. A somewhat delicate term with many nuances, including religious ones, the subsidiarity principle when applied to the public sector proposes that if a particular service or administrative function can be carried out at the local level of government just as well as at a higher level, then it should be assigned to the former.[1] While difficulties arise when this principle is used to discuss the relationship between private and public spheres, in the more general federalist manner in which we will apply it the argument is that the federal government and higher levels of government should play a subsidiary role in the affairs of local government and governance.

We introduce the concept at this stage to signal one of the strands that will be picked up in our overall conclusion: that of taking the design and ideas of subsidiarity more seriously. The creation of effective metropolitan-wide governance will require that national and subnational states recognize that many areas of policy making need to be vested in some form of metropolitan authority and, more specifically, that many of these activities can best be undertaken at local levels — within municipalities, towns, and counties of metropolitan areas, and even at the local neighborhood level. Conversely, conurbations need to recognize that some of these functions — especially the spatially interconnected — cannot be carried out at the local level but should be "handed up" to higher orders of government and governance. In the European Union, the discussion of multilevel governance in the context of international, national, and subnational relations addresses the assignment of governmental functions as, in part, a problem of nesting functions at various governmental levels (Hooghe and Marks 2003; Bache and Flinders 2004). These discussions may also be relevant in the federalist metropolitan context.

Policy challenges can be addressed not only through the reassignment of functions to different levels of government but also through intergovernmental coordination, either vertical across levels of government or horizontal among governments at the same level. We have found two models for policy coordination that are helpful for our analysis. Figure 1.1 depicts Metcalfe's (1994) Policy Coordination Scale, which assigns a position to each level of coordination (higher levels involving much greater coordination than lower levels), while figure 1.2 depicts a spectrum of

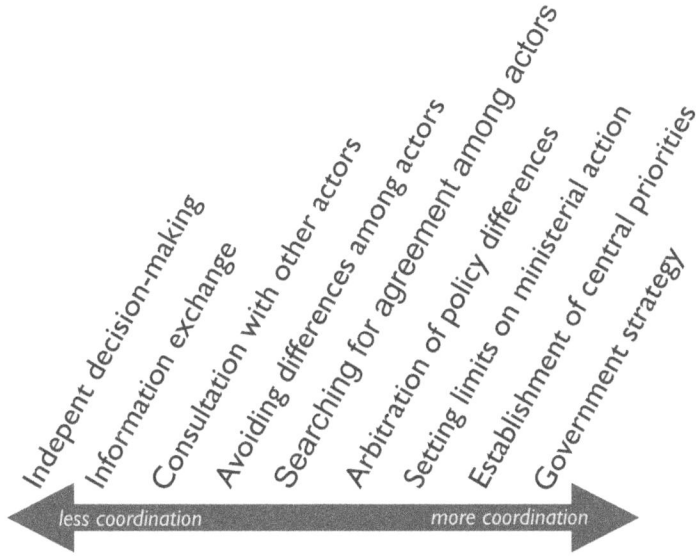

Figure 1.1. Policy Coordination Scale
Source: Based on Metcalfe (1994), cited in Paiva (2003, 43).

types of coordination in three broad bands of political difficulty (Mitchell-Weaver, Miller, and Deal 2000; Walker 1987).

At the "relatively easy" end of the scale are informal cooperation arrangements, interlocal service agreements, regional councils, and contracts with private vendors. "Moderately difficult" coordination involves local special districts, a transfer of functions, annexation, or the creation of regional special districts or metropolitan multipurpose districts. "Very difficult" to achieve politically are one-tier consolidation (the melding of two or more jurisdictions into one) or changes that require the creation of a new metropolitan tier of government as part of the federal structure, implying constitutional change and reform.

But how best to address the challenge of institutional complexity in metropolitan governance is clearly a theme that is increasingly present on the planning and democratic agenda, as are the many possibilities of action and arguments for best approaches. Boundaries can be redrawn, multiple local governments can coordinate their actions in one or more areas, agencies can be created, and authority can be devolved upwards or downwards from one level of government to the next. More likely, as the

Relatively easy
1. Informal cooperation
2. Inter-local service agreements
3. Joint power agreements
4. Extraterritorial powers
5. Regional councils of government (COGs)
6. Federally encouraged single-purpose districts
7. State planning and development districts (SPDDs)
8. Contracting from private vendors

Moderately difficult
9. Local special districts
10. Transfer of functions
11. Annexation
12. Regional special districts and authorities
13. Metropolitan multipurpose districts
14. Reformed urban country

Very Difficult
15. One-tier consolidation: city-county and area-wide consolidation
16. Two-tier restructuring: federal structures
17. Three-tier reform: metropolitan-wide structures

Figure 1.2. Types of Intergovernmental Coordination, Governance,
and Government, by Level of Political Difficulty
Source: Based on Mitchell-Weaver, Miller, and Deal (2000) and Walker (1987),
cited in Paiva (2003, 43).

title of our research design suggests, the answer will lie in the conceptual opening generated by the notion of governance, involving governments and other actors, and, we hope, will entail a move away from the "line of least resistance" approach, which postpones action, perhaps with the hope that the issue will disappear.

Unitary versus Federal Systems and the Implications
for Metropolitan Governance

To conclude this section on governance and institutions, we return to our decision to examine only those countries in the Americas with federal systems (Rosenn 1994). Constitutionally the architecture of federal governments differs markedly from that of unitary systems, and within each there is also marked variation. This is one of the principal reasons why we chose not to look at metropolitan government across the Americas as a whole but instead to examine those experiences common to a single arrangement—that of federal countries in the Western hemisphere. We also chose, wherever possible, to be comprehensive in our data collection and to include most if not all metropolitan areas in our countries, thus better serving the growing discussion on metropolitan governance in the Americas by complementing previous studies that have adopted a more mixed, city-focused approach (for example, Rojas, Cuadrado-Roura, and Guell 2008).

Under most federal arrangements, lower levels of government authority have constitutionally defined rights and relative autonomy from the federal government. Usually they comprise large populations and/or spatial entities — Brazil, the United States, Mexico, and Canada are good examples, as are other federal states such as India, Russia, and Australia. A unitary state is one that is governed as a single unit, with one constitutionally created legislature. Unitary governments are in the majority worldwide in part because they often comprise relatively small populations that would not justify the creation of distinct internal territories (although counterfactual examples also exist — Belgium and Switzerland, for example — both of which are small, yet federal and have important regional linguistic and ethnic minority variation within their national boundaries).

Unitary governments may also delegate or devolve powers to lower (regional or subregional) levels, but the principal difference is that the central government has the capacity to recall such devolved or delegated powers if it so chooses. A good example here is the United Kingdom, where there were growing and ultimately successful demands that Parliament create regionally constituted assemblies for Scotland, Wales, and Northern Ireland. While Scotland has its own legal system and laws, these can be overridden by UK national legislation (and/or by EU laws). In the same vein, what Parliament gives it can also take back — as it did when the Thatcher government abolished the metropolitan authority of the Greater London Council in 1986 — in large part because it was controlled by another party (Labour) and was pressing ahead with policies that were anathema to Margaret Thatcher's (Conservative) government. In 2000, after a referendum, the Blair (Labour) government restored the (now) Greater London Authority, though with somewhat different powers and with a directly elected mayor and a London Assembly.

However, just as unitary governments may create federal-like arrangements (always with the proviso of revoking them), so may federal governments contain unitary arrangements. In both the United States and Canada, for example, the federal government has only those powers expressly delegated to it; the powers and functions of the states or provinces are mandated by the nation's constitution, enabling each internally to operate in a unitary manner. States control the allocation of powers to the substate level, to counties, cities, municipalities, special district boards, and the many different arrangements that make up the subnational United States. Mexico operates similarly, although the federal government has traditionally held sway (Wilson et al. 2008), and in Brazil's constitutionally designed system both states and municipalities have designated roles and responsibilities, though with certain common obligations.

So what do these federal-versus-unitary differences mean for metropolitan governance and for our analysis in this book? We argue that there are two important implications. First, if the key to metropolitan management is to create a new tier — an independent metropolitan government — then it is probably easier to achieve in a unitary state, since the central government can legislate to create a new tier of government — as in Quito, Ecuador, where in 1993 the metropolitan district was forged out of the county district surrounding the old city of Quito. The very fact that a simple act of Parliament or of Congress can create and revoke a metropolitan area, and do so without engaging in a major constitutional reform, makes such arrangements feasible (though sometimes politically difficult and even requiring the expedient of a referendum, as in the case of London). In cases where states have cultural and ethnic regional variation, then some level of autonomous government may be highly appropriate and may avoid conflict and possible secession.[2]

A second implication for our analysis is that while on the surface it may be difficult in federal systems to conceive constitutional changes that would create a new tier of government with powers separate from states, municipalities, and federal government, these federal structures do allow state and local governments to engage formally in intergovernmental relations, as well as in collaborative arrangements. Where municipal autonomy exists, either of a constitutional or a practical nature, intermunicipal arrangements and state-municipal arrangements can offer viable means of constructing some level of metropolitan governance.

Together, both implications suggest that the constraints and opportunities within which institutional and organizational actors function may offer space for local leadership to innovate without necessarily changing the institutional and organizational status quo. Holding the broad constitutional arrangement constant, even though considerable variety exists in the way our six federal countries function, enables us to look for these homegrown alternatives. In doing so we suspend judgment on the nature of and need for strategies of metropolitan management per se and argue instead that just seeking midrange strategies for metropolitan governance is a good first step. Moreover, even if unitary governments were "better placed" to deal with metropolitan issues, it is extremely unlikely that any one of our six countries would change its basic constitutional arrangements. Findings from other federalist systems may confirm or further illustrate potentially useful approaches — as the constant dialogue in the Forum of Federations demonstrates[3] — and we will address these further in the final chapter along with a discussion of the broader implications of our findings.

POLICY CHALLENGES IN METROPOLITAN AREAS

A devil's advocate could argue that the apparent lack of success in developing effective metropolitan organization is primarily a problem in the mind of the planner or the institutional designer and that, pragmatically, some kind of passive incremental approach is best, especially one that can be left to existing governmental units. However, humankind's so far less-than-able response to the challenges of metropolitan urbanism suggests to us that more active alternatives need to be found. High-density, closely linked metropolitan areas are increasingly vulnerable, for example, to natural disasters such as earthquakes, hurricanes, and other extreme climatic events, all of which are present in the countries that we are studying. Economic disparities in the global economic arena are another source of vulnerability, and here, too, coordinating actions across jurisdictions requires different approaches to resource distribution and redistributive economic investment in order to generate more equal opportunity for different economic actors. But if there is an overriding argument for the need to break away from the current, almost permanent state of precrisis adaptation and to search for serious alternatives, it is the need to significantly increase social and economic equity and to better attend to the collective well-being of metropolitan inhabitants.[4]

Economic Efficiency of Public Service Provision

As populations grow large, the profile of public service requirements changes. While one may argue that many basic functions such as public security, education, sanitation, and road maintenance are necessary in all urban areas regardless of size, scale requirements in large cities and conurbations lead to fundamental changes in the way they are provided. A small town might allow for the disposal of wastewater on dwelling premises through septic tanks, but with larger urban areas wastewater systems must be established. In transportation, city streets and pathways will need streetcars or subways. Furthermore, new services and regulatory activities become necessary or possible as large numbers of people reside in close proximity. Here the economics of efficiency enters the policy agenda.

The term *economies of scale* refers to the variation in per-unit cost of production as the quantity produced increases. This idea, derived from microeconomics and developed in the context of private sector businesses, is also highly relevant to the provision of public services. For many public services, such as the provision of drinking water, the cost per unit provided declines as the level of production increases because of the large, so-called "lumpy" investments that are required to get such systems up and running or to move them from one level of service provision to another. In the case of water supply, the large feeder mains of the primary and secondary networks are quite expensive, but as their costs can be spread over many users who can be connected to these networks for little more than a few yards of pipe and a meter, the average cost of provision drops considerably. However, at some point the average cost of provision may well start to rise again because of *diseconomies of scale,* as in transportation systems that become inefficient because of congestion. For some types of services, especially those where face-to-face interactions are required, diseconomies of scale may occur at fairly low levels of service. Here there will be greater efficiencies in more localized delivery systems. Choosing which way to go — scale up or scale down — for which service is a constant theme in the metropolitan debate, in relation to both the economics of city size and the incentives for cross-jurisdictional activity.

Charles Tiebout (1956) formulated the problem of optimizing provision of public services by focusing attention on the diverse set of demands for services across different population groups. For example, families with children might place a higher priority on education than would those without children. Some groups might place a higher priority on public transportation than other groups. Tiebout proposed that the problem of collective choice of local governmental services could be resolved if local jurisdictions were small and residents of those jurisdictions had similar preferences for local services and taxation. Citizens would be encouraged to move to jurisdictions that had an array of services with particular quality levels and, implicitly, tax rates that would meet their preferences, thereby optimizing the provision of services across all individuals. Although this conceptualization of the provision of local services has generated much discussion in policy communities, and provides a partial rationale for the strong preference of local government control found in several countries, such as the United States, it would be difficult to imagine this strategy as effective in the large conurbations being discussed in the book because of pervasive externalities. A resident might work, live, and shop in different jurisdictions, and consume public services in a jurisdiction in which he or she did not pay taxes. In extreme instances, a community might decide not to offer public education, thereby reducing local taxes but imposing the public costs of education on other jurisdictions. Here we encounter the problem of externalities.

First presented by the economist Arthur C. Pigou in his *Economics of Welfare* ([1920] 2002), *externalities* arise when the total benefit, positive or negative, of a transaction is not accurately incorporated into the price associated with the transaction. In cities, services are usually provided on a geographical basis, with taxpayers in the jurisdictions sharing the expense equally. Yet differences in the consumption of services may well vary among taxpayers. The amount of domestic refuse produced or the number of cars parked on the roadside all generate consequences beyond what a single user consumes and pays for. Solid waste (garbage) landfills can become exhausted, or school buses can find themselves with lengthy holdups, and policy makers and service coordinators find themselves struggling to propose alternatives. While this generates one class of issues within a single jurisdiction—linked to regulation and costs—the issues grow for multiple jurisdictions, as in most of our metropolitan regions. Resident taxpayers in one jurisdiction may consume a service in an adjacent jurisdiction but not pay taxes there. For example, parks and leisure activities paid for by one municipality may be used by residents from other areas; investments in roads and street lighting may provide safer routes home for workers crossing from one municipality to another.

Assessing efficiency in the delivery of local public services has been of interest to research communities (Afonso, Schuknecht, and Tanzi 2003; Peter C. Smith and Street 2005). Neoliberal policies, decentralization of the state, and, in some countries, taxpayer revolt have all contributed to pressure for increased efficiency. Privatization of public services is an option advocated for increased efficiencies (Christoffersen, Paldam, and Würtz 2007). Interest in subsidiarity and possible changing of economies of scale because of technological innovation has led scholars, especially in Europe, where adjustments to the formation of the European Union are in play, to investigate the assignment of public service functions among levels of government (Hülsemeyer 2000; Reifschneider 2006).

Tackling issues of intergovernmental collaboration or the redefinition of service areas among jurisdictions is often high on the agenda
of decision makers as efficient means of providing services are sought
(Feiock 2004).[5] Since externalities are affected by both the nature of the
service and the demand for the service, jurisdictional expansion to inter-
nalize them can be a solution. Alternatively, to achieve appropriate scale
in the provision of services, local jurisdictions across metropolitan areas
can attempt to coordinate urban development strategies, land use planning, water and drainage infrastructural development, transportation,
social services, public security, environmental policy, and so on. The extent to which these activities are likely to be transmetropolitan will affect whether they should be primarily publicly or privately provided and
whether implementation and oversight are nested hierarchically or coordinated horizontally to maximize efficiency, access, and equity.

One area in which these questions of the economics of efficiency and
the consequences of externalities looms large is that of sustainability and
global warming. Metropolitan areas are major sources of global emissions,
despite having a relatively small per capita carbon footprint, and there is
little doubt that within the next two decades efficiency measures will
need to incorporate energy and emissions considerations in the delivery
of public services. Currently on the national agenda, this issue is likely
to become a large-city (metropolitan) one in the near future and will no
doubt go on to include the challenges brought about by cross-state and
cross-national urban corridors.

Equity and Resource Disparities

The issue of equity in metropolitan areas arises in three ways. First, at
the macro level, metropolitan areas tend to have higher personal income
disparities than those found nationally (United Nations Habitat 2010).
Even though urban areas are the major economic engines for most countries, they are also the home of substantial socioeconomic disparities that
accompany much of today's development. In Latin America, some recent improvements in income equality in many countries, driven by both
labor market developments and public policy (Lopez-Calva and Lustig
2010), are encouraging, but urban poverty remains a prominent issue
(Fay 2005), as will be discussed in the case studies below. A second form
of disparity occurring within metropolitan areas results from the uneven
geographic distribution of fiscal capacity and public service needs. Metropolitan areas in the Americas tend to be subject to high levels of poverty-

based socioeconomic segregation (Roberts and Wilson 2009; Sabatini 2003; Telles 1995, 44; Duhau 2003; Fischer 2003; J. Rodríguez and Arriagada 2004; Wheeler and La Jeunesse 2006). Areas within the metropolis with lower-income populations tend to have less adequate tax bases than the more affluent areas. In fact, within most metropolitan areas one finds wealthy municipalities and poor municipalities. In the poor municipalities, inadequate government revenues impede progress on education, health, poverty, and even economic development policies. Such geographic disparities are manifest at other scales, such as those between states or provinces. Disparity between tax bases and policy needs are present in both the North and Latin American countries studied here.

Higher levels of governments can adopt redistributive policies to address such disparities, as when national governments redistribute resources across states and/or municipalities. For example, transfers to distressed communities or equalization in revenue systems can remedy resource disparities. However, redistribution within metropolitan areas represents a dilemma if there is no metropolitan-level governmental institution that can articulate and implement it. Furthermore, the lack of metropolitan institutions impedes the formation of consensus in other metropolitan-wide policy areas, such as economic development strategies. Among lower-income municipalities, the pursuit of narrowly drawn and poorly funded strategies is commonplace.

A third and often commented-on issue of equity in a number of our country studies refers to the differential access to channels of political participation, especially in relation to policy formulation and implementation. Racial and ethnic minorities and the poor rarely have the organizational clout to effectively articulate their interests in the same way that business and other elites do; public transportation deficiencies and a lack of available time can place serious obstacles to the creation of interorganizational networks, forums, and broader movements for change.

In a different direction, decentralization may exacerbate the challenges to equitable development in metropolitan areas, since local governments are usually expected to become more self-sufficient, pursuing strategies through their own resources. In terms of resource base, decentralization usually implies that local governments will also be asked to assume greater responsibility for raising their own sources of revenue. Such sources generally rely on taxes, most notably property, value-added, or sales taxes, but as these are inherently linked to the strength of the local economy, the lower-income municipalities may find themselves in an increasingly vicious circle.

The Research Design and the Countries

The Research Questions

The central question that we set out to examine in this volume is *whether the current and emerging initiatives and structures of governance are capable of meeting the challenges of collective life in these large and complex metropolitan areas.* This broad central question can be disaggregated into three more specific groups of research questions.

(1) *What are the key characteristics of the institutional and organizational forms of metropolitan governance initiatives? How frequently do they appear, and what policy issues do they address?* This first step of our analysis is largely descriptive. In establishing categories of forms, we will later test the extent to which these can provide analytical purchase in answering our other research questions. The preceding discussion about public services and demographic and institutional diversity suggests that some issue areas will be more likely addressed at the metropolitan scale than others. Given the comparative approach, we will also be able to identify differences across countries, should they exist.

(2) *What factors shape the emergence and dynamics of these metropolitan-based systems?* This is our key analytical question. From the earlier discussion of metropolitan areas and their challenges, we expect that five types of factors will be found to influence the appearance, or absence, of metropolitan initiatives: (i) the constitutional and/or state-attributed powers of local government, including fiscal capacity; (ii) jurisdictional geography of local government; (iii) technical and organizational characteristics of service delivery systems; (iv) political systems and the practice of politics; and (v) demographic and civic pressures

In relation to the first factor, *constitutional provisions and/or state-attributed powers,* we note that of the six countries examined here, only one has metropolitan arrangements by a formal constitutional designation (Brazil). But even where this is absent, state or provincial governments can — through their own constitutional authority — have profound effects on the emergence of local government as well as metropolitan arrangements. Fiscal incentives can play a part in decentralization, and the strengthening of subnational governments can be expected to affect the emergence of metropolitan-wide functions. In relation to the second factor, *jurisdictional geography* and the spatial patchwork of local government, we seek to identify how the multiplicity and complexity of government structures and the distribution of populations and their different socioeconomic characteristics affect the emergence of metropolitan governance.

As for our third factor, public goods have *technical and organizational characteristics of service delivery* that affect economies of scale or thresholds of demand, which in turn affect the metropolitan agenda. Hence we should expect to find metropolitan initiatives in those policy areas where significant economies of scale or externalities may be achieved. In some policy areas, such as the network features of infrastructure and transportation systems, the benefits of collaboration among all jurisdictions within the metropolitan area will be more clear-cut. For others, the benefits to be derived from metropolitan-wide action will be less apparent and more debatable. So far as the fourth factor, *political systems and the practice of politics*, is concerned, we ask whether and how political parties, interest groups, and advocacy coalitions are organized for and engage in metropolitan issues. Equally, in the absence of venues for metropolitan agendas to be considered, we ask whether the organization of political systems reinforces existing governmental structures and thus impedes the formation of metropolitan political systems.

In relation to the final factor, *demographic and civic pressures*, we outlined earlier that even in countries with strong primate cities such as Argentina, Mexico, and Venezuela, large and complex second-tier cities are today also emerging and growing rapidly, and those countries are thereby having to redefine their governance challenges as public pressure for an effective policy agenda increases. Across our countries, citizens are putting civic pressure on local government for solutions to many policy issues. Under these circumstances, we ask what the possibilities are for locally based issues to assume metropolitan-wide salience.

(3) *Are the initiatives offering opportunities for democratic governance and creating incentives for citizens to participate? Are they thereby acquiring political legitimacy?* Democratization has been an important development in many countries in the world, including several of the countries studied here. The democratization process has highlighted various mechanisms for establishing legitimacy, such as elections; public debate on issues of policy; and public participation in policy making and a sense of collective identity. We wish to evaluate whether and how these existing and emerging forms of metropolitan governance adhere to democratic practice in both its representative and direct forms and to assess the extent to which they can be viewed as legitimate institutions and arrangements. In essence, we ask who is effectively determining the public good.

Six Federalist Experiences and Polities

As already noted, the six countries included in this book all share a federalist constitutional structure with three levels of government: federal, state/provincial, and local. With the exception of Canada, all are presidentialist systems with a clear separation of governmental functions between the three branches — executive, legislative, and judicial. Canada is a constitutional monarchy with a parliament and prime minister but with a federalist system of provincial legislatures. Although all six are similar, they are at the same time very different in terms of the extent and exercise of powers at the federal, state/provincial, and local levels. In Canada the federal government has a low profile, with almost all of the effective powers falling to the provincial parliaments. In Venezuela the central government is everywhere, not least since President Hugo Chávez centralized powers in the presidency. In Mexico, Argentina, and the United States, federal and state governments play important roles in regional government, with a common trend toward the strengthening of regional and local governments in each case under "new" federalist arrangements (in Mexico and the United States). Only in Brazil municipalities form part of the federal pact and are institutionally autonomous; elsewhere they are under the aegis of the regional (state/provincial) governments.

Our six countries vary markedly in size — both geographically and in population terms. Brazil, Canada, and the United States are huge territorially (over three million square miles), yet Canada is at the lower end of the population rankings, quite close to Argentina and Venezuela, and its vast space and small population give it a very low population density (see table 1.2). Brazil (almost 200 million people), Mexico (108 million), and the United States (over 300 million) all have huge populations, whereas the other three countries are in the 25 to 40 million range. Similarly the number of local jurisdictions and governments corresponding to those populations varies, with the United States' enormous raft of local governments representing the extreme outlier. All have a number of metropolitan arrangements — defined in different ways — and these will be the focus of following chapters.

The politics of these six countries and the depth of consolidation of their democracies vary. The recent past of Argentina and Brazil was until the 1980s dominated by military authoritarian regimes that eschewed democracy and civil society engagement. Both have new constitutions, and through competitive elections their democracies have survived the "two-turnover test."[6] Venezuela, also under dictatorships for a significant

Table 1.2. The Six Case Study Countries Compared

	Canada	United States	Mexico	Venezuela	Brazil	Argentina
Size of country (sq. miles)	3,851,807.61	3,717,811.29	761,605.50	352,144.33	3,282,921.75	1,068,301.76
Size of country (sq. km)	9,976,136	9,629,087.04	1,972,549	912,050	8,502,728	2,766,889
Total population (2008)[a]	33.3 million	304.1 million	106.7 million	27.9 million	189.6 million	39.7 million
Population density (sq. miles)	8.7	81.8	140.1	79.3	57.8	37.2
Total urban population (%)[a]	80.2	76.5	77.0	88.0	84.36[b]	90.9
Number of cities 500,000–1 million	7[c]	24	28	2[d]	22	2
Number of cities 1–3 million	2[c]	7	9	2[d]	12	2
Number of cities > 3 million	–	2	1	1[d]	2	–
Number of metropolitan areas	33 (CMA)[e]	366 (MSA)[f]	90	N/A	36[g]	NA
Federalist Territories						
Number of states	10 provinces and and 3 territories	50 states and 1 district	31 states and 1 Federal District	23 states and 1 Capital District	26 states and 1 Federal District	23 provinces and 1 Autonomous City
Total number of municipalities/counties	5,600	3,142	2,438	334	5,565	1,144

Table 1.2. The Six Case Study Countries Compared (*cont.*)

	Canada	United States	Mexico	Venezuela	Brazil	Argentina
Economic Data (in US$)[h]						
GDP total[i]	1.34 trillion	14.1 trillion	874.8 billion	326.1 billion	1.59 trillion	307.2 billion
GNI (Atlas method; 2009)[i]	1.32 trillion	14.0 trillion	860.3 billion	323.5 billion	1.56 trillion	297.7 billion
GNI per capita (Atlas method; 2009)[i]	41,980.00	46,360.00	8,960.00	10,090.00	8,070.00	7,550.00
GDP per capita (2009)[i]	39,599.00	45,989.00	8,143.00	11,490.00	8,230.00	7,626.00

a. *Source:* United Nations Population Division (2006).

b. *Source:* IBGE (2010).

c. Statistics Canada (2012a).

d. 2005 estimates.

e. In Canada, Census Metropolitan Areas (CMAs). A CMA is an urban area with a population of at least 100,000, including an urban core with a population of at least 50,000. Statistics Canada (2012b).

f. In the USA, Metropolitan Statistical Areas (MSAs). An MSA contains a core urban area of at least 50,000 population.. It comprises the central county or counties containing the core, plus adjacent outlying counties having a high degree of social and economic integration with the central county or counties as measured through commuting ("Notices," *Federal Register* 75, no. 123 [June 28, 2010]: 37252).

g. Formally designated in federal or state legislation as of 2010.

h. GNI (or gross national product in the terminology of the 1968 United Nations System of National Accounts) measures the total domestic and foreign value added claimed by residents. GNI comprises GDP plus net receipts of primary income (compensation of employees and property income) from nonresident sources. The World Bank uses GNI per capita in U.S. dollars to classify countries for analytical purposes and to determine borrowing eligibility. When calculating GNI in U.S. dollars from GNI reported in national currencies, the World Bank follows its Atlas conversion method, using a three-year average of exchange rates to smooth the effects of transitory exchange rate fluctuations. Gross domestic product (GDP) is the sum of value added by all resident producers plus any product taxes less subsidies not included in the valuation of output). Growth is calculated from constant price GDP data in local currency. GDP per capita is gross domestic product divided by midyear population. See Finfacts (2011).

i. *Source:* World Bank (2009).

part of the twentieth century, emerged from dictatorship somewhat erratically in the 1960s, which began with a power-sharing arrangement between the two major parties. And while that transitional democracy was more effectively consolidated in the 1980s and 1990s, its democratic institutions have become increasingly fragile under Chavez, though Chavez has mobilized civic involvement of low-income groups to support his political project and centralized control. Mexico, long regarded as "inclusionary authoritarian" under the aegis of a dominant single party for over seventy years until 2000, today has a consolidating democracy with three principal parties sharing the majority of the seats in Congress and vying for the presidency. Both Canada and the United States have consolidated democracies. Canada is a parliamentary democracy with four major parties in the Ottawa Parliament, and while there are periodic claims for secession in Quebec, thus far those claims have been accommodated within the federalist structure without a breakup. The United States has two principal parties and a stable democracy with strong traditions of civic participation in local government, although here too there are cycles in which the role of the federal government waxes and wanes under "New Federalism" and even "New New Federalism" (Wilson et al. 2008).

The Research Design and the Structure of the Book

Although we come to this collaborative study from the perspective of different academic traditions, our research agenda seeks answers that we hope will be relevant to all those who engage in public policy. As academic researchers we adopt a range of disciplinary perspectives and methods to formulate and examine questions of governance. Ours is an empirically grounded, interdisciplinary perspective, but in all cases our goal is to reflect upon what our findings say for policy and governance.[7] Thus in the following chapters we look across these differences to assess the different experiences observed and to explain the rationales and behaviors that shape metropolitan governance in such different polities — even while we hold uniform their underlying federalist nature. Though the chapters have a common framework, from the outset we also wanted to ensure that the uniqueness of each country's metropolitan governance structure and vision should come to the fore and not be obscured by forced comparisons of the lowest-common-denominator type.

In retrospect this has been just as well, since our respective case studies show a great diversity in experiences and outcomes, driven by a number

of factors that we will explore. And while we see far less institutionalization of metropolitan governance than we expected, the issue continues
to play an important part in the democratic conversation in each of the
six countries. Indeed, another of our principal concerns was prompted by
the question: What are the future prospects for effective metropolitan
governance — what needs to be done and by whom, and what might be
the levers to achieve it? Given that metropolitan governance is not yet a
mature field of study and even less a robust field of public policy, our final
chapter will provide conclusions about the future that we hope will engage the policy community.

The order in which the chapters appear is neither north to south nor
alphabetical. Rather, chapters are ordered according to a certain logic that
appears from the case studies. Canada, the United States, and Brazil (chapters 2–4) have more decentralized systems, and the institutional rules
and possibilities are, despite variability, relatively clear, with responsibilities resting primarily at the state level. In Mexico, Argentina, and Venezuela (chapters 5–7), where government is more centralized and metropolitan affairs are more politicized, the order here reflects a spectrum from
Mexico showing these features less than the other two cases to Venezuela
showing them the most.

For Canada, Andrew Sancton shows that provincial governments are
the primary tier of government and that where the principal cities are rapidly suburbanizing — as most are — the provincial government promotes
the central city to annex and/or merge its surrounding cities. Only in Vancouver do we find an example of a genuine metropolitan government
and governance structure — indeed, it is probably the sole example within
the six countries — but even here the arrangement grew out of agreement
and consensus of a confederacy of municipalities. In general, however,
the metropolitan question plays out differently in each province.

Robert Wilson shows that in the United States, as in Canada, city
governments are creations of state governments and that the response
to metropolitan challenges varies significantly across states. Many states
allow cities to annex and incorporate by agreement. But the element
unique to the United States is the propensity for single-purpose governments to be created, with their own governance structure. This makes for
metropolitan governance that is conducted normally through a huge raft
of local governments; it may not be pretty, but this fragmented structure is
the prevailing model, partly because of urban-suburban political conflict.
Several counterfactual examples — two-tier arrangements — also exist, and
these are discussed and analyzed with a view to explaining why, in certain

circumstances, states and cities do grasp the nettle and construct a new tier of governance.

The third case study is that of Brazil, which, as Peter Spink, Marco Antonio Teixeira, and Roberta Clemente describe, was the only country to have systematically created metropolitan regions as part of its constitutional structure during its period of military government. Metropolitan governance was further extended to some twenty-five metropolitan regions after the 1988 democratic constitution. Here too, however, metropolitan regions are under the aegis of state governments: while they are empowered in juridical terms, the authors show that they are almost uniformly weak, poorly articulated, and not popularly supported. This contrasts with a more positive feature of the Brazil local governance scene: the noninstitutional presence of intermunicipal agreements and consortia used to coordinate infrastructure or to collaborate on environmental and social policies such as health and economic development. These arrangements do appear to elicit a sense of identity and support from local citizens, yet they are technical and managerial rather than democratic in approach.

The cases of Mexico, Argentina, and Venezuela show less systematic and less predictable trajectories of constructing metropolitan governance and highlight how (partisan) politics often plays a big part in shaping the outcomes. Peter Ward and Hector Robles show that in Mexico the concept of the metropolitan is federally defined and that while consultative arrangements are mandated for conurbations these have neither executive functions nor outcomes: they are at best "indicative." The authors analyze five different metropolitan case studies, ranging from the single-municipality case of Ciudad Juárez to multijurisdictional Mexico City, which straddles two states and comprises over fifty boroughs. In between are Guadalajara, which has a flawed metropolitan council, and Monterrey, where the state executive takes effective control of matters metropolitan. While the results point to the importance — as in the previous three cases — of a more active role for state-level government, it is much less clear how this will play out in the future.

In Argentina, although the states (provinces) have primary responsibility for activating and overseeing metropolitan governance arrangements, the high levels of partisanship among the executive and legislative bodies, the dominance of a single central municipality and competition and distrust among the others, and political rivalry between mayors and the state executive all make serious and sustainable collaboration difficult at the metropolitan level. As Pedro Pírez demonstrates, the federal government becomes involved only when two states share a metropolitan area that straddles their common borders and where the possibility of recourse to a third (higher) authority does seem to enhance metropolitan organization and effectiveness; otherwise it is largely absent.

Finally, David Myers documents that Venezuela has always been highly politicized and centralized in relation to urban questions. Even though the postdictatorship period from the 1960s onwards has seen some interest in and advocacy of municipal reform, efforts in this direction have come to nothing because partisan political control exercised from the center has restricted local autonomy and metropolitan initiatives. Only in Caracas has there been serious experimentation with a metropolitan structure, but even here it is partisan controlled: Myers's analysis reveals that it, too, is wholly driven by the Chávez political project. If politics undermines the possibilities of metropolitan governance in Venezuela, the only good news is that some large cities are embedded in a large single (municipal) district, so that interjurisdictional integration is less of an issue.

The final chapter, by Ward, Spink, and Wilson, places the experiences of the six countries in the context of the original research questions outlined in this chapter. Two conclusions stand out. First there is a clear and urgent need to conceive and create new governance structures for metropolitan affairs that will enable metropolitan-wide policies to be formulated and implemented and will meaningfully engage citizens living there. Although this finding applies to a full range of public policies, given the context of metropolitan-wide socioeconomic and public resource disparities it is particularly relevant to the alleviation of poverty and reduction of social inequities and, more generally, to improving people's lives. The second set of conclusions concerns how best to achieve this and move forward. The case studies suggest that while regional governments — states and provinces — are the most practical initiators of an effective architecture of metropolitan governance, there is no single route to get "there" from the "here and now" and certainly no single overall normative imperative that should be taken as best practice. Several midrange strategies and possible conclusions can be offered, but states and localities will need to work out the politics and management structures that work best in their own polities and localities. The result will very likely be different approaches within the same country, any one of which may be similar to approaches in other countries, thus confirming one of the practical benefits of comparative studies — the identification of opportunities for conversation. Achieving effective metropolitan governance will require the day-to-day negotiation of many changes in existing patterns of incentives and disincentives. Overall, however, we believe that the principle of federalist subsidiarity, used sparingly and conceived both from the bottom up and from the top down, may serve to retain local control while scaling up the functions of metropolitan governance, and, hopefully, developing a sense of citizen commitment and identification to the broader metropole.

Notes

1. The religious nuances are due in part to the term's early appearance, in the writings of the bishop of Mainz (Wilhelm von Ketteler, 1811–77), in the proposition that policies performed by the most appropriate level of the social order achieve results without overcompensating, which would breed dependency, or undercompensating, which would fail to fully satisfy needs relative to the common good. Ketteler's proposition was a major influence on Pope Leo XIII's formulation of the *Rerum Novarum* (1891), the document that signaled the Catholic Church's entry into the ideological dispute over the nature of society and the state.

2. Similarly, so-called federacy arrangements, while relatively rare, accord one or more regions or states more independence and autonomy than the nation or kingdom accords its substate units. Examples here would be the United Kingdom's Channel Islands and the Isle of Man; Nicaragua's North and South Atlantic Autonomous Regions; and Denmark and Greenland's Faroe Islands, among others. Spain is another country where autonomous internal regions are constantly redefining the subnational arena. This is sometimes called "asymmetric federalism" (Stepan 1999).

3. The Forum is an independent organization that was initiated in Canada and is supported by many countries and governments. Its primary focus is to discuss the contribution of federalism to the maintenance and construction of democratic societies and governments (www.forumfed.org).

4. The formation of policy communities and international organizations, including UN Habitat (www.unhabitat.org) and United Cities and Local Governments (www.cities-localgovernments.org), that are concerned with analyzing urban issues and sharing best policy practices attests to the increasing recognition of the importance of these issues.

5. This issue is by no means a new concern; see Ostrom, Tiebout, and Warren (1961).

6. Huntington's two-turnover test proposes that a fledgling democracy is not tested until it has undergone two changes of party in government (Huntington 1991).

7. While our approach is interdisciplinary, the various disciplines represented among the authors include social psychology (Spink); geography and sociology (Ward and Pírez); urban and regional planning (Wilson); and political science (Myers and Sancton).

Chapter 2

Metropolitan Governance in Canada

ANDREW SANCTON

Despite the country's vast territory, Canada's population is concentrated in a few urban areas not far from the border with the United States. The border is important because the Canadian approach to governing urban areas is quite different from the American. Growth in Canada's population is restricted almost exclusively to urban areas and to nearby towns and villages, and the challenges for the institutions of urban governance are great.

The aim of this chapter is to describe and analyze the various approaches adopted within Canada to address the problems of metropolitan governance over the past fifty years. This has been a period of exceptionally rapid urban growth, especially in areas immediately outside the boundaries of central-city municipalities. Such growth has caused the various provinces constantly to seek changes in local governmental institutions so as to adapt to this growth and to attempt to shape it efficiently and effectively.

POLITICS AND FEDERALISM IN CANADA

Canada is a parliamentary democracy whose head of state is Queen Elizabeth II. Except when the queen is in Canada, she is represented by the

44

governor general, who is appointed by the queen on the advice of her Canadian prime minister. The Parliament of Canada comprises the queen, the Senate (whose members are appointed by the prime minister), and an elected House of Commons. The prime minister and his or her cabinet must retain the confidence of the House of Commons to remain in office. As the government, they exercise the formal authority of the governor general, leaving the latter to exercise only the symbolic responsibilities of a head of state. Canada has two official languages, English and French. The main political parties are the Conservatives, New Democrats, and Liberals, but the Conservatives and Liberals are the only ones to have formed federal governments.

Of considerably more importance to this chapter is the fact that Canada is a federation, initially established by the British North America Act, 1867, now the Constitution Act, 1867. After 1867 Canada progressively detached itself from British authority, but it was only in 1982 that Canadians formally obtained the legal authority to amend all aspects of their constitution without reference to the British Parliament. In 1867, the Canadian federation comprised four provinces; six more were subsequently added, all from territory previously under some form of British control. Each province is formally headed by another representative of the queen, the lieutenant governor, and each has its own unicameral legislature, whose confidence the provincial government (headed by a premier) must always retain. There are also three northern territories, each of which has its own elected legislature but remains under the ultimate authority of the federal government.

Canada is probably the most decentralized federation in the world, meaning that the provinces are extremely powerful. Most of their legal authority derives from § 92 of the Constitution Act, 1867, which lists specific legislative powers that are allocated to the provinces. One such power is "municipal institutions in the province." Unlike the federal system in the United States, the federal parliament in Canada was granted all of the legislative authority not explicitly granted to the provinces. While the American federal government generally grew stronger over time, in Canada it was the provinces that won the biggest victories in the battle for legislative supremacy. Many such victories were the direct or indirect result of the political influence of the province of Quebec. In large part Quebec has this influence because it is the only state or province in North America with a French-speaking majority, and its political leaders have fought tenaciously to maintain all the power needed to protect Quebec's majority language and culture. Other provinces have been pleased to benefit from Quebec's gains. The result has been that no federal government in Canada (unlike its American counterpart with respect to American states) would ever attempt to influence provincial decisions about such matters as public education or welfare policies for poor people. Some observers (especially in Quebec) even go so far as to say that federal policies explicitly aimed at cities are illegitimate because they impinge on provincial legislative responsibility for "municipal institutions." Another important sign of real provincial autonomy in Canada is that most political parties in most provinces have no institutional connection with any party at the federal level. This includes all provincial political parties with the words *liberal* or *conservative* in their official names.

Unlike the federal and provincial governments, the municipal institutions established by the various provinces do not act on behalf of the Crown. They do not have parliamentary systems of government but rather possess internal structures similar to those of municipal governments in Britain and the United States. Most Canadian municipal elections are conducted on a nonpartisan basis. Where political parties do exist and where elections are partisan, as in Montreal and Vancouver, they are separate in name and organization from parties at both federal and provincial levels, meaning that citizens in these cities have three distinct sets of parties to contend with as they decide for whom to vote on three separate election days.

The Importance of Metropolitan Areas

In 2001, Statistics Canada for the first time provided data for a new kind or urban entity: *major urban regions.* Only four regions in the country qualified: the Extended Golden Horseshoe (Toronto); Montreal and Its Adjacent Region; the Lower Mainland and Southern Vancouver Island; and the Calgary-Edmonton Corridor. In 2001, these major urban regions had a combined population of 15.3 million, or 51 percent of the entire Canadian population, up from 49 percent in 1996 and approximately 41 percent in 1971. Between 1996 and 2001, the four major urban regions grew by 7.6 percent, compared to a 0.5 percent increase in the rest of the country (Statistics Canada 2003). For more information on these major urban regions, see table 2.1.

Population data in this chapter derive from the 2006 census, but no data were provided for the major urban regions. We must rely instead on the much more firmly established census metropolitan areas (CMAs).

Table 2.1. Canada's Four Major Urban Regions, 2001

	Share of Canadian Population	Population in Millions	% Increase from 1996	% Share of Relevant Provincial Population
Extended Golden Horseshoe	22	6.7	9.2	59
Montreal and Its Adjacent Region	12	3.7	2.8	52
Lower Mainland and Southern Vancouver Island	9	2.7	7.3	69
Calgary-Edmonton Corridor	7	2.15	12.3	72

Sources: Statistics Canada (2003).

Statistics Canada states that "a census metropolitan area (CMA) . . . is formed by one or more adjacent municipalities centered on a large urban area (known as the urban core). A CMA must have a total population of at least 100,000 of which 50,000 or more must live in the urban core. . . . To be included in the CMA . . ., other adjacent municipalities must have a high degree of integration with the central urban area, as measured by commuting flows derived from census place of work data" (Statistics Canada 2007).

In this chapter, we are focusing on CMAs having populations of more than five hundred thousand (see table 2.2). The main difficulty in using this list of CMAs relates to Toronto. The five CMAs of Toronto, Oshawa, Hamilton, Kitchener, and St. Catharines-Niagara are contiguous, forming a continuous built-up urban area often known as the Golden Horseshoe because of the horseshoe shape it forms as it wraps around the western tip of Lake Ontario. The Extended Golden Horseshoe used by Statistics Canada to describe Toronto's major urban region, is, of course, based on this name (figure 2.1). Only two of the CMAs in the Extended Golden Horseshoe — Toronto and Hamilton — have populations of over five hundred thousand. For the purposes of this paper, each will be treated separately.

Table 2.2 shows that there is considerable variation in the demographic characteristics of Canadian metropolitan areas. Between 2001 and 2006, five of the nine metropolitan areas grew faster than the national average of 5.4 percent, with Calgary and Edmonton growing at

Table 2.2. Canada's Census Metropolitan Areas with Populations over 500,000 in 2006

CMA	2006 Population	% Increase since 2001	% of Population in Central City	% of Labor Force in Manufacturing and FIRE Employment	Median Annual Earnings (full-time workers)	% Visible Minority	% Foreign Born
Toronto	5,113,149	9.2	49.0	24.7	$45,350	42.9	45.7
Montreal	3,635,571	5.3	44.6	20.0	$39,419	16.5	20.6
Vancouver	2,116,581	6.5	27.3	15.9	$43,215	39.6	41.7
Ottawa-Gatineau	1,130,761	5.9	71.8	9.3	$50,298	16.0	18.1
Calgary	1,079,310	13.4	91.4	13.6	$46,189	22.2	23.6
Edmonton	1,034,945	10.4	70.6	13.6	$44,515	17.1	18.5
Quebec	715,515	4.2	68.6	15.9	$38,851	2.3	3.7
Winnipeg	694,668	2.7	91.1	17.5	$38,773	15.0	17.8
Hamilton	692,991	4.6	72.8	22.0	$46,146	12.3	24.3
CANADA	31,612,897	5.4		17.8	$41,401	13.4	18.4

Sources: Statistics Canada (2008).

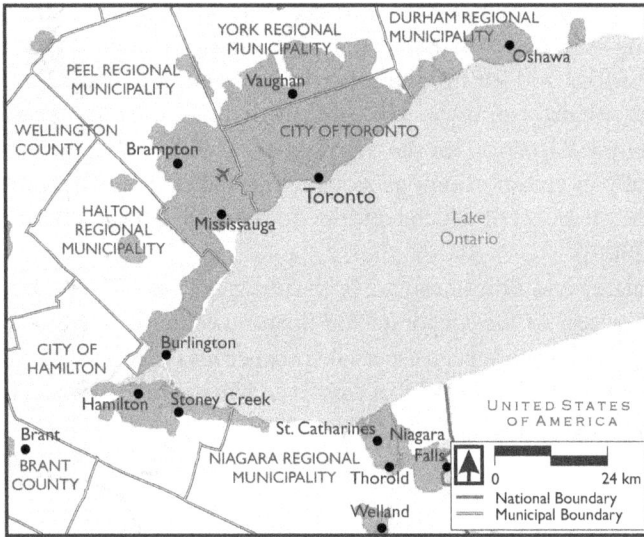

Figure 2.1. The Golden Horseshoe in Ontario

the astounding rates of 13.4 and 10.4 percent respectively. At the opposite end of the scale was Winnipeg at only 2.7 percent. Probably the most significant demographic differences among these CMAs relate to the diversity of their respective populations as measured both by the percentage of visible minorities and by the percent foreign born. Here both Toronto and Vancouver rank extremely high, attracting immigrants of all racial backgrounds from all over the world and thereby enhancing their reputations as globalizing cities. At the opposite end of this scale is Quebec City, with numbers so low that they confirm the city's image as a governmental center populated by provincial civil servants and as a regional center for Canadians whose French origins go back many centuries. Despite these variations among Canadian CMAs, there is no evidence that the presence or absence of high numbers of immigrants has had any effect on the nature of metropolitan governance.

Toronto and Vancouver are both globalizing metropolitan areas with significant population growth fed by very high immigration levels. Montreal — once Canada's largest urban area — continues its secular decline in relation to Toronto but retains its role as the metropolis of the increasingly dynamic and self-confident French-language community based in Quebec. Although not as attractive to immigrants as Toronto and Vancouver, Montreal has increasingly become a magnet for French-speaking immigrants from places such as Haiti, Vietnam, Lebanon, and North Africa and for immigrants who are willing to learn French as a second or third language. The result is that Montreal has become the main physical location for the transformation of French Canada from an ethnically and racially homogeneous community to a much more diverse one, the members of which continue to share a language (Germain and Rose 2000).

Calgary and Edmonton are both riding a resource boom led by rising oil prices. As the corporate and financial center of the Canadian oil industry, Calgary has been especially prosperous in recent years, but neither place is a significant global city. Even less so are the remaining metropolitan areas listed in table 2.2.

The Framework for Addressing Policy Issues

Canada is a highly urbanized and highly decentralized federation. Under the Canadian Constitution, provinces have direct responsibility not only for municipal institutions but also for education and health care facilities. This means that many of the most important decisions about public sector institutions within Canada's metropolitan areas are under provincial jurisdiction. In theory at least, the federal government can spend money on such provincial matters as education and health, but it cannot attempt to regulate them by enacting legislation. There is no constitutional obligation for provinces even to establish municipalities and other locally controlled decision-making bodies, let alone devolve authority to them.

Most provinces have articulated strategic land use policies, which municipalities are expected to follow. Most provinces have also been highly interventionist with respect to municipal structures, so that Canadian metropolitan areas over time and in different provinces have experienced almost every kind of institutional arrangement imaginable. The fact that provinces have been heavily involved has meant that nongovernmental actors have been less important in metropolitan governance, certainly in comparison with metropolitan areas in the United States, where involvement of private sector and voluntary agencies has been a hallmark of what has often been labeled the "new regionalism" (Sancton 2001).

Among the nine CMAs in Canada with populations over five hundred thousand, there are effectively four different types of institutional arrangements for metropolitan governance:

1. No metropolitan level of government; various single-purpose authorities; and strong provincial involvement in metropolitan issues. This is the institutional arrangement for Toronto.
2. A multifunctional metropolitan-level institution covering all or most of the CMA, as found in Montreal, Vancouver, and Quebec City.
3. A federal government institution (the National Capital Commission) with multifunctional capability in the National Capital Region, which straddles the provinces of Ontario and Quebec.
4. A single municipality that covers all or most of a CMA, making another level of metropolitan government unnecessary. This is the arrangement for each of the remaining CMAs, including Ottawa in Ontario and Gatineau in Quebec, which are the dominant municipalities within the National Capital Region. Ironically, it is also the situation in Quebec City, where the central city comprises more than 70 percent of the population of the CMA *and* there is a form of metropolitan government.

Each arrangement will be described in turn.

No Metropolitan Level of Government,
Single-Purpose Authorities: Toronto

The municipality of metropolitan Toronto (1954–97) was probably Canada's best-known municipal institutional innovation. "Metro" and its constituent municipalities became the textbook example of a successful two-tier system. The upper-tier Metro council was created by the province of Ontario in 1953, primarily to solve a service crisis in the rural and suburban municipalities surrounding the city of Toronto. These municipalities had been unable to cope with the infrastructure demands in the Toronto region caused by the explosive growth of the postwar economy. With its functional responsibility for water supply and sewage treatment systems, arterial roads, and regional planning, Metro facilitated, in a relatively orderly way, the continued growth of the Toronto CMA in the late 1950s and 1960s (Frisken 2007).

By the 1970s, however, the Metro system in Toronto was facing at least three major problems. First, suburban municipalities within Metro had collectively surpassed the population of the central city, largely because of the infrastructure paid for through taxes collected within the central city. Once in the majority, suburbs seemed unwilling to use Metro to help rebuild deteriorating infrastructure within the central city, and political tensions between the two sides mounted. Second, most of the new urban growth within the Toronto CMA was taking place outside the boundaries of Metro, but the provincial government did not extend its boundaries, thereby ensuring that Metro's regional planning functions would become increasingly irrelevant. Third, because the upper-tier authority was spending an increasing share of total municipal revenues, there was increasing pressure to have members of the upper-tier council directly elected to serve only at that level, rather than to have Metro councilors chosen by the lower-tier councils from among their own members. After the new arrangements for direct election were implemented in 1988, jurisdictional battles and disputes between elected politicians at the two levels became more common, and the two-tier system was increasingly seen as dysfunctional.

In late 1996 the government of Ontario announced that the municipality of metropolitan Toronto and its constituent parts would be merged into one new city of Toronto. The primary stated purpose of this policy was to save money. The policy caused a huge political battle that has been well documented elsewhere (Frisken 2007). The key point for this chapter is that the controversial amalgamation had nothing to do with metropolitan governance. In 2006, the population of the new city was 2.5 million, while that of the Toronto CMA was 5.11 million. In fact, as already noted, Toronto's metropolitan area really contains more like 6.7 million within the Extended Golden Horseshoe. All the difficult issues associated with metropolitan growth were taking place *outside* the new city's borders.

From 1998 until 2001, a Greater Toronto Services Board had a territory and mandate similar to what has just been proposed. It was replaced by a Central Ontario Smart Growth Panel with a territory closer to that of the Extended Golden Horseshoe, but its only mandate was to produce a report about how to manage future growth, a mission it accomplished in 2003. Since then, the province itself has taken responsibility for strategic infrastructure planning in the area that it calls the Greater Golden Horseshoe (Sancton 2008, 121–27).

Multifunctional Metropolitan Institutions: Vancouver, Montreal, Quebec City

In the late 1960s the legislature in British Columbia established a network of "regional districts" throughout the entire province that remains in

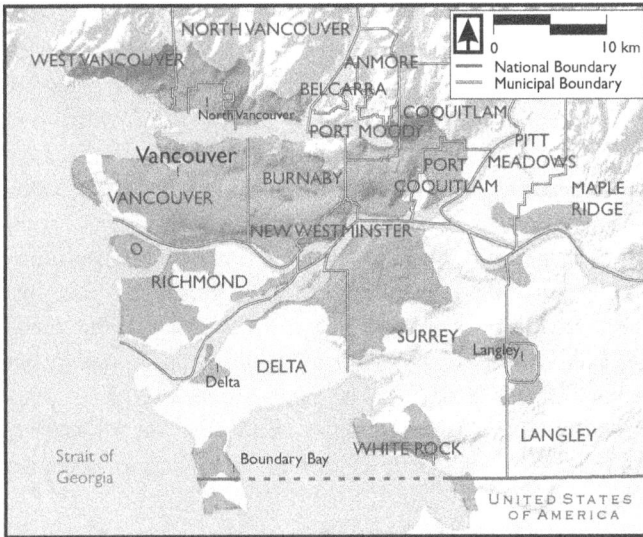

Figure 2.2. Vancouver Metropolitan Area

place today. The Greater Vancouver Regional District — now known as Metro Vancouver — provides a mechanism for metropolitan government in British Columbia's most populous CMA (figure 2.2; Cashaback 2001).

The provincial government in British Columbia was anxious to emphasize that a new level of government was not being created. The regional districts were to include many existing intermunicipal special-purpose bodies and to act as an institution through which increased intermunicipal cooperation could be encouraged. Regional districts are governed by a board of directors, not a council; directors are all themselves elected members of municipal councils, and they have multiple votes depending on the size of the population they represent; municipalities can opt out of many regional services or, if they are near the outer boundaries, opt into the services being provided by a neighboring district; the districts were created without changing any existing municipal boundaries. Although there have been some calls for direct election to the boards of directors of regional districts (Patrick Smith and Stewart 1998), no government has moved toward implementing such a change, presumably because of a concern about the jurisdictional conflicts that would likely ensue.

Metro Vancouver has twenty-one member municipalities and a population in 2006 of 2.117 million. Its territory corresponds exactly to that of the Vancouver CMA. The population of the city of Vancouver was 578,041. The suburban city of Surrey is not far behind, with a population of 394,976 (Statistics Canada 2008). In short, by Canadian standards, the municipal system of the Vancouver CMA is quite highly fragmented, but Metro Vancouver acts to provide services concerning regional planning, water and sewage, garbage disposal, and regional parks. Although it is impossible to determine objectively an ideal institutional model for metropolitan governance, it is hard to imagine a mechanism that could better combine local self-government through established municipalities with the existence of an institution at the metropolitan level that provides both a degree of consensual metropolitan leadership and a framework (the strategic plan) within which municipalities can voluntarily cooperate with each other.

In 2000, the Quebec Legislature established somewhat similar institutions, called metropolitan communities, for Montreal and Quebec City. The territory of the Montreal Metropolitan Community (MMC) corresponds very closely to that of the Montreal CMA. It comprises the territories of the city of Montreal plus eighty-two other municipalities. The MMC has potential responsibilities relating to regional planning, waste disposal, regional parks, coordination of public transport, economic development, regional infrastructure, and cost sharing for public housing. It is governed by an indirectly elected twenty-eight-person council that is chaired by the mayor of Montreal, who is the MMC's main political spokesperson.[1] Similar structures are in place for the Quebec (City) Metropolitan Community, which comprises twenty-seven municipalities on both sides of the St. Lawrence River and on the historic Ile d'Orleans. It is still far too early to assess the effects of the new metropolitan communities on Quebec's two major CMAs, although initial indications are that they have not had much impact.

The National Capital Commission: Ottawa and Gatineau

Canada's fourth-most-populous CMA is Ottawa-Gatineau, with a 2006 population of 1,130,761. Of this number, 812,129 lived in the city of Ottawa, Ontario, and 242,124 in Gatineau, Quebec. The territory of the CMA is roughly coterminous with the territory of the National Capital Commission (NCC), an agency of the federal government that has existed in its current form since 1959. The commission comprises fifteen members appointed by the federal government. In its earlier institutional manifestations it played a major role in drawing up and implementing a regional plan for the entire area, the most notable feature of which is a Greenbelt around the original city of Ottawa. The NCC is also responsible for significant green spaces and recreational areas on the Quebec side of the river. An important constitutional ruling of the Supreme Court of Canada in 1966 held that the federal government had the power to plan for the National Capital Region and to expropriate land for its purposes, including land for the Greenbelt (Fullerton 1974, 1–14). Such a power related exclusively to the fact that the area in question was the federal capital. Similar federal powers do not exist in other Canadian CMAs.

In the last few decades the NCC has built parkways, removed railway tracks from Ottawa's downtown, renovated historical buildings, provided sites for national museums, and created a winter skateway on the frozen Rideau Canal. In short, it has done many of the things that are often expected of metropolitan governments. The difference, of course, is that metropolitan governments are generally accountable in one way or another to metropolitan residents. In the case of the NCC, board members are accountable only to the federal government that appointed them. Although there have been many examples of localized objections to NCC actions, most residents of Ottawa-Gatineau are highly appreciative. They should be: the NCC spends money from all Canadians to provide urban amenities for the approximately 3 percent of Canadians who live in the National Capital Region.

A Single Municipality That Covers All or Most of a CMA: Calgary, Edmonton, Winnipeg, Hamilton

Calgary is Canada's fifth-most-populous CMA, with a 2006 population of 1,079,310. The 2006 population of the city of Calgary was 988,193, meaning that there was no possible reason for a distinct metropolitan level of government. The city's territory has increased incrementally over many decades as a result of a continuing series of annexations. Some have been controversial and have generated intense opposition. Decisions on annexation applications from cities in Alberta are made by a quasi-judicial body, the Local Authorities Board (LAB). The usual pattern in the past has been for Calgary to ask for very large annexations and for the LAB to grant less than what it asked for (Masson and LeSage 1994, 164–66).

The creation of a single-tier metropolitan authority without there having been a strong two-tier system is likely to be possible only within metropolitan areas that do not have large populations. Calgary is perhaps the exception that proves the rule. Its annexations have been facilitated by the absence of long-standing urban municipalities nearby (Parker 2005). Simple as single-tier structures are, they are not without their problems. Annexation battles—even in Calgary—are often slow, messy, unpopular, and expensive; occasionally the provincial government has to step in directly to sort out intractable disputes.

The territory of the city of Edmonton has also increased dramatically over the years through use of the same Alberta laws and practices that were in force in Calgary. The difference in Edmonton is that incorporated suburban municipalities are nearby and have generally fought hard against forced annexation. As a result, while the 2006 population of the Edmonton CMA was 1,034,945, the population of the city was only 730,372, or 70.6 percent of the total CMA population. Although this percentage is small compared to Calgary, it is high compared to most North American central cities. There is no pressure from anyone for a distinct level of metropolitan government. However, the City of Edmonton has often called for municipal amalgamations over the years, while the suburban municipalities have claimed that voluntary intermunicipal cooperation is quite sufficient. The latest institutional vessel for such voluntary cooperation was the Alberta Capital Region Alliance, created in 1995, comprising twenty-two distinct, incorporated municipalities. But the City of Edmonton withdrew in frustration in 2006, thereby dooming the voluntary approach. In response, the government of Alberta in 2008 created the Capital Region Board, comprising a provincially appointed chair and the mayors and representatives of twenty-five contiguous municipalities. The board's initial priorities are "to create a long-range plan for regional land use and infrastructure such as roads and transit; develop an electronic system to share geographic information; and develop a strategic plan for social and affordable housing." The board can do nothing without the support of both the City of Edmonton and a large majority of the suburban and rural municipalities. Although each member has one vote, "If a decision of the Capital Region Board is to be made by a vote, the decision must be supported by not fewer than seventeen representatives from participating municipalities that collectively have at least 75 percent of the population in the Capital Region" (Capital Region Board 2008).

Winnipeg is Canada's eighth most populous CMA. In 1970 the New Democratic Party (the social democratic party that at the time controlled the Manitoba Provincial Legislature) decided to create a single City of Winnipeg—a "unicity"—to replace a two-tier system of municipal government comprising the Corporation of Greater Winnipeg and its twelve constituent municipalities. The main declared objective of the provincial government was to equalize taxes and service levels within the territory of the new unicity (Brownstone and Plunkett 1983).

The Manitoba New Democratic Party believed at the time that it could establish a single, amalgamated city and simultaneously create innovative mechanisms for decentralization and citizen participation. Indeed, there was great initial optimism that a new era in municipal government was being launched. The first unicity council had fifty members, each of whom sat on one of thirteen community committees that would advise the main council on matters of more local concern. These committees were in turn advised by residents' advisory groups whose members were chosen at open community meetings. Over time, enthusiasm for consultation and advice waned, especially as it became evident that the unicity council could not possibly do what every councilor and local group wanted. By 1992, the council had been reduced to fifteen members and much of the special machinery for citizen participation had eroded or been abolished. Since then, the provincial government has seemed concerned more with managing growth outside the unicity's borders than with the institutions within (Province of Manitoba 2003). In 1991, the unicity comprised 94.5 percent of the population of the Winnipeg CMA. In 2006, the equivalent figure was 91.1 percent, meaning that the CMA area beyond the unicity's boundaries was growing faster than the unicity itself.

The remaining CMA with a population above five hundred thousand is Hamilton, which is immediately west of Toronto and is now considered by Statistics Canada to be part of the Extended Golden Horseshoe. As in Winnipeg in 1970 and Toronto in 1998, Hamilton's two-tier system of metropolitan government was completely amalgamated in 2001.

Agenda Setting, Political Representation, and the Exercise of Power

Not surprisingly, the politics of metropolitan areas varies quite dramatically, depending on the institutional settings that are involved. The institutions are determined by the provincial governments, and their respective approaches are quite disparate, causing a great variety in Canadian arrangements for metropolitan governance. Nevertheless, some significant generalizations apply more or less to all major Canadian metropolitan areas. First, no metropolitan governments are themselves the subject of great political loyalty, conflict, or functional importance. As we have seen, the city governments of Calgary, Winnipeg, and Hamilton can be seen as metropolitan governments because of their wide territorial scope and because they include such a high proportion of the population of their respective metropolitan areas. These governments are seen as important, but not because they are metropolitan. They are important because they do the normal things that city governments do. The Montreal and Quebec Metropolitan Communities are so new, so functionally weak, and so overshadowed by recent debates about municipal amalgamation and de-amalgamation that only a tiny proportion of the metropolitan population would even know that they exist.

Because provincial governments play such important roles with respect to policy making for health, income security, education, and social services, none of these policy areas are thought of by Canadians as having a particularly metropolitan focus. Social housing is often considered to be more of a municipal function in Canada, but metropolitan institutions, to the extent that they exist at all, have no direct operational role with respect to housing. At best — notably in the province of Quebec, and more recently in Edmonton — they have a potential role as planners for the territorial distribution of social housing.

Above all, the metropolitan agenda in Canada is about urban infrastructure (roads, rapid transit systems, sewers, water supply systems) and the regional planning that is required to build such infrastructure in a reasonably effective manner so that the inefficiencies resulting from uncontrolled urban sprawl are at least minimized, if not prevented. To the extent that there is popular interest in such issues, it comes from commuters caught in traffic jams, truckers who cannot move their cargoes, developers concerned about servicing capacities, and environmentalists of many different stripes, whose concerns in most cases are antithetical to those of the other groups. But these conflicts are not manifested in a metropolitan political arena. They sometimes play themselves out in local municipal politics, but more often in provincial politics.

Outward and explicit evidence of conflict in metropolitan policy making is not often found in election platforms, political advertising, or the other kinds of political activity that usually attract the attention of the media. Instead, the conflicts are often buried in municipal official plans, consultants' reports, and the assumptions made by developers as they compete with each other in a complex marketplace. At various times and in various provinces, there have been requirements that some kind of metropolitan institution come up with a regional plan. The making of such plans sometimes reveals the real stakes in metropolitan politics, but just as often, unfortunately, the plans simply paper over political conflicts so as to meet the technical requirements of the plan-making exercise. Worse still, regional plans sometimes get formally adopted but are then ignored as circumstances change, new governments come to power, and items that were once political priorities (such as homelessness) seem to fall off the political agenda.

Because metropolitan issues are often seen as technical and specialized, they rarely provoke significant political mobilization. Perhaps because provincial governments are usually seen as having the capacity—and sometimes even the political will—to tackle metropolitan infrastructure problems, it is relatively rare for urban business interests to attempt to build community coalitions designed to act as substitutes for governments. Such coalitions are famously prevalent in American cities, precisely because governments appear so often to be unwilling or unable to address metropolitan issues.

In recent years Toronto has perhaps become the Canadian exception to the rule. In the absence of any metropolitan governmental structure for this area, a business-led group now called the Greater Toronto CivicAction Alliance has emerged to attempt to provide some leadership with respect to city-region issues. Like its counterparts in the many American city-regions that also lack formal mechanisms for city-region governance, the Alliance brings together representatives from many of Toronto's various communities and attempts to arrive at some consensus as to how public and private resources can be used to confront the area's many problems and to enhance its global competitiveness (Toronto City Summit Alliance 2003).

With respect to managing growth, it now appears that the provincial government itself is taking the initiative. A common argument advanced in Canada in general and in Toronto in particular in recent years is that in this age of global city-regions the ten provinces that comprise the Canadian federation have no long-term future as viable units of government. Instead, they will somehow give way to institutions of government that are based on the most important of the city-regions, Toronto being a prime example. But new initiatives from the government of Ontario to shape the nature of Toronto's long-term growth and to provide for greenbelts and other conventional mechanisms of regional planning suggest that the role of the provincial government with respect to urban affairs might well be increasing, rather than decreasing (Province of Ontario 2005). Indeed, it is likely that the provincial governments, instead of simply fading away, will consolidate their roles as the real strategic authorities for Canada's city-regions (Sancton 2008).

METROPOLITAN POLICY

In addition to the formal metropolitan structures described previously, almost every other conceivable mechanism for addressing metropolitan issues can be found in one Canadian city or another. For example, inter-municipal agreements are a mechanism through which the City of Toronto provides water for two of its northern suburban neighbors (White 2002). Similarly in Toronto, a special-purpose authority provides fixed-rail transit for the larger Toronto metropolitan area, although there is continuing controversy as to exactly who should be subsidizing what. Because, as we have seen, regional planning for Toronto has largely been taken over by the province, there are no longer any metropolitan institutions concerned with crucial government functions.

In British Columbia, on the other hand, there has been much controversy about the extent to which regional land use plans formulated by the regional districts should have precedence over the local plans of their constituent municipalities. Regardless of the legal technicalities, regional districts have played a major role in managing growth, aided by the provincial Land Reserve Commission, which is charged with protecting agricultural and forest land from undue urban development (Bish and Clemens 1999, 127).

Unlike Vancouver, in Calgary almost all the metropolitan area is governed by one municipality, the City of Calgary. The city's official objective is "to maintain at least a 30-year supply of developable land within its boundaries. Having this land supply allows for the long-term planning necessary to accommodate Calgary's high rate of growth and to facilitate the planning and budgeting of infrastructure (sewers, roads). Periodic annexations are proposed to maintain a long-term land supply." The city claims that its annexation policy is a key part of Calgary's "growth management strategy." "It helps ensure that sprawl does not occur, that is, haphazard development, often at very low density. Calgary's planned suburban communities now achieve densities of 6 to 8 dwelling units per acre. This is almost 40 percent denser than communities built in the 1970s and 1980s, and some twelve to sixteen times more land efficient than existing rural residential development outside Calgary's borders" (City of Calgary 2005).

In Winnipeg's metropolitan area there is similarly only one significant municipal government. The expectation of the creation of the unicity
in 1971 was that the growing tax base of suburban areas could be used to
support the deteriorating position of the central city. But as suburban political strength grew over time within the unicity council it became increasingly obvious that such an outcome was far from automatic. Tax levels might be equal, but decisions about infrastructure investment were
always the result of a political process that depended largely on where the
votes were. Parts of the central city of Winnipeg remain among the most
troubled in any city in Canada. To the extent that they have been assisted
by new infrastructure investment, the source of the funds has been the
federal government rather than suburban Winnipeg taxpayers.

Although Winnipeg has long been a grateful recipient of federal
bounty, other cities are now beginning to benefit from a deliberate attempt by the federal government to enhance its role in urban policy making, mainly through the provision of funds for renewing urban infrastructure. Although the Liberal government headed by Paul Martin (2004–6)
took an activist stance in relation to cities, the Conservative federal government headed by Stephen Harper has been much more cautious and
respectful of its traditional jurisdictional constraints. It has, however, extended previous federal commitments for the funding of infrastructure
while continuing to emphasize that its main interlocutors on this matter
are the provincial governments, not the cities themselves.

Urban municipalities in Canada are overwhelmingly dependent on
the property tax for their revenues. This is one of the major reasons
why they have recently been so aggressive in seeking new federal financial aid. In only a few cases do they have direct access to taxes collected
by the provinces. For example, the City of Montreal receives from the
Quebec government 1.5 cents per liter of the provincial gasoline tax
collected within its boundaries. South Coast British Columbia receives
11.5 cents per liter and turns it over to the Greater Vancouver Transportation Authority, which manages public transit and planning for major
traffic arteries throughout the region. The federal and Ontario governments are now sharing gasoline tax revenues as well, but such sharing
is not targeted at the largest CMAs. There is no municipal income or
sales tax in Canada.

The term *metropolitan governance* now has virtually no political salience in Canada. As we have seen, in seven of Canada's largest CMAs
the municipality of the central city is sufficiently significant in its territorial scope to itself act as the government of the metropolitan area. Metro

Vancouver is clearly a form of metropolitan government even if officially it is primarily a mechanism to facilitate intermunicipal cooperation. The Montreal Metropolitan Community is so functionally weak and so recent in its creation that it has not entered the public consciousness. Only in Toronto is there any serious concern about how metropolitan issues can be confronted. But even here it is becoming increasingly obvious that an institutional solution is in sight — the provincial government of Ontario is taking direct control itself.

Possible Future Shapes of Metropolitan Governance

Of the major CMAs being analyzed here, only Vancouver has a distinct metropolitan-level institution of government with any real functional capabilities. But even here it acts as a kind of umbrella institution for various special operating authorities for water, sewerage, and transportation. Metro Vancouver is obligated to adopt a regional planning document, but it must mobilize significant local municipal consent before its own plan is legally enforceable.

It is impossible to imagine, even in the Canadian context, that there will ever be a single municipality encompassing more than 70 percent of the population of the country's three most populous CMAs (Toronto, Montreal, Vancouver). But what of the others that have populations of over five hundred thousand? Is the large-central-city or single-tier model worthy of emulation? In all of these places, boundary extensions or outright municipal amalgamations have been extremely controversial and have been accomplished without the approval of the people who were forced to join the central city (Sancton 2000). In many countries, certainly including the United States, such a mechanism for extending municipal boundaries is simply out of the question.

But if such changes were politically possible elsewhere, would they be desirable? The Canadian experience is ambiguous at best. In Winnipeg, where a social democratic provincial government legislated complete municipal amalgamation largely to equalize tax rates, suburban politicians quickly dominated the new council and were reluctant to invest in severely deprived areas of the central city. Meanwhile, secession movements sprang up (one of which, in Headingley, was successful), and urban growth took place at a faster rate outside the city's boundaries than within them, causing policy makers to fret about the need for planning arrangements covering both the (relatively) populous city and the mainly rural municipalities that surround it. In Edmonton, annexation battles have been extremely controversial; the central city has not attained the complete consolidation it has been seeking for many years; and the province has imposed its new Capital Region Board.

Ottawa and Hamilton—both in Ontario—have large rural areas within the city boundaries, yet the boundaries are still not so perfect that they eliminate the need for difficult negotiations with their municipal neighbors, especially around transportation and planning issues. In both places there are concerns about the representation of rural areas in city decision making, and in both places there are rural secessionist movements, the strength of which is difficult to gauge.

Calgary would appear to be the single-tier system that has worked most smoothly, but questions remain about how long it can continue its apparently ceaseless expansion across the prairie and toward the Rocky Mountains. Eventually, it will come up against significant towns in its hinterland and the traditional intermunicipal metropolitan conflicts will inevitably break out.

Governance arrangements for the CMAs of Vancouver and Calgary appear to have been sufficiently successful to offer potential models for other countries. The new metropolitan communities in Montreal and Quebec City might one day—after they have become better established—offer yet another model. But it is Toronto that appears to be the model of how *not* to govern a metropolitan area. In the early 1990s it looked as though the provincial government was moving toward establishing a form of metropolitan government for much of the Toronto CMA and beyond. But this plan was rejected by a provincial government of a different political stripe and with much strength in the outer suburbs. This government chose to ignore the larger issues of metropolitan governance and to invest its political capital in sponsoring a forced merger of the components of the municipality of Metropolitan Toronto into a single City of Toronto. The result was a municipal behemoth with a population of more than two million but no capability to influence growth patterns in the suburbs beyond its borders. The next provincial government to face the problem has effectively chosen to become itself the metropolitan government. This model might well turn out to be functionally effective, especially in the eyes of those who favor greenbelts and limits on urban sprawl. But it will confound those who believe that city-regions should govern themselves and that Canada's provinces are outmoded relics of the days when Canada was a rural nation rather than an urban one.

NOTES

An earlier version of this chapter has been published as "A Review of Canadian Metropolitan Regions: Governance and Government," in *Governing Metropolitan Regions in the Twenty-First Century,* ed. Don Phares (2009). Permission from M. E. Sharpe to make use of that paper in this volume is gratefully acknowledged.

1. See the MMC's website under "Qui sommes nous," the subheads "Institution" and "Conseil" (http://cmm.qc.ca/qui-sommes-nous/institution/ and http://cmm.qc.ca/qui-sommes-nous/conseil/, accessed January 18, 2012).

Chapter 3

Metropolitan Governance in the United States

Is Fragmentation an Effective Strategy?

ROBERT H. WILSON

As cities grow larger, the nature of demand for public services changes dramatically. During the urbanization process in the United States new forms of local government emerged to meet these demands. The federalist system of government formed by the U.S. Constitution, ratified in 1788, has proven remarkably flexible in addressing the problems and challenges arising from urbanization. State governments, in particular, have facilitated the emergence of new forms of local governments and themselves have expanded into new policy arenas relevant to urban populations (Elazar 1987).

Today, the United States is fundamentally a metropolitan nation, with over 80 percent of the population living in what are designated as metropolitan areas (Frey et al. 2004). The spatial organization of metropolitan areas emerging after World War II has presented challenges to the provision of services and governance. Rapid suburbanization during this period has had a significant socioeconomic and racial dimension, with central cities exhibiting higher levels of poverty and minority population than suburban areas in the same metropolitan area. The socioeconomic disparities embedded in the spatial organization of metropolitan areas and the political representation shaped by the highly fragmented local government systems create significant impediments to metropolitan-wide governance initiatives. State governments hold critical authority over local governments and thus represent another potential source of approaches and policies addressing metropolitan challenges. But this authority is only rarely exercised, and states, in general, have been indifferent to concerns of large cities with relatively high levels of poor and minority populations.

Although examples of innovative responses have emerged, the patterns of metropolitan governance are far from uniform, and the wide range of approaches emphasize local control, that is, control by local governmental jurisdictions within metropolitan areas, with little authority ceded to metropolitan-wide initiatives. In some instances citizens have approved new forms of specialized (especially single-purpose) governments, while elsewhere the federal and state governments have encouraged collaboration and coordination. Concerns over efficiency and service provision play a leading role in most initiatives. But broadly speaking, metropolitan polities, institutions, and governing bodies that focus upon a metropolitan policy agenda are rare in the United States, and the metropolitan challenge is met largely through fragmented, ad hoc initiatives. The practice of fragmented governance is proving to be both a pragmatic and a reasonably effective response — at least in the U.S. case. This chapter will explain why this pattern of ad hoc metropolitan initiatives has emerged as the dominant form. It will be found that the significant socioeconomic disparities in the country's metropolitan areas and the fragmented local government structure with great value placed on local control contribute to this outcome. The chapter will also assess the ability of this unique governmental framework and its policy-making capabilities to address metropolitan issues.

Metropolitan Areas in the United States: Historical Origins and Contemporary Profile

The United States became an urban nation as it industrialized. Prior to the second half of the mid–nineteenth century, cities and towns largely served as trade and supply centers for a natural resource–based, largely agrarian, economy. Cities such as New York and New Orleans grew to significant size as a result of critical trade functions. With industrialization, urban growth followed a new dynamic and a new set of cities emerged.

Rapid population growth followed, and by 1900 one-half of the country's population already lived in cities. The development of the industrial city can be separated into two distinct phases, the first based on center-city growth and reinforced by railroad networks and the second defined by suburbanization and transportation systems relying on the internal combustion engine. The initial movement of manufacturing and residential population to the suburbs, following the appearance of trams, the omnibus, and automobiles, began in the early decades of the twentieth century, but by midcentury it had become the dominant pattern and had established the geographic foundation of metropolitan America. The suburbanization process was further encouraged by public policy that supported the housing industry, home ownership in particular, and the underlying infrastructure (Jackson 1985).

As we observed in chapter 1, a later and equally dramatic change took place in the urban structure of the United States during the 1960s and 1970s with the rapid growth of cities and the formation of metropolitan areas in the so-called Sunbelt, a region stretching from the South through the Southwest and up the western coast (Abbott 1993). Indeed, several metropolitan areas in the Sunbelt, such as Atlanta, Dallas, Los Angeles, and Seattle, eventually surpassed the population of most northern cities, with the principal exceptions of New York and Chicago.

This reshaping of the metropolitan structure toward the end of the twentieth century can be observed through population data for the largest metropolitan statistical areas (MSAs; the standard definitional unit adopted in the United States).[1] The share of national population in the largest twenty-five MSAs has been fairly stable, around 40 percent, even though the share of the largest ten and the single largest (New York MSA) declined somewhat between 1970 and 2000 (see table 3.1). This reflects the quite rapid growth of several smaller cities that were considered second tier at the beginning of the period, such as Dallas, Phoenix, and Houston. Today, the nine major census regions of the country have sizable metropolitan areas.

This pattern of urbanization was in large part driven by national economic restructuring during the last three decades of the twentieth century, briefly characterized by a relative decline in the size of the manufacturing sector and the expansion of several service sectors, especially the financial, insurance, and real estate sector (FIRE). The twenty-five largest MSAs reflect this change (see table 3.2), with a somewhat smaller share of the nation's employment in manufacturing relative to their share of population on account of a decentralization of manufacturing activity

Table 3.1. Population in Metropolitan Areas, 1970 and 2000

Metropolitan Area	Share of National Population 1970	2000	Growth Rate of Population, 1970–2000 (%)
New York metro region[a]	9.6	7.5	8.8
Top 10 metro areas	28.4	26.8	31.0
Top 25 metro areas	40.5	39.6	35.3

Sources: Calculations by authors from "Demographic Characteristics" data provided by State of the Cities Data System (http://socds.huduser.org/Census/Census_Home.html?) based upon 1970 and 2000 U.S. Censuses, using the 1990 definition of metropolitan areas (www.census.gov/population/metro/).

a. The New York CMSA, which includes the primary metropolitan statistical areas of New York – Northern New Jersey – Long Island and New York – New Jersey – Connecticut.

Table 3.2. Share of National Manufacturing and Financial Sector Employment in Metropolitan Areas, 1970 and 2000 (percent)

Area	Manufacturing 1970	2000	FIRE 1970	2000
New York metropolitan region[a]	9.4	5.8	15.1	10.3
Top 10 metro areas	28.7	25.6	37.3	31.2
Top 25 metro areas	39.7	38.0	55.0	46.2

Sources: Calculations by authors from "Characteristics of Workers by Place of Work" data provided by State of the Cities Data System (http://socds.huduser.org/Census/Census_Home.html?) based upon 1970 and 2000 U.S. Censuses, using the 1990 definition of metropolitan areas (www.census.gov/population/metro/).

a. The New York CMSA, which includes the primary metropolitan statistical areas of New York–Northern New Jersey–Long Island and New York–New Jersey–Connecticut.

to midsize cities and rural locations in recent decades (Wilson 1993). In contrast, these same MSAs have a relatively high share of national financial sector employment, although this, too, has shown a modest decline over the thirty-year period. Thus these twenty-five MSAs will be increasingly important to the country's economic prosperity, especially as leaders in the postindustrial economy and, to a lesser extent among the smaller of the twenty-five, as leaders in manufacturing.

In the United States, unlike most of the other countries examined in this volume, ethnicity and race are important public policy issues, particularly in MSAs where the demographic and ethnic structure differs from that of the country as a whole. African Americans tend to be concentrated in the large MSAs much more than whites and Hispanics (table 3.3). In addition, foreign-born nationals are rapidly increasing their share of the national population, and in 2000 nearly two-thirds of this population lived in the twenty-five largest MSAs, even though new immigrant gateways are found in some smaller cities and rural areas (Singer 2004; Rogers and Ward 2008). In sum, the diverse demographic composition of the United States is not evenly dispersed spatially; rather, minority and foreign national groups are relatively concentrated within metropolitan areas.

Furthermore, within individual metropolitan areas, significant demographic and socioeconomic differences exist across central cities and suburbia. With the exception of the New York MSA, only around 20 percent of the white population in MSAs lived in central cities (more precisely, the county in which the central city was located) in 2000 compared with the much larger proportion of blacks and Hispanics (see table 3.4). However, the central-city share of minority populations declined between 1980 and 2000 as minority populations suburbanized. Indeed, measures of racial segregation in metropolitan areas have declined in recent decades (Massey and Denton 1994; Iceland 2002). Nevertheless, central cities continue to have a larger share of minority and foreign-born populations than do suburban areas of MSAs.

In addition to differences in demographic composition, metropolitan areas display the complex socioeconomic conditions of the broader society (Altshuler et al. 1999). Between 1970 and 2000 poverty rates declined in the country as a whole, but they increased in metropolitan areas (table 3.5). But by the end of this period poverty rates in central cities were much higher than the national average. Moreover, the poverty rates in central counties were almost three times those of suburban counties in 2000 (table 3.5). In other words, poverty in the nation can become relatively concentrated in central cities. Other measures of economic well-being show similar central city–suburban differences. Real median household income was almost 50 percent higher in suburban counties than in central cities in 2000, a substantial increase over the 1970 differential (table 3.6). But recent studies have found that the share of middle-class families in many metropolitan areas has declined since the 1970s (Booza, Cutsinger, and Galster 2006).

Table 3.3. Percent of National Population by Race/Ethnicity, 1980 and 2000, and Percent Foreign Born, 1970 and 2000, in Metropolitan Areas

Area	White		Race/Ethnicity African American		Hispanic		Foreign-Born	
	1980	2000	1980	2000	1980	2000	1970	2000
New York metropolitan region[a]	7.1	5.2	10.7	9.9	3.1	5.6	25.7	16.7
Top 10 metro areas	22.7	19.3	35.8	35.2	11.4	18.6	53.1	50.1
Top 25 metro areas	34.3	30.8	46.6	46.0	17.0	26.7	68.3	66.3
Share of U.S. population	83.4	75.1	11.7	12.3	6.4	12.5	5.7	11.1

Source: Calculations by authors from "Demographic Characteristics" data provided by State of the Cities Data System (http://socds.huduser.org/Census/Census_Home.html) based upon 1970, 1980, and 2000 U.S. Censuses, using the 1990 definition of metropolitan areas (www.census.gov/population/metro/).

a. The New York CMSA, which includes the primary metropolitan statistical areas of New York–Northern New Jersey–Long Island and New York–New Jersey–Connecticut.

Table 3.4. Composition of Central City and Suburban Populations by Race/Ethnicity, 1980 and 2000 (percent)

	1980 Central City	Suburbs	2000 Central City	Suburbs
Area				
White				
New York metropolitan region[a]	32.4	67.6	37.6	62.4
Top 10 metro areas	25.4	74.6	21.5	78.5
Top 25 metro areas	25.0	75.0	20.7	79.3
Black				
New York metropolitan region[a]	74.1	25.9	69.4	30.6
Top 10 metro areas	71.6	28.4	56.9	43.1
Top 25 metro areas	69.8	30.2	55.3	44.7
Hispanic				
New York metropolitan region[a]	75.1	24.9	64.4	35.6
Top 10 metro areas	53.7	46.3	43.8	56.2
Top 25 metro areas	50.7	49.3	41.4	58.6

Source: Calculations by authors from "Demographic Characteristics" data provided by State of the Cities Data System (http://socds.huduser.org/Census/Census_Home.html?) based upon 1980 and 2000 U. S. Censuses, using the 1990 definition of metropolitan areas (www.census.gov/population/metro/).

a. The New York CMSA, which includes the primary metropolitan statistical areas of New York–Northern New Jersey–Long Island and New York–New Jersey–Connecticut.

Table 3.5. Poverty Rates by Metropolitan Areas, 1970 and 2000 (percent)

Area	1970 Total	Central City	Suburbs	2000 Total	Central City	Suburbs
New York metropolitan region[a]	10.0	14.9	5.8	12.9	21.0	6.7
Top 10 metropolitan regions	9.7	14.6	5.8	11.9	21.0	7.5
Top 25 metropolitan regions	9.8	14.6	6.3	11.4	19.8	7.6
U.S.	14.7	n/a	n/a	11.8	n/a	n/a

Source: Calculations by authors from "Demographic Characteristics" data provided by State of the Cities Data System (http://socds.huduser.org/Census/Census_Home.html?) based upon 1970 and 2000 U. S. Censuses, using the 1990 definition of metropolitan areas (www.census.gov/population/metro/).

Note: Poverty rates are measured as the percent of households with income below poverty level.

a. The New York CMSA, which includes the primary metropolitan statistical areas of New York–Northern New Jersey–Long Island and New York–New Jersey–Connecticut.

Table 3.6. Median Household Income by Central City and Suburbs, 1980 and 2000 (in constant 1999 dollars)

| | 1980 | | 2000 | |
Area	Central City	Suburbs	Central City	Suburbs
New York metropolitan region[a]	34,745	49,297	43,670	62,159
Top 10 metropolitan regions	39,147	51,404	41,062	62,408
Top 25 metropolitan regions	38,906	50,779	41,803	61,019
U. S. national median	35,851		41,994	

Source: Calculations by authors from "Demographic Characteristics" data provided by State of the Cities Data System (http://socds.huduser.org/Census/Census_Home.html?) based upon 1980 and 2000 U. S. Censuses, using the 1990 definition of metropolitan areas (www.census.gov/population/metro/).

a. The New York CMSA, which includes the primary metropolitan statistical areas of New York–Northern New Jersey–Long Island and New York–New Jersey–Connecticut.

To summarize, the urban structure of the country has become less hierarchical in terms of its size distribution, and metropolitan areas with large spatial reach have emerged in all regions of the nation. Metropolitan areas have become the principal loci of national wealth generation, yet, as the data demonstrate, many of the socioeconomic, racial, and ethnic disparities of the country are accentuated there. Thus, increasing economic prosperity and inequality occur within the same geography. These demographic and socioeconomic conditions, especially the central city–suburban differences, are important to the analysis of metropolitan governance in the United States and represent major impediments to any effective metropolitan-wide collaboration.

FEDERALISM, POLITICS, AND URBANIZATION: SHAPING LOCAL GOVERNMENT IN THE UNITED STATES

The U.S. Constitution provides a federalist structure of government composed of three branches (executive, legislative, and judiciary) and two governmental levels, a form of so-called dual federalism. The first level consists of a single federal government headed by a president, elected every four years and able to be reelected once, and a bicameral Congress: the House of Representatives, with 435 members elected every two years, and a Senate, with one hundred members (two from each state) who serve staggered six-year terms. The second level is composed of multiple governments created by the fifty sovereign states, which are empowered to form their state and local governments and electoral systems. Although the precise forms of state and local governments vary substantially, because of constitutionally protected powers of states, they all have separation of branches, with direct elections for governor and bicameral legislatures (with the exception of a single house in Nebraska).

Under the Constitution, and ratified by nineteenth-century court decisions, definitions of local government structures and their powers and attributes are vested exclusively in state governments. The result is very significant variations in substate governments across the nation, as also seen in the Canadian case. Furthermore, the nature of local government itself has evolved quite significantly over the last two centuries in response to urbanization and, later, to metropolitanization (Frederickson, Johnson, and Wood 2004).

Urbanization, or more specifically higher residential densities found in cities, has created new types of demands for a range of services typically provided by government, as illustrated by New York City, which was a pioneer among American cities in confronting the public service demands of a large and rapidly growing population (Benjamin and Nathan 2001). The growing need for more powerful local governments able to mobilize resources to build infrastructure and transportation systems and the technical competence needed to address problems of public health and safety produced a qualitative change in local governments.

This ratcheting up of government capacity coincided with the incorporation of large immigrant populations into the political life of cities. New service demands and political dynamics spawned the urban reform movement in the early years of the twentieth century. Whereas machine politics were originally built on wards—that is, spatially defined areas with "winner take all" electoral districts—the reform movement argued for citywide elections, since it was thought that officials elected "at large" would be better able to define the best interests of the city, as opposed to the parochial interests of officials in the ward-based (and often "political machine") system. There was also an important dimension of class conflict underlying this debate, with middle-class and increasingly suburban interests anticipating more favorable outcomes for their interests through citywide elections. Even though many large cities, such as Chicago, did not adopt the full range of these government reforms, this period made evident some of the political conflict generated by the spatial organization that was emerging in urban America.

Since the early 1900s two political parties, Democrats and Republicans, have dominated the political system. The party system is relatively decentralized, with important regional and urban dimensions in both parties. The political realignment and policy interventions of Roosevelt's New Deal (1930s) consolidated an urban constituency in the Democratic Party heavily based on an industrial unionism (Mollenkopf 1983). The Democratic Party controlled Congress for much of the period from the Great Depression until the late 1980s and the presidency for much of the period through the 1960s. But with rapid suburbanization, which favored the Republican Party, the two parties became much more competitive at the national level (Orfield 2002). In the 1980s and later, despite brief periods with one party controlling both branches, a divided government with one party holding the presidency and the other a majority in at least one house of Congress has been the predominant pattern.

The regional basis of power of the two parties has also evolved. After being heavily Democratic for most of the twentieth century, the southern states became a bastion for the Republican Party by the end of the century. In northern states, the Democratic Party had some advantage, especially in states with large urban areas, but overall the parties have been fairly competitive. The West Coast states have become more heavily Democratic, while in mountain and plains states the pattern is more mixed but with fairly competitive politics in some states. Central to the changing prospects for parties are two important constituencies: religious social conservatives, favoring the Republican Party, and Hispanics, favoring the Democrats.

Elections to national and state offices are partisan (i.e., candidates are party based), but elections for local government offices are mostly nonpartisan, or at least not formally partisan, with exceptions in larger cities. In many states, suburban political interests are dominant in state legislatures, but the authority of state governments in the relatively decentralized federalist system is only occasionally used to address metropolitan-wide issues, as discussed below. And nonpartisan local elections further diminish the incentive for political parties to develop urban or metropolitan agendas.

State Government Paramountcy and Home Rule

State governments have the constitutional authority to create and define the powers and authorities of local government, as noted above. The exercise of this authority in granting "home rule" charters to local governments, a practice that was widely adopted by the mid–twentieth century, created the basis for strong local governments (Christensen 1995, 80–81).

Under home rule provisions, state governments relinquish policy-making authority to city government. Even in states that resisted the strengthening of local government powers, such as southern states with Reconstruction Era constitutions, home rule powers were provided to larger cities.

In addition to significant authority and financial flexibility provided by home rule provisions, many states gave city governments the authority to change their boundaries through annexation and other means, further discussed below. The ability to annex proved helpful as population growth began to spill over city boundaries into adjacent areas. In some regions, such as the Northeast, cities expanded their boundaries until reaching a neighboring city's boundary, ending the possibility for further annexation.

State governments have the authority to intervene or assume the functions normally assigned to local government. Such actions can be justified on the basis of the inability of local governments to control negative externalities. The institutional incentives and requirements that states can impose on local governments can be observed in the field of growth management. Closely related to transportation planning, the management of metropolitan growth cannot be effectively addressed by a single local government because of the various spatial externalities created by land use patterns that affect adjacent jurisdictions (Fisher 1999). Beginning in the 1990s, several state governments adopted a wide range of initiatives to enable local government to more effectively address this policy challenge (Wilson and Paterson 2003). Not all states engage in growth management policy, because of either political culture (i.e., a predisposition to minimize governmental involvement in land use decisions) or a perceived lack of demand or need. But some states have adopted more assertive positions, from encouraging cities to submit plans and collaborate with adjacent jurisdictions to requiring that local planning be consistent with state-level plans.

This legacy of urbanization, the strengthening of local governments, and the nature of local politics are key to understanding contemporary metropolitan governance in the United States, as discussed in more detail below. The critical role of state government in defining powers and authority of local governments has been noted (Christensen 1995, ch. 4; Miller 2002). But several authors writing in the 1970s argued that many state governments had seemingly lost interest in the metropolitan question, if they were not actually beginning to impede progress toward some level of metropolitan integration (Frisken and Norris 2001). Moreover, during the decentralization of the public sector after the 1970s, federal-state relations took precedence and state-local actions were largely neglected (Wilson et al. 2008). But with home rule powers in hand, a permissive environment for local government initiatives was created within the framework defined by state governments. Just as some states choose not to exercise prerogatives, local governments may choose not to exercise land use control authority made available to them by states, as in the cases of Los Angeles and Houston (Gainsborough 2001). The authority assigned by state governments leads policy and institutional choices of local governments that vary significantly within and across states. But it is also important to note that suburban political interests, partly because of the suburbanization of the urban population discussed above, are increasingly dominating state legislatures. This will undoubtedly strengthen suburban interests in defining the sorts of metropolitan governance initiatives enabled by state governments.

The Role of the Federal Government and Support for Metropolitan-Wide Initiatives

Despite constitutional limitations, the federal government affects cities and metropolitan areas in several significant ways. Some roles emerged in the New Deal programs of the 1930s, constituting what can be characterized as a federal urban policy (Mollenkopf 1983). These included urban infrastructure investments, low-income housing, and health and labor programs, all very much targeted to urban working-class populations and urban development. In the 1950s, under a Republican president, federal involvement in large urban areas was reshaped, with greater benefits accruing to suburban areas through support for the construction of the interstate highway system, as well as for the automobile and oil industries. With the return in the 1960s of Democratic presidents, federal aid to states and, especially, local governments expanded substantially to a wide range of policy areas, including community development and housing, social services, transportation, and environmental policy (Glickman and Wilson in press). Starting with Republican president Ronald Reagan in the 1980s, growth in federal transfers to state and local government slowed significantly and became much more heavily weighted toward state governments—a pattern that continues to this day.

This proliferation of federal programs in the 1960s created a need for coordination, not only among the federal programs, but also with state and local governments, and intergovernmental relations became important in both urban and rural areas. The federal government encouraged the formation of regional bodies, the councils of governments (COGs), to coordinate federal programs and regulations with local governments. The

COGs rarely became significant policy actors, but this form of coordination remains present today in metropolitan areas. Under the Intermodal Surface Transportation Efficiency Act (ISTEA) of 1991, coordination of multimodal systems of transportation in metropolitan areas was achieved by the federal requirement for the creation of metropolitan planning organizations (MPOs). The collaboration of local governments, including state governments, through the MPOs was a condition for federal transfers. Some MPOs evolved from the COG experience, but regardless of the specific origins they have become critical elements of today's institutional landscape in metropolitan America. Moreover, several federal regulatory and enforcement roles affect metropolitan governance. Air quality control boards are mandated for those metropolitan areas not in compliance with federal air quality standards. Although not yet fully implemented, these boards will have quite strong authority for imposing policies designed to improve air quality in metropolitan areas.

Some metropolitan governance initiatives are subject to federal laws dealing with individual rights. For example, initiatives that involve formal voting systems are subject to the federal Voting Rights Act (VRA). Miami–Dade County consolidation, discussed below, adopted single-member districts to ensure that there was no dilution of the voting strength of minority populations as mandated by the VRA. And initiatives involving federal funding are subject to federal provisions concerning citizen consultations.

But the effect of the federal government on metropolitan governance is largely limited to those policy areas where federal policy affects local revenues, as in fiscal transfers for transportation investment, or where metropolitan areas contain natural systems subject to federal regulations—such as environmental quality and natural resource management. But among the range of federal roles in metropolitan issues, the most significant leverage is that of the purse.

LOCAL GOVERNMENTAL STRUCTURES IN METROPOLITAN AREAS

The unique complexity in local government structure, with significant variation across states, results from the authority vested in state governments, as discussed above (Miller 2002). Although all territory within states is subdivided into nonoverlapping and mutually exclusive jurisdictions, denoted as counties (or townships in some states), many other local

Table 3.7. Structure of Local Governments in the United States

Year	Counties	Municipalities	Towns and Townships	School Districts	Special Districts	Totals
1932	3,062	16,442	19,978	128,548	14,572	182,602
1942	3,050	16,220	18,919	108,579	8,299	55,067
1952	3,049	16,778	17,202	56,346	12,319	105,694
1962	3,043	17,997	17,144	34,678	18,823	91,685
1972	3,044	18,517	16,991	15,781	23,885	78,218
1982	3,041	19,076	16,734	14,851	28,078	81,780
1992	3,043	19,279	16,656	14,422	31,555	84,955
1997	3,043	19,372	16,629	13,726	34,683	87,453
2002	3,034	19,429	16,504	13,506	35,052	87,525
2007	3,033	19,492	16,519	13,051	37,381	89,476

Source: Years 1957–97 from Stephens and Wikstrom (2000, table 1.2, p. 8). Data for 2002 and 2007 from U. S. Census Bureau (2003, 2008).

government jurisdictions are superimposed on this same territory. These other jurisdictions can be general-purpose governments, such as incorporated cities, or a range of special districts (table 3.7). A specific function, such as public education, may be assigned to a general-purpose government or an independent school district. State governments have the authority to create special districts and the powers assigned to them. The resulting raft of local governments means that within a single state different types of local governments may be authorized to offer the same service, thus creating competition among these governments (Carr 2004).

New patterns of local government emerged during the twentieth century, as described above (Frederickson, Johnson, and Wood 2004). Particularly notable was the massive consolidation of school districts following World War II (table 3.7). The principal reason for this consolidation is highly relevant to our later discussions concerning metropolitan America. The consolidation of the many small, often rural, school districts was called for because larger high schools could efficiently offer a more specialized curriculum due to economies of scale. But the long-term decline in the total number of governments was reversed in the 1970s as the growth of special-purpose districts more than compensated for the decline in the number of school districts. The creation of utility districts represented an alternative to provision by a local general-purpose municipality in rapidly expanding suburban areas.

Table 3.8. Structure of Local Governments in Metropolitan Areas

Geographic Area	Counties	General-Purpose Governments	Special Districts	Total School Systems	Total Governments
Total No. of Government					
New York Metro Area[a]	25	824	723	753	3,149
Top 10 metro areas	113	2,583	3,428	2,217	10,924
Top 25 metro areas	190	4,350	5,728	3,065	17,683
Average No. of Governments					
Top 10 metro areas	11	258	343	222	1,092
Top 25 metro areas	8	174	229	123	707
Average Population					
New York Metro Area[a]	847,995	25,728	29,322	28,154	6,732
Top 10 metro areas	668,380	29,240	22,032	34,067	6,914
Top 25 metro areas	585,888	25,590	19,434	36,319	6,295

Source: U. S. Census of Governments, GCo2-1 (P), July 2002 (http://www2.census.gov/ govs/cog/2002COGprelim_report.pdf). Population calculations by authors from "Demographic Characteristics" data provided by State of the Cities Data System (http://socds.huduser.org/Census/Census_Home.html?) based upon 2000 U. S. Census, using the 1990 definition of metropolitan areas (www.census.gov/population/metro/).

a. The New York CMSA, which includes the primary metropolitan statistical areas of New York–Northern New Jersey–Long Island and New York–New Jersey–Connecticut.

Today, metropolitan governance structures in the United States comprise multiple local government jurisdictions — many more so than for any other case discussed in this volume (Phares 2004). Among the largest twenty-five MSAs there are over seventeen thousand local governments (table 3.8). The average number of governments among the ten largest metropolitan areas is no less than 1,092, and among the largest twenty-five the average is 707. The range, however, is significant: New York, Los Angeles, Chicago, Philadelphia, Houston, St. Louis, and Pittsburgh metropolitan areas all have at least eight hundred local governments. At the other extreme, the Miami metropolitan area has only forty local governments, Baltimore has fifty-seven, and several have less than two hundred. The use of special districts and school systems, the categories responsible for a majority of governments, also declines by size of MSA, as does the average population per district. This observation is consistent with the finding of Mitchell-Weaver, Miller, and Deal (2000) that fragmentation,

Table 3.9. Special Districts by Type in the Twenty-Five Largest Metropolitan Areas

Type of Special District	*Number of Districts in 25 Largest MSAs*
Water management	440
Waste management	901
Water supply and sewage, and other multifunction districts	984
Highways	103
Transportation facilities	56
Public mass transit systems	87
Electric and gas utilities	205
Health	171
Education	39
Housing and community development	508
Libraries	315
Parks and recreation	340
Fire protection	985
Other	612
Total in MSA	5,646

based on level of expenditures of individual governments within a metropolitan area, declines as population size increases.

The use of special districts varies substantially by governmental function (table 3.9). Special districts among the largest twenty-five MSAs are most common for provision of fire protection; water and sewerage; waste management; housing and community development; parks and recreation; and libraries. But no discernible patterns of use by function across the metropolitan areas can be observed. New York, Chicago, and St. Louis rely heavily on special districts for fire protection, but seven metropolitan areas have no such special districts. The Pittsburgh MSA has 107 special sewerage districts, while thirteen other MSAs have fewer than five such districts and six have none. In other words, the use of special districts tends to be skewed across all functions, with relatively few metropolitan areas demonstrating exceptionally high numbers of districts. The creation of special districts, although broadly affected by size of the metropolitan areas, seems to depend greatly on enabling provisions of state laws and local political choices rather than on any inherent characteristic associated with the production of the services (Stephens and Wikstrom 2000, 132).

Forms of Metropolitan Governments
in the United States

The complex institutional structure of local government, with significant involvement of federal and state governments and choices made by local government officials, contributes to the country's rather wide range and multiple forms of metropolitan initiatives. The simplest form of local government structure occurs when a single jurisdiction encompasses most of an urbanized area, as in El Paso County in Texas and Honolulu County in Hawaii, and as we see in several municipalities in Argentina, Canada, Mexico, and Venezuela. In these cases, a single government has, potentially, the policy instruments and citizen accountability procedures, namely elections, in hand to address issues of large metropolitan populations.[2] Leaving aside these relatively few cases, this section proposes a categorization of initiatives where multiple local governments are present and provides examples of each. In addition, this section will discuss why these types of initiatives emerged, why some forms are rare, and the initiatives' implications on a number of governance dimensions.

Metropolitan initiatives in the United States can be classified into three types: (1) Restructuring of local governments, including geographical redefinition; (2) Confederation of local governments for metropolitan-wide collaborations; and (3) Ad hoc collaborations, including the creation of single-purpose authorities.

In the first category, the powers and responsibilities of local governments are restructured, including instances where geographical boundaries of governments are redefined. This alternative will typically affect only governmental activities within a single governmental jurisdiction, such as a county or city, and thus may not truly incorporate a metropolitan agenda beyond the locality itself. The city-county consolidation represents the most substantive form of restructuring, and state-enabling legislation usually requires a vote by citizens to approve changes (Kemp 2003; Carr and Feiock 2004). Starting with the vote to consolidate the five boroughs of New York City in the 1890s, elections can be highly contentious (Benjamin and Nathan 2001). This type of initiative is found in Miami–Dade County, which was consolidated in 1957 (box 3.1, figure 3.1). Even after consolidation, Miami–Dade County represented well less than a quarter of the population in the Miami metropolitan area. Such consolidations are not easy to achieve, however, and fall at the "difficult" end of the spectrum that we discussed in chapter 1 (see figure 1.2). Indeed, despite many

BOX 3.1

RESTRUCTURING LOCAL GOVERNMENT
The Case of Miami-Dade County

One of the oldest examples of governmental restructuring is found in Miami. After two failed referenda (1948 and 1953), voters approved the formation of a two-tier governmental structure for Miami and Dade County in 1957, but even then by only 51 percent, and the approval of the referendum was due to several unique features of the city (Marando 1974). The area had previous experience with functional consolidation for specific policy systems, including public education, fire protection, and port facilities. In addition, as an area of rapid growth and heavy tourism Miami–Dade County had few community interest groups, and the number of established municipalities in the county was small. These factors explain the lack of organized opposition. The lower tier of local government (i.e., the thirty-five municipalities) provides public security, zoning, and code enforcement. The upper tier, the county, provides emergency management, transportation services, public housing, and health care services from taxes assessed throughout the county. Other taxes are assessed either by the county, for incorporated property, or by municipalities to fund services. The county and municipalities conduct separate elections for officeholders.

attempts at consolidation, only thirty-two have been implemented since the first in 1805 (New Orleans), and only five have occurred since 1990, representing an estimated 15 percent of those proposed (Carr 2004; Leland and Thurmaier 2004, 3; Marando 1974).

But restructuring can be spatial in nature, involving changes in the geographic jurisdictional boundaries through consolidation, mergers, and annexation (leaving aside the creation of altogether new governments, a topic discussed below in the case of special districts [Carr 2004]). Restructuring is subject to state-enabling legislation, and the specific incentives created will influence the type of restructuring advocated by policy entrepreneurs (Carr 2004). The authority to annex has been extensively used by a few cities, including Albuquerque, Houston, and Indianapolis, to greatly expand their territorial boundaries (Rusk 2003). But in general the strategy is more piecemeal and has limited practical effect in addressing the issues of metropolitan areas (Brierly 2004; Rusk 1998).

An important characteristic of initiatives to restructure government is their strong public accountability systems. With consolidation and an-

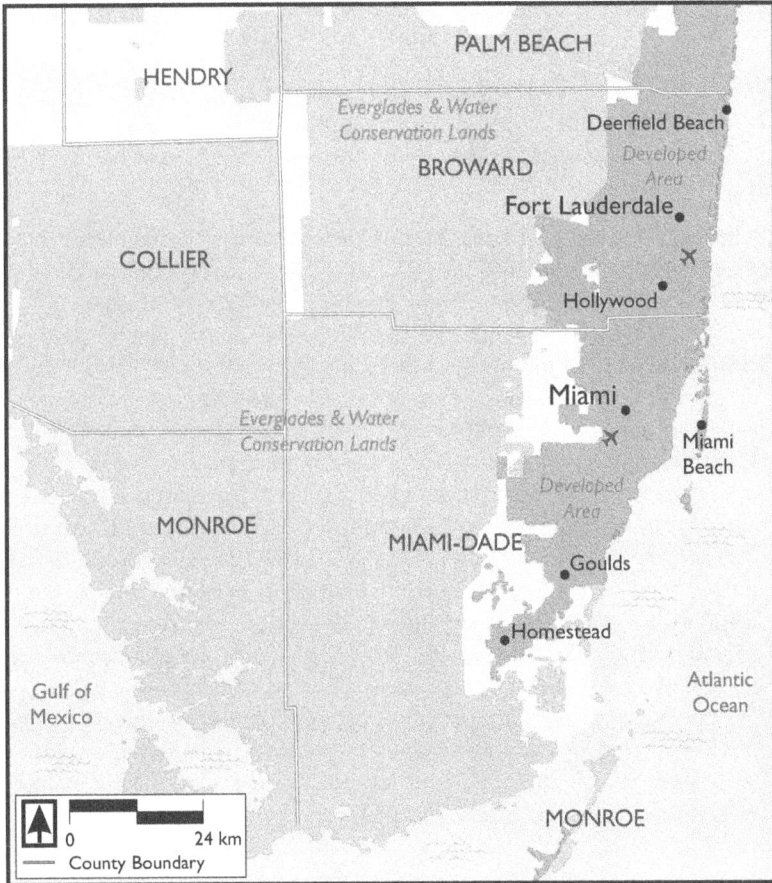

Figure 3.1. Miami–Dade County

nexation, preexisting electoral processes remain largely intact, although the number of elected officials may change. Most electoral systems consist of single-member districts, several of which were adopted following a review of the VRA, but some use at-large systems. In the latter, the dilution of voting strength of minority communities under proposed consolidations can be an issue, as noted earlier (Crooks 2004; Marando 1974; Swanson 2004). In addition, initiatives to restructure government rely on institutionalized revenue systems, another important feature of this category of initiative. Preexisting tax systems, with their full measure of accountability and legal frameworks, remain largely intact, although property rates may be equalized between the city and the annexed territory or

BOX 3.2

THE CONFEDERATION FORM IN
THE MINNEAPOLIS–ST. PAUL METROPOLITAN COUNCIL
Top-Down Construction after Bottom-Up Cooperation

Minneapolis and St. Paul had gained experience in region cooperation from their creation of a sanitary district (in 1933) and an airport commission (in 1943). The Twin Cities Metropolitan Council was approved by the state legislature in 1967 as a planning agency for the seven-county (approximately three hundred local government jurisdictions) Minneapolis–St. Paul metropolitan area. The concept was promoted by moderate Republicans in the state legislature and by land developers who sought efficiency in the development of infrastructure systems needed for urban growth. In the following decades the expansion of the council's authority into additional functions was approved by the state legislature, partly because of the council's effectiveness in fulfilling its obligations in previous years. A unique feature of the council is a tax-sharing system for commercial and industrial properties through the metro service area. The council coordinates the development of several area-wide services, including sewage and water systems, transportation, and major land uses. The council develops a "blueprint" for services and implements it through a variety of tools (Orfield 2002). To control the physical growth of the metro area, expansion of sewer service must follow the service area established by the council. The governor appoints the council's seventeen members, sixteen of whom represent specific geographic districts.

between urban and rural locales in county government reform (Leland and Thurmaier 2004).

The second category of initiatives involves metropolitan-wide collaboration or confederation of existing local governmental units in a multi-county metropolitan area. This can be voluntary or induced by higher levels of government, but it rarely leads to a new formal government and is best viewed as a confederation of governments with jurisdiction over at least one service function that has a fairly broad geographic scope. The specific form of confederation adopted in a metropolitan area is constrained by state-enabling legislation and the politics of the approval process. Two of the most notable cases are the Minneapolis–St. Paul Metropolitan Council (box 3.2, figure 3.2) and the Portland (Oregon) Metro. These types of organizations follow a general pattern: (1) a recognition that no single local government has the appropriate geographical authority

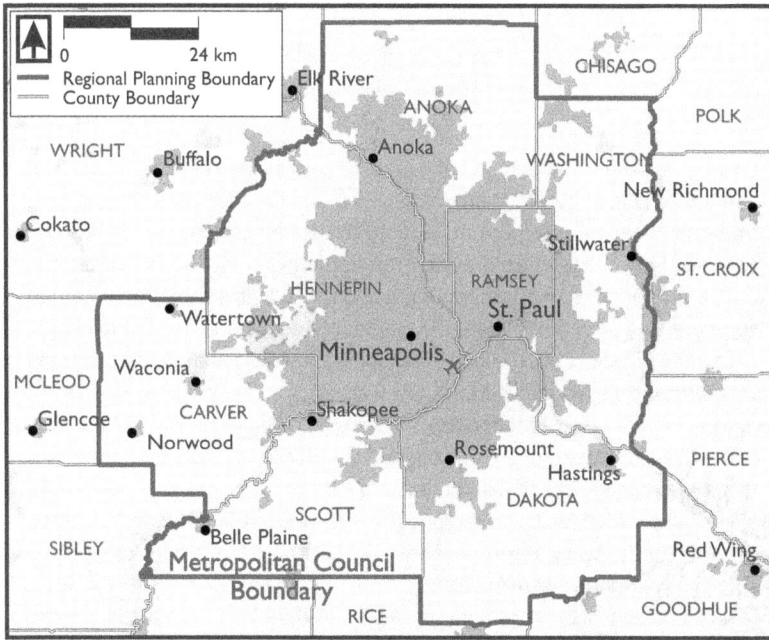

Figure 3.2. Minneapolis–St. Paul Metropolitan Area

or the fiscal capacity to address the problem(s); (2) a request by the local governments to the state legislature for the authority to create the metropolitan council, subject to voter approval; and, if approved, (3) a gradual evolution of the powers and responsibilities of these confederations over time, depending in part on their performance as perceived by the local population. Council members are appointed, by the governor in the case of Minneapolis, and by election in Portland Metro. In the Portland and Minneapolis–St. Paul cases additional powers have accrued over time, but the revenue structure of these bodies and the ability to increase revenues, by taxation or otherwise, are quite constrained. Reasons for the relatively few cases of metropolitan-wide collaboration are discussed below.

Initiatives in the third category, ad hoc cross-jurisdictional collaborations and special authorities and districts (McCabe 2004), are by far the most common in the United States. These can be formed to address the provision of public services within one or more counties and usually focus on a single type of service, as found in the single-purpose special districts as discussed above. St. Louis exemplifies the adoption of the ad

BOX 3.3

THE CASE OF ST. LOUIS
Ad Hoc Metropolitanism

Local governance has been a concern in St. Louis since the late nineteenth century. To gain efficiency in urban management, the city was "emancipated" from the county government in 1876 by the state legislature. In 1926, the Missouri State Legislature provided the authority for city-county consolidation, but reunification attempts failed and the two governments remained separate. In 1949, the Bi-State Development Agency was created to coordinate transportation, but the lack of authority granted to this agency produced very few tangible results. In 1954, growing sewer problems generated public health concerns, and a metropolitan-wide service district, under the authority of the Missouri Constitution, was created. In 1955 a proposal was presented for a Metropolitan Transit District, but it failed over the issue of public ownership of the transit facility to replace the 125 uncoordinated transit companies. In the following three decades, two additional attempts at city and county consolidation were made, but to no avail. The second, in 1987, was an initiative to consolidate the various cities within the county into a single-city government, and though it was approved by voters it was later determined to be unconstitutional by the U.S. Supreme Court, since it forced incorporation and stripped authority from the county government. In response to this setback, several single-purpose commissions were created to coordinate services in the metropolitan area. Hundreds of single-purpose governments were also created. Solid waste management for all cities and counties was consolidated into a single body in 1991. Similarly, districts or commissions were established for higher education, cultural institutions, justice information, medical centers, and an airport. The St. Louis Metropolitan Planning Organization (created in the 1970s, following federal guidelines) and the East-West Gateway Council of Government attempt to coordinate governmental activities across the metropolitan area, and a number of nonprofit organizations attempt to facilitate coordination. In 2002, 801 units of local government exist despite many attempts to consolidate governmental services.

hoc strategy, across many types of services, following failed attempts at redefining general-purpose local governmental structures (box 3.3, figure 3.3). Because of both voter opposition and, in some instances, judicial proceedings brought by affected governments, St. Louis turned to alternative strategies, including the creation of single-purpose governmental entities.

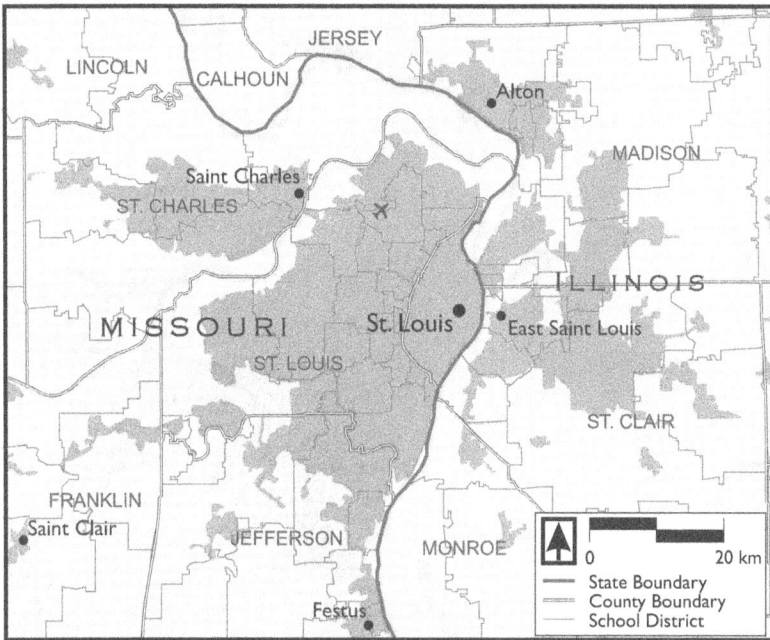

Figure 3.3. St. Louis Metropolitan Area

The creation of special authorities (Mitchell 1992) and districts is generally justified, in terms of public finance, by potential economies of scale in the provision of a particular service and/or the need for a quasi-public body to make long-term investment decisions. The New York Port Authority was established in 1921 initially to overcome market failures in the private sector provision of transportation services (Benjamin and Nathan 2001), but it subsequently expanded into a range of functions. Transportation services, in particular, are amenable to cross-jurisdictional collaboration. In the case of business improvement districts, services formerly provided by a city government are provided by a quasi-public entity and often involve nongovernmental organizations (Morçöl and Zimmerman 2006). In the special case of airport authorities, federal regulatory bodies may, to achieve economies of scale and facilitate air traffic control, force adjacent cities to collaborate in the provision of services, as in the case of the Dallas–Fort Worth Airport. The officials in special authorities are generally appointed by local general-purpose government officials and, occasionally, state government officials, whereas special districts typically hold elections for their leaders, as discussed below.

The categorization of initiatives presented in this section and the three illustrations provide a framework for reviewing several dimensions of local governance, including the way citizens are engaged and the effectiveness of the technical and administrative features associated with the initiatives. It will be observed that each of the three types has different strengths and weaknesses across these dimensions. These strengths and weaknesses help explain the frequency of occurrence of the various types of initiatives.

THE PROSPECTS FOR METROPOLITAN GOVERNANCE IN THE UNITED STATES

Policy-Making Capability

Of the forms of metropolitan governance examined here, the restructuring of local government through consolidation of city-county governments or expansion of the power of counties offers the most promising alternatives for policy making. In theory, these forms of government are likely to be the most effective because they are subject to federal laws guaranteeing political rights of citizens and their administrative capacity is predicated on a reliable tax base under the stewardship of elected officials. But in practice consolidation has not yet realized these potential benefits and, given the rate of referendum failure discussed earlier, proponents have not been able to convince citizens of its advantages (Carr and Feiock 2004). At the same time, under the prevailing fragmented metropolitan governance system, as observed in St. Louis, there appear to be few venues for coordinating regionwide, multipurpose governmental strategies (Dodge 1996). Rather, there is a heavy reliance on special districts and authorities, suggesting that policy actions will be largely determined on narrowly defined considerations. It has also been found that per capita expenditures for a particular function are higher in areas that rely on special districts than where the function is performed by a general-purpose government (Foster 1997).

Many argue that the fragmented system is the more desirable framework, a view endorsed by citizens. According to the Tiebout framework, discussed in chapter 1, small jurisdictions offer the opportunity for like-minded citizens to choose where to live on the basis of both the tax structure and services consistent with their preferences. Such a framework, it is argued, recognizes the multicentric nature of metropolitan areas and

will generate competition among local jurisdictions, presumably leading to more efficient government and thus increasing citizen satisfaction. Under this approach, communities may collaborate on some issues,
as in the creation of the Dallas–Fort Worth Airport, and compete in
other arenas.[3]

Political Representation and Citizen Participation

Citizen participation in metropolitan governmental organizations varies
substantially across the three categories of initiatives (Dodge 1996, ch. 6).
The most well-established forms of participation, through election of representatives and officials, are in those arrangements with formal governmental status, such as upgraded urban counties, consolidations, and annexations. Despite the apparent citizen preference for the fragmented,
small-government approach, Kelleher and Lowery (2004) find that election turnout is lower in metropolitan areas with higher levels of governmental fragmentation.

The voting strength of minority populations located in the central
city may be relatively diluted in countywide elections following a city-
county consolidation, even though their formal participation in elections
is secured by provisions of the VRA to ensure that minority neighborhoods are adequately represented. There also is the distinct possibility
that malapportionment in the prereformed urban county, with its multiple local election systems, will be eliminated under a countywide electoral
system. For the various interlocal arrangements, citizens may be able to
exercise some degree of accountability through elections, but participation in actual policy making is likely to be effectively curtailed because of
the technical nature of the interlocal arrangements. Similarly, the proliferation of special districts places burdens on citizens, who become voting
members in multiple, overlapping local governments, a situation that
probably leads to lower citizen participation in policy making.

But beyond within-county participation, incentives for citizen participation in metrowide organizations are, for the most part, ineffective.
Multicounty authorities and confederation bodies rarely have direct elections; instead, officials are appointed to represent the participating governments. In these bodies, means for citizen participation may be quite
limited. Although openness in government and forums for citizen participation are abundant and required by federal government, actual participation imposes real costs on citizens. In contrast, special districts involve the election of officials by citizens within the district, since taxing

power is usually assigned to the district, but voter turnout for special-district elections is generally quite low (Burns 1994; Stephens and Wikstrom 2000, 133).

The creation of a metropolitan identity that might enhance the legitimacy of a metropolitan governmental body can be difficult to forge (for the case of New York City, see Benjamin and Nathan 2001, ch. 3). Residents of center cities and suburban cities may not relate to a broader metropolitan identity. However, several mechanisms are available for generating this type of identity, such as public relations campaigns, sports franchises, metropolitan-wide infrastructure systems, and even metropolitan elections. Good-government organizations frequently lead campaigns to create metropolitan-wide governance structures. But in many metropolitan regions the tensions and competition between suburban areas and central cities (and in some cases among suburban areas within a single metropolitan area) make it quite difficult to form a metropolitan identity.

Agenda Setting and Assignment of Functions

The policy agendas of metropolitan bodies are linked to the specific functions and activities assigned to them, which, as noted above, vary substantially. The relatively rare instances of governmental restructuring in metropolitan areas generate governmental bodies with general-purpose government responsibilities, but instances of single-purpose or limited-purpose initiatives are much more common.

Under city-county consolidation and annexation, the preexisting functions and activities are maintained or even enhanced, subject to the enabling legislation of state governments. The Miami–Dade County consolidation resulted in increased authority for the county government (Stephens and Wikstrom 2000). Consolidation can be constructed as a tiered system, with one tier for general countywide services and another tier for enhanced services for urban areas (Stephens and Wikstrom 2000, 71). But it has been noted that the benefits of consolidation are not entirely realized when services within a county are not fully integrated, thus leading to inadequate coordination of service delivery, as in the case of Indianapolis (Stephens and Wikstrom 2000, 85). In addition, even with consolidation there is no guarantee that the majority of the metropolitan population will reside within the jurisdiction, as in the case of Miami–Dade County consolidation.

The choice of single-purpose authorities or districts seems to be affected by the particular service in question. It is common for physical infrastructure systems, such as ports, water, and waste management, largely because these systems rely heavily on major investments with substantial economies of scale and long time horizons. Thus the reassignment of these functions from general-purpose governments might be expected. The nationwide consolidation of school districts in the 1950s provides another example. But special districts can also be formed because of spatial service gaps. County governments, for example, may not adequately serve population growth occurring just beyond the service boundaries of cities, thereby creating a geographical service gap that can be corrected by the creation of special districts.

Metropolitan bodies, including both confederations and voluntary associations such as metropolitan planning organizations, are usually involved in land use and transportation planning, two policy areas with very substantial externalities (Wilson and Paterson 2003). These types of organizations may also address those services where a unified effort can realize potential economies of scale, such as zoos, port and airport facilities, and solid waste disposal.

Implementation and Effectiveness Issues

Administrative and Financial Capacity

A wide range of capacity is found among governmental organizations in metropolitan areas (Dodge 1996). The formal local governmental structures, such as city-county consolidation and annexation, will generally have substantial bureaucratic systems and taxation authority. Consolidation itself has been justified as a mechanism to modernize local administrative structures, although some argue that the transaction costs of such governments outweigh the benefits of scale economies in service provision (Brierly 2004). Intergovernmental relations with co-federated forms of metropolitan governance also help determine the effectiveness of these forms. Even under tiered city-county consolidation, determining the unit of government—that is, county government or cities within the county—to provide a service continues to be an issue. In both Miami and Indianapolis, coordination of service provision has not been entirely resolved, although it is important to note that in these cases a formal governmental venue for resolving service provision disputes is available (Stephens and Wikstrom 2000, 61). In Indianapolis, the incomplete consolidation of taxation districts contributed to intergovernmental tensions (Stephens and Wikstrom 2000, 85). And a study of the effectiveness of consolidations found that agreeing to a common purpose and collective action among participants is more easily achieved in economic development initiatives than in services leading to redistribution of resources from suburbs to center cities (Leland and Thurmaier 2005).[4]

The capacity of special districts is, by definition, more constrained. But the limited scope of special districts' missions means that their capacity can be focused on a single function. At the formation of a special district, revenue sources are defined. Despite a relatively steady stream of revenues guaranteed for special districts, expanding or altering revenue streams can be difficult and subject to approval from some other governmental jurisdiction.

Interjurisdictional Collaboration in Service Provision

As the impetus for reform of governmental structures in metropolitan areas has waned, there has been an increase in the use of special districts (as outlined above) and forms of interjurisdictional collaboration (see table 3.9). Some of these forms of collaboration are entirely voluntary; others can be encouraged to various degrees by state and federal governments (Kemp 2003). The COGs, MPOs, and environmental boards are designed by the federal government to induce collaboration and coordination among local and state actors. State governments have additional policy levers available, and the degree of aggressiveness in applying those levers is related, in part, to the seriousness of the problem and the extent to which it transcends the geography of local government jurisdictions (Wilson and Paterson 2003, 65–68). The increasingly frequent use of these types of strategies has even encouraged the adoption of new terminology — that of metropolitan governance — to reinforce the fact that these initiatives do not lead to the formation of formal metropolitan government (Feiock 2004; Post 2004). Although state government plays a role in defining the options available for local governments, their implementation depends heavily on the local political and institutional context.

The adoption of interlocal collaboration appears to be the result of pragmatic decisions by local policy makers (Dodge 1996, ch. 7; Thurmaier and Wood 2002), but conducive institutional and political cultures also play a role (Thurmaier and Wood 2002). Frameworks for the analysis of collective action, or governance, have been developed, partly on the basis of the capacity of participating governments (Feiock 2004; see figure 1.2 in chapter 1). The underlying nature of the policy issue being addressed can lead to inefficient service provision by a single unit of government as the issue transcends its geographic boundaries. Or a particular government may have inadequate capacity to deliver a service efficiently and may make an agreement with a neighboring government. A county government may enter into an agreement with a city government that has the capacity to provide services, such as emergency medical services, to nonincorporated areas of the county. Or a strong county government may deliver services to small municipalities within the county. Since these arrangements are contractual and voluntary, common interests and efficiencies in service provision, as well as political leadership, are critical factors.

Indeed, interlocal agreements are found for a wide range of urban services but seem to be more common for social service delivery. In these systems, the extensive interaction between agencies and clients may lead to a potential for economies of scale and scope in spatially distributed delivery systems. Local governments with greater administrative capacity may be better able to serve geographic areas of low-density demand than the alternative local government structure. Hence a municipal government in a small city will contract for services with a county agency or agencies of larger, nearby cities. As such, interlocal agreements for services represent an alternative either to governmental consolidation or to the formation of special districts.

Such interlocal agreements for metropolitan collaboration are institutionally more fragile than the restructured governments previously discussed, but their very flexibility and absence of permanent obligations make them an attractive option. Although these arrangements can be based on formal commitments (including contracts) between participating governmental units, they are often subject to periodic review and thus to change. Nonformal arrangements, such as the MPOs, rely on resources found within participating units of governments, and, given the possible dissolution of the arrangements, the sustainability of administrative capacity is even less certain.

EXPLAINING METROPOLITAN GOVERNANCE IN THE UNITED STATES

The range and frequency of metropolitan initiatives in the United States provide strong evidence of new policy challenges arising in metropolitan areas. It should not be surprising that elements of the country's federalist design, historical legacies of institutional choices, the spatial organization of metropolitan areas, and the tradition of local control in U.S. political culture all contribute to the complex institutional and fragmented structure of local government. This section will first highlight special roles of federal and state governments in shaping governmental institutions in metropolitan areas, roles that are particularly important given that local government is not defined or assigned attributes in the U.S. Constitution, and then seek to explain why some forms of metropolitan initiatives are more common than others.

Although the current role of the federal government in urban and metropolitan issues is modest compared to its role in the 1960 and 1970s, an important institutional legacy is evident. First, the restructuring of the federal government in the creation of the Departments of Transportation and of Housing and Urban Development and the Environmental Protection Agency aligned the federal executive branch with a modern, urban society and led to the diffusion of similar structures in the executive branch of state governments. But its most important legacy of concern here is a specific form of collaboration, the metropolitan planning organization. Dating back to a federal initiative of the 1960s, MPOs are now pervasive in metropolitan areas, primarily because of the requirements imposed by the federal government. The importance of a steady funding flow, such as the federal government provides in urban transportation policy, is recognized as a powerful incentive to ensure collaboration. In addition, the federal government's funding of water and wastewater systems and its regulatory role in aviation and environmental quality can induce collaboration among local governments. But in the special cases of metropolitan areas that cross state boundaries, such as St. Louis and the New York MSA, or national boundaries, such as El Paso–Ciudad Juárez and San Diego–Tijuana, the constitutionally defined authority of the federal government to address interstate or international issues is not being fully exercised. The latter case, however, reminds us that the tendency toward decentralization in the federalist system, initiated in the last decades of the twentieth century and continuing in the twenty-first, has meant that state and local governments are more fully responsible for devising solutions to challenges faced in metropolitan areas.

As the federal role in metropolitan matters has receded, the paramountcy of states has been reasserted. The relative autonomy assigned to state governments under the dual-sovereignty provision of the U.S. Constitution in defining local governmental structures creates substantial variation, if not experimentation, across states in approaches to metropolitan governance, as discussed above. States have occasionally imposed metropolitan service delivery and statewide plans (Stephens and Wikstrom 2000, 61; Wilson and Paterson 2003), especially in those with higher population densities and more intense land use conflicts. But more commonly the initiative for exercising prerogatives and options provided by state governments rests with local governments and thus is responsive to local priorities and political culture.

Turning now to explaining the emergence of metropolitan initiatives themselves, we have observed that initiatives in two categories, restructuring of local government and confederation, are relatively rare. The scarcity of these types of initiatives is due in no small measure to the spatial organization of political interests in metropolitan areas. Suburban residents may have no interest in being absorbed into a government that must address, and fund, the higher-cost services in central cities. And, in the other direction, minority populations in central cities that have achieved a majority of the polity may be reluctant to allow their political influence to be diluted by incorporation into a broader entity. Arguments about efficiency in service delivery and promotion of metropolitan-wide economic development seem to be trumped by political considerations (Rusk 1998; Norris 2001; Swanstrom 2001). The high rate of failure in public referendums for more robust metropolitan authorities reflects the fear of many voters that their particular interests would not be adequately represented under a government representing the entire metropolitan region. For example, the fragmentation of school systems within metropolitan areas, with relatively wealthy suburban independent school districts having no interest in merging with inner-city school districts, illustrates the impediments created by local self-interests. These politics are replicated in resistance to the formation of metropolitan governments or councils. Two of the most notable exceptions to this finding, Minneapolis–St. Paul Metropolitan Council and Portland Metro, confirm that a political culture supporting metropolitan areas is very rare and requires nurturing to survive.

In contrast, the ad hoc arrangements, including interlocal arrangements and single-purpose authorities and districts, are widely used to address policy issues in metropolitan areas. That is to say, the preferred method of realizing the potential for increased efficiency in service delivery and coordination is through interlocal collaboration or single-purpose districts rather than through metropolitan initiatives with larger geographic service and broader policy-making authority. These ad hoc initiatives serve a wide range of policy areas but are especially common for major infrastructure systems, such as transportation (the domain of the MPOs), where the benefits of economies of scale and networks to metropolitan-wide collaboration are clear. Many suburban jurisdictions, generally with relatively small populations, enter interlocal agreements with larger neighboring jurisdictions for many types of urban services.

When the suburban jurisdictions are large, the incentive for cooperation is lessened (Lewis 2004), again reflecting the importance of scale in
the provision of urban services. But public officials in specialized service
areas that endorse these initiatives understand the potential for efficiencies in these narrow, and technical, types of arrangements, which contributes to their proliferation.

The single-purpose special districts, one form of the ad hoc strategy,
have an important political dimension and reflect the significance placed
on local control by U.S. citizens. A single-purpose government is constrained, by definition, and thus is unlikely to grow into a multipurpose
government or to expand its geographic jurisdiction. Though popular,
single-purpose districts do not necessarily have a metropolitan-wide reach,
and significant proportions of metropolitan residents may fall outside geographic service areas of special districts and thus further fragment metropolitan governance systems.

It is useful to end this section by reflecting on an apparent contradiction between the relative frequency of adoption of initiatives and their
political legitimacy. The form of initiatives that would lead to a full-
fledged election system to hold officials accountable, that is, restructured
governments, is rarely accepted by voters. Even the metropolitan-wide
entities, whether formal, the confederation type, or MPOs, usually feature indirect representation through the appointment of officials elected
in local governments in the metropolitan region. But the more common
initiatives, ad hoc collaborations, have relatively weak accountability systems. Furthermore, ad hoc collaborations for service usually utilize a fee-
for-service concept and therefore do not address underlying disparities
in resources or redistributive policies. In other words, the preference for
ad hoc initiatives, that is, voluntary arrangements focused on a narrow
policy issue, does not provide an effective venue for raising and addressing concerns of low-income or underserved populations.

Some ad hoc metropolitan initiatives have achieved high visibility,
such as the New York Port Authority and the Dallas–Fort Worth Airport
Authority, and in the long term these may, despite relatively weak and
certainly not very transparent public accountability measures, establish
legitimacy through the efficiency and effectiveness of their activities. But
at the same time, metropolitan entities can also be viewed negatively as
lacking in legitimacy because of their ineffectiveness in resolving metropolitan problems. Traffic congestion comes to mind. Given the diverse
and often conflicting political interests in metropolitan areas, establishing legitimacy for metropolitan initiatives that tend to have weak or lim-

ited authority is a major challenge. The institutional weakness of ad hoc metropolitan initiatives means that engaged polities are unlikely to be formed, thus undermining effective metropolitan governance.

Despite the numerous examples of metropolitan initiatives, the resources and capacity of the public sector are not being brought fully to bear on metropolitan issues. The overwhelming majority of the more significant governmental efforts for metropolitan planning and service provision rely on voluntary cooperation of submetropolitan governmental units. There is disagreement over the degree of efficiencies realized through such metropolitan cooperation (Swanstrom 2001), and metropolitan-wide political expression and consensus are clearly elusive. Although examples of relatively successful multipurpose metropolitan agencies exist, the alternative — that of single-purpose and narrow collaboration with accompanying institutional fragmentation — is clearly the strategy of choice. In fact, some argue that the most effective strategy to address metropolitan issues is to rely on the creative impulses of local initiatives to create a competitive environment vis-à-vis neighboring jurisdictions. But in turning to issues of social disparities, the lack of a metropolitan perspective and strategy reinforces social inequities (for the case of affordable housing, see Basolo and Hastings 2001). Yet it is on this very issue that the interests of central cities and suburban jurisdictions are most divergent.

Metropolitan Governance in the Future: The Possibilities

The extraordinary range in form and function of metropolitan initiatives demonstrates the remarkable flexibility and adaptability of the U.S. governance system in responding to the nation's metropolitan challenges. As in the past, this system continues to provide creative responses to societal change, as demonstrated in the adoption of home rule provision for cities during the initial phase of rapid urbanization in the early twentieth century. But in broad measure, metropolitan governance initiatives, while numerous and occasionally significant in impact, are largely ad hoc and shaped by a highly fragmented local government system. The prospects for the wider use of restructured metropolitan governments are extremely limited. Given this bleak outlook for reform or redefinition of formal government structures, many scholars and policy activists argue that a "New Regionalism" approach and regional coalitions should be promoted (Frisken and Norris 2001; Oakerson 2004; Mitchell 1992). Indeed, one element of this approach is already often in place, namely that of the increased use of horizontal collaboration of local governments. But because of both institutional and political resistance, metropolitan-wide issues are unlikely to be addressed, at least not without inducements by higher-level government. Despite some signs that decentralization pressures are receding, the federal government is not likely to take a leadership role in the foreseeable future beyond the one effectively exercised in the MPOs, leaving the potential leadership role largely to state governments. A wide range of approaches across states can be observed: in smaller, high-population-density states such as Rhode Island or Delaware, the politics and intensity of the urban growth challenges are different than in geographically large states with metropolitan areas occupying a relatively small share of that geography, such as Arizona.

To date, though, the metropolitan question in the United States is simply not on the nation's agenda — certainly not for the federal government and rarely for state governments. Although local governments and citizens confront a range of policy issues in metropolitan areas, rarely are these issues being framed as metropolitan-wide and within metropolitan governments or institutions. And the creation of a metropolitan agenda, whether at the national or the state level, is problematic for several reasons. The spatial organizations of metropolitan areas in the United States, characterized by significant demographic and socioeconomic differences both within and between them, represent major impediments to creating a metropolitan policy agenda. With few exceptions, there are no governmental venues for political consensus building and regionwide political leadership. Political parties do not organize at the metropolitan level, an alternative that might provide a counterweight to technocratic governance focusing on independent jurisdictions. Moreover, the common strategy — that of fragmentation and proliferation of limited-purpose structures — appears to work reasonably well and reduces the incentives that might otherwise lead to metropolitan consolidation and coordination.

NOTES

1. The U.S. Bureau of the Census has developed the most commonly used definition of metropolitan areas in the United States. Metropolitan statistical areas (MSAs) are based on variables defined at the county (or township in some states) level. Although the U.S. Census Bureau adopted a new method of defining

metropolitan areas in 2003 (see chapter 1), the earlier system will be used in this chapter (Frey et al. 2004). A county is declared a MSA if it has an incorporated city of over fifty thousand population. Although a single county can be defined as an MSA, many MSAs are composed of adjacent counties. In 2000 there were 313 MSAs, consisting of 848 counties with a population of 226,207,070, or 80.4 percent of the nation's population (Frey et al. 2004, 6–7). To ensure comparability of data with the other federalist counties in the United States, tables provide information on the largest MSA (the New York Metropolitan Region), the ten largest MSAs, and the hundred largest metro areas. In the latter grouping, the smallest of the twenty-five MSAs is San Francisco, with a population of 1,731,000 in 2000.

2. In Texas, unlike most states, county governments have quite constrained powers and therefore are not able to address many challenges of large urban populations.

3. Feiock (2004) uses a collective action framework to explore the circumstances under which collaboration and competition emerge.

4. See also Johnson and Neiman (2004) on competition and cooperation in economic development.

Chapter 4

Metropolitan Governance in Brazil

Institutions, Organizations, and Lessons
from Intermunicipal Consortia

PETER K. SPINK,
MARCO ANTONIO C. TEIXEIRA,
AND ROBERTA CLEMENTE

In Brazil, metropolitan regions emerged as an explicit and debated urban phenomenon in the second quarter of the twentieth century and would later be included in the formal public sector institutional framework in the mid-1970s during military rule (1964–84), when a technocratic version of military developmentalism was strongly in evidence (Souza 2003). The first regions to be formally designated by the legislation fit the broad descriptors that have been used for this comparative study (large, multi-jurisdictional, and with continuous urban development), but later the state governments would designate other, much smaller regions with more scattered municipalities simply as a way of imposing regional planning. Out of the thirty-six existing regions designated as metropolitan, some twenty can be considered as typical conurbations, occupying together less than 2 percent of the landmass and being home to some 39 percent of the national population. While Brazil's 1988 democratic constitution reconfirmed the metropolitan concept, it failed to provide the necessary guidelines for governance. As a result, in places like Greater São Paulo, nearly twenty million people in thirty-nine municipalities attempt to improve living conditions

100

using the same institutional framework as a rural municipality with fewer than one thousand inhabitants and in which the entire adult population can meet together in the local civic center or church hall. In this chapter we look at the recent history of metropolitan governance in Brazil and ask what possibilities exist for a more effective response to some very urgent social demands. In seeking an answer we find ourselves drawn to some fairly classic questions about organization and institutionalization and to the argument that—at least in Brazil—metropolitan issues are strong in description and debate but weak in governance and action, placing federalism at a crucial fork in its development.

URBANIZATION AND THE GROWTH OF
THE METROPOLITAN REGIONS IN BRAZIL

Most reviews of Brazil's urban history point, with varied emphasis, to four specific stages. In the first, initial concentrations along the coast served as links between the country's plantation economy and the Portuguese metropolis, Lisbon. Here, Salvador, which was the first capital between 1549 and 1763, was a focal point for most of the trade between Brazil and Portugal and also, as its architectural heritage shows, an institutional center for the Catholic Church. The commodity that marked this earlier period was sugar, and even though this could be found in various parts of the coastal region, its early imprint was strongest from the southern half of the state of Bahia through to Pernambuco. Salvador, also the capital of Bahia, remained the most populated city in the country until Rio de Janeiro began to increase in importance and population as a result of the increasing flow of minerals from inland Minas Gerais to the nearest coastal ports and became the country's second capital from 1763 to 1960. In 1808, with the arrival of the Portuguese royal family in retreat from Napoleon, Rio was transformed into the seat of the Portuguese empire, a role it assumed until 1821. With independence, Rio remained the national capital, serving also as the port for the export of sugarcane and coffee (which would become the next boom commodity) from the surrounding regions.

Another coastal town that experienced considerable expansion due to sugarcane would be the port of Recife, the capital of Pernambuco in the Northeast. The port, protected by the reefs that provided its name, not only was a growing center for distribution but also served as the residential center for many of those involved in the sugarcane industry, which grew up in the semicoastal region. Coffee in São Paulo would later generate a similar effect, although here the port outlet was Santos and the farms were inland well beyond the coastal range. The town of São Paulo sat at an altitude of 2,500 feet on a plateau within the coastal mountains where rivers flow inland to make the natural boundaries of the River Plate basin. For much of its early life it was a simple staging post, and when independence was declared in 1822 it had a population of only twenty-five thousand. Coffee was to be the stimulus for change. The railroad links between the interior and the port of Santos were built in the 1860s. By the 1880s the coffee boom was well under way, and coffee went on to represent over 50 percent of exports by the early twentieth century. Housing the urban residences of the new coffee magnates who imported most of their goods from France, the more temperate São Paulo was preferable to coastal Santos, which was hot, humid, and the site of numerous epidemics.

In the second stage of urban growth, which began with the end of slavery in 1888 and the declaration of the Republic in 1889, the sugarcane industry entered into decline and would pick up again only with mechanization in the latter third of the twentieth century. Rio de Janeiro could not compete with the state of São Paulo's growth as a coffee producer, and from this moment on São Paulo, also a state capital, began to increasingly assume a role as an important political and population center, attracting people from the rest of the country and abroad.

The third period of urban growth was linked to industrialization, initially in the beginning of the twentieth century and more noticeably with the economic transformations of the 1950s and 1960s in São Paulo and Belo Horizonte. During this period, São Paulo would overtake Rio de Janeiro in size, and Belo Horizonte would quickly exceed the perimeters of its original design. Iron, steel, and chemical production and oil refining would increase internal migration to a number of secondary areas linked, in part, to the primary manufacturing cities.

The final stage, at least for now, has been characterized by continuing migration to the existing major urban centers as a result of climate change, job loss in agriculture, and a lack of effective public services in the smaller, very rural municipalities. In the center of the country, the new Federal District and the capital city Brasília have served as another magnet for migration, initially in relation to construction work, as in the case of the capitals of other newly formed states. More recently, with relocation of industry and a boom in agricultural commodities, plus a measurable increase in municipal competence following the 1988 Constitution, the

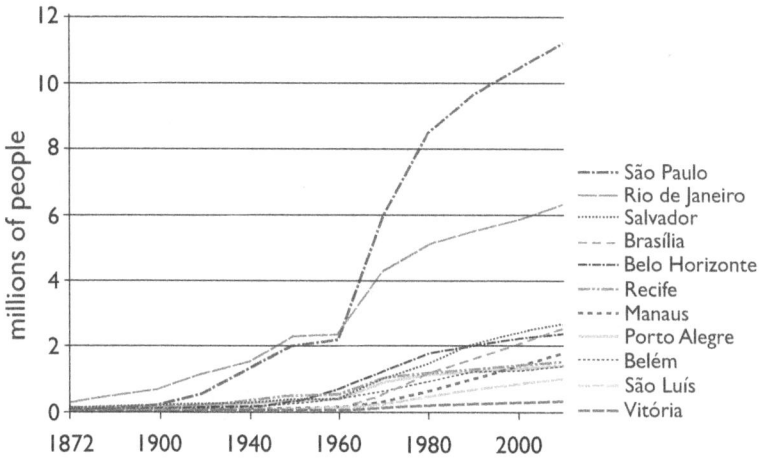

Figure 4.1. Evolution of the Urban Population in the
Principal State Capitals, 1872–2010

number of secondary centers has increased. But the importance of the
original "entry points" into Brazil is still key to an understanding of the
country's urban and largely coastal demographic landscape.

Figure 4.1 shows the evolution of the urban population in the principal state capitals from 1872 through to 2010. The legacy of the original
entry points and early logistic centers for Portugal's plantation economy
remains strong (Keating and Maranhão 2008). In 1872, Rio de Janeiro
(274,972 inhabitants), Salvador (129,109), and Recife (116,671) were the
three main urban areas of the country. São Paulo, with only 31,385 inhabitants, was ninth on the list (just before the boom)—a very different position from that of the year 2010, when there would be some 11,000,000
residents just within the city of São Paulo. By then Rio de Janeiro
(6,000,000) and Salvador (2,700,000) would already be lagging far behind it in population. With the exception of Belo Horizonte and the Federal District (Brasília), all the major centers lie along, or close to, the coast.

The demographic growth of the country affected not just the leading
capital cities but also the villages and towns that were growing up around
them, generating conurbations that quickly removed what natural barriers
existed between one and the other. Whereas in some areas the additional
growth would be less significant, in others, such as Greater São Paulo and
Greater Rio de Janeiro, the result would be a doubling in size. With the
process of urbanization accelerating during the 1960s and clearly out of

step with the capacity of what were then extremely state-dependent municipal authorities to provide adequate services, it was perhaps inevitable that the introduction of institutional arrangements favoring cooperation between municipalities would be suggested. Architects and planners began to debate this issue at the end of the 1950s, and at the beginning of the 1960s they engaged in some early experimentation (Azevedo and Mares Guia 2004; Klink 2008). Rolnik and Somekh (2004) point to an important seminar on housing and urban reform, hosted in São Paulo by the Brazilian Institute of Architects (IAB) in 1963, that in its final report proposed the need for administrative agencies for large urban areas made up of different municipalities that could articulate the resolution of common problems. But it would be during the military regime following the coup of April 1, 1964, that the first formal metropolitan regions would be created.

The Creation of Metropolitan Areas

The early steps were a number of "embryonic" experiences (Rolnik and Somekh 2004), such as the São Paulo State government's formation of the Executive Group for Greater São Paulo in 1967 and the establishment of similar organizations in Porto Alegre, Belém, Salvador, and Belo Horizonte. In Rio de Janeiro, a different experiment was taking place. After the move of the capital to Brasília and the (new) Federal District in April 1960, Rio de Janeiro had assumed the role of a city-state, being named the state of Guanabara until 1975. In 1967, a presidential commission proposed that metropolitan regions be defined as municipalities that form part of a given socioeconomic community and that their role as regions should be restricted to carrying out "common services," a reflection of concerns with preserving municipal autonomy. Inclusion was to be obligatory (there was no provision for opting out). In her analysis of this early period, Guimarães (2004) mentions that other proposals present at this time, such as one that allowed states and municipalities to come together in more voluntary consortia, were clearly set aside in favor of a centralist and authoritarian federal mandate.

The first eight regions were created in 1973, with the ninth (Rio de Janeiro) following in 1974 (table 4.1). The choices made clearly show that the centralist economic development model was dominant and that the various other experiments in intermunicipal cooperation were ignored (Araújo Filho 1996). Even attempts by the federal statistical bureau (the Brazilian Institute of Geography and Statistics [IBGE]) to create more

Table 4.1. Waves of Metropolitan Regions

Region	State	Geographical Location	Year	No. of Municipalities
Belém	Pará	North	1973	5
Belo Horizonte	Minas Gerais	Southeast	1973	34
Curitiba	Paraná	South	1973	26
Fortaleza	Ceará	Northeast	1973	13
Porto Alegre	Rio Grande do Sul	South	1973	31
Recife	Pernambuco	Northeast	1973	14
Salvador	Bahia	Northeast	1973	13
São Paulo	São Paulo	Southeast	1973	39
Rio de Janeiro	Rio de Janeiro	Southeast	1974	18
Vale do Aço	Minas Gerais	Southeast	1995	4
Vitória	Espírito Santo	Southeast	1995	7
Aracajú	Sergipe	Northeast	1995	4
Baixada Santista	São Paulo	Southeast	1996	9
Campinas	São Paulo	Southeast	1996	19
Natal	Rio Grande do Norte	Northeast	1997	9
Foz do Rio Itajaí	Santa Catarina[a]	South	1998–2010	5
Florianópolis	Santa Catarina[a]	South	1998–2010	9
Londrina	Paraná	South	1998	8
Maringá	Paraná	South	1998	13
Maceió	Alagoas	Northeast	1998	11
Norte/Nordeste Catarinense	Santa Catarina[a]	South	1998–2010	2
São Luis	Maranhão	Northeast	1998	5
Vale do Itajaí	Santa Catarina[a]	South	1998–2010	5
Carbonífera	Santa Catarina[a]	South	2002–2010	10
Goiânia	Goiás	Center-West	1999	20
Tubarão	Santa Catarina[a]	South	2002–2010	3
Macapá	Amapá	North	2003	2
João Pessoa	Paraíba	Northeast	2003	12
Sudoeste Maranhense	Maranhão	Northeast	2005	8
Grande Manaus	Amazonas	North	2007	8
Chapecó	Santa Catarina	South	2007	16
Cariri	Ceará	Northeast	2009	9
Campina Grande Vale do Rio	Paraíba	Northeast	2009	23
Cuiabá	Mato Grosso	Center-West	2009	4
Agreste	Alagoas	Northeast	2009	20
Lages	Santa Catarina	South	2010	2

Source: EMPLASA (2011); Garson, Ribeiro, and Rodrigues (2010).

a. Downgraded to planning districts in 2004, eliminated in 2007, and reinstated in 2010.

definitive statistical criteria (e.g., population, territory, conurbation, economic and social integration and complexity) were of little effect. Had they been adopted, they would have led to the inclusion of Santos, Campinas, and Goiânia, all clearly metropolitan in statistical terms at that time but excluded from the metropolitan definition by the military government of the day (Guimarães 2004).

The law creating the regions provided for a special fund to finance metropolitan activities and policies. The services listed as potentially sharable within the metropolitan regions were: integrated planning for economic and social development; water supply, sewage, and solid waste; land use; transport and roads; production and distribution of gas mains; management of water resources; and control of environmental pollution. Other services could be included as a result of the decision of the region's deliberative council. The deliberative council and another consultative council would be responsible for articulating the work of the municipalities involved. On paper, this was a fairly orthodox design favored by many planners of the time; in practice, given the political climate, the deliberative councils were presided over and largely filled by state authorities, who in turn were selected over the federal government. The consultative councils, largely filled by the municipalities, could only make suggestions and had no decision-making power (Rolnik and Somekh 2004).

Following redemocratization and the debates leading to the1988 Constitution, metropolitan regions stopped being a prerogative of the federal government and instead became part of the urban planning responsibilities of state governments: "States can, through their own laws, create metropolitan regions, urban agglomerations, and micro regions, made up of sets of linked municipalities, in order to integrate the organization, planning, and delivery of public activities of common interest" (art. 25, § 3). Nineteen metropolitan regions were added to the list between 1995 and 2003, and then a further eight between 2005 and 2010. However, the majority of these more recent regions are hardly metropolitan in the usual sense of the word and certainly could not be described as the "splashes of light" mentioned in the introductory chapter. For example, in Santa Catarina, the state government used the metropolitan format extensively as part of a strategy for bringing smaller municipalities together for regional planning, even though the areas identified were hardly metropolitan in the normal use of the term. Indeed, they were so unmetropolitan that six of the Santa Catarina regions were downgraded to planning districts in 2004 and then were eliminated in 2007. The state government, however, seems still undecided and has recently reinstated the six as well as creating two more.

Souza (2005) has argued that in simultaneously maintaining the previous generic conceptual framework forged under military developmentalism—an example of path dependency—while passing the responsibility for new regions to the states, Congress failed to provide the incentives necessary for effective cooperation. A key opportunity to make a break with centralist planning was lost. Edésio Fernandes, in his introduction to Gouvêa's (2005) study on the metropolitan question, remarks that at the time a proposal was submitted by representatives of the various metropolitan regions to consider the political nature of the metropolitan regions and to include them as part of the federal pact along with states and municipalities. However, given the intensely municipal orientation of the Constitutional Congress (which also weakened the power of the states), the "baby was thrown out with the bathwater" (Gouvêa 2005, 15). Indeed, there were very few proposals for alterations to the constitutional project (an indication of lack of congressional interest), and all of these, including one that would transform all metropolitan regions of over five million inhabitants into states (echoes of the Rio de Janeiro–Guanabara city-state), were set aside. The result provided very little guidance for the metropolitan regions and certainly no obligatory financial support (Gouvêa 2005).

Whether from institutional inertia, lack of political interest, or the difficulty of articulating effective advocacy, the result has been the application of very minimalist metropolitan legislation to a variety of contrasting settings. In the following tables and comments we have focused attention on a subset of metropolitan regions that fit within two broad sets of criteria. First, we have considered only those areas that have been included within the list of formal metropolitan regions, all of which are multijurisdictional. This enables us to look for similarities and differences within a common constitutional and legal framework. Second, we have concentrated on those that broadly fulfill the working definition that was provided in the opening chapter: namely that they comprise large contiguous built-up areas of more than five hundred thousand people and involve more than one government jurisdiction. This relatively broad consensus position, derived from statistical descriptions and the field of urban affairs, provides a minimum guarantee that in our comparative studies we are looking at similar socio-spatial phenomena and provides us with a solid basis for examining questions of governance and

Table 4.2. Relative Population Balance in the Principal Metropolitan Regions

Metropolitan Region	Pop. of Total RM, 2010	Central or Pole Municipality	Pop. of Central or Pole Municipality, 2000	% of Total Metropolitan Pop.
Vitória (ES)	1,685,384	Vitória	297,489	17.65
Baixada Santista (SP)	1,663,082	Santos	407,506	24.50
Porto Alegre (RS)	3,960,068	Porto Alegre	1,365,059	34.47
Campinas (SP)	2,798,477	Campinas	1,024,912	36.62
Recife (PE)	3,688,428	Recife	1,536,934	41.66
Belo Horizonte (MG)	5,413,627	Belo Horizonte	2,375,444	43.88
Curitiba (PR)	3,168,980	Curitiba	1,678,965	52.98
Rio de Janeiro (RJ)	11,711,233	Rio de Janeiro	6,323,037	53.99
Maringá (PR)	612,617	Maringá	349,860	57.10
São Paulo (SP)	19,672,582	São Paulo	11,244,369	57.15
Goiânia (GO)	2,173,006	Goiânia	1,256,514	57.82
Natal (RN)	1,340,115	Natal	785,722	58.63
João Pessoa (PB)	1,198,675	João Pessoa	716,042	59.73
Londrina (PR)	764,258	Londrina	493,358	64.55
Aracajú (SE)	835,654	Aracajú	552,365	66.09
Belém (PA)	2,040,843	Belém	1,351,618	66.22
Fortaleza (CE)	3,610,379	Fortaleza	2,447,409	67.78
São Luis (MA)	1,327,881	São Luis	966,989	72.82
Salvador (BA)	3,574,804	Salvador	2,676,606	74.87
Maceió (AL)	1,156,278	Maceió	917,086	79.31

Source: IBGE (2010).

performance.[1] The result is the subset of twenty metropolitan regions shown in table 4.2.

One interesting feature of table 4.2 is the considerable differences between regions with regard to the weight of the principal municipality. In some metropolitan regions the central municipality is very dominant in terms of population, with upwards of 65 percent (Maceió, Salvador, São Luis, Fortaleza, Belém, and Aracajú); in others the central municipality holds 50 to 65 percent of the population (Londrina, João Pessoa, Natal, Goiânia, São Paulo, Maringa, Curitiba, and Rio de Janeiro) and in still others less than half the total metropolitan population resides in the central municipality (Belo Horizonte, Recife, Campinas, Porto Alegre, Santos, and Vitória). Santos has only 25 percent of the population of the

Figure 4.2. Locations of the Principal Metropolitan Regions

"Santista" metro area, and Vitória has only 18 percent of the population of "Greater Victoria."

Figure 4.2 shows the geographical locations of this subset of twenty metropolitan regions; they are still very much a coastal phenomenon. Important to watch, however, will be the two connected corridors from Santos through São Paulo to Campinas in the state of São Paulo and from São Paulo through to Rio de Janeiro (where plans are being made for a high-speed train link). This almost L-shaped pattern of conurbation has been referred to by the São Paulo Metropolitan Planning Organization (EMPLASA) as a macrometropolis. We have included the Federal District on the map as a locator but not as a metropolitan area. Its own, somewhat curious urban characteristics—11 percent (270,000) of the population, essentially its middle- and upper-middle-class elite, live in the originally planned and futuristic city of Brasilia, while the remaining 2.2 million are spread across a number of "satellite towns" in a wider interstate configuration—will be discussed later.

Metropolitan Inequalities

The municipalities that are grouped together in the metropolitan regions are, in most cases, not only significant population centers but also significant contributors to the tax base of the country. In the 1960s and 1970s this reflected the largely urban location of the country's industries (for example, the motor car industry in São Paulo), whereas in more recent years, with the centrifugal process of factory relocation, industrial sector jobs have been partly replaced by jobs in the service sector. Income tax data are normally aggregated by tax district, and in some cases, especially in smaller states, one tax district can cover the state as a whole. However, as a general guideline to income concentration, such metropolitan regions as Salvador, Porto Alegre, and São Paulo are responsible for between 55 and 65 percent of the total income tax collected in their respective states; in Belém and Rio de Janeiro this rises to 89 percent, while in Curitiba, Florianopolis, and Belo Horizonte it is around 35 to 40 percent.

Such a significant contribution to income tax should not, however, be taken to suggest that the metropolitan regions are islands of equality in a country of inequalities. In fact, they are very much the opposite. In general, the municipal regions show the same income disparities present in the country as a whole, aggravated by industrial relocation toward the interior of the country and a change in the metropolitan profile toward service industries, in which wage disparities are more extreme. Together, the shortage of decent housing, the shortage of jobs, inadequately distributed public services, and clear signs of a growing socio-spatial segregation (Ribeiro 2004b) create a very serious challenge for policy makers, service managers, and, above all, citizens themselves.

In a recent study using the 1992–2004 national sample census data, André Urani, the director of a leading independent economic and social research think tank, described the metropolitan regions as "beached whales" (Estado de São Paulo 2006).[2] While the overall level of the UNDP Human Development Index is slightly higher for the metropolitan areas than for the state of which they form a part, the changes over time show an inverse picture:[3] the percentage of people below the poverty line fell nearly ten points for the country as a whole between 1992 and 2004, yet the drop in regions like São Paulo was almost negligible. Average income in the country as a whole rose almost 10 percent in the same period, but in the metropolitan regions the increase was only 1 percent, and in São Paulo there was a drop of nearly 3 percent. In contrast, if in the country as a whole the 10 percent poorest had a 63 percent rise in income levels (in part because of federal interventions), those in the metropolitan regions had an increase of only 10 percent (while the gains for the 10 percent most wealthy were over 22 percent). In 2007, unemployment rates, which had been at very high levels throughout the country, began to show signs of changing for the better, wavered under the events of the 2008 global economic crisis, and then started to improve again in 2010. But even here the change was slower in the metropolitan regions, and in a number of them unemployment rates were still between 3 percent (Porto Alegre) and 10.7 percent (Salvador) in December 2010.

The national intermediary sample census gives a partial picture of the economic structure of the labor force from the data in the nine most important metropolitan areas.[4] Table 4.3 shows the population distribution for different income groups in terms of the Brazilian official minimum salary in 2011 (around US$320 a month). As can be seen, nearly 30 percent of the population of the country declared themselves as economically active yet were earning less than the minimum salary.[5] This proportion ranged from 12.6 percent in São Paulo to 44.3 percent in the metropolitan region of Fortaleza. Cost-of-living factors play a part here, but it is important to register that in overall terms a minimum salary is by no means a guarantee of a necessary minimum income for everyday life. In São Paulo, for example, the Joint Trades Union Statistical Service (DIESSE) places the necessary minimum income at some four to five times the value of the minimum salary. By this definition, over two-thirds of the region's employed workforce could be described as receiving substandard incomes.[6]

Poverty and illiteracy indicators show similar differences in distribution between the regions. In terms of income, the population beneath R$75.50 per capita per month (normally understood as the poverty line) varies from 14 percent in Greater São Paulo and 18 percent in Rio de Janeiro to 37 percent in Recife, 39 percent in Fortaleza, and 43 percent in Maceió.[7] Conditional cash transfers, including the federal *bolsa família,* have played an important role in alleviating extreme poverty, but the overall disparities remain in place both within and between regions. Within any of these indicators, there are also marked differences with

Table 4.3. Distribution of Average Incomes in Nine Metropolitan Regions

Metropolitan Region	Total occupied workforce	Without income or only on benefits	Up to ½ min. Salary (%)	½–1 min. Salary (%)	1–2 min. Salaries (%)	2–3 min. Salaries (%)	3–5 min. Salaries (%)	Above 5 min. Salaries (%)
Brasil	92.689.253	10,9%	9,7%	19,7%	31,8%	10,7%	9,2%	8,0%
Belém	947.903	7,4%	11,1%	29,8%	30,7%	8,3%	6,8%	5,9%
Belo Horizonte	2.660.434	5,2%	5,4%	19,3%	36,4%	12,2%	10,7%	10,8%
Curitiba	1.729.803	4,0%	3,7%	10,8%	37,4%	16,2%	14,7%	13,2%
Fortaleza	1.638.158	4,5%	12,3%	32,0%	29,5%	7,7%	7,0%	7,0%
Porto Alegre	2.019.163	5,8%	4,1%	11,8%	39,6%	15,7%	11,9%	11,1%
Recife	1.516.857	4,8%	11,0%	29,8%	30,0%	9,7%	7,2%	7,5%
Rio de Janeiro	5.331.054	6,8%	3,3%	14,9%	37,4%	12,6%	12,5%	12,5%
Salvador	1.886.311	3,5%	14,1%	26,6%	30,4%	8,3%	8,3%	8,8%
São Paulo	9.555.279	7,8%	3,2%	9,4%	38,6%	15,6%	13,4%	12,8%

Source: IBGE (2009b).

regard to gender and ethnic origin: for example, Afro-descendants as having higher levels of unemployment and lower income levels than Euro-descendants, and women as having higher levels of unemployment and lower income levels than men.

The metropolitan regions, seen as large and complex conurbations, face many social and environmental challenges, and much has been written about them in these terms.[8] Substandard houses of wood or brick, multiplying up the sides of unstable hillsides and occupying unused municipal land, such as that along the banks of rivers and creeks; people living or working on the streets, traffic chaos; urban waste; air and water pollution; and security and urban violence are among the many topics that provide a stream of photographs and examples for international reports.[9] But we now turn to a rather different question: whether these are in any way regions in practice, as opposed to merely a descriptive technical or statistical category. Specifically, we ask whether these areas are "metropolitan" in their structures of government and processes of governance; the extent to which planning and service provision take place on a metropolitan scale; and whether the organizational and institutional responses developed are able to meet the challenges posed by metropolitan expansion and the inequalities identified above.

Current Constitutional Provisions and Options for Intermunicipal Cooperation

Brazil's federation is made up of three interlocking and contiguous types of jurisdiction. These are municipalities, which are also federal entities;[10] states, made up of municipalities; and the Federal Union itself. The broad political model is one of an elected executive at each level (president, governor, and mayor) for a four-year term of office (open for a single reelection), and a separately elected set of representatives with no limits for reelection. At the federal level there are two houses (Senate and Chamber of Deputies) and one chamber at the state and municipal levels (the State Assembly and the Municipal Chamber). Executive elections are based upon a majority vote, while representative elections are organized on the basis of closed party lists and proportional representation without the possibility of "write-in" or independent candidates. Senate elections are for an eight-year term and are split, with part of the Senate being renewed at each period. Municipal elections take place two years after the federal and state elections.

Brazil has twenty-six states, a Federal District (similar in status to a state but without municipalities), and currently some 5,565 municipalities. Given that municipalities are contiguous to each other, new municipalities can be formed only by the division of existing municipalities, a process referred to as "emancipation," which, following a boom of new municipalities after the 1988 Constitution, has been considerably restricted through a new constitutional amendment. Indigenous peoples also have territorial rights and are self-governing in their own areas, though still under the stewardship of the federal government.

An important background variable in the Brazilian political system is the large number of political parties spanning the political spectrum, some of which have a national presence and others of which are more regional. Party orientation can also vary from place to place so that, with a few exceptions, party membership is not necessarily a clue to ideological positioning. It is rare that any one party can gather enough votes to form a clear representative majority, with the result that alliances, coalitions, fronts, and political bargaining are part and parcel of day-to-day politics. A large number of public managerial positions are up for grabs within a modified spoils system—a result of a constitution that provides for a permanent civil service but not for permanent careers within it. In management terms, budgeting is an executive-led process that must be approved by the appropriate assembly, but even then the function of the budget is to "indicate" the direction of investments and expenses; it does not obligate the executive other than in very broad terms. Brazil's recent Fiscal Responsibility Law places constraints on executive overspending, but there is still much room for maneuvering.

Important also as background is the current 1988 Constitution, which formally ended the transition from military rule (1964–84) and played an important role in opening up many areas of social policy to wider social control through an extensive matrix of deliberative or consultative councils at the state and municipal levels. Tripartite health councils, as well as councils for the environment, for children and adolescent rights, and for gender and many other issues are subtly turning the country's previous *clientelista* representative model into, at minimum, a structure with more open debate, and in certain parts of the country popular participation has made direct democracy a significant part of the governance arena. In Portuguese there is no easy translation for the word *accountability*, but in recent years the expression "transparency" has grown in use to refer to very much the same phenomenon: the requirement that governments and elected representatives be clear about what they are doing and how they are spending public funds.[11]

However, despite this growth in popular participation and public control, the democratic model is still very much executive driven at all levels. The model is a very homogeneous one, with the federal constitution specifying many things that have to be followed at the state and municipal levels. Many administrative processes are repeated throughout — such as accounting, budgeting, and planning — and although there are formal divisions of taxes between tiers, in recent years there has been a slight drift of fiscal and financial power back to the federal government. This process, in part a result of neoliberal policies favored by successive governments, has led to increasing discussion about how federal Brazil's Federal Republic actually is (Souza 2001), and to increasing calls for decentralization and for greater real autonomy at state and local levels.

The current 1988 Constitution recognizes three different types of formal intermunicipal arrangements for cooperation in planning and policy implementation, each of which grew up in a different way at a different time. The first provision is for "metropolitan regions," the second for "intermunicipal consortia," and the third for "integrated development regions." In the 1988 Constitution, the previous concept of metropolitan regions, dating from the early 1970s and military rule, remained in the statute book. However, as mentioned above, the responsibility for introducing new metropolitan regions was transferred to state governments as part of their specific arrangements for public policy planning in the urban field. The involvement of municipalities remained coercive and adscriptive, for they were left without the possibility of declining membership (in a few cases, state legislation allows for other municipalities to request inclusion).

The second type of intermunicipal arrangement — the consortium — has a different origin, characterized by local and subregional decisions to increase cooperation and association between municipalities. While the possibility of municipal association for "improvements in common interests" can be found as far back as 1891, these were at the time subordinated to the approval of the corresponding state authority.[12] In the twentieth century there were many restrictions on local government spending in extraterritorial policy arenas, which again made consortia a somewhat heroic solution. Yet despite adverse conditions, examples started to increase.

One of the earlier experiences came from within the state of São Paulo in the 1960s, with the Consortium for Social Development of the

Region of Bauru, and, later, in the 1970s, with the Consortium for the Development of the Paraíba [River] Valley. In Santa Catarina, a number of intermunicipal associations were set up around the same period with a focus on integrated planning and service provision. São Paulo would be the testing ground of the first intermunicipal health consortium in the 1980s (Cruz 2002). The consortium as a mechanism for horizontal cooperation would enter a boom period in the state of São Paulo during the first democratic government after military rule and under the direct leadership of Governor André Franco Montoro (1983–86), who saw in this arrangement a simple way for municipalities to get together for microregional development, at a time when more sophisticated arrangements could involve complex legal and accounting questions. Very soon, intermunicipal consortia would be found all over the country (Bremaeker 2001).

The consortium was formally included in the 1988 Constitution as an option for intermunicipal organization, but it was not detailed at the time; instead the Constitution simply stated that the "Union, States, Federal District, and Municipalities would develop the necessary laws for public consortia and cooperation agreements between the different federated entities, authorizing the associative management of public services as well as the total or partial transfer of charges, services, people, or goods essential for the continuity of transferred services." The implicit approval in the word *would* provided a signal of intention. In March 2005, Congress finally passed the necessary law. By that time there were over 3,495 consortia in existence (Rodrigues 2006).

The third type of intermunicipal arrangement, the integrated development region, was instituted by federal legislation and is the only one to have retained the status of being an initiative of the Union. Its focus is the territorial linkages of different states and municipalities that together make up a federal development initiative for regional territorial organization and social and economic development. The classical example is the Federal District, which is contiguous with other states and municipalities, parts of which are inevitably drawn into the matrix of activities and different forms of planned or unplanned urban development that the creation of the capital brought about, involving altogether almost three million inhabitants. The others are the region of Teresina, which brings together the 1,100,000 inhabitants of fourteen municipalities in Piaui and Maranhão, and the Juazeiro-Petrolina region on both sides of the São Francisco River in the adjoining states of Bahia and Pernambuco, which together form a major irrigated agricultural development zone.

The Federal District and Brasília are, to many Brazilians, one and the same place. In fact, the Federal District, as a whole, forms an area of 5,800 square kilometers and has a relatively low population density (some 400 inhabitants per square kilometer as opposed to 2,400 inhabitants per square kilometer in São Paulo or 7,700 in Fortaleza). Conceived as a somewhat hybrid "state-district-municipality," it is divided into administrative areas, but these — despite carrying individual names such as Taguatinga, Ceilandia, Sobradinho, Planatina, and Gama, and having a population far greater than that of the "pilot plan" of Brasilia itself (some 2.2 million versus 270,000) — are still treated as satellite towns. Using as a basis the 2000 national census, the "pilot plan" contained 16 percent of the population, Taguatinga and Ceilandia 29 percent, and the remainder 55 percent.

The Federal District does not have a capital, and its constitution is similar to that of the municipalities, yet at the same time its principal executive is considered to be a governor. More recently, its influence has spread across the state borders of Goiás and Minas Gerais to include some seventeen municipalities and a further million people. It remains, however, a mixed blend of federal office workers, multiple service providers, and people employed in commerce, farming, and agriculture.

The Question of Metropolitan Authority: Administration, Government, and Governance in the Metropolitan Regions

While the metropolitan regions share a common organization — the National Forum of Metropolitan Entities — more detailed information about the way each metropolitan region is organized and managed and, more importantly, about their similarities and differences is not collectively available.[13] The Forum itself has had a varied existence, lapsing into inactivity after 2002 but recovering in 2008 and 2009 to elect a new directorate in June 2009 at a time when a number of positive changes were taking place and many attempts were being made to get the metropolitan issue on the agenda. Congress, for example, had set up a special commission to examine a previous 2004 proposal for a metropolitan planning statute, and an interfederal work group on metropolitan management had been created within the President's Office in 2008 with support from the Inter-American Development Bank. However, both these and other efforts produced little result, partly because of a general difficulty at the federal level in facing the interjurisdictional and institutional issues involved in metropolitan affairs. This can be seen for example in the problems faced by the interfederal working group. Created with representatives from all parts of the federation, actively supported by the Forum, and supported by expert witnesses, the group still was unable to reach consensus on key questions, was never reconvened after its initial report, and never met the objective of producing a common metropolitan agenda (Ravanelli 2010).

The problem, however, appears more extensive. As commented previously and until very recently, with the exception of Azevedo and Mares Guia (2004) on state constitutions, Rezende and Garson (2004) on tax incentives, and Gouvêa (2005) on governance options, Brazil's excellent and vibrant research tradition on urban policy questions has tended to leave aside the managerial, organizational, and institutional aspects of metropolitan government and governance — other than in terms of general comments on a lack of effectiveness — and the few that have raised these points have been single- or small-sample case studies focusing on, for example, the more internationally known urban centers of Belo Horizonte, Recife, Rio de Janeiro, and São Paulo. Indeed, as a number of colleagues have also noted (for example, Azevedo, Mares Guia, and Machado 2008), there has been a conspicuous lack of an effective contemporary discussion of metropolitan management and of the organizational and institutional possibilities for government or governance, and metropolitan management and governance have not been able to find a permanent place on governmental agendas.[14] Fortunately there are signs of change at least on the academic front, with more extensive work on fiscal issues (Garson 2009), and important volumes of collected essays in a comparative framework (E. Castro and Wojciechowski 2010; Klink 2010), as well as a special issue of the Brazilian journal *Cadernos Metropole* dedicated to the theme of metropolitan management, which attracted papers from most of the active researchers in the field but also showed the size of the agenda-building challenge (Ribeiro and Bógus 2009).

To develop a more comprehensive overview for this chapter, we carried out an intensive archival study of the state and federal legislation available for each of the principal metropolitan regions in table 4.2 and also of other public documents available. We followed this up by personal contacts with representatives of the metropolitan agencies involved, which in turn led to visits, telephone conversations, and, in a number of cases, follow-up questionnaires. Even in cases where agencies had been deactivated it was always possible to trace somebody who had played an active role and could bring us up to date. Given the volatility of Brazilian political organization, the picture we present may be lacking in one or another specific item, and innovations may have emerged of which we are unaware; but the overall picture that we have been able to build is consistent with and extends previous work (Azevedo and Mares Guia 2000, 2004; Gouvêa 2005; Ribeiro 2000) and is probably one of the first attempts to effectively systematize the situation across the principal metropolitan regions at a single point in time.

Most laws or supporting documents have specified the areas in which it was envisaged that metropolitan action could and, presumably, would take place. To group these together for comparative purposes, we used a list of forty-six policy areas that had been developed in the course of a long-term study on subnational government innovation (Spink 2000). Table 4.4 shows the distribution of the areas in which the main twenty metropolitan regions are mandated to act, alongside those areas highlighted in the original 1973 legislation. As can be seen, no single area is common to all, but of those areas in which over 50 percent of the regions have a mandate to act, all but one — housing — were part of the original 1973 legislation during the military regime. However, it is probable that their continuity has more to do with urban pragmatics than with path dependency.

Metropolitan Planning Activities

As is clear from table 4.4, the main statutory emphasis in 60 to 90 percent of the regions concerns the broad theme of urban infrastructure and regulation, especially public transportation and highways, pollution control, water and sewage, and planning and economic development. Housing is perhaps the only area in which direct action is required, a situation that reflects Brazil's chronic housing deficit, currently estimated around seven million units. A secondary emphasis is placed on mechanisms of linkage, on key social policy areas, on industry and commerce, and on information systems (25 – 50 percent), followed by some very specific issues such as hillside risk slippage prevention. This considerable range of possibilities is what the legislation provides for by enabling the metropolitan regions to act. The question that naturally follows is: How many metropolitan regions are in fact doing this? A widespread and general impression given by urban observers is that, in fact, very little is taking place, at least not substantively (Devas 2005; Klink 2008, 2010; Rodriguez-Acosta and Rosenbaum 2005; Souza 2003). As Ribeiro

Table 4.4. Main Statutory Policy Areas for Action as Set Out in the Legislation for Each of the Leading Metropolitan Regions

Policy Area	Frequency among the 20 Leading Metropolitan Regions	Included in the Original 1973 Legislation
Public transportation	17	Yes
Pollution control	15	Yes
Water and sewage	15	Yes
Local and regional development	15	Yes
Urbanism and use of territory	15	Yes
Transit and highways	14	Yes
Ecosystem preservation	14	Yes
Management and planning	14	Yes
Housing	12	No
Public sanitation	12	Yes
Water supply and irrigation	12	Yes
Intergovernmental relations	7	No
Social welfare	6	No
Industry and commerce	5	No
Information systems	5	No
Intragovernmental relations	5	No
Workforce training and job creation	5	No
Energy and mineral resources (gas)	4	Yes
Education	4	No
Health	3	No
Accident prevention in areas of risk	2	No
Finance and budget	2	No
Policing	2	No
Agrarian reform	1	No
Agriculture and fishing	1	No
Food supply	1	No
Intermunicipal consortia	1	No
Popular participation	1	No
Public buildings	1	No
Science and technology	1	No
Working conditions	1	No

(2004c) and others have commented in referring to a paradox in Brazilian society, as metropolitan problems accumulate, they gain increasing social and economic relevance, but they remain orphans of political interest. To check this impression we turned to the data available from our interviews with staff involved in the different metropolitan agencies.

Certainly actions for public transportation can be found in some manner in all the metropolitan regions, and in the administrative structure of many states there is a specific secretariat for metropolitan transportation. In many cases, there are also mechanisms of structure planning *(planos diretores)*. But even though plans and policies may be developed by the metropolitan agencies, very little is actually implemented, either because of reported budget constraints at the state or municipal level or because the municipalities have "difficulty in effectively working together." At times there can even be problems between secretariats and agencies of the same state. The practice is indeed very different from the design; very little is taking place that could be directly or even indirectly linked to the presence of a formally instituted metropolitan region. Only two of the metropolitan regions have common metropolitan-wide schemes for the effective management of solid waste disposal, and it appears that in most places the smaller member municipalities continue to resist the prospect of becoming the metropolitan "garbage dump" or landfill. On a positive vein, the Metropolitan Region of Greater Vitória has consolidated an effective metropolitan scheme for water resource management that involves pollution control and the recovery of polluted areas. Each metropolitan region has provision for a formal agency—always a creation of the state government—to serve as a management body for metropolitan affairs. Their names vary from place to place and are often lodged within a corresponding state-level secretariat. For example, in Ceará the body is within the office of the state secretary for infrastructure, whereas in Belo Horizonte the agency is within the planning secretariat. Legislation also provides for some kind of metropolitan council, but with only a few exceptions these tend to be administrative arrangements restricted to the technical staff of the municipalities concerned and in a substantial number of cases are inactive or have not been institutionalized.

Metropolitan in Name but Not in Financial Provision

The presence of agencies within the public sector is an indicator of the presence of budgets, but here again the practice is very different from what would be imagined. Public budget legislation in Brazil makes a distinction between the budget as planned and approved — seen as authorizing expenditure — and the budget as actually applied, which may be different. A certain amount of leeway is allowed, and apart from certain statutory areas there is no requirement to spend all that has been authorized. Budget analysis is therefore something of an acquired art, but one that has become clearer with the widespread use of information technology and requirements for transparency. On examining the State Budget Laws as approved for 2008, we found that only six of our subset of major metropolitan regions had more substantive budgets allocations of US$20–40 million, four had budget allocations of US$1.75–2.5 million, and the remainder had from US$500,000 down to nothing. However, even the six more significant allocations — mainly around transportation — were themselves less than 1 percent of the corresponding state budget (Curitiba 0.28 percent, Porto Alegre 0.24 percent, Recife 0.43 percent, São Paulo 0.06 percent, Goiânia 0.39 percent, and Vitoria 1.04 percent). Thus it would seem that, discounting transportation investments, specific allocations for the metropolitan regions within state budgets are normally very low indeed, corroborating other information about current practices. (All states will, however, provide substantive transfers to individual municipalities.)

The results suggest that there is little stimulus for metropolitan-wide spending; that which does take place is largely a result of the specific local organizational structure and the human agency of individual decisions. Here our data confirm the result of studies by Rezende and Garson (2004, 2006) and Garson (2009), who point to the very high imbalances in per capita budgets between the different municipalities that make up the different metropolitan regions, a result of the complex formulas used for revenue sharing and of the differences in municipalities' own local tax-raising possibilities. In the absence of major state-level funding specifically at the metropolitan level, there is little incentive for municipalities with a higher per capita budget to, in effect, transfer funds to those with less investment power. Each will negotiate directly with the state to resolve specific municipal issues in individual policy fields.

Metropolitan Government and Governance: Real or Illusory?

Table 4.5 shows what we have been able to gather from documents and interviews about the formal institutional design and current organizational practice for our subset of twenty metropolitan regions. First, the table indicates whether the specific metropolitan design is one for government, governance, or merely administration (through an agency of the state or subordination to a state secretariat). By *government* we mean a specific democratic jurisdictional arrangement with elected representatives and a mandated authority over a certain territory and set of affairs (Dahl 1972). By *governance* we refer to mechanisms for dealing with a broad range of problems and/or questions and/or issues in which different groups and interests regularly arrive at mutually satisfactory and binding decisions by negotiating and deliberating with each other and by being prepared to cooperate in the implementation of these decisions (Schmitter 2002). With the exception of Rio Grande do Sul and Pernambuco, where state legislation allows for other municipalities to request to join a metropolitan region, the municipalities, and specifically their residents, have very little say and cannot decide to withdraw from the region (a feature that places some restriction on the use of the term *governance*). Only in a few cases and despite the prevailing democratic climate, as Azevedo and Mares Guia (2004) also noted, were the states to include provisions to require prior consultations with municipalities and residents before declaring a metropolitan area.[15] As can be seen, the dominant design is that of governance (normally through metropolitan-wide councils), and there is no provision for metropolitan government as such.

Second, table 4.5 describes the current design as far as we have been able to ascertain in relation to service implementation and access. In thirteen of our twenty metropolitan regions, the scope is restricted to planning, and in only seven are there indications of implementation. In terms of access to the overall metropolitan-wide body, we made a distinction between those regions where access is restricted to executive branch authorities of the municipalities involved and those where it is also open to the legislative branch and/or to civil society. Again the results are that structures are overwhelmingly restrictive: in only five of the governance-oriented models are provisions made for the involvement of other institutional and local actors, and when they are, the offers are more symbolic rather than substantive.

In practice, so general is the overall trend toward a lack of effective metropolitan-wide action that the exceptions—few of which can be seen as innovative—can be reported individually. Significantly, perhaps, six of them are to be found among the regions that have a more equal population distribution between the different municipalities constituting the metropolitan areas (see table 4.2): Vitória, the Baixada Santista, Porto Alegre, Campinas, Recife, and Belo Horizonte. First, in terms of service provision, the Greater Vitória Region both plans and implements water

Table 4.5. Governance in the Metropolitan Regions

Design	Action		Access	
	Restricted to Planning	*Involving Planning and Implementation*	*Restricted to Executive Branch Authorities*	*Includes Legislative and/or Civil Society*
Governance	13	6	7	8	5
Administration	7	7	0	7	0
Government	0	0	0	0	0
(Total)	20	13	7	15	5

resource policy, tourism, and education through a development council and a development fund. Funds are split, with 60 percent from the state and 40 percent from the municipalities. The development council is deliberative, with parity between state and municipalities (seven from each) and with the deciding votes held — in the case of a tie — by civil society and social movements.

In the Baixada Santista Metropolitan Region, which contains the coastal towns of São Paulo State around the port of Santos, the metropolitan deliberative council is composed of the nine mayors plus nine officials from different state agencies that were defined as relevant to the metropolitan region. Here a metropolitan agency was created for organizing investments, and a metropolitan fund was built up on the basis of a R$1 per annum per inhabitant contribution from each of the municipalities (totaling R$1,500,000) and a matching value from the state. A measure of its progress has been the recent decision by the state to raise its contribution to R$2 per capita, thus turning the value of the fund to R$4,500,000 per annum (equivalent to US$2,700,000). However, this value, as we saw before, is low in terms of budgetary commitment, and the overall value of the fund for the period 1999–2010 was some US$32 million. In a recent study Lippi (2011) has commented that for many of the political and technical actors involved the value was seen as bordering on the symbolic. Nevertheless, some ninety small projects have been completed, mainly in the areas of road maintenance, public transportation, public security (police posts), and health centers. There is, however, no provision for open consultation or any involvement of the region's different legislatives. The result is an executive-oriented agency for regional investment that is moving incrementally forward but, in the view of most of those involved, could have advanced much further.

In Porto Alegre, a state-level planning foundation is responsible for projects both in the metropolitan area and in other conurbations and serves as the coordinating body for transportation. Here a metropolitan public transportation council has some oversight powers, but its heavily weighted composition in favor of the state executive, with only one representative each from the transportation sector, trade unions, and community groups, places it very low down on any scale of effective social control.

In Campinas, also in São Paulo State, the structure developed is similar to that of the Baixada Santista, with a development fund and representatives from each of the municipalities and the state in equal numbers (nineteen). There are no provisions for anyone in the legislative branch or civil society to serve as a permanent member but at least there is provision for six members of civil society to take a consultative role.

The Metropolitan Region of Recife, in the Northeast of the country, has been one of the entities that was at one time very active, only to fall dormant and to emerge again, for a time assuming an active role in the National Forum of Metropolitan Entities. Its development council is made up in a similar way to the others (equal representation for the state and the municipalities), with the inclusion of three state deputies and one member from each municipal legislative chamber in a consultative role. There is no participation of civil society organizations. Recently questions of public transportation, water and sanitation, poverty reduction, and hillside slippage prevention have been the focus of a number of interjurisdictional activities, including steps toward creating a metropolitan parliament similar to the Natal Common Parliament (discussed below). Perhaps the most promising step has been to build on the previous experience of a municipal transportation company (one of the few successful experiences in the country) to consolidate in 2008 the Greater Recife Transportation Consortium for the metropolitan region as a whole. Beginning with the two main municipalities (Recife and Olinda) plus an active role by the state government, the consortium—which uses the 2005 public consortium legislation to be discussed later—hopes to gradually expand and cover the metropolitan region as a whole. This is the first time public transportation has been treated in this integrated manner in Brazil, and it is raising considerable interest, not the least for the use of the consortium approach to building a metropolitan agenda (Best 2011).

Belo Horizonte has had a previous and unsuccessful experience of a metropolitan assembly composed of the mayors and two municipal councilors from each municipality, as well as members of the state judicial, legislative, and executive branches, totaling some eighty-four members. After considerable discussion between state and municipal leaders, plus interaction with university centers and civil society, major reforms are now in place. The role of the assembly has been reduced, and a deliberative council has been created that is made up of sixteen members: five from the state executive branch, two members of the state assembly, seven municipal representatives (two from the central municipality of Belo Horizonte, one each from the other two large municipalities, and three representing the remaining thirty-one small municipalities). In addition there are two representatives from civil society organizations, which are nominated by and report to a civil society forum. The main focus is currently on transportation, with funds drawn from state and municipalities. Important here has been the learning process and the break with jurisdictional parity in favor of population balance (Azevedo, Mares Guia, and Machado 2008).

The João Pessoa Metropolitan Region was created in 2003 and never really got off the ground. To that extent it can be considered yet another case of failure. However, given the need to face the demand for a solid waste landfill, the state government put pressure on the members to create a consortium in 2007 in which five of the nine municipalities took part. In a similar way, Rio de Janeiro has a common waste disposal strategy and landfill, but this was imposed during the military period. The Natal Metropolitan Region also introduced waste disposal soon after the creation of its development council in 2005. In Salvador the metropolitan agency, a state-owned firm, plans and implements urban actions mainly in the area of Salvador itself.

The metropolitan development council of Natal was showing signs of slowing down by 2007, but here attention should be drawn to the body that brought this about: the Natal Common Parliament (Parlamento Comum de Natal), made up of all the members of the municipal legislatures within the region. The latter began as an initiative of Natal's municipal legislature, gathering support from surrounding municipal chambers and the Brazilian Law Association (OAB). Created as a vehicle that would not be superimposed on the existing legislatives, its role was defined as that of organizing the metropolitan agenda. It had no physical location, and its task was seen as that of identifying common problems and guaranteeing solutions (Clementino 2003). Despite early success it has had a checkered existence, falling into disuse. In 2009 attempts were begun to bring it back into activity, and these received an added boost when Natal was chosen to be one of the sites for the 2014 World Cup.

Thus from what we have been able to observe, with the exception of Natal, where 42 percent of the state's population is located in 5 percent of its territory, the most effective advances seem to be in metropolitan regions where less than 50 percent of the metropolitan population resides in the core or central municipality. This does not mean that advances are impossible elsewhere, but perhaps the more equal balance may help horizontal discussion (A. Fernandes 2004). However, and despite the advances, the overall picture and the results of nearly twenty or more years are, to say the least, disappointing.

Metropolitan Regions: Contradictions and Limits

As noted in this book's introduction, the incentives and disincentives present in the various "metro-meanings" are often contradictory, and Brazil is no exception; *metropolitan* seems to mean all things to all interest groups, both positively and negatively. On the other hand, there are often strong and clear incentives for municipalities to be municipalities. Brazil has had municipalities throughout its history, and, in contrast with municipalities in most of Spanish-speaking Latin America, these have a strong emotional and symbolic presence — so much so that in the 1930s the *movimento municipalista* argued for the recasting of the federalist pact as a federation of municipalities without states, and though it was unsuccessful there is little doubt that this tradition remained in the drafting of the 1988 Constitution. Even today, the creation of new municipalities is a bottom-up process whereby people vote to be "emancipated" (as the expression goes) from an existing municipality or from a part of an existing municipality. People may physically move throughout a metropolitan conurbation, but they will express their identity in terms of their municipal or local microregional location. The question "Where do you come from?" will invariably bring a precise local answer. People from Santo André in the São Paulo Metropolitan Region may say Santo André or refer to the more local ABC (the motor car region of Santo André, São Bernardo, and São Caetano), but they will never say, "From São Paulo." Mayors are elected by their individual municipal residents, and, as is well known, municipal elections are about potholes in the roads, public transportation, health, jobs, and schools.

This municipal tendency has increased rather than decreased as the result of two major federal decisions. First, the Constitution of 1988 transferred a number of key social policy responsibilities to the municipality. Second, the recently enacted law of fiscal responsibility limits municipal borrowing and provides for the suspension of political rights and even jail sentences for mayors who do not keep their finances in order or who pass an unsolvable debt to their successor. Put together, the two decisions require mayors to be much more focused on what is taking place within their municipal limits and almost require them to regard what happens outside as a subordinate issue or question. As we pointed out, a miniscule proportion of state budgets is specifically earmarked for metropolitan issues, but at the same time all state secretariats will be involved in transferring significant funds for municipal activities or will be engaged in other complementary actions that affect the everyday lives of people in the places where they live. Equally, the substate planning regions and the different structures of coordination to be found across policy sectors will also often follow the lines of significant conurbations.

Given the distinctively different force fields of municipalities and metropolitan regions, we need to ask whether there is any future for serious development and extension of the metropolitan regions as they currently stand and for metropolitan regions *as such*. Certainly the legal framework that set up the regions provided the municipalities with, at the best, only a secondary supporting role in their institutional architecture, and in most cases a very passive and bystander role in their design. However, lack of interest as a result of a top-down decision process cannot alone explain metropolitan regions' inability to develop and implement public policies. The legal provisions of a number of them leave open real possibilities for participation and decision making, not just by the municipalities themselves but also by civil society. Equally, many examples from other spheres of action have shown how political, technical, and societal actors can "reuse" existing institutional structures for more democratic objectives, in the same way that the hermit crab finds its protection in cast-off shells.

One of the possible and very pragmatic reasons for metropolitan regions' lack of success could lie in extreme differences in demography and economy between member municipalities, making the task of developing common policy in other than very basic areas such as transportation and water very difficult. For example, in the São Paulo Metropolitan Region, São Paulo has some eleven million inhabitants while São Lourenço da Serra had less than eleven thousand inhabitants in the 2010 census, and the GDP of São Paulo City is five thousand times bigger than that of its tiny neighbor. Most of the people living in the capital have never even heard of São Lourenço and certainly have no idea that it is one of thirty-nine municipalities in Metropolitan São Paulo (Abrucio, Carneiro, and Teixeira 2000).

Similarly, the central municipality is usually the biggest in the metropolitan region—in terms of both population and economy—and this, allied to the name of the region (the central municipality normally is the "flag carrier"), tends to create a situation in which the smaller surrounding municipalities come to expect a bigger contribution from their more powerful partner. Certainly the results of our "search for action" suggest that a more balanced situation helps, but that is hardly likely to persuade the more concentric metropolitan regions to break up their core cities. However, centrality aside, demographic densities (inhabitants per square kilometer) can vary alarmingly, from 178 in the Londrina metropolitan region to 2,500 in the Rio de Janeiro and São Paulo Metropolitan Regions, and rising to 6,000 and 7,000 inhabitants per square kilometer respectively in the two core municipalities. As Davidovich (2004) has commented, contrary to the homogeneous image that the generic term *metropolitan* evokes, metropolitan regions are as different among themselves as they are within. For federal policy makers such variety presents difficulties, and for those more directly involved in transferring solutions from one part of the country to another, the disparities can easily become barriers.

The demographic weight of the central municipality is also usually a clue to its political importance both historically, as shown in figure 4.1, and currently in terms of sheer voting weight. If, within Brazilian political tradition, the governor of an important state is almost automatically a potential candidate for the presidency, so the mayor of one of the major population centers is a natural candidate for governor and thereafter also for president. Some 23 percent of the country's electorate resides in the focal (center) cities of the metropolitan regions, rising to 42 percent of all the state of Rio de Janeiro's voters in the city of Rio de Janeiro. The 28 percent of the São Paulo State voters that reside in the city of São Paulo provide its mayor with a powerful national voice, in addition to the economic power that the state capital carries. For example, the rise of the Workers' Party (PT) to national prominence was certainly influenced by its performance in key capital cities such as Porto Alegre, Belo Horizonte, and São Paulo.

The political power of the focal city in many of the metropolitan regions can create a series of dilemmas for state-level relations and consequently for metropolitan affairs. Azevedo and Mares Guia (2004) suggest that while state and municipal governments formally recognize the metropolitan issue, they tend to see it as a "zero-sum game" in which greater metropolitan power will mean less state power. What incentives are there, for example, for a state governor to invest heavily in a metropolitan region in which the leader of the focal town and the metropolitan "flag carrier" may be a political opponent or even a potential rival for party nomination to the presidency? Given the two-year gap between municipal and state elections and the well-known voting reactions to governments in office, the possibility of having different political parties in power at the different levels is very real. Following the 2004 municipal elections, the situation in the fifteen most important central cities of the different metropolitan regions was one in which parties were in direct opposition to one another in nine state-city relationships and allies in only six.

However, Brazil's many political parties will often behave at the state level in entirely different ways and with different coalitions than they will at the national level. On the positive side, Recife has benefited by the continued commitment to joint action coming from the governor's palace despite a change in political party, and one of the key features of the Belo Horizonte revival has been the window of opportunity created by a pact for progress between state and municipal leaders from different parties (Azevedo, Mares Guia, and Machado 2008). Behind the Baixada Santista story is a history of the mayors of the nine municipalities meeting with representatives of state agencies ever since the first democratic state government was installed in 1983, and long before the creation of the metropolitan region in 1996. Even the name Baixada Santista refers not to a focal city but to a regional identity, including the region's famous football team. People may come from Guarujá, Cubatão, or Praia Grande, but it is a sure bet that at game time on Sunday afternoon they will be *santistas*.[16]

In contrast, the São Paulo Metropolitan Region is an extremely diverse set of municipalities with complex home-to-work travel patterns and many different football clubs; nobody would describe it as a positive example of metropolitan management. Yet within its conurbation different subsets of municipalities have been developing highly innovative activities using the previously mentioned model of the intermunicipal consortium, thus suggesting that interorganizational competence and interjurisdictional concern are indeed possible and not necessarily part of the problem. It is to the "consortium effect" that we now turn.

THE INTERMUNICIPAL CONSORTIUM:
ALTERNATIVE, COMPLEMENT, OR SOURCE OF IDEAS?

Intermunicipal consortia are based on an agreement at the municipal level made by the executive and legislative branches of the local government to cooperate with an adjacent or nearby municipality on one or more shared topics of interest. As pointed out above, they began to emerge in the 1960s and the 1970s but blossomed in the 1980s and today can be found all around the country. Unlike the metropolitan regions, the consortia feature a voluntary agreement that is made independently by the different municipalities involved.

The early consortia were not metropolitan in scope, and only over the years has the "consortium effect" moved from the smaller, rural, often river basin or watershed areas of microdevelopment through collective health provisions to some of the major issues facing the larger urban conglomerates. Data on the presence of the consortia are difficult to aggregate, as their mechanisms of association are very simple and are registered only at the municipal level. Indeed, as we commented earlier, one of the many interesting features of the "consortium effect" is that beyond a single clause recognizing the possibility of consortia in the 1988 Constitution there was never any guiding legislation until 2005 (an observation that undermines the theory that Latin legal frameworks work against innovation by requiring detail before action).

The most recent census of municipal information was carried out in 2009 by the Brazilian Institute for Geography and Statistics (IBGE). It reported data on intermunicipal consortia in the areas of health, education, housing, culture, and urban development (including waste management). Table 4.6 shows the overall numerical distribution of consortia and also the percentage difference in terms of municipal size.

The data for this table come from a series of questions in the municipal survey and may or may not be cumulative. Municipalities were asked about different types of consortia but not about multithematic consortia that can include several policy areas. Further, the questions referred to only certain types of consortia and not all possible consortia that might exist. However, the survey does provide a reasonable glimpse of the potential size of the "consortium effect," and comparing this data with data from a previous IBGE study in 2001, which included education and health, enables us to see how the tendency is increasing (15 percent in health, 39 percent in education). The results tend to show that the "consortium effect" follows fairly closely the demographic distribution of municipalities

Table 4.6. The Presence of Intermunicipal Consortia

Population per 1,000	Number of Municipalities in Country	Health	Education	Housing	Culture	Urban Development
Total	5,565	2,323	398	170	336	847
< 10	2,551 (46%)	1,241 (53%)	144 (36%)	59 (38%)	109 (32%)	316 (37%)
10–< 20	1,370 (24%)	531 (23%)	102 (26%)	38 (22%)	91 (27%)	183 (22%)
20–< 50	1,055 (19%)	355 (15%)	92 (23%)	48 (29%)	85 (26%)	211 (25%)
50–< 100	316 (6%)	116 (5%)	26 (7%)	8 (5%)	31 (8%)	68 (8%)
100–< 500	233 (4%)	73 (3%)	25 (6%)	13 (5%)	19 (6%)	61 (7%)
≥ 500	40 (1%)	7 (1%)	9 (2%)	3 (2%)	2 (1%)	8 (1%)

Source: IBGE (2009a).

within the country even across policy areas, suggesting that despite their early origins in small municipalities, consortia are now a general presence on the interjurisdictional landscape. There are very slight differences among types of consortia—for example, a higher percentage of the health consortia are in very small municipalities (fewer than ten thousand inhabitants)—but the overall picture suggests that consortia are becoming an organizational option in many spheres, and the 2009 IBGE study reports their links and partnerships with private sector and civil society organizations. Not surprisingly, the consortia are attracting international attention (Kellas 2010).

Three very different examples illustrate the range, evolution, and potential contribution of the consortia. The first is the Quiriri Consortium, which was formed by four municipalities linked by the headwaters of the River Negro in Santa Catarina, with a focus on environmental preservation and sustainable development that has brought together all sectors of the local society (see Jacobi and Teixeira 2000). Quiriri became a model for at least seven other consortia in Santa Catarina set up on similar lines: Iberê (with seven municipalities), Lambari (sixteen), Bem Te Vi (four), Rio Benedito (five), Esmeralda (six), Babitonga (six), and Piracema (eleven). Significantly, and following the earlier discussion about the potentially negative contribution of major cities as the flag carriers of the metropolitan title, none of these names, including Quiriri itself, has any link with any specific municipality; all are names of animals, birds, rivers, or fishes.

Second, at the other end of the country, is the Intermunicipal Consortium for Agricultural Production and Food Supply (CINPRA; see Barboza and Lemos Arouca 2002). It links the capital city of São Luis in the state of Maranhão and thirteen surrounding municipalities in an extensive network of food production and small family agricultural development, including schools and export facilities, and has served as a model for five other consortia in the same state involving, in all, over 25 percent of the state's municipalities.

Perhaps most emblematic for the discussion of metropolitan governance is a third consortium formed in the ABC automobile industry region within the megametropolis of São Paulo (Abrucio and Soares 2001; Clemente 1999; Cunha 2004; Jacobi 2001; Kellas 2010; Machado 2009; Rolnik and Somekh 2004). Its most visible moment was the launching in 1997 of the Greater ABC Chamber (Camara de Grande ABC), an intergovernmental open forum for public policy formulation and implementation covering seven municipalities and involving more that one hundred different organizations from the private and civil society sectors and state and local governments. Its antecedents go back to 1990 and the creation of an intermunicipal consortium (among Santo André, São Bernardo do Campo, São Caetano do Sul, Diadema, Mauá, Ribeirão Pires, and Rio Grande da Serra). This, significantly, was a reaction to the failure of previous metropolitan-wide plans in the area of solid waste disposal, coupled with the need to urgently protect a vital set of river basins. With time and experience, the consortium began to focus on other intermunicipal questions, especially—following a series of major structural changes in the automobile industry—those of economic and social development. After a while these discussions snowballed, and the result was the creation of the chamber itself. In this case the deliberative council also included the state governor and key state secretaries; the seven mayors; the presidents of the local legislatures; state and federal deputies with representation in the region; five representatives from the Citizenship Forum; five representatives from the trade unions; and five representatives from the business sector.

Thematic groups were formed on a variety of issues, such as the strategy of the chamber's Agency for Economic Development; ways of increasing the competitive competence of the area's productive chains; professional training and job creation; macro water management; improvements to the road system and public transport; water basin management; children and adolescents; literacy programs; working hours and contracts; civil defense; integrated health policies; and housing. The role of the deliberative council is to approve the proposals of the thematic

groups and to guarantee that these are coherent with overall development aims. Decisions are made on the principle of consensus. Continuity within the chamber and the consortium has been relatively constant,
despite some major political upsets in the region, including the tragic
death of one of its leading institutional architects, Celso Daniel, the progressive mayor of Santo André. Today, despite this loss and considerable
political changeovers in the region, the consortium and chamber continue to move forward.

The ABC consortium is not the only consortium operating within the
São Paulo metropolitan region. There are at least two other major blocs,
one to the southwest of the region with six municipalities and one to the
east with eleven municipalities. There are also some ten neighboring consortia in which one or more municipalities of the metropolitan region are
taking part. Of the thirty-nine municipalities, only eleven, including the
City of São Paulo itself, are individual players. While these data go against
the thesis of municipal isolation, they do perhaps suggest that the process
of forming intermunicipal linkages is slow and somewhat hesitant.

The Future of Metropolitan Governance in Brazil

During its more heroic period, the field of intermunicipal action tended
to borrow and adapt a variety of administrative and organizational arrangements, usually hand built with the support of local legislatives and
legal advisors and often classified as *informal*. The 2005 "consortium"
law provides the necessary legal support for many of the activities that
the existing consortia had been carrying out, but it also brings in subtle
modifications, leaving out any mention of contiguous relations and extending the range of actions to the union, states, federal district, and
municipalities—that is, to all federal entities. Theoretically, therefore, the
union, states, federal district, and municipalities can create public consortia to achieve objectives of common interest, in almost any combination
or form for virtually any objective, linking one municipality in the extreme
north with another in the extreme south, some six hours' flying time away.
What is more, the resulting consortia can be set up as either public or private associations.

There is no doubt that the framers had in mind the needs of the existing consortia, which were struggling in a number of gray areas to organize collective services, but their zeal to provide a more general institutional framework could produce a number of unforeseen developments if

those active in the less public-minded areas of municipal affairs chose to explore the limits of the legislation. However, the new legislation also provides us with a clear example of the difference between two very contrasting approaches to public action at which we have already hinted. In the first approach (much loved by lawyers, neoinstitutional economists, and, consequently, many international development agencies), the key to effective public action lies in the careful design of institutions that will, if set up correctly and given the necessary skills, training, and plenty of social capital, deliver what is expected of them. According to the second approach (supported by those who see institutions as a pragmatic consequence of human action), it is by working things out in practice that problems are solved and knowledge is built. The role of the legislator is to confirm and support rather than to predict and produce. Institutions here are products not of design but of social processes that ascribe value to practices that work, or, to use Philip Selznick's formulation, "infuse with value beyond the technical requirements of the task at hand" (1984, 17). Institutions work because their loyalty and importance are earned rather than required. Despite the 2005 legislation and the framing of the idea of a public consortium, many existing consortia continue as they were, and unless there is significant state or federal level leverage new consortia are just as likely to adopt the previous ad hoc approach as the new. As Strelec (2011) has pointed out in a study of consortia in São Paulo State (a very early stronghold for consortia practices), it seems that the new legislation is seen as providing yet another alternative to be added to previous possibilities, and the jury is still out on whether it will be a success or not.

At the same time that the consortia emerge as a potential practical means of facing up to the metropolitan governance challenge, very few of the consortia that we have studied over the years, including the previously mentioned Quiriri and CINPRA examples, provide for anything other than more competent technical management of policy implementation with some local consultation. The ABC experience has advanced further, but there are doubts about its long-term sustainability (E. Fernandes 2005). As Rolnik and Somekh (2004) confirm, there remain very few concrete examples of increased governance, active community participation, and deliberative democracy. The case of the metropolitan transportation authority in Recife may provide further examples, given the commitment of a number of the municipalities involved to participatory governance approaches, and Belo Horizonte is also a case to watch. On the positive side, results to date do suggest that intermunicipal cooperation is possible, that intermunicipal actions can be adequately articulated, and that the skills for their adequate management are present. The idea of municipalities getting together to solve common problems is not therefore an impossible dream or a bottomless pit of despair into which history, political traditions, legal frameworks, and genetic administrative incompetence have thrown the country's metropolitan regions.

At the same time, to suggest that the future of Brazil's large, extensive, and cramped metropolitan population should be left to the voluntary dispositions of local government officials to cooperate may gain favor from Pollyanna but seems to exclude most of the same population from the answer to our opening question in this volume: *Metropolitan for whom?* The same question also applies to those who argue that if things get much worse they will eventually get better. Fortunately, however, as Azevedo and Mares Guia (2004) point out, the "tragedy of the commons" scenario is not one to which many would morally subscribe. Constitutionally, Rezende and Garson (2004) have pointed out, state legislation can define the composition of metropolitan regions, set directives, call for coordination, and create plans but must respect municipal autonomy. Equally, however, the same constitution binds the municipalities to cooperate in matters of common interest and requires the federal government, states, and municipalities to assume joint responsibility in many policy areas without establishing any level of differentiation. It also requires municipalities of over twenty thousand inhabitants to have their own individual structure plans.

It would appear from the data we have been able to gather that, unfortunately, few state governors, mayors of capital cities, or federal agencies give much priority to metropolitan-wide issues as such and that when they do they see them as urban questions rather than as questions of governance. Ribeiro (2004a) of the Observatório das Metrópoles research network has even suggested that the current situation should be characterized as one of increasing *ungovernability* brought about by the size, complexity, and accumulation of problems; institutional fragmentation; and a lack of political interest and of values that might drive collective actions.

In this chapter we have identified some of the reasons that may have brought Brazil's metropolitan regions to what we could call a federalist crossroads and that lead to the questions: What options are available, and in which direction should we turn? How far can and should states go, and what are the limits to municipal autonomy? How might Brazil move forward in the difficult area of joint responsibility for matters of extremely urgent common interest?

In looking for options, we have avoided seeking international comparisons, for that is a task that will be taken up in the final chapter. Instead, we look at the prospects of field-grounded possibilities. We accept a certain degree of path dependency to the extent that naturalized practices and frameworks tend to be suggestive and the transaction costs involved in creating Brazil's version of cooperative federalism (Grodzins 1966) tend to be high, but at the same time we find ourselves closer in position to the potentially emancipatory perspective provided by Giddens (1979) when discussing structuration.

One option is to take seriously the technical role of the existing metropolitan agencies — that is, the model as given — and put it into practice within the current democratic context, emphasizing the role of metropolitan councils in guiding policy. Here there would be a need to seriously rethink the basis of tax revenue sharing and to create effective and substantial metropolitan funds for metropolitan management. The experiences of Belo Horizonte, Greater Victoria, and Baixada Santista have shown possibilities, and certainly formulas can be created to allow for differences in municipal per capita budgets.

As an extension of the first option, the creation — or strengthening — of effective metropolitan parliaments or participative councils may well be also key not only to the control of such funds but, as Rolnik and Somekh (2004) have suggested, to the construction of effective metropolitan agendas and to the overcoming of the more technocratic approach to planning that has tended to dominate the metropolitan scene. Here the example of the Natal Common Parliament shows that this route is possible. Ward (1999) also emphasized the importance of democratic metropolitan governance in his analysis of Latin American megacities, placing it as the first of his six principles for large city administration.[17]

A third route would be to recognize that effective metropolitan governance seems a long way off and to pin hope on a new generation of intermunicipal associations (Cunha 2004). Azevedo and Mares Guia (2004) have used the expression *incremental institutionalization* to refer to a process of gradual association between adjoining municipalities and state-level agencies, formalized through cooperation agreements and councils. Here the experience of the Greater ABC Chamber offers several lines to be explored, especially in relation to a multithematic agenda and lower transaction costs (Machado 2009). This "line of least resistance" approach (either voluntary or in part compulsory) was the one favored by many of the political actors in the ill-fated Inter Federative Working Group of 2008 (Ravanelli 2010), although the Supreme Court would not be in favor of "compulsory cooperation," given that municipalities are also original members of the federal pact.

A fourth option would be the establishment of monothematic consortia, or single-purpose agencies, such as the ones in health and education that crisscross metropolitan regions and often involve adjacent municipalities (Garson 2009). The experience of Greater Recife would be important to follow in this respect.

A fifth approach would be the explicit and voluntary transfer of control over certain activities (for example, water, sewage, transport, health, and education) from the metropolitan municipalities back to the state, so that the state could in turn centralize their coordination and implementation through a single state monothematic or multithematic metropolitan agency. The argument here is that if decentralization has proved possible the reverse may also be potentially viable. (For example, in the São Paulo Metropolitan Region, while there is a state-supported metropolitan health research network covering and providing information on the whole region, response to day-to-day health needs and threats is organized by municipality, in seven separate health regions, rather than according to demographic or epidemiological considerations.)

A sixth line of thinking would follow Gouvêa's (2005) argument that some level of institutionalization is a sine qua non for metropolitan affairs and that the prospects for the future democratic and participative development of policy priorities will depend on the presence of a sufficient level of collective power to sustain a "metropolitan conscience." Here several "institutional practices" are close at hand. The metropolitan municipality is already almost a reality in metropolitan regions such as Salvador and Maceió, where the central municipality is home to close to 80 percent of the population. Another practice would draw on the experience of the city-state of Guanabara (Rio de Janeiro) or the model of the Federal District, where, in effect, a number of different areas are brought together in a single jurisdiction with semistate status. In a similar vein, and recalling the historical significance of the relation between representation and taxation for democratic life, creating a more effective and explicit tax base for metropolitan-wide action—which Rezende and Garson (2004) regard as an essential step for any progress—could provide an important incentive for a new phase of democratic metropolitan-wide governance. Reverse emancipation may seem hard to bring about, especially given Brazil's culture of *municipalismo,* but it may be institutionally more comfortable than many think. The state of Rio de Janeiro, with its capital, Niteroi, and the state of Guanabara, with its capital, Rio de Janeiro, lived side by side until 1975, when they were fused into the state of Rio de Janeiro and Rio de Janeiro became the capital city. Turning Brazil's metropolitan districts into urban states would shake up political power structures, but it could also be a way to provide greater equity for their populations and to require greater responsibility of their governments.

Notes

1. Gouvêa (2005) follows a similar line by noting the lack of precision in the 1988 Constitution and the need to distinguish, as certain states have done, between metropolitan regions, urban agglomerations of intermediary scale, and microregions.

2. The Brazilian Census takes place every ten years, and for 2010 only basic demographic data have been released. Hence most of the analytic studies cited will use either the 2000 data or the intermediary sample studies.

3. The UNDP Human Development Index is a weighted index that takes into consideration income, longevity, and education.

4. Belém, Recife, Fortaleza, Salvador, Belo Horizonte, Rio de Janeiro, São Paulo, Curitiba, and Porto Alegre.

5. A contradiction in terms, given that the Constitution guarantees that no worker can earn less than the minimum salary.

6. Current statistics are showing that of every ten jobs being created in the formal market, nine are being offered with salaries equal to two minimum salaries or less and require only the very minimum of literacy skills.

7. Statistics are from the EMPLASA website (2007) and use information from the 2000 full census: "Tabela 5: Regiões Metropolitanas Nacionais, População abaixo da Linha de Pobreza: 2000," 2007, www.emplasa.sp.gov.br/emplasa/Brasil/tabela_Metropoles/Tabela5.htm (accessed February 29, 2012).

8. See the important volume edited by Ribeiro (2004b), as well as Ribeiro (2010) and the ongoing work of the national research network Observatorio dos Metropoles (www.observatoriodasmetropoles.net).

9. For example, the recent report on the state of the cities in Latin America and the Caribbean by the regional office of United Nations Habitat (2010).

10. Brazil's federalist model is unusual in that both states and municipalities are part of the federal pact.

11. For greater detail on Brazil's subnational institutional arrangements, see Wilson et al. (2008).

12. In the first—republican—constitution of the state of São Paulo.

13. The Forum is currently housed at the São Paulo Agency of EMPLASA.

14. At the 2009 Congress of State Secretaries of Administration, a major gathering of public sector management specialists, only two of the some two

hundred papers presented dealt with the theme of metropolitan management, and in 2011 none did.

15. The cases of Espírito Santo, Maranhão, Paraíba, and Rio Grande do Sul.

16. A colleague who was carrying out research in the region used the expression "Santos Metropolitan Region" in a conversation with a member of the council. He was quickly corrected: "Santos is Santos, the Baixada Santista is something else."

17. The others were transparency of procedures; a single authority for key responsibilities; the decentralization of all other responsibilities (subsidiarity); maximization of public participation; and fiscal autonomy.

Chapter 5

Metropolitan Governance in Mexico

Mission Impossible?

PETER M. WARD
WITH HÉCTOR ROBLES

THE METROPOLITAN IMPERATIVE

In earlier work one of us discussed a number of the challenges that face metropolitan areas in developing a tiered structure of democratic government and governance both in Latin America generally and in Mexico specifically (Ward 1996, 2004).[1] These challenges are not new, of course: during the 1960s many cities created special-purpose authorities designed to reduce externalities and achieve efficiencies, but these were often frustrated and boycotted by opposition from local governments and from vested interest groups. Ultimately they often failed, in large part precisely because they ignored the inclusion of public voice and accountability—the essence of the idea of governance as the term is used in this book. And later, during the 1990s, a second "wave" of metropolitan governments, including fully fledged single metropolitan authorities as well as two-tier systems, appeared in a number of countries. In other countries—including that of Mexico considered here—a less institutionalized approach of inter-municipal collaboration has been adopted, though more ephemeral in its success and sustainability.

Each of the chapters in this volume wrestles with many of the issues of how to achieve effective governance for large metropolitan areas given their large and often highly differentiated populations and their (often) multiple and overlapping administrative and governmental jurisdictions, usually charged with ensuring both representational *and* participatory democracy. In many respects each of the authors is asking how to get "there" from "here"— whether by constructing a new tier of metropolitan government within Latin American federal and unitary systems, by merging existing governments into a single city, or by recasting the opportunities, incentives, or demands for cooperation and collaboration between the various units, agencies, and actors. Read thus, it will be clear that for some — us included —"public choice" arguments and rationality in favor of maximizing the autonomy of local governments are probably not an appropriate way forward when governments are subsumed within a metropolitan area or region. Instead, it might be argued that some modest level of governmental reach *across* jurisdictions is probably required to ensure integrated planning and some level of redistributive functions across the highly differentiated urban space that metropolitan areas inevitably represent.[2] The question that confronts us is how best to create this new architecture of metropolitan government and governance — and in this chapter we propose to explore several different experiences from Mexico, working within the country's three-tier federalist structure, as well as to explore the feasibility of developing a new (fourth) metropolitan tier of government and, if that is not feasible or desirable, then the means of best achieving more effective metropolitan governance.

The introductory chapter to this book outlined several imperatives that appear to be informing this conversation and the search for a new metropolitan governance architecture; they include democratization, decentralization and devolution, the technocratization of administrative and governmental procedures, a demographic slowdown, and pressures for greater efficiency and competitiveness. These have all been driving forces in Mexico since the 1990s.

POLITICS AND FEDERALISM IN MEXICO

Mexico's constitution provides for a federal structure that today comprises (1) a single federal government headed by a president elected for six years, with no reelection, and a national congress with a lower house of five hundred seats, to which members are elected every three years (two hundred by segmented proportional representation), and an upper house (senate) of 128 members (four from each state) — again without immediate reelection; (2) thirty-one sovereign states and a single Federal District, each with a governor elected directly for a nonrenewable six-year term; a single house legislature of varying size with local deputies elected for three-year nonrenewable terms; and (3) some 2,500-plus municipalities, which by the federal pact are accorded municipal autonomy under the aegis of the state and the local congress. Municipal presidents head the *ayuntamiento* (city government and council) and are elected for three-year nonrenewable terms, with an elected council *(cabildo)* of varying size integrated from party lists according to the party vote. A national and state judiciary makes up the third branch of the federalist system.

Two features of the Mexican political system stand out. The first is that the PRI (Party of the Institutionalized Revolution) had total and uninterrupted domination for seventy-two years until the National Action Party (PAN) won the presidency in 2000 and then again in 2006. Throughout that period the PRI also dominated at the state and local levels, and not until 1989 did a state fall to a non-PRI government. Since that time a significant number of states and cities have been governed by all three principal parties — including the Federal District, where the Party of the Democratic Revolution (PRD) has won all elections since the 1996 political reform allowed for direct elections in that entity. Thus Mexico's current political landscape is a patchwork of parties in power, with frequent electoral alternation and with different parties simultaneously governing at the federal, state, and local levels.

A second feature has been the tradition of a strong centralized political system vested within the presidency. Thus the hegemony of one party, together with the power vested in a strong presidentialist system that controlled both the party and federal bureaucracies, meant that until recently the second and third tiers (states and municipalities) of the federalist system had neither effective autonomy nor true sovereignty. Similarly, the other two branches (legislative and judicial) did not exercise effective checks and balances upon the executive branch. Nevertheless, democratic change from the late 1980s onwards, electoral and political reforms, and the rising plurality of parties in power led to a weakening in the traditional domination of the center and the national president, and to the strengthening of a "new" or more "authentic" federalism since 1994 (Ward and Rodríguez 1999). Today Mexico has a federalist structure that accords effective powers, responsibilities, and autonomy to the levels as well as to the branches (Camp 2006, 2010). True decentralization—both vertical and horizontal—is now a feature of Mexico's inter- and intragovernmental relations, but it has been in place for less than two decades (Wilson et al. 2008).

In the national legislature, power was more or less shared between the PRI and PAN between 2000 and 2006, with the PRD making up the third force. That changed in 2006 when the PAN narrowly defeated the PRD, pushing the PRI back into third place. In 2012 the PRI won back the presidency and again became the majority party in both chambers. Thus partisan politics drives the political processes in Mexico, although the constitutional prohibition on immediate reelection makes for little personal performance incentive, while maximizing the control and influence of party bosses over the career tracks of their politician members.

METROPOLITAN STRUCTURES IN MEXICO

Metropolitan Areas and Economic Activity

Table 5.1 presents data for the sixty-seven metropolitan areas and cities (of over one hundred thousand inhabitants) of Mexico in 2000 and displays several important dimensions: namely, the population, the number of municipalities that each embraces, and the gross production values (GPVs) generated for the principal sectors of each city. Several of the cities are highlighted because, although often quite large, they comprise a single municipality and as such in Mexico are not considered to be metropolitan, since they are not conurbations of two or more municipalities (see below). Indeed, seven of the top twenty-three cities on the list are single-municipality cities with a population of over half a million, and considering at least one of these cases allows us to explore the counterfactual examples of cities that should not, at least in principle, be dogged by challenges of divergent politics, multijurisdictional conflicts, or the need to collaborate across multiple jurisdictions. Our analysis explores one such case—that of Ciudad Juárez.

An idea that implicitly underpins many of the arguments for change is that some sort of integrated government of an urban or metropolitan area is desirable to promote economic growth by making the area more productive and allowing it to be competitive, whether through economies of scale, maximized efficiency, or innovation, and by directing urban

Table 5.1. Metropolitan Areas of Mexico, Showing Population and Sectoral Share of GDP

Rank	Metropolitan Area/ City	Population in 2000	No. of Municipalities	No. of States	Share of Total Industry	GPV in 1998 per Commerce	Economic Sector Services
1	Mexico City	17,380,709	40	3	43.29%	40.94%	15.77%
2	Guadalajara	3,539,706	7	1	53.74%	38.70%	7.56%
3	Monterrey	3,211,393	10	1	56.09%	32.23%	11.68%
4	Puebla	1,701,662	17	2	67.02%	26.79%	6.19%
5	Tijuana	1,214,085	2	1	38.16%	50.00%	11.84%
6	**Ciudad Juárez**	**1,205,648**	1	1	**52.35%**	**36.58%**	**11.07%**
7	León	1,129,801	3	1	50.74%	41.21%	8.05%
8	Toluca	939,929	10	1	75.61%	20.34%	4.05%
9	Torreón	815,992	4	2	56.72%	35.47%	7.80%
10	San Luis Potosí	798,782	2	1	69.46%	25.75%	4.80%
11	Mérida	779,180	4	1	35.04%	54.70%	10.26%
12	**Chihuahua**	**657,876**	1	1	**58.03%**	**33.18%**	**8.79%**
13	Cuernavaca	638,776	5	1	57.53%	33.19%	9.28%
14	Aguascalientes	633,839	3	1	64.69%	28.12%	7.19%
15	**Acapulco**	**620,656**	1	1	**15.51%**	**45.73%**	**38.76%**
16	Tampico	603,105	4	2	43.18%	44.42%	12.40%
17	Saltillo	599,951	3	1	79.42%	15.43%	5.15%
18	Querétaro	599,463	3	1	68.97%	23.70%	7.34%
19	Veracruz	560,101	2	1	42.48%	43.42%	14.09%
20	**Morelia**	**549,996**	1	1	**29.29%**	**60.34%**	**10.37%**
21	**Mexicali**	**549,873**	1	1	**52.17%**	**39.91%**	**7.91%**
22	**Hermosillo**	**545,928**	1	1	**56.39%**	**34.86%**	**8.76%**
23	**Culiacán**	**540,823**	1	1	**17.55%**	**72.15%**	**10.30%**
24	Reynosa	483,858	2	1	59.14%	31.44%	9.42%

Table 5.1. Metropolitan Areas of Mexico, Showing Population and Sectoral Share of GDP (*cont.*)

Rank	Metropolitan Area/ City	Population in 2000	No. of Municipalities	No. of States	Share of Total Industry	GPV in 1998 per Commerce	Economic Sector Services
25	Tuxtla Gutiérrez	473,248	3	1	26.81%	63.05%	10.14%
26	Xalalapa	433,837	3	1	37.93%	50.11%	11.96%
27	**Durango**	427,135	1	1	44.85%	46.75%	8.39%
28	Cancún	407,215	2	1	4.10%	58.25%	37.66%
29	Oaxaca	397,462	9	1	14.05%	66.28%	19.67%
30	Celaya	379,537	3	1	60.06%	34.08%	5.86%
31	**Matamoros**	376,279	1	1	55.17%	32.48%	12.34%
32	**Villahermosa**	330,846	1	1	12.73%	71.40%	15.87%
33	**Mazatlán**	327,989	1	1	32.03%	46.73%	21.24%
34	**Irapuato**	320,914	1	1	47.86%	44.96%	7.18%
35	**Nuevo Laredo**	308,828	1	1	36.90%	41.06%	22.05%
36	Monclova	293,182	4	1	81.57%	13.88%	4.55%
37	Tepic	289,533	2	1	34.23%	58.69%	7.08%
38	Coatzacoalcos	281,795	3	1	51.36%	40.57%	8.07%
39	Pachuca	261,399	2	1	35.42%	54.29%	10.29%
40	Orizaba	255,422	8	1	79.05%	16.25%	4.70%
41	**Cd. Obregón**	250,790	1	1	38.40%	53.17%	8.43%
42	**Cd. Victoria**	249,029	1	1	15.34%	63.55%	21.11%
43	**Uruapan**	225,816	1	1	29.10%	60.35%	10.55%
44	Cuatla	225,266	4	1	54.93%	37.14%	7.93%
45	**Ensenada**	223,492	1	1	42.49%	44.99%	12.52%
46	Minatitlán	219,819	5	1	58.22%	32.44%	9.35%

Table 5.1. Metropolitan Areas of Mexico, Showing Population and Sectoral Share of GDP (*cont.*)

Rank	Metropolitan Area/ City	Population in 2000	No. of Municipalities	No. of States	Share of Total Industry	GPV in 1998 per Commerce	Economic Sector Services
47	Poza Rica	206,235	4	1	13.08%	66.11%	20.81%
48	**Tehuacán**	**204,598**	1	1	**54.77%**	**40.44%**	**4.79%**
49	**Los Mochis**	**200,906**	1	1	**24.26%**	**66.57%**	**9.18%**
50	Puerto Vallarta	198,606	2	2	3.24%	51.39%	45.37%
51	Colima	196,318	2	1	12.65%	71.00%	16.34%
52	Zacatecas	192,826	2	1	13.15%	76.13%	10.72%
53	**Campeche**	**190,813**	1	1	**23.29%**	**62.04%**	**14.73%**
54	**Tapachula**	**179,839**	1	1	**21.41%**	**68.92%**	**9.66%**
55	Tlaxcala	175,726	7	1	70.15%	25.96%	3.89%
56	Zamora	171,078	2	1	33.46%	60.61%	5.93%
57	Córdoba	163,382	2	1	42.78%	50.17%	7.05%
58	**La Paz**	**162,954**	1	1	**13.10%**	**73.21%**	**13.68%**
59	**Nogales**	**156,854**	1	1	**43.57%**	**43.21%**	**13.22%**
60	**Chilpancingo**	**142,746**	1	1	**7.05%**	**79.14%**	**13.72%**
61	**Salamanca**	**137,000**	1	1	**67.25%**	**27.27%**	**5.49%**
62	Guaymas	136,126	2	1	28.35%	54.54%	17.11%
63	**San Luis Rio Colorado**	**126,645**	1	1	**36.84%**	**54.77%**	**8.39%**
64	**Piedras Negras**	**126,024**	1	1	**54.38%**	**37.71%**	**7.90%**
65	**Cd. Del Carmen**	**126,024**	1	1	**4.51%**	**52.76%**	**42.73%**
66	**Chetumal**	**121,602**	1	1	**17.74%**	**54.61%**	**27.65%**
67	Delicias	118,113	2	1	46.92%	47.44%	5.64%

Source: Sobrino (2003).

Note: Bolded lines indicate cities of 100,000 population contained in a single municipality and therefore nor deemed "metropolitan."

growth to achieve these ends. Yet exactly how these spatial interconnections occur or are achieved is poorly understood, often being subjective and based upon ad hoc or scattered empirical findings (Paiva 2003). That fact notwithstanding, in table 5.1 the relative importance of Mexico's metropolitan areas is expressed in terms of their gross product by sector and per capita. Mexico City is far and away the most important, but its role as an industrial powerhouse has declined in recent years (although it still generates three times as much industrial product as Monterrey). Compared with most other places Mexico City is more significant in commerce and services, as are Morelia and Merida, both tourist centers and state capitals, and Acapulco, a tourist center. Significant industrial centers in table 5.1 are those associated with export-oriented growth — Puebla, Toluca, Querétaro, San Luis Potosí, Saltillo — each of which generates 65 to almost 80 percent of its gross product from industry. These same cities also have significantly higher per capita GDP rates (Saltillo is the highest, with over sixty-one thousand pesos GDP per capita). Generally cities with highly export-oriented industrial economies generate higher levels of GDP per capita — over forty thousand pesos — while the more commercial and service-oriented cities, and those that are national rather than global industrial production centers, such as León, come out much lower.

Definitions of *Metropolitan*: The Term's Ambiguity in Mexico

Within Mexico's federal constitution there is no provision for metropolitan government. Mexico's federal system provides for a federal (central) government and for state (regional) and local (municipal) governments — nothing else. Thus any metropolitan collaboration and coordination must be done informally or formally through state-mandated programs and/or through arrangements prescribed by state law so long as these do not contradict the Constitution. In practice, therefore, definitions of *metropolitan* have emerged in the rather ad hoc and often somewhat subjective fashion outlined in chapter 1.

Since 1950 a settlement with more than 2,500 inhabitants has been officially considered "urban" in the census, a low threshold by international urban classifications. Later, the first full Urban Development Program (Programa Nacional de Desarrollo Urbano, 1989–94) created the following classification: *small cities,* those with a population between fifteen thousand and one hundred thousand inhabitants; *medium cities,* those with over one hundred thousand to one million inhabitants; and *large cities,* those with more than one million inhabitants. In Mexico only a city whose urban zone spreads across more than one municipality is considered a "metropolitan" area. To our thinking this is problematic, since it leaves out Ciudad Juárez, ranked sixth in population with over 1.2 million inhabitants, as well as several other cities of more than 500,000 (table 5.1). Moreover, it is necessary to differentiate between a *metropolitan area* and a *metropolitan zone.* Following Sobrino (2003), metropolitan areas encompass an urban (built-up area) that extends over two or more municipalities, embrace land uses that are nonagricultural, and are physically contiguous. A metropolitan zone, on the other hand, also includes the whole municipal territories that touch upon the metropolitan area irrespective of whether they are contiguous (or primarily urban or agricultural in land use). Thus the boundaries of the metropolitan zone are congruent with the limits of the municipalities that form part of the respective metropolitan area, and in reality they form part of an urban "conurbation." Indeed, in Mexico the term *conurbation* is the preferred legal term to provide for metropolitan definitions and coordination.

However, the term *conurbation* is also riddled with ambiguities. In 1994, CONAPO published a study in which it established four metropolitan zones and thirty conurbations (embracing eighty-seven municipalities), whereas the Programa Nacional de Desarrollo Urbano, 1995–2000, used different criteria, proposing as it did 125 municipalities that conformed to twenty-nine conurbations. In short, there is no "official" rule for delimiting which localities to include in defining metropolitan areas. Only two articles of the Constitution refer to metropolitan zones or cities, but neither is helpful in clarifying what should constitute a metropolitan zone or how membership is determined. Article 115 on the municipality states: "When two or more urban centers located in municipal territories of two or more different states form or tend to form a demographic continuity, the national government, the states, and the respective municipalities, within their entitlements, will jointly and in coordination plan the development of those centers abiding by the respective laws on the topic." This article offers the possibility (and expectation) of creating metropolitan agencies for cooperation and coordination but not that of creating a metropolitan government, since only the municipality has autonomy and authority over the municipal jurisdiction—subject to the municipal codes of the regional (state) legislature.[3] Article 122 on the Federal District indicates that localities or municipalities in conurbation with the D. F. may coordinate among themselves and with the federal government to provide services through so-called metropolitan commissions. The regulation of these commissions is subject to the agreement of their members, but once again they do not have the character or authority of government.

In the National Law of Human Settlements (1976; reformulated in 1993), a conurbation is defined vaguely as "the physical and demographic continuity that forms or tends to form two population centers," while a metropolitan zone is described as "the territorial space under the dominant influence of a population center." With this ambiguity the law recognizes the necessity of coordination between the national government and the subnational and local levels in zones where there is a conurbation, and it gives states and municipalities the faculties to jointly administer public services in these zones. Specifically, article 21 of the law indicates that all levels of government should be involved in the delimitation of a conurbation zone where the geographical, urban, and economic characteristics of two or more population centers from neighboring states require it.

Thus Mexican law recognizes the existence of conurbation zones, but their establishment and delimitation depend on the willingness of two or more municipalities (and their respective state/s) to formally make an agreement to create a commission for the conurbation. The agreement defines the limits of the conurbation as well as the responsibilities of the national government and the corresponding states and municipalities. To take effect, the agreement must be published in the *Diario Oficial de la Federación*. What this basically amounts to is that conurbation commissions are responsible for urban development planning, but they do not have a precise structure defined by law, nor does the law specify the means whereby they are expected to achieve their purpose. Thus the strength or weakness of a conurbation commission depends heavily upon the specific faculties that states and municipalities assign to it. As we shall observe below, commissions have invariably lacked "teeth," but for the purposes of this chapter and looking to the future we should note that the law does allow for commissions to exercise effective powers, provided that there is the political will to do so (Cieslik 2007; López Pérez 2003).

Besides the provision of urban conurbation commissions, there are laws and regulations that, if adopted, can require coordination of different governments to provide certain services in metropolitan zones. A good example is the law that establishes the coordination bases of the National System of Public Security. This law allows for the establishment of coordination agreements among different levels of government, as well as between neighboring municipalities, and it specifically allows for the creation of intermunicipal bodies to provide public security in a metropolitan or conurbation zone.

Opportunities for Intergovernmental Collaboration

Given the lack of any empowered and constitutionally mandated metropolitan structure within Mexico's federal system, it might be helpful to outline some of the opportunities that provide for intergovernmental collaboration. One recent positive step that we highlight below has been the councils of mayors and governors. Political parties have sought to offer training that will strengthen municipal governance, not least because of the high turnover of personnel every three years (due to a prohibition of consecutive reelection of mayors) and the low baseline skills that have traditionally existed. Also, the federal government has an office within the Interior Ministry responsible for municipal governments, an important function of which was to oversee decentralization and municipal strengthening in the wake of the 1983 reform of article 115 of the Constitution. Also, governors are now playing an increasingly important role through the national Council of Governors (CONAGO) and are pressing their case for a greater share of fiscal resources and for a widening of taxation opportunities at the regional level (Ward and Rodríguez 1999). An important part of a governor's job has always been to leverage federal resources, but in Mexico's new democratic environment this is less likely to depend upon personal loyalty and closeness to the president and now relates much more to his effectiveness in creating appropriate institutional structures that will enable projects to go forward — whether these are statewide or metropolitan. Having a good and effective technical team is paramount. Governors are also working together — as the recent cases of Tamaulipas, Nuevo Léon, Coahuila, and Chihuahua demonstrate (González Parás 2003) — even sometimes crossing party lines. Until 2000 such collaboration of "all for one and one for all" was anathema in Mexico's highly centralized and hierarchical traditions. But in the first two decades of the twenty-first century perhaps the idea has greater traction as cities seek greater metropolitan collaboration, a point to which we return later.

CASE STUDIES IN METROPOLITAN COORDINATION

Nationally there are sixteen urban centers with more than five hundred thousand inhabitants in which two or more municipalities form a conurbation and jointly create a metropolitan zone (table 5.1).[4] It is precisely these centers that especially need coordination between governments to provide services and to guarantee sustainable development of the city. The most salient cases in this respect are the three largest metropolitan areas, Mexico City, Guadalajara, and Monterrey, and these are discussed in greater detail below.

Mexico City: Is Metropolitan Government "Truly Mission Impossible"?

As table 5.1 and figure 5.1 show, the metropolitan area of Mexico City is extreme in the complexity of its composition. Today it comprises twenty million people, spread almost equally over two federal entities: the state of Mexico and the Federal District (and also touching upon the state of Hidalgo in a single municipality to the north). The overall conurbation (metropolitan zone, following Sobrino's definition) embraces no less than forty separate municipalities plus sixteen *delegaciones* in the D. F. Considering only the contiguous urban area — what I will call the "metropolitan area"— reduces slightly the total number of municipalities (to thirty), plus the sixteen *delegaciones.* Several of these municipalities and *delegaciones* are very large in their own right, with more than a million people (Ciudad Nezahualcóyotl and Ecatepec). Thus the metropolitan area comprises a patchwork of governments in which all three federal levels of authority are likely to be heavily invested, with the regional governments of the D. F. and the state of Mexico being the primary players. The fact that this is also the national capital, involving the intersection of federal, regional, and local governments, inevitably makes Mexico City something of an outlier in any systematic analysis of the Mexican case.

The past is littered with attempts to create a consultative council for the conurbation commission, as well as occasional attempts to coordinate activities between adjacent municipalities and between the D. F. and larger contiguous municipalities in the neighboring state of Mexico. But such collaborations have been ephemeral (Ward 1998b) and have usually failed badly (Alfonso Iracheta, qtd. in Ward 2004, 513). Some statutory metropolitan commissions have worked reasonably well in the past, most notably that of public rapid transit (Metro) through COVI-TUR. Today, the Estatuto de Gobierno del Distrito Federal includes (in its third section) a whole set of articles for metropolitan coordination. Basically the statutes establish that the D. F. must coordinate with its neighboring municipalities in the areas of human settlements planning; environmental protection and ecological preservation; transportation; water and sewerage; treatment and disposal of waste; and public security.

Figure 5.1. Mexico City Metropolitan Area

The main mechanisms for this metropolitan coordination in Mexico City are metropolitan commissions, and the government of the Distrito Federal can commit material, human, and financial resources for the operation of the commissions, but the amount of these resources must be authorized by the Legislative Assembly. Moreover, any agreement at the metropolitan level must be published in the *Diario Oficial de la Federación* and in the *Gaceta del D.F.* Thus, regardless of the traction and success that these commissions achieve — and prima facie the evidence is that their success is only partial at best — the sheer size, extent, and multijurisdictional structure of the Mexico City metropolitan area pose huge challenges. To that extent Mexico City needs dramatic remedial action of the "very difficult" kind (see Mitchell-Weaver, Miller, and Deal's model [2000; figure 1.2] in chapter 1)—namely, constitutional reform.

These challenges notwithstanding, the D. F. in particular has made great strides since 1997 in developing more democratic and effective representative and participatory governance structures, both regionally, through the activity of the legislative assembly, and locally in the sixteen *delegaciones* (Ward 2004; Ziccardi 2003). The quality of government is generally better today, and the knowledge and participation of citizens at the local level are much improved. But the "big picture" of primary-level decision making and effective coordination between the D. F. and the Edo de México still needs to be addressed.

Several lessons may be learned from this extreme case, among which is the imperative of creating some level of integrated metropolitan authority and vision that might ensure a degree of equity and redistribution between better-off and less well-off areas of Mexico City. While the same can be argued for any major city, the scale of Mexico City and the substantial socioeconomic inequality *between* as well as *within* administrative jurisdictions make some level of compensation desirable. However, the creation of a new tier of metropolitan authority seems very unlikely. Any attempt to annex or amalgamate half of the city by the governments of either the D. F. or the State of Mexico would be strongly resisted and remains "Mission Impossible." Nevertheless, some level of integrated and collaborative planning and executive decision making may emerge, probably through metropolitan commissions. To the extent that these can be empowered to report to the respective constituent elected assemblies—the Asamblea Legislativa del D. F. and the State of Mexico Congress—then one might envisage an arrangement whereby agreements could be ratified—rather like international treaty arrangements. This would create the basis for an integrated level of effective governance with public oversight and would be a major improvement on the current structure.

Some improvement in governance in Mexico City occurred as a result of the political reform of 1996, which after 1997 facilitated direct elections for the head of the D. F. government as well as the head of each borough *(delegación)*. This new regime of representative government heralded a significant improvement in the process of participatory democracy and transparency of local governance. But to the extent that this was rectifying an anomaly (the D. F. was the only area where previously there had been no direct elections), it is hardly a lesson in replicability. Applying the principle of subsidiarity to this hierarchy of intergovernmental re-

Figure 5.2. Guadalajara Metropolitan Area

lations and activities also has much to commend it and could be useful both in Mexico City and elsewhere. Thus some form of regional metropolitan commission and authority over certain sectors of activity might be created — with or without direct elections — that would report back to the regional congress (or both congresses in this case), and in which municipalities would retain control over local services and functions under the principle of subsidiarity, as in the case of Montreal discussed in chapter 2.

Guadalajara: Metropolitan Governance via Councils and Commissions—*a medias?*

Guadalajara, the second-largest metropolitan area in the country, with over 3.5 million population, lies singly within the State of Jalisco and embraces seven municipalities within its conurbation, six of which form part of the contiguous metropolitan area (figure 5.2). Of these, Guadalajara Municipality itself has 1.6 million residents, followed by three other principal municipalities: Zapopan (910,000), Tlaquepaque (460,000), and Tonalá (315,000).

Coordination among municipalities in the metropolitan zone of Guadalajara is hardly recent. Formal instances of it first appeared in 1977, when the Congress of Jalisco enacted the Ley de Asentamientos Humanos after the national law of 1976 was enacted. The state law regulated intermunicipal coordination for metropolitan development using the federal scheme of conurbation commissions. Municipalities collaborated mainly for physical planning. In 1978 the Commission for the Urban-Regional Development of Guadalajara (Comisión para el Desarrollo Urbano-Regional) was created. The commission consisted of the state minister of government and the nineteen municipal presidents of what was then called the Guadalajara Region. This commission elaborated and approved the Plan de Ordenamiento de la Zona Conurbada de Guadalajara, completed in 1982. However, this was fairly typical of the "paper" plans of the day (i.e., plans with little or no executive authority), mandated by the 1976 law and the National Urban Development Plan of 1978.

However, Guadalajara is especially interesting in that it does have a metropolitan institution responsible for the planning and funding of public works: the Council of the Metropolitan Zone of Guadalajara, created in 1989 for coordination and conciliation of actions that had an intermunicipal scope in the metro zone. Initially, the members of the council came from some departments and offices of the national and state governments as well as the local governments of Guadalajara, Tlaquepaque, Tonalá, and Zapopan. Later, the *ayuntamientos* of El Salto, Ixtlahucán de los Membrillos, Juanacatlán, and Tlajomulco de Zúñiga also became members of the council. It was not until 1993 that the state law of urban development gave the city council formal recognition as the principal governmental entity responsible for governmental coordination across the metropolitan zone. According to the state law the principal responsibilities of the council are

Ordering and regulating the urban growth in the city
Finding alternatives for the efficient operating and administering of public services
Agreeing on the main alternatives for executing public works of relevant
    magnitude in the areas of infrastructure and equipment
Solving, under a metropolitan scheme, the problem of solid waste management
Tackling the problem of urban pollution

The council operates through five commissions coordinated by the state ministry that deals with each of these arenas: Urban Development,

Public Transportation and Road Issues, Water and Drainage, Environment and Natural Resources, and Financing. Within these commissions most technical and political development planning takes place, with the main political weight and influence being exercised by the governor, especially when it comes to decision making related to public works. A Metropolitan Fund exists to generate resources for the operation mandated to the city council and comprises contributions from the national government and the private sector, as well as the permanent contributions from the state government and participating municipalities. Projects that are approved by the plenary council establish the relative contributions of state and local governments, assessed according to a formula that takes account of the population of each municipality and the fiscal transfers received by the state and local governments from the national government. Once the amounts of contributions are defined, municipal presidents present a request for resources to their respective *cabildos* so that these can be incorporated into the municipal budget of the next year, with the state government also setting aside the funds in its annual budget. In 2001 roads took the lion's share of the Metropolitan Fund (64 percent), while water, drainage, and solid waste took 21 percent and public transportation 10 percent. But even so, the total amount assigned was less than US$50 million. In 2004 contributions were fifty/fifty from state and local governments, with each providing around US$13 million to create an overall pot of US$26 million.

Another mechanism to achieve intermunicipal coordination is the agreement between municipalities. In Jalisco services in the arena of transportation and roads are mainly the responsibility of the state government. However, the Ley de los Servicios de Vialidad, Tránsito y Transporte del Estado de Jalisco establishes in its chapter 6 that *ayuntamientos* in the conurbation can develop agreements among themselves and the state government, as well as coordinated public road and transportation works. This can occur either through the city council or by the establishment of commissions.

Guadalajara — like Mexico City and Monterrey — has a metropolitan system of transportation overseen by a decentralized public agency, Sistema de Transporte Colectivo de la Zona Metropolitana (SISTECOZOME), to administer and operate urban transportation systems in the metropolitan zone of Guadalajara. SISTECOZOME is administered by an administrative council and a general director. The council includes the state government, the municipal presidents of Guadalajara, Zapopan, and Tlaquepaque, representatives of the private sector, and representatives of different unions of workers. In effect, though, the fact that five of the twelve councilors are from the state government gives primary decision making to the governor. At the beginning SISTECOZOME operated mainly through public funding and subsidies. However, since 1982 the participation of the private sector has become increasingly important, particularly the "light load" and microbus concessions. The private sector operates most routes of SISTECOZOME by subcontracting service provision, although tariffs are set by the state government, which also provides some level of subsidy.

In 2001 the council proposed to create a Metropolitan Planning Institute for the municipalities of Zapopan and Guadalajara, but politics intervened and different actors and sectors defended or attacked the proposal. Specifically three of the six conurbation municipalities refused to sign the agreement, concerned that they would lose authority and that the institute would, in effect, create a tier of organization that would contravene their autonomy. As elsewhere, the principal functions and services for which municipalities are responsible include water and sewerage; public lighting; solid waste collection, treatment, and disposal; markets and *centrales de abasto;* cemeteries; slaughterhouses; streets, parks, and open spaces; and public security within their jurisdiction. Besides these functions, municipalities can coordinate through conurbation commissions in areas of human settlements; environmental protection; public transportation; solid waste management; and public security. The state is responsible in the metropolitan areas for providing public education; public health services; environmental protection; the water and sewer system (jointly with municipalities); social security; public security; culture and libraries; some national parks in conjunction with the federal government; housing; urban development; and tourism.

In the most recent iteration (2007), an "intermunicipal association" was proposed by the majority party (PAN), ostensibly as a new initiative, although the proposal was hardly new. And as one of us (Robles, then a council member for Zapopan) argued publicly at the time, given the legal constraints of empowering this level of government (discussed earlier), the proposed association is unlikely to move forward effective collaboration unless other major actors are also involved (federal and state) and unless serious consideration is given to resource allocation. In the event, in December of 2007 the state congress approved a constitutional reform that made obligatory metropolitan collaboration between the municipalities.

Guadalajara highlights the difficulties that intergovernmental frictions often pose to prevent effective collaboration. It also demonstrates that there is often intense competition between jurisdictions and that these conflicts and divisions are not necessarily anchored primarily in party politics (since all of the governments in Guadalajara were PANista until 2009, when the PRI swept the board, doing so again in 2012).

More than anywhere else in Mexico the city has experimented with the structure of a metropolitan council — since 1997 — and it represents a significant initiative in the Mexican case. However, the lack of adequate resources has undermined its potential. Finally, in the case of Guadalajara it seems likely that the recent attempts to create a Metropolitan Planning Institute will also flounder given the competition, jealousies, and party rivalries between and within the various entities, making it at best a half-hearted *(a medias)* attempt to construct a structure of metropolitan governance. To date, the evidence suggests that planning institutes work best where they are vested in a single jurisdiction (as in León and Ciudad Juárez), although this should probably remain a hypothesis rather than a definitive finding.

Monterrey: Metropolitan Coordination through the Regional Powers of State Government (the Firm and Guiding Hand Approach)

Monterrey's metropolitan zone comprises nine municipalities and 3.2 million inhabitants, 1.07 million of whom live in the central municipality of Monterrey, and the bulk of the remainder in the adjacent eastern and northern municipalities of Guadalupe (535,000), San Nicolás de los Garza (437,000), Apodaca, and General Escobedo (about 100,000 each), and to the south, in its protected valley, the "richest" municipality in the country, San Pedro Garza García (113,000) (see table 5.1 and figure 5.3). Because Monterrey is an important state capital, some federal offices are located there and work in especially close conjunction with the central government. Almost 85 percent of the population of Nuevo León State resides in the metropolitan area, this having increased from 74 percent in 1970 (Aguilar Barajas 2004). Inevitably, therefore, the state government's attention is firmly focused on the metropolitan area.

As in the previous two cases, municipalities carry out the local functions and activities, and the regional government coordinates the metropolitan level of planning and sectoral activities in transportation, infrastructure, environmental protection, and security. Such coordination is achieved in one of three principal ways: through bilateral agreements between municipalities; by decentralized regional public agencies; or by regional government (state secretariats) through which the governor has

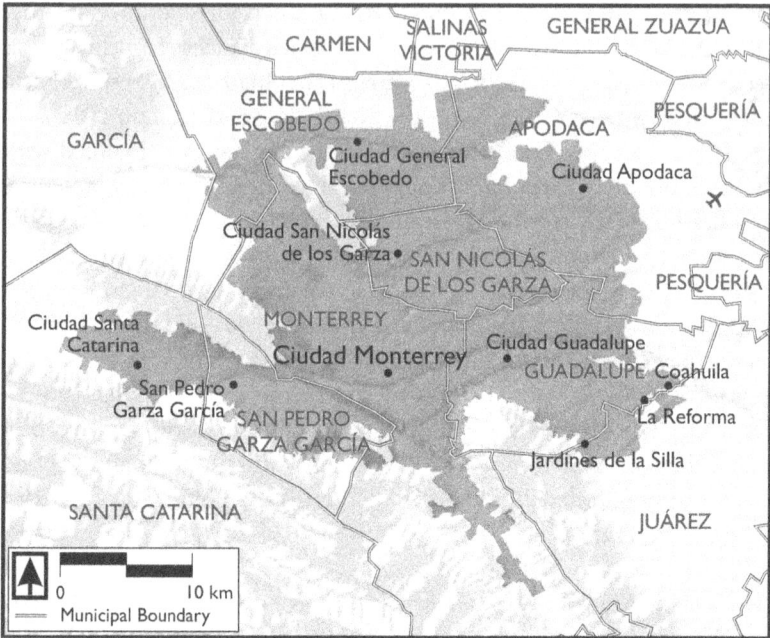

Figure 5.3. Monterrey Metropolitan Area

the most say. Metropolitan (conurbation) commissions in Monterrey have not worked well in the past. In the transportation arena, the Metropolitan Council for Transportation is all-important, dominated by the regional (state) government (Paiva 2003, 185). The urban rail company METRORREY is a one-purpose agency responsible to the state government through the Public Works Secretariat and also participates in the council. As in Guadalajara, the Metropolitan Council for Transportation plans and undertakes investment and sets tariffs, and the state government is the primary power behind the whole structure, ruling on pricing and urban transportation routes. The Metropolitan Council for Transportation is a "strong agency that is adequate in terms of territory. Its strength lies in the state legislation that ensures that urban transport decisions are taken at the state level" (Paiva 2003, 213). Individual municipalities are responsible for implementation of regulations and issuing permits, a process that has become streamlined in recent years with decentralization (Paiva 2003, 203), which has given municipalities greater local control and responsibility. Municipalities also serve as agents of the central and regional governments in ensuring monitoring of public transportation with respect to the environment and the quality of service. Thus, while autonomous, they also remain firmly within the reach of the central and regional governments.

This tendency for the regional government and the governor to take firm control of strategic areas at the metropolitan level is also demonstrated by the 2000 law that created a decentralized agency called Metropolitan System of Solid Waste Processing (SEMIPRODESO), which, while leaving all direct collection in the hands of the municipalities, provides for direct state government control of the dump sites, as well as for the reception and processing of garbage and waste. Perhaps more than in most metropolitan areas in Mexico, this case shows that it is the state government in Monterrey that has the most effective metropolitan reach, this being largely explained by Paiva (2003, 62), as the result of its relative independence from the center of Mexico (given that it is a northern border state) and its role as a manufacturing and export center (see also Garza Villareal 1996). As we observed in table 5.1, Monterrey maintains its profile as a manufacturing powerhouse. The relative success of metropolitan coordination in Monterrey, therefore, derives in large part from the strong intervention and control exercised by the state government and by the governor's office in particular. The fact that such a large proportion of the state's population live within the metropolitan area and that the city contains a very rich municipality within its bounds, as well as having very considerable economic importance nationally, means that the opportunity costs of failure and of metropolitan inefficiency would be high.

Toluca: Metropolitan Coordination between Polynucleated Centers
(a Cities-within-the-City Approach)

The dynamic growth of the metropolitan area of Toluca (ranked seventh in size in table 5.1) was from the mid-1960s onwards closely tied to industrial expansion along the highway axis that runs eastward from the center toward Mexico City. Industrial plants were established in small (private) ranches on the northern side of the highway, which was itself converted into a grandiose and tree-lined city entry highway called the Paseo Tolluacan, with functional feeder roads running alongside it to service the factories. This industrial park development led to metropolitan expansion and was driven by strong gubernatorial leadership tied to the then governor's elite support base associated with the town of Tlacomulco and therefore identified as the "Tlacomulco group." In Toluca a key economic elite has consistently played a primary or at least significant role in shaping the economic base of the city as well as its physical growth.

However, the population distribution across the metropolitan zone is quite unusual and makes for administrative complexity. The Toluca metropolitan area has a total population of over eight hundred thousand, yet its metropolitan zone formally comprises ten municipalities — as many as Guadalajara, which is much larger, of course. Strictly speaking, this is the Toluca conurbation, and not all of these municipalities are actually part of the contiguous built-up area (see figure 5.4). But the interesting feature of Toluca is that the metropolitan area comprises a series of municipal capitals *(cabeceras)*, or cities within the city, and a very large number of pueblos within its metropolitan structure, so that it can be best characterized as a metropolitan area of conurbation townships *(pueblos conurbados)*. Figure 5.4 depicts some sixteen small townships embedded within the four municipalities. Besides Toluca, there are three other principal municipalities: Metepec, San Mateo, and Zinacantepec (figure 5.4). These latter three municipalities, along with many of the pueblos immediately to the north of Toluca's downtown core, retain their old pueblo atmosphere and a *cabecera* (or a sub-*cabecera*) structure: namely a historic core with a plaza, commercial and administrative buildings, markets, and low-income rental housing surrounding the central area. In some cases these pueblo cores still have agricultural land parcels stretching out beyond the urban fringe extending to the next pueblo. With industrial growth and metropolitan expansion, these pueblos — both their cores and their *ejido* lands — became the focus of population infill by a working-class population, and residential estates developed on the erstwhile farms and smallholdings. Thus the metropolitan area began to coalesce, with each municipality taking charge of its own development, while the state government sought to create adequate transportation routes and linkages between the pueblos, the northern industrial zone, and Toluca's downtown, where most people worked. Urban development plans at the state level aimed to maintain the integrity of these outlying pueblo cores and their populations within the municipalities while making for a functional unit by ensuring the movement of people to their workplaces — a task in which they have only had partial success.

It is difficult to draw too many lessons about the Toluca experience, not least given its somewhat sui generis polynucleated structure and the fact that much of the metropolitan focus of the state government is directed thirty miles to the east, where ten million people live in that half of Mexico City that lies within the state's boundaries. However, for Toluca

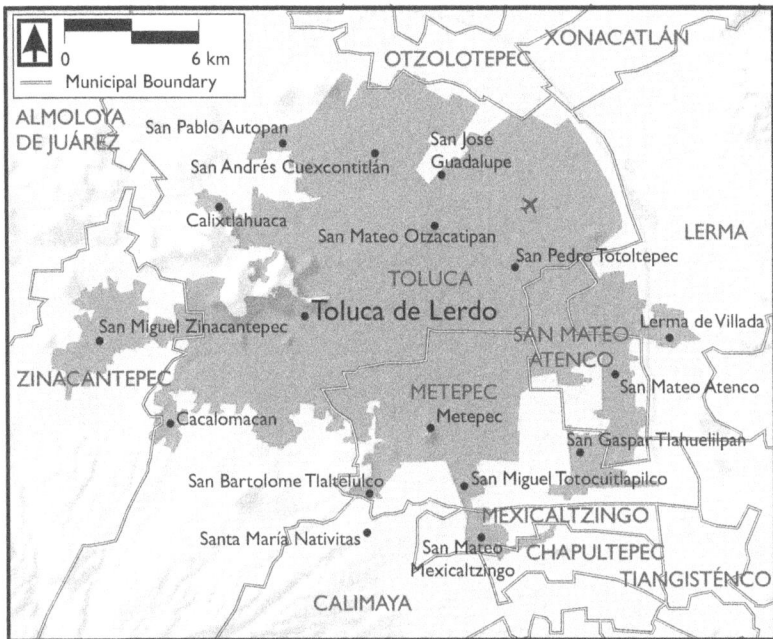

Figure 5.4. Toluca Metropolitan Area

it is apparent that the influence of a powerful state elite has been a major determinant in the city's development. Moreover, the state's coordination of the conurbation municipalities and their pueblo cores can provide an important axis in achieving a significant level of integration, especially if this embodies the principle of subsidiarity at the local level.

Ciudad Juárez: Metropolitan Government in a Single Jurisdiction — the Case of Public and Private Partnerships

As noted earlier, Mexico has seven individual city municipalities, each with over half a million population, that are not classified as metropolitan areas since they do not form part of a conurbation. In these cases the whole urban area falls within a single municipal jurisdiction. In declining order of size, these are Ciudad Juárez, Chihuahua, Acapulco, Morelia, Mexicali, Hermosillo, and Culiacán (see table 5.1). This means that in these cities the responsibility for providing services belongs to a single government, so prima facie there should be at least a citywide vision unencumbered by jurisdictional rivalries and by the need for coordination

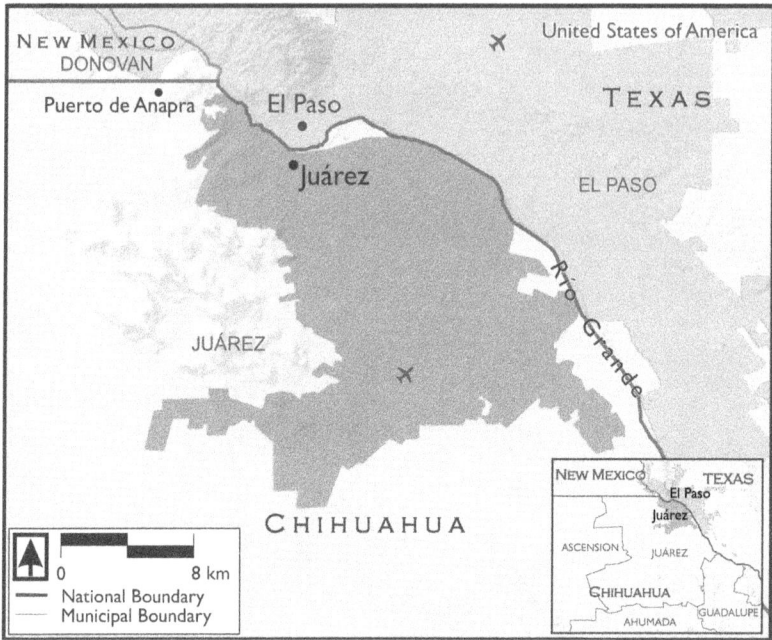

Figure 5.5. Municipality of Ciudad Juárez

with other municipalities. A metropolitan tier of governance or inter-municipal consortia arrangements are not imperative. Here, we look in more detail at one of these cases — Ciudad Juárez — to evaluate how far this singular governmental structure makes a difference in providing for easier and more effective urban governance. Does it offer a counterfactual example to those considered previously?

Although Ciudad Juárez is a single municipality, strictly speaking it too is part of a wider metropolitan zone by virtue of its geographical position bordering El Paso, Texas, and Sunland Park (contiguous to El Paso but actually in New Mexico). This is not untypical of many U.S.-Mexico border cities, and in effect Ciudad Juárez, with over 1.2 million people, is part of a single metropolitan area of approximately two million, though spread across two countries and three states (figure 5.5). However, while there has always been a strong tradition of transhumance and of cross-border communication and dialogue, as well as intercity cooperation around issues of common concern, when it comes to planning, social development, and infrastructural provision responsibility has always been firmly vested in the municipality and in its single government. Moreover, the city is distinctive in that an entrepreneurial elite has traditionally exerted a strong influence on the direction and nature of city growth and planning. The case of Ciudad Juárez illustrates how a single municipal entity offers a greater opportunity for economic elites to exercise direct influence, especially when there is a considerable degree of consensus and common vision among that elite.[5]

The existence of this strong private sector dates back to the presence of several major Chihuahua economic "elite" families engaged in the city's economic development primarily through the Border Industrialization Program anchored around *maquila* (in-bond assembly) industries in the city. As urban planning began to emerge from the late 1970s onwards, the key players in the private sector — industrial entrepreneurs mostly — found that they could invariably protect their interests and shape the city's growth through backroom negotiation with the municipal president and the governor. With the ascendance of the PAN in the city and state in the early 1990s, and the PAN's experimentation of devolving responsibility for city planning to a mixed quasi-public, quasi-private planning institute, these entrepreneurial elites had even greater direct and (now) quite transparent access to shaping city development through the Grupo Progreso de la Fundación de Empresariado Chihuahense, which emerged during the administration of Governor Francisco Barrio (1992–98) and was sustained even after the PRI won the state back in 1998 (Padilla Delgado 2005). However, there was always the feeling that this group was acting at least in a partially self-interested manner, and its corporatist style led to some suspicion among broader-based civic groups (Padilla Delgado 2005, 507). In 2000 another association, the Plan Estratégico de Juárez A. C., was created, comprising not only the entrepreneurs *(socios impulsores),* but also public and private sector institutions *(los promotores),* and finally *los socios numarios,* the small and middle-size entrepreneurs, individuals, and private developers. The plan adopted as its model the success story of the urban redevelopment of Spain's city of Bilbao (Padilla Delgado 2005).

Without entering into the details of the plan here, we seek to demonstrate how a single administrative unit with authority over metropolitan planning is more able to develop an integrated vision for the whole city, whether primarily through public or private sector leadership. In the Juárez case the presence of a well-organized elite economic group has meant that the private sector has been more important than would normally be expected where a metropolitan area had several autonomous jurisdictions or where the elite was less influential. The case of Juárez shows how the participation of a concerted elite can shape the nature of urban planning and growth — in this case articulated through a single municipal jurisdiction (compared with Toluca, where elite interests were articulated through the state government). Juárez also shows how a metropolitan planning institute can work best where it embraces the participation of all sectors but also gains support from the most powerful stakeholders within the private sector. However, as was the case for Toluca, such findings do not make for easy normative replicability.

STRATEGIES FOR IMPROVING METROPOLITAN GOVERNANCE IN MEXICO

These case studies illustrate some of the options being played out in Mexico as metropolitan governments seek to address common problems of integrated planning, environmental protection, security, and transportation, while at the same time fostering greater citizen engagement in urban governance. In the final section of this chapter we briefly outline some of the strategies that might usefully be considered.

The Possibilities for Creating New Instances of Metropolitan Government: Merger, Annexation, and Executive Metropolitan Councils

Creating a new tier of metropolitan government is certainly the most difficult task to achieve politically and is especially unlikely in Mexico, since it would conflict with existing power holders and local interests. For example, while one-half of Mexico City (the D. F.) may ultimately be converted into the thirty-second state of Anahuac (as has been proposed and debated over many years), merging the D. F. and the State of Mexico and thereby creating a single metro area would create a "superstate" even more powerful than its already two powerful parts. It would almost be a country within the country. Even in metropolitan areas such as Guadalajara where a new tier might be feasible, strong local interests will almost certainly prevail. Moreover, such a merger might not be desirable, since citizen identity and engagement are much easier to achieve at the more local level.

Nevertheless, some new additional "tier" with specific responsibilities for certain functions (macro urban planning, environmental controls, security, transportation, primary infrastructure networks, etc.) could make a lot of sense. It would need to have executive functions, be appropriately funded by federal and regional authorities, and be transparent and accountable — probably to an elected metropolitan council or congress. The model of the Greater London Council comes to mind, as well as numerous other examples (London, Department of the Environment 1997; Rojas, Cuadrado-Rooura, and Guell 2008). However, such a body would require major constitutional change and would need approval from two-thirds of Congress and half plus one of the states. While the idea might fly, pragmatically there are easier ways of achieving integration that would at least need to be seriously tested before any recasting of the federalist structure could become likely.

Working within existing structures is more realistic — for example, by experimenting with special-function councils or by making new arrangements for metropolitan coordination that would report to local legislatures, whether at the state or the local level. In Mexico City this would require new institutional executive arrangements reporting to two legislative chambers: the Legislative Assembly of the D. F. and the State of Mexico Congress in Toluca. Other cities would require an arrangement in which each *ayuntamiento* (an executive body with quasi-legislative functions) was an equal stakeholder to which the new metropolitan council would report. The arrangement would be feasible, since it would operate within the existing legislation that we discussed earlier. However, to be effective, it too would probably require some constitutional changes to create a mandate that would ensure it was (1) appropriately funded; (2) sustainable beyond electoral term limits; (3) and not subject to different ideologies operating in the individual units. This would be a difficult task, but if the mandate was restricted to macro-level activities that were in the common interest, and if accountability was ensured, such a strategy might provide a way forward, especially if it was also tied to the principle of subsidiarity.

As we have outlined in earlier chapters, subsidiarity implies vesting responsibility and decision-making authority at the local level, passing up to the next (higher) level only those decisions and tasks that cannot be effectively handled locally. One could see how this might work well in the D. F., with its structure of sixteen *delegaciones,* as well as in other metropolitan areas where the principle of subsidiarity would apply to the bottom-up hierarchy of neighborhoods: submunicipal districts, municipalities, metropolitan councils to regional governments. Once again, though, in order to work and be sustainable beyond the term limits of the constituent jurisdictions, it would probably need to be institutionalized formally.

Strengthening Metropolitan Government through
Existing Arrangements and Practices

This chapter has demonstrated that in Mexico the term *metropolitan* is
ambiguous and that there is no formal entity of metropolitan government. A metropolitan area is a built-up area that spreads across more
than one administrative jurisdiction. A metropolitan zone, on the other
hand, includes the whole municipality, regardless of whether it is part
of the built-up area. It is akin to a conurbation, and Mexican law does
allow for the creation of commissions at the conurbation level. Various
arrangements exist that seek to achieve some level of metropolitan coordination, but with different levels of success. Thus, even though one may
talk about "metropolitan" areas and zones in Mexico, this is not a level
of government, nor is there the notion of a governance structure to accommodate the needs of populations living in metropolitan areas. However, this analysis does suggest that government entities that form part of
a metropolitan area are realizing the need to achieve better-integrated
government and governance in a number of ways — albeit often improvised and partial — in order to attend to common challenges facing the exercise of government and governance across their jurisdictions. We have
suggested that capital city metropolitan areas — in this case that of Mexico
City — may be special cases because of federal and sometimes regional involvement beyond that of local municipalities. Also, the politics are more
in the front line, and executive positions often serve as a springboard or
stepping-stone to higher office; thus the stakes are greater. In general the
emergence of metropolitan initiatives appears most likely to be shaped
by (1) the density (number and population) of governmental entities in
a given metro area, and the relative weight and importance of the metro
population vis-à-vis those of the state's total population; (2) the predisposition of the state government to support collaboration between municipalities and entities; and (3) the extent of political initiatives to improve governance.

As we outlined in the case of Monterrey, there are situations where
more effective metropolitan government can be achieved through
strengthening the capacity and leadership of regional (state) government,
whether by empowering statewide agencies or by creating special sectoral
commissions. The creation of metropolitan councils as in Guadalajara
sounds fine in principle, but in practice their success depends upon the existence of political will and consensus across the primary stakeholder governments. Experience suggests that this is most likely to be precipitated by

a particular moment of urgency or crisis, but then it will probably affect some areas more than others. Another weakness is the lack of continuity from one administration to the next. Certain sectors of activity—such as primary water and drainage provision or transportation—may commend themselves more easily than others to metropolitan councils or commissions, especially where these require "lumpy" (major) public investment or are politically difficult to manage locally. While provincially driven forced annexation and amalgamation along the lines of the Canadian case would not work in Mexico, the fact that municipalities are subservient to state government does offer the latter the capacity to create executive commissions for certain metropolitan functions. However, these will be successful only insofar as they are adequately funded. The state (governor)-driven example that Monterrey provides probably offers the best mechanism for achieving metropolitan governance.

Coordination between municipalities can also be achieved in a number of other ways, such as consortia, *mancomunidad* arrangements, and bilateral agreements.[6] Still another mechanism is to privatize, placing local jurisdiction responsibilities in the realm of private enterprise, whose reach is always likely to be much greater. Public-private partnership arrangements, in which local jurisdictions retain a formal voice and responsibility but work in conjunction with the private sector, is another alternative, though little used to date. Whatever institutional architecture is adopted, there will always be the need to strengthen metropolitan governance and provide some fiscal autonomy and provision of metropolitan agency funding, or direct funding to service providers. But Mexico is still a long way from creating some truly effective level of representative and participatory democratic governmental structures at the metropolitan level. It seems likely that the muddling through and ad hoc practices of collaboration will continue, probably along the lines of the cases presented here.

NOTES

1. By *government* we refer to the structures and functions of government in the city; *governance* includes forms of public action beyond that of the government alone (Lefèvre 1998) and focuses upon the relationships and processes in and around government and the delivery of public goods.

2. It should also be noted that some public choice advocates recognize that certain services and functions are more efficiently and effectively provided on a metropolitan-wide basis (Hamilton 2000).

3. Since 1983, municipalities within the same state have been allowed to associate and coordinate in order to provide services in defined conurbations, but it was not until the 1999 constitutional reform that municipalities were allowed to coordinate with municipalities from other states in the conurbation—and only then with the approval of their state congresses. Such opportunities would apply only in the occasional cases where two or more states form part of a metropolitan zone (see table 5.1, the cases of Mexico City, Puebla, Torreón, Tampico, and Puerto Vallarta).

4. We might also include two additional cases, Reynosa and Tuxtla Gutiérrez, since these were very close to the five hundred thousand cutoff point in 2000.

5. In this respect Juárez differs from Toluca and Monterrey, both of which have strong elites but not the same level of consensus and cohesion. In both those cities elite groups tend to cycle in and out of power across the six-year cycles of state government.

6. A *mancomunidad* is a joint trust created between two or more entities to co-manage a particular set of functions. Most usually in Mexico it is formed for the management of forests and water basins and other natural resources across municipal jurisdictions.

Chapter 6

Argentina

The Political Constraints to
Effective Metropolitan Governance

PEDRO PÍREZ

THE POLITICAL CONTEXT OF ARGENTINE FEDERALISM
AND METROPOLITAN GOVERNANCE

Argentine federalism is in large part the result of struggles between groups led by provincial *caudillos* during the first half of the nineteenth century. The new federal structure, consolidated in 1880 with the federalization of the city of Buenos Aires (which prior to this time was the capital city of the province of the same name, as well as the national economic center), was supported by the provincial oligarchies with regional influence and power. This structure, strongly presidential with a centralized national government, prevailed until the 1930s and provided for Argentina's insertion into the international economy on the basis of the export of food products and raw materials.

Since the end of the nineteenth century and particularly during the first decades of the following century, Argentina received a huge influx of European immigrants who settled in its cities and especially in the capital, Buenos Aires (Scobie 1974). This population integrated economically and socially, providing the basis for the development of an urban middle class, which began to participate and mobilize politically. Electoral reform

171

helped the Unión Cívica Radical (UCR) Party to win the presidency in the national elections of 1916, and the UCR kept power until 1930, when the first of what were to be several military coups during the century returned the traditional oligarchs to power.

However, in Latin America as elsewhere, the international crisis of the 1920s accelerated the process of economic transformation and from the middle of the 1940s strengthened an incipient process of industrialization around an import-substituting industrialization (ISI) orthodoxy. That same decade, and after further military disruptions, (then) colonel Juan Perón began to meld the new industrial workers with union activists and politicians from different origins (labor, radicals, conservatives, socialists) and created a movement that supported him to win both the 1946 and 1952 elections. These administrations were characterized by what Torre and Pastoriza (2002) call "welfare democratization," which sought to integrate urban and rural workers through corporatist state policies on an increasingly "populist" basis. This movement was further consolidated through the creation of a political party with deep social movement roots, the Partido Justicialista (PJ).

The second half of the twentieth century was characterized by instability. Until 1973 the PJ was banned, with the armed forces keeping a tight rein on political life. In 1973 some political liberalization was granted, aimed at preventing the radicalization of urban political protests and the development of armed groups within Peronism and the Left. This allowed the PJ to return to power for a short but critical period of time.[1] However, early 1976 saw yet another military coup in which a junta sought to ensure the transformation of society and politics through policies of economic liberalization and deindustrialization, causing unemployment and poverty, and subduing society through state repression.

Only after the end of the military dictatorship in 1983 were traditional political parties able to recapture their roles in local, provincial, and national elections. The UCR won the 1983 elections, but it was forced to vacate the presidency six months prior to the end of its term because of the economic crisis. With the exception of a brief period of the Alianza government (1999–2001), the PJ in its various guises ruled the country under Carlos Menem between 1989 and 1999, after a constitutional reform in 1994 allowed for his reelection. Even though Menem won the election on a populist and developmentalist platform, his governments followed a firm and orthodox neoliberal path of economic deregulation, decentralization, privatization, and international liberalization. After several years of strong economic growth (though accompanied by increasing unemployment and rising poverty), the country was plunged into a severe period of recession shortly after the end of his 1999 term. The PJ recovered politically from this episode with the 2003 election of the late Néstor Kirchner, former PJ governor of the province of Santa Cruz. Earlier devaluation of the currency and the declaration of default and subsequent renegotiation of the external debt provided for a policy of protection of national industries, which, taken together with the increase in commodity prices, allowed for some economic recovery with four years of growth over 8 percent per annum. In 2007 Kirchner's wife and former senator Cristina (Fernández de) Kirchner was elected president and then reelected for a second term in 2011.

Since the 1980s the traditional political parties have undergone major transformations. The UCR never recovered from its 1989 failure in office, and its influence was effectively relegated to governing in some provinces and municipalities. The crisis of 2001, in which the president of the Radical Party was forced to resign, vacating the presidential palace by helicopter, marked the near demise of the (Radical) party in the subsequent national elections. The PJ had changed from a union-based party to one shored up by territorial control, and after the 1983 elections it was this power in provincial and municipal governments that helped to sustain the party's influence.

Constitutional reforms in 1994 replaced the indirect election and electoral college with a system of direct election for the offices of the president and vice president. This reform increased the political weight of those territories with large populations, especially the province of Buenos Aires, and in particular some of the municipalities within the metropolitan area of Buenos Aires (hereafter the BAMA). Thus the ability to win and control these votes became increasingly important for all levels of government (local, provincial, and federal). Moreover, the provincial governments consolidated, becoming especially influential in the successful economic management of their territories.

Provincial governments are responsible for the economic and urban infrastructure and are the principal conduits for the transfer of federal funds from the center. Because municipal governments are responsible for the disbursal of provincial and federal funds as well as social policies affecting low-income populations, they are key actors in relation to these groups. This has led to the consolidation of strong clientelist relationships (Auyero 2001; Trotta 2003) that are tied to a process of building and sustaining political capital from the local grassroots level through the provincial and federal levels.

By the beginning of the twenty-first century Argentine politics had become largely devoid of any strong ideological motivations or visions for public policy reform and had become, instead, a system of relationships oriented toward power accumulation. Hence the frustration and the public venting of *"Que se vayan todos"* (Out with all of them!) during the 2001 crisis. Almost nobody left, however; the PJ was able to resurrect itself and continued to win national elections, holding a number of key districts such as the provinces of Buenos Aires and Córdoba, even though the PJ has by now come to represent substantially different social sectors and economic interests.

METROPOLITAN AREAS IN ARGENTINA

The Evolution of Metropolitan Areas in Argentina

Argentina is one of the so-called "early-urbanizer" societies in Latin America. During the late nineteenth and early twentieth centuries, Argentina's urban population increased dramatically, primarily as a consequence of overseas immigration. In this respect the country's urbanization pattern somewhat resembles those described in earlier chapters on the United States and Canada. However, from the 1930s through the 1950s, continued urban growth was primarily a consequence of internal migration from the interior provinces.

Table 6.1 presents data compiled from the last five censuses.[2] It shows clearly the variation in population distribution and the urbanization rates from the 1960s through to 2001. Specifically, since 1960 the growth rate of the overall population has remained relatively low, with a further noticeable decrease in growth after the 1980s. This has occurred across all regions regardless of city size. Nevertheless, urbanization has continued, though at a decreasing pace: in 2001 the urban population represented 89.31 percent of the total.

Even the most populated area (the BAMA) has experienced a slowdown in growth, as have other urban centers of over fifty thousand inhabitants (excluding the BAMA) since 1991. On the other hand, centers between five thousand and fifty thousand inhabitants have been the most dynamic. Moreover, those towns and cities located outside the Pampa Region (also excluding the BAMA data) have shown the highest growth rate during that period.[3] As a consequence of these trends, since 1970 the

Table 6.1. Argentina's Urban Population by Region, 1960–2001

	Urban Population (in millions)					Growth Rate (%)					Proportion of Total Population (%)				
	1960	1970	1980	1991	2001	60–70	70–80	80–91	91–01	60–01	1960	1970	1980	1991	2001
Total population	**20.01**	**23.36**	**27.95**	**32.62**	**36.22**	**1.56**	**1.81**	**1.47**	**1**	**1.45**	**100**	**100**	**100**	**100**	**100**
Total population without BAMA	13.27	14.89	17.94	21.29	24.18	1.15	1.88	1.64	1.21	1.47					
Centro	2.06	2.38	2.79	3.27	3.72	1.47	1.59	1.54	1.22	1.45	10.27	10.19	9.97	10.04	10.26
Comahue	0.30	0.42	0.63	0.90	1.03	3.24	4.16	3.43	1.3	3.01	1.51	1.79	2.24	2.75	2.83
Cuyo	1.18	1.36	1.66	1.94	2.20	1.44	2.05	1.48	1.19	1.53	5.88	5.81	5.95	5.95	6.07
Buenos Aires MA	6.74	8.48	10.01	11.32	12.05	2.32	1.68	1.17	0.59	1.42	33.67	36.28	35.81	34.71	33.25
NE	1.62	1.81	2.25	2.82	3.36	1.13	2.2	2.18	1.68	1.8	8.08	7.74	8.04	8.65	9.28
NW	2.07	2.25	2.85	3.46	4.17	0.8	2.4	1.85	1.79	1.71	10.36	9.61	10.19	10.6	11.51
Pampeana	5.84	6.39	7.36	8.32	8.99	0.9	1.42	1.17	0.75	1.06	29.19	27.35	26.33	25.5	24.83
Patagonia	0.21	0.29	0.41	0.59	0.71	3.45	3.46	3.51	1.85	3.06	1.03	1.24	1.46	1.8	1.96

Sources: Lindenboim and Kennedy (2003).

proportion of the total urban population in the BAMA and in other settlements containing over one million people has declined.[4] Since 1970 the proportion of the population living in centers of between ten thousand and five hundred thousand inhabitants has consolidated. In short, there has been a "double decentralization" process at work, with centrifugal movement out across the national territory (from Buenos Aires), as well as a shift in growth patterns to lower orders of the urban hierarchy (Lindenboim and Kennedy 2003).

Nevertheless, according to the 2001 census, the contemporary urban structure still has two-thirds of the total urban population living mainly in the BAMA itself and in centers between ten thousand and five hundred thousand inhabitants. No less than 37.2 percent live in Buenos Aires, while only 16 percent live in other centers of more than five hundred thousand inhabitants. This means that although since the 1960s the population dynamics have shifted toward a more balanced distribution, the actual concentration of population has not changed much. Nearly half of the national urban population lives in three metropolitan areas of over one million inhabitants (Buenos Aires, Córdoba, and Rosario), although there remains a huge difference between the size of the first city and that of the next two.

Definition of Metropolitan Areas

The concept of *metropolitan* in Argentina hinges on the concept of locality in the physical sense. The Instituto Nacional de Estadísticas y Censos (INDEC, the Statistics and Census National Institute) defines a metropolitan area as a geographic space occupied by population settlements that are either "simple" or "compound," being made up of provinces, departments (or districts), or one or more local governments.

Since the focus of this book is that of governance, we will define metropolitan areas as urban agglomerations either partially or totally occupying the territory of two or more municipalities. These agglomerations usually occur when the metropolitan center expands outwards into neighboring municipalities. It is only since 2001 that the census has recorded this information by municipalities. Prior to 2001 information was organized according to departments; thus it was difficult to identify metropolitan regions as outlined above. Indeed, in the provinces of Buenos Aires, Mendoza, and La Rioja, departments remain the territorial area of municipal governments for which census data are gathered. Some attempt has been made to make the 2001 data compatible with those of the 1991 census by breaking down the data at the municipal level, although it has not always been possible to achieve this (for example, in the province of Córdoba). Therefore, it is not possible to disaggregate data prior to 1991, nor is it possible to do so for either 1991 or 2001 in the case of the Córdoba Metropolitan Area. (In those cases, we will use the information for the localities that form part of the metropolitan area.)

According to these criteria, by 2001 there were twenty metropolitan areas in Argentina with over fifty thousand inhabitants, twenty of which exceeded one hundred thousand inhabitants. These metropolitan areas accounted for more than half of the total population and almost two-thirds of the country's urban population. Metropolitan population growth rates are lower than those of the urban population and are closer to that of the national population.

The Importance of Metropolitan Areas in Argentina

The lack of adequate data makes it difficult to estimate the economic importance of Argentina's metropolitan areas, although, as one would expect, economic activity is highly concentrated in urban areas: no less than half of the country's Geographic Gross Product is generated by the Buenos Aires Metropolitan Region (Escolar and Pírez 2004).[5] Metropolitan areas made up 58 percent of the national labor force in 2001, and the proportion of total wage earners was slightly higher. Post-2003 economic changes have placed greater priority on rural and regional areas of economic activity, so the role of metropolitan participation in the national economy may have decreased somewhat. However, the metropolitan areas remain the principal sites of Argentina's domestic economy.

Within the metropolitan areas themselves there are marked spatial inequities, with the central-city core showing a concentration of population and economic activities, higher incomes, and better urban infrastructure (housing and services, etc.). This is especially evident in the BAMA, where the metropolitan center (the Autonomous City of Buenos Aires, ACBA) has relatively low basic unmet needs, with these increasing as one moves outward into the *segunda corona* (second ring). Similar metropolitan inequities and center-periphery variation appear in other cities. Taking the data for three different metropolitan areas of different population sizes and regions across the country, we have created a simple indicator of inequity in the distribution of the population with health insurance, those living in overcrowded conditions (both relative to the total metropolitan population), and those classified as "employers" in relation to the metropolitan "economically active population."

Other figures and graphs (not shown here) provide insights about provincial metropolitan areas. The Rosario Metropolitan Area (located in the central region of the country) is one of the three cities that exceed one million inhabitants. In the metropolitan center—Rosario City—a significant portion of the population lacks health insurance and lives in overcrowded conditions, yet at the same time there is a surplus in the concentration of employers. According to these indicators of levels of inequitable distribution, Rosario City's center, compared to the overall metropolitan area for the first two variables, has a lower percentage of population without health insurance but higher numbers of people living in overcrowded dwellings. Compared with the metropolitan economically active population on this last variable, it has a higher level of employers and self-employed.

A similar pattern emerges in the metropolitan area of Mendoza, located in the Cuyo region and containing a population close to one million in 2001. Two of its subareas appear to have higher concentrations of better urban conditions. These are located in the city of Mendoza (the capital of the province and the metropolitan central city) and the municipality of Godoy Cruz, both of which also show high levels of population without health insurance and living in overcrowded conditions. However, in the municipality of Luján de Cuyo these variables are relatively flat and unchanging, while the rest of the metropolitan area shows an overall improvement. Not surprisingly, employers are concentrated in the capital city (as in Rosario). The Tucumán Metropolitan Area in the northwest of the country had a population of 730,000 inhabitants in 2001. There, too, graphs show that the capital city of the province, San Miguel de Tucumán, stands out by having a higher population without health insurance and living in overcrowded conditions, yet containing a high number of employers—as does the municipality of Yerba Buena.

Since the latter part of the twentieth century these center-periphery distributions were expected to attenuate somewhat as the suburbanization process embraced the upper-middle and middle classes, although significantly modified structures have not yet been observed (Pírez 1994, 1996, 1998). To date the distribution of economic activities—at least those in the BAMA—remain strongly concentrated in the central city (ACBA—see Pírez 2005).

Metropolitan Governance: A Public Framework for Addressing Policy Issues in Metropolitan Areas

In Argentina there is no formal provision for the creation of an independent entity of metropolitan government. Instead, the federal structure provides for three clear levels of government: the national level, the federal government; an intermediate provincial government (equivalent to states); and the local (municipal) government. Local government is responsible not just for cities but for the broader municipality or spatial unit. Thus there are two types of municipal government: the first is the physical area of the city and its area of expansion; the second is the municipality/department, a much broader area containing urban and rural settlements—such as the departments in the province of Buenos Aires. These larger departmental territorial areas are political administrative units. Therefore, it is possible to have one or more cities within a broader departmental jurisdiction. Not all municipal systems are similar; they depend upon the attributes that are assigned by provincial constitutions and laws, and these vary by province, as in the cases of the metropolitan areas of Buenos Aires, Córdoba, Rosario, and Mendoza. Several of these examples will be described in detail later, but suffice it to say here that the principal differences accorded by law are the relative autonomy to regulate urban land, the capacity to levy property taxes, and the power to enact their own local constitutions—the *cartas orgánicas.*

Together with the surrounding municipalities of the province of Buenos Aires, the metropolitan area also includes the Autonomous City of Buenos Aires, which is both the seat of the federal government and the federal capital of Argentina. This local government is not a municipality but an "autonomous city." Its institutional design is similar to that of the provinces,[6] a point to which I will return later in the analysis.

Once a town expands across its municipal boundaries, no provision allows for a formal government for the single urban area. Instead, the government becomes split between the municipalities and the province. Municipalities are generally a weak level of government in Argentina. Cities have no control over national policies, even those that directly affect them, and given that metropolitan areas are invariably highly fragmented, they do not carry much weight in the political game either. However, they can influence provincial politics and political relations, especially where they are the provincial capital or an important city such as Rosario. Moreover, the Autonomous City of Buenos Aires has a status and weight like that of a province, and because it is at the heart of the national capital it has added influence in political, institutional, social, and economic affairs.

To understand the current situation in which municipal governments find themselves, it is important to recognize that during the 1990s there was a dual process of decentralization (figure 6.1). On the one hand, as part of public spending cuts and a downsizing policy implemented by the federal government, a number of services were transferred to provincial governments — namely education and health care — that had actually been legislated for implementation much earlier, in the late 1970s. Thus provincial governments extended some new roles to municipal governments, which, while giving them greater powers, were not always undertaken with a concomitant transfer of resources. In addition, the National Housing Fund (FONAVI) was eliminated and replaced with budgetary items that were now transferred to the provinces. This period was also accompanied by an emerging social crisis as a result of rising unemployment and an increase of at-risk, low-income populations. This placed greater pressure for social policy making upon municipal governments, which now have a number of new responsibilities such as community food production programs, housing and urban infrastructure provision largely aimed at helping people build their own houses, and so on. In short, the role and importance of local government have increased in the last two decades because of decentralization. However, while the 1994 constitutional amendment accelerated and consolidated the process of decentralization by acknowledging the autonomy of municipal governments, some provinces have not incorporated the provisions into their local constitutions — including Buenos Aires, Santa Fe, and Mendoza Provinces.

Nevertheless, the process of decentralization has consolidated the role and powers of provincial governments, and the provinces have been the true beneficiaries of decentralization. As we can see in figure 6.1, during the 1990s state resource distribution was modified at all three levels, with slightly over 90 percent of the total budget remaining in the hands of the federal government and the provinces and less than 9 percent going to municipalities. This means that provinces play an important role in any metropolitan governance initiative. Since the 1990s, municipal governments have mainly sought to develop social policies carrying out welfare plans designed and financed by the federal government, and to a lesser extent by provincial governments. Accordingly, municipalities allocate half of their resources to social purposes (Iturburu 2000, 16). However, there is a great financial dependence upon such transfers. Between 1993 and

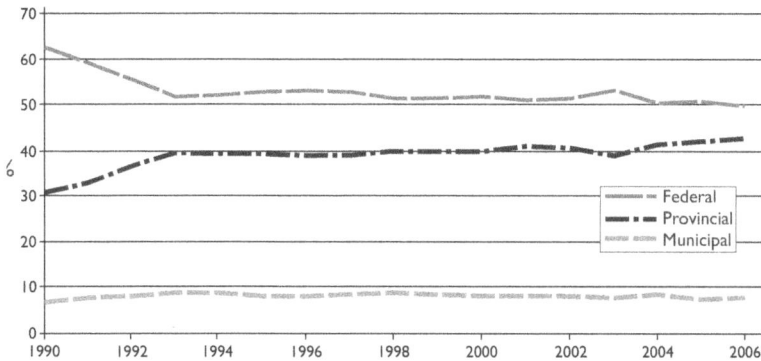

Figure 6.1. Distribution of Public Expenses among Government Levels,
1990–2001
Source: Dirección de Análisis (2011).

1997, transfers from federal and provincial government accounted for between 37 and 41 percent of total municipal resources. On the other hand, municipal taxes account for more than 70 percent of municipal resources (MEOySP 1999, 20), which grants them some flexibility in developing local policies. However, these funds are limited, since the lion's share goes to payroll and administration: data for 1993 to 1997 show that only 12 to 17 percent of funds went into capital investment projects *(inversiones)* (MEOySP 1999, 20).[7] Further, except for a small number of rare exceptions, municipalities lack skilled personnel and necessary equipment to carry out their functions adequately.

Thus, while Argentine municipal governments have a relatively strong political-institutional capacity to govern, they have not been able to build governmental institutions to exercise power and authority. Management at the municipal level is consequently often ineffective and inefficient. Argentina has never promoted a serious "metropolitan agenda," although there have been a number of half-hearted attempts. For example, in the late 1980s an entity within the Ministry of Interior of the federal government (the National Commission for the Buenos Aires Metropolitan Area [CONAMBA]) offered a diagnosis that laid the basis of a metropolitan agenda, but it had little impact outside academe (CONAMBA 1988).

Since the 1990s, a number of "strategic plans" have been developed in many cities, some of them in metropolitan areas. However, such plans usually correspond to one particular municipal territory and were developed with different degrees of participation of the local community.

They failed to reach across the larger region in which those municipalities were located, and by planning independently they de facto negated any reference to the larger metropolitan area.

The most compelling initiatives have taken place in three central cities in the country's most important metropolitan areas: Buenos Aires, Córdoba, and Rosario. However, those metropolitan plans were constructed largely around a vision of the central city (i.e., the most important "core" municipality), rather than growing out of a genuine attempt to develop a metropolitan-wide agenda, and the product was more a statement of objectives than a realistic and serious plan constructed around concrete proposals. And while the roles have been expanded and the importance of municipal governments has increased, a genuine metropolitan agenda has still not come to fruition. Even in the BAMA, where outside the central city area (ACBA) some of the conurbated municipalities have developed strategic plans, these have been undertaken in a fragmented way and without including a broader metropolitan perspective. However, while the formal development of a metropolitan agenda by governments is limited, civil society does appear to be making incipient attempts to create some impetus for reform. Yet there is still insufficient recognition of the fragmentary nature of metropolitan areas, which are in most cases an amalgam of individual municipalities.

There are two main reasons for this metropolitan fragmentation. The first is institutional: namely, that city government is not acknowledged as part of a metropolitan area but rather is seen as one of the three territorial levels (national, provincial, or local — which may be city or part metropolitan). The second is political: in Argentina the tendency has always been for political power to be tied to hierarchically and partisan-driven clientelistic linkages. In addition to hindering democratic development, these ongoing political practices inhibit the creation of intermunicipal metropolitan links and undermine the possibilities of shaping new institutional organizations with effective political legitimacy. This hinges on the orientation of municipal politics toward ensuring electoral support as well as the heavy dependence for financial resources upon provincial (and federal) governments, which are similarly oriented to garner electoral support. Thus a focus on electoral support often distorts the specific issues and challenges that municipalities face, these being replaced by concerns about accumulating political power. The focus on electoral support is particularly pronounced in gubernatorial and representative elections, which are often marked by intense partisanship and rivalry. Therefore, pressures often prevent local governments from developing cooperation and linkages, further inhibiting the development of common platforms and the emergence of municipal associations supportive of joint management structures. In metropolitan areas this becomes even more problematic as partisanship and political clientelism prevent the creation of "intrametropolitan" coordination and cooperation.[8] Indeed, in metropolitan areas political representation and power accumulation are especially likely to be fragmented.

Municipal political weakness also derives from the fact that municipal territories do not coincide or overlap with provincial electoral districts. In general, representatives to provincial legislatures are elected for an area that encompasses several municipalities. Moreover, at the national level provinces with fewer inhabitants — usually the ones with lower relative economic development — are overrepresented in Congress (Escolar and Pírez 2004). Similarly, urban municipalities have a relatively lower legislative representation than rural ones. However, research into a number of cases (especially in Buenos Aires) that address these metropolitan issues has had limited influence among decision makers.

METROPOLITAN CASE STUDIES

As mentioned above, metropolitan areas in Argentina are highly fragmented, and the design of these administrative arrangements varies across provinces. For the purpose of this analysis, we will examine the several jurisdictional arrangements that exist. We will begin with the simplest and most common situation: that of metropolitan areas located within the boundaries of a province. Then we will analyze two more complex cases: a metropolitan area that encompasses two different provinces, and finally the case of BAMA, which includes a province and the government of ACBA. The provincial government has sole responsibility for intermunicipal affairs, and this comes to the forefront in the case of metropolitan areas. Similarly, and at a higher level, interprovincial issues involve the intervention of the federal government, forming the "jurisdictional centralization" that impinges upon fragmented metropolitan areas.

Provincial Metropolitan Areas

We will briefly analyze three cases that show the variation in this metropolitan universe: the metropolitan areas of Córdoba, Rosario, and Mendoza.

Metropolitan Area of Córdoba

Defined strictly, the contiguous built-up area of the Córdoba Metropolitan Area in 2001 had a population of 1,348,892, of whom 1,267,774 lived in the city of Córdoba itself.[9] The metropolitan area includes the central city and six other localities: Villa Allende, Mendioloza, Saldán, Malvinas Argentinas, Estación Juarez Celman, and Unquillo (Tecco and Fernández 2005, 89). Toward the west, this continuous urban sprawl stops abruptly at the Sierras Chicas, the mountain range closest to the city that also abuts a large area of military bases. The broader metropolitan area encompasses the following five towns: La Calera, Malagueño, Río Ceballos, Salsipuedes, and Parque Norte. All included the total population of the Córdoba Metropolitan Area would total 1,400,665 inhabitants.

Because the territory of the capital municipality is so large, the city of Córdoba practically covers the whole metropolitan area, with 90 percent of the population concentrated here. However, the presence of some twelve additional local jurisdictions within the effective city area greatly fragments decision-making processes and consequently leads to the "interjurisdictional conflicts that occur in relation to traffic, transportation issues, public health, provision of drinking water, management of water basin, etc." (Tecco and Fernández 2005, 92).

Under the Córdoba Provincial Constitution, the municipalities are responsible for establishing regulations for and management of everything related to their territorial organization, land use, and building activities within the municipal territory and the "area where municipalities render services"— also defined by a provincial law. The provincial government is responsible for oversight of the water supply in the capital city, previously provided by a state-owned company later privatized. Today the provincial government controls service provision.

In the municipalities that surround the capital city, local authorities are responsible for water services, and these services are provided either by cooperative organizations or by municipal companies. Only the capital city receives waste disposal and sanitation services. In the capital city, the municipality is responsible for the sewage infrastructure and the other provincial municipalities have no service. Municipal governments are responsible for disposal of all solid waste generated and collected in their area.

Urban transportation service is a municipal activity carried out through concessions to private companies, but intermunicipal services are regulated and controlled by the provincial government. In the same way, urban maintenance (road and street lighting) are managed by the municipalities, while interurban roads are a provincial responsibility. Environmental regulation and control responsibilities are shared by the provincial and the municipal governments. However, the municipalities are in charge of garbage collection and street cleaning, normally through concessions with private companies. Education services (preschool, elementary, secondary, and nonuniversity tertiary levels) are regulated and provided by the province of Córdoba. Only in Córdoba City are there municipal schools (since 1984). Finally, social assistance and social policies are carried out primarily by the municipalities but usually with some provincial administration and with federal (and in some cases provincial) resources.

In 1995 the city of Córdoba completed a local strategic plan (Plan Estratégico de Córdoba, PEC), which was the first in Argentina. On the basis of the plan, in the following year the municipality of the city of Córdoba began negotiations with the metropolitan municipalities to make progress toward some level of metropolitan-wide arrangements. However, the elections that year halted these initiatives because of intense competition between the governor and the mayor of Córdoba, even though both were from the same political party (the UCR). Not until 2007, when the PJ was in charge of the provincial government and a coalition (formed in part by the UCR) was in charge of the city, did the mayor of Córdoba launch an initiative for metropolitan negotiations. This gave way to a technical/political meeting closely related to the provincial elections the following year in which the mayor of Córdoba ran for the governorship. However, when the PJ won those provincial elections, the metropolitan negotiations again stalled.

The Rosario Metropolitan Area
The metropolitan area of Rosario is the third largest in Argentina, with a population of 1,165,749 inhabitants (figure 6.2). It includes the city of Rosario and ten municipalities: Villa Gobernador Galvez, San Lorenzo, Gral Baigorria, Capitán Bermúdez, Pérez, Funes, Fray Luis Beltrán, Roldan, Puerto General San Martín, and Soldini. Unlike Buenos Aires and Córdoba, Rosario is neither an autonomous city nor a provincial capital. Its importance as a metropolitan center lies in its diversified economic activities and its port. The city of Rosario has 909,397 inhabitants, which represents 30 percent of the Santa Fe Province population, whereas the metro area accounts for 39 percent of the province's population. In economic terms the metropolitan area of Rosario generates approximately 50 percent of the province's gross product (about 5 percent of the Argentinean total).[10]

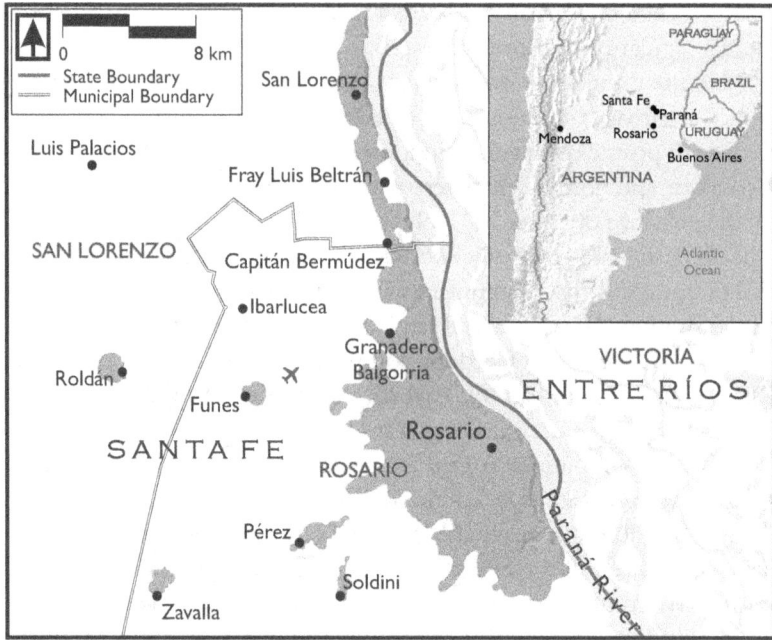

Figure 6.2. Rosario Metropolitan Area

Historically, the port of Rosario has played an important role in the economic development of the city and is one of the most important in Argentina. In 1994 the port authority was transferred from the federal government to the province of Santa Fe and is administrated by the Ente Regulador del Puerto de Rosario (ENAPRO). Rosario is the only municipality included in the directory of ENAPRO. In political terms, the area has a checkered history. Rosario, the central city, has been governed by the Socialist Party since 1989, whereas most of the municipalities and communes have been governed by the PJ. However, since the end of 2007 the Socialist Party has been in control of the provincial government: indeed, the former mayor of Rosario was the incoming governor.

The provision of services in the metropolitan area of Rosario is highly fragmented. Each municipality provides most of the services within its territory. Water and sanitation services are provided mainly by a public company (Aguas Santafesinas SA) and in some cases by municipal or local cooperatives. Aguas Santafesinas SA is a public company jointly held by the provincial government (51 percent), the municipal governments (36 percent) that are covered by the service, and employees (10 percent).

Aguas Santafesinas provides the service to the municipalities of Rosario City, Cap. Bermudez, Granadero Baigorria, Funes, and Villa Gobernador Galvez. The regulation and control of the provision of water and sanitation are a provincial responsibility carried out by a single agency—the Ente Regulador de Servicios Sanitarios. Bus public transportation within each municipal jurisdiction is the responsibility of the municipal government, while public transportation linking more than one municipality is under provincial jurisdiction. In the case of the city of Rosario, the Ente del Transporte de Rosario has authority over the funding, planning, and regulation of public transportation in the city. Finally, garbage collection and public lighting are provided by the municipalities. In the case of the city of Rosario, the garbage collection is under concession to two private companies, while actual solid waste disposal is in all cases a municipal matter.

The metropolitan area of Rosario provides an interesting metropolitan planning case study.[11] The Strategic Metropolitan Plan (Plan Estratégico Metropolitano—PEM) was developed in 2004 out of a 1998 strategic plan initiative for Rosario. The main purpose of the plan was to jointly set the guidelines "to facilitate the strategic management of territorial development on a regional scale." These guidelines were developed with the participation of ten municipalities, eight communes, the provincial government, and around sixty public and private organizations.

On the initiative of the mayor of the municipality of Rosario (at the end of 2003 and beginning of 2004), there was an attempt between the municipality of Rosario and the provincial government to work cooperatively. However, in the following months (March and April 2004) the provincial government tried to take the lead in this "regional process" through its vice governor, who was a native of Rosario. The provincial government figured that the plan could offer them greater control over the central municipality (in the hands of the Socialist Party) and thus over the metropolitan region, and it called upon the mayors and technicians from the municipalities to work on issues of common interest for the metropolitan area at large. This was proposed through a top-down approach whereby the provincial government designed the strategies and the local governments implemented them. The initiative was limited in what it could achieve, in part because the vice governor's team comprised only four people and was never able to form a joint task force with the municipality of Rosario, and as such its decision-making capacity over the metropolitan territory was restricted.[12] Therefore, the provincial initiative slowly faded. By 2006, the municipality of Rosario had achieved some level of its own dynamism around common problems and issues by working with various agencies (the Coordinated Commission, the General Board, the Technical Office of Planning, and the Technical Advisory Board) and with some lesser provincial involvement within a flexible and pluralist process involving multiple groups, sectors, and social actors working together. It was the Technical Office of Planning that showed the political leadership and planning knowledge on behalf of the government of Rosario and established different working methods (commissions over specific subject matters, discussion forums, participatory workshops, meetings with experts, and so on), with the purpose of strengthening action and consensus on certain critical issues, as well as developing programs and projects (Durand 2006).

In this case it was evident that the leadership of the municipality of Rosario drove the process forward. At the same time private sector actors understood the metropolitan territorial needs and began to take action. The local mayors, too, began to see opportunities for development as a bottom-up process and began to establish innovative and democratic rules, which strengthened this type of process (Durand 2006). The Metropolitan Strategic Plan addressed four main metropolitan issues: metropolitan coordination, the metropolitan economic system, infrastructure and environment, and welfare and quality of life.

In both of these cases, ultimately the lack of a strong commitment to metropolitan planning and integrated governance per se appeared to be unimportant, since only a relatively low percentage of the metropolitan population resided outside the capital (central) city area. However, to the extent that city expansion is projected to occur outside the central city area, this may become more important in the future.

Metropolitan Area of Mendoza
The metropolitan area of Mendoza encompasses six municipalities:[13] Mendoza Capital, Godoy Cruz, Guaymallén, Las Heras, Luján de Cuyo, and Maipú (figure 6.3). As we mentioned earlier, the metropolitan population by the year 2001 was 986,341 inhabitants. Unlike the metropolitan areas of Rosario and Córdoba, where the actual capital city municipality contains most of the population, in the metropolitan area of Mendoza most of the population is located in the adjacent municipalities of Guaymallén (251,339 inhabitants), Godoy Cruz (182,997), Las Heras (182,962), and Maipú (153,600), while Mendoza Capital has a population of 110,993 and the other departments have a population of 104,470 inhabitants. Moreover, the capital city is the only one in which

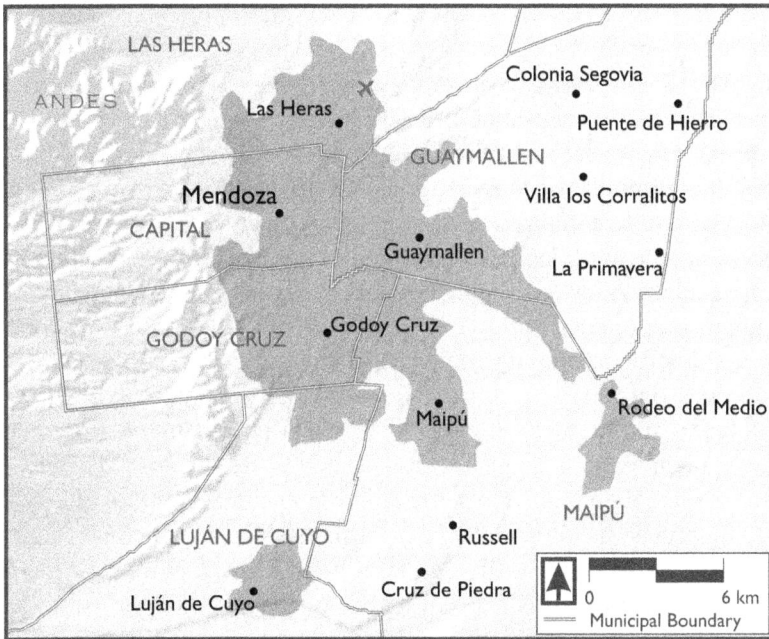

Figure 6.3. Mendoza Metropolitan Area

the population has declined from the previous census (1991), indicating the process of suburbanization that occurred during the 1990s. This makes it an interesting comparative case, since here some level of integration and collaboration at the metropolitan level becomes imperative.

The province of Mendoza is located in an arid area of the nation, with an economy of oasis-based irrigation agriculture.[14] Vineyards and olive groves have been its traditional economic activities, and Mendoza, together with the neighbor province of San Juan, are the largest wine producers in Argentina. During the 1990s, winemaking went through important technological changes, with a strong increase in investments, mainly from abroad. This led to reactivation of the industry, increasing the types of grapes for making red wine and champagne, a process that was harnessed to the increase of exports. These processes largely took place in the rural areas of the metropolitan municipalities, especially in Luján de Cuyo, Maipú, and Guaymallén (Alvarez and Ruiz de Lima 2001). The process of suburbanization raises questions about the organization of access to the two principal but scarce resources associated with such so-called "oasis" economies, namely, land and water, which lead to particular pressures on the way the economies of the metropolitan area and the province operate.

The municipalities of the province of Mendoza have limited autonomy, since they do not enact their own local constitutions (cartas orgánicas) and cannot raise taxes. Since 1994, they have been authorized to establish intermunicipal cooperation boards in order to participate in the processes of decentralization and regionalization of the province. Furthermore, the municipalities can enter into agreements for different purposes: common services, human resources, policy planning, purchase of equipment, promotion and development, educational coordination, joint works, coordination with the provincial government, public services coordination, and environmental issues (Usach 2005). After the loss of municipal autonomy during the 1976–83 dictatorship, the provincial government sought to regulate urban growth in the Mendoza Metropolitan Area through regulations and land use zoning. However, this was based upon an overly uniform and general territorial planning concept that did not account for the problems and particular characteristics of local communities. After the return to democracy in 1983 this issue was not addressed again until 1992, when the provincial government took the initiative, in 2002 finally presenting a Territorial Planning and Land Use framework bill. However, this bill was not approved.

Waste collection and disposal are under the municipal jurisdiction. In an attempt to coordinate the transportation and disposal of urban solid waste, the provincial Ministry of Environment and Public Works (Obras Públicas), together with all the municipalities in the metropolitan area, in 2002 joined in making a Provincial Urban Solid Waste Plan (Plan Provincial de Residuos Solidos Urbanos). An intermunicipal consortium was created to carry out and manage the investment program for building treatment plants and/or for final disposal of urban solid waste.[15] This need to coordinate waste disposal appears to increase when many municipalities need to dispose waste in a single site or a few sites. No one wants to receive everyone else's garbage or to be the sole dump site for the metropolitan region, which probably explains why the provincial government steps in to manage the process. We will return to a similar case below (Buenos Aires).

By the end of the 1990s the municipalities of the metropolitan area of Mendoza attempted to formulate a strategic plan provided for under the 1994 Reformed Organic Law (Ley Orgánica). In 1998, the intermunicipal structure Mendoza Strategic Development (Desarrollo Estratégico de Mendoza — DEM) was created to formulate a plan with the following principal objectives: to transform the metropolitan area into a recognized entity at the regional, national, and international levels; to strengthen public and private cooperation: to establish guidelines for individual and collective decision making; to create a sustainable, efficient, and integrated urban model; to promote strategic thinking; to promote the optimization of municipal management; and to promote citizen participation.[16] However, only a preliminary diagnosis and an institutional analysis were done. A Board of Technical Coordination was formed, which together with a Consultant Board began discussing issues such as traffic and roadwork planning, economic enterprises, joint purchases, the unification of building codes, employment, and workers' training (Barbosa and Salinas 2000). Yet by the 2000 elections the DEM had stopped functioning,[17] and indeed it had weakened during the election campaign. Furthermore, the DEM had a major financial problem, given that the largest municipalities that contributed were reluctant to commit resources that favored the poorest municipalities. Any equilibrium that existed tipped in favor of the capital municipality, even though it had not promoted its metropolitan leadership role (Usach 2005).

Interprovincial Metropolitan Areas

Here I propose to address two rather special metropolitan cases: first, a metropolitan area whose jurisdiction crosses two provinces (Neuquén and Río Negro); second, the rather special case of the BAMA, which includes two major provincial-level players, the province of Buenos Aires and the ACBA.

Metropolitan Area of Neuquén–Río Negro
The provinces of Neuquén and Río Negro were formed in the late 1950s. Up to this time there had been two federal territories, but since their creation each has had a municipal regime with considerable autonomy. The Neuquén Metropolitan Area is formed by the provincial capital, the city of Neuquén, and the city of Plottier, which is only about thirteen kilometers from the capital. In 2001 this provincial metropolitan area had 228,376 inhabitants, of whom 203,190 lived in the capital city and 25,186 in Plottier. However, the province of Río Negro also has twelve cities located in a 100 km strip (between Contra Almirante Cordero in the west and Chichinales in the east), called the Alto Valle del Río Negro, that links to Neuquén and Cipoletti by a major bridge across the Neuquén River. This area has a total of 262,256 inhabitants. The population on

the Río Negro corridor is primarily distributed between two cities with more than seventy thousand people each (General Roca, 78,275, and Cipoletti, 75,078), along with ten smaller cities and towns (Villa Regina, 31,209; Allen. 26,083; Cinco Saltos, 19,819; General Fernández Oro, 6,813; Ingeniero Huergo, 6,483; Cervantes, 5,173; Chichinales, 5,060; General Enrique Godoy, 3,823; Contra Almirante Cordero, 2,782; and Mainqué, 2,658). Overall this interprovincial metropolitan area has 500,632 inhabitants almost equally split between the subarea of Río Negro and that of Neuquén City.

Regardless of the higher concentration of population in Neuquén compared with its subarea neighbors, the city of Neuquén is the provincial capital, whereas the capital of Río Negro is the city of Viedma, located far to the west on the Atlantic coast. For this reason, although the two cities form a single metropolitan area (albeit spread along a corridor), the presence of the provincial government differs in the two subareas, which are two political, internally fragmented units: the Neuquén subarea, which has two municipalities; and the Alto Valle del Río Negro subarea, which has twelve. However, there is no institutional recognition of the region other than the need for the involvement of the federal government for the region to function effectively.

It has also been suggested that the cities of Santa Fe and Paraná could be seen as forming a single metropolitan area (see figure 6.4). Both are capital cities of the provinces of Santa Fe and Entre Ríos respectively, and they are separated only by the Paraná River. However, the fact that they are the provincial capital cities with their own conurbations means that these units are much more self-contained.

The Buenos Aires Metropolitan Area (BAMA)

Governance of the BAMA (figure 6.5) is much more complex than that of any other metropolitan area in the country and merits more detailed discussion for several reasons.[18] First, it has a very complex political-institutional structure. The government of the ACBA (formerly the "Ciudad Capital"); many municipalities of Buenos Aires Province (the number varies according to the criteria for defining *metropolitan* but is between twenty-four and thirty-five); the government of Buenos Aires Province; and the federal government. Second, almost one-third of the national population reside in the metropolitan area, and half of the National Geographic Gross Product is produced there (Escolar and Pírez 2004), giving it national prominence and importance.[19] A third complicating factor is that its status as the capital city, with its economic and demographic

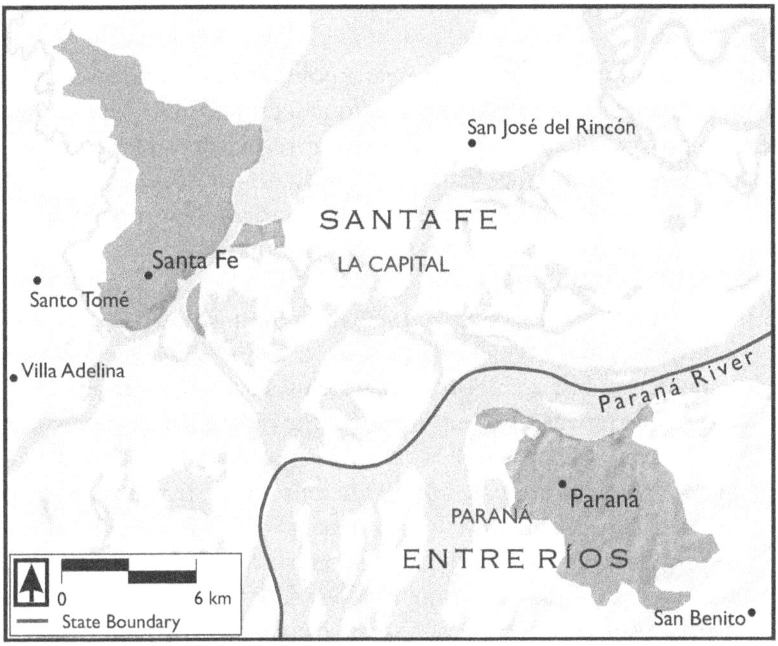

Figure 6.4. Santa Fé-Paraná Metropolitan Area

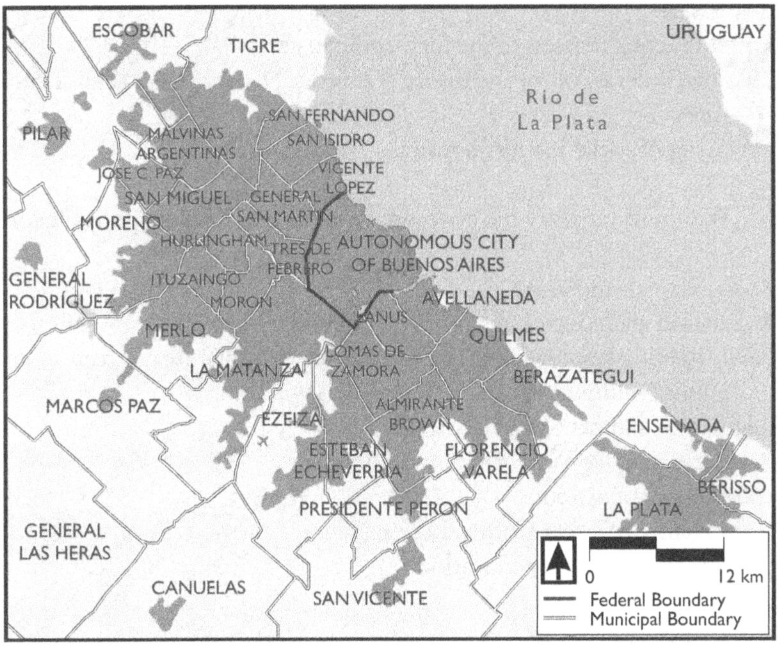

Figure 6.5. Buenos Aires Metropolitan Area

importance, gives it inordinately greater political weight and leverage in national affairs. It also makes for a unique set of relations between the federal, provincial, and autonomous city governments and the municipalities within the metropolitan area of greater Buenos Aires.

Below we will briefly analyze the role of each of these governments. The federal government is responsible for the following:

Infrastructure systems (water and sewage, power and natural gas supplies)[20]

Metropolitan public transportation systems since their privatization. This government level is in charge of the regulation and control of the railway system as well as of the Buenos Aires City subway network.[21] It is also responsible for the bus service that links Buenos Aires City to the metropolitan municipalities.[22] This service is run by private companies through government concessions.

Regulation and control of communications. The telephone network has been privatized and is managed by two companies, while the mobile phone system is managed by several private companies.

The national road network, where it provides access to the metropolitan Buenos Aires City

Universities

Environmental matters in the metropolitan area

Security (Federal Police) and justice (Ordinary National Court) in Buenos Aires City

Financing of social interest housing

Within its territory the government of the ACBA is responsible for:

Road network and signs

Regulation and control of land use and building activities

Public lighting system and urban maintenance (public areas, green space, public buildings, etc.)

Regulation and control of city traffic

Regulation and control of the environment

Solid waste collection

Maintenance of street stormwater drainages

Primary and secondary education

Health services

Social interest housing

The government of Buenos Aires Province, in the metropolitan area that lies outside ACBA, is responsible for:

Intermunicipal road network
Land use regulation
Intermunicipal automotive transportation regulation
Regulation and control of electrical power distribution (beyond those areas covered by federal responsibility), which has been privatized
Regulation and control of water and sewage networks
Primary and secondary education and health
Security (provincial police) and justice (ordinary provincial courts)
Land use and social interest housing

The metropolitan municipalities also have a number of responsibilities, including collection of domestic solid waste, maintenance of roads and public areas, and public lighting provision. Provincial regulations concerning the environment apply, as well as land use and building controls. Municipalities supply primary health services and distribute welfare resources that are received from the federal and the provincial governments.

Buenos Aires has three significant metropolitan organizations. The first is the Coordinación Ecológica del Área Metropolitana Sociedad del Estado (Ecological Coordination of the Metropolitan Area State-Owned Company, or CEAMSE), which belongs to the governments of Buenos Aires Province and of the city of Buenos Aires and is responsible for the final disposal of solid waste for the whole area. The second is the Mercado Central (Central Market), which belongs to the province of Buenos Aires, the city of Buenos Aires, and the federal government, which has oversight of the provisioning of perishable vegetables coming into the metropolitan area. The third is the Autoridad de la Cuenca de los Ríos Matanza-Riachuelo (Matanza-Riachuelo River Basin Authority), which is in charge of planning and developing works in that metropolitan basin.

The latter has an interesting history beginning in 1993, when the federal government created an Executive Committee for the Matanza-Riachuelo, which included the municipality of Buenos Aires and invited the province of Buenos Aires to participate. Three years later this committee was replaced by an Executive Committee of the Plan for Environmental Management and Control of Matanza-Riachuelo Basin, which was coordinated by the federal government with the participation of the governments of the city of Buenos Aires and the province of Buenos

Aires. On both occasions these were federal agencies that included the other two governments, though in a rather subordinate role. Metropolitan municipalities were not involved. However, the evident failure of these initiatives, given the basin's extremely high levels of pollution, drove the municipal neighbors to bring a legal suit against the state. In 2006 the Supreme Court supported the claim, acknowledging the citizens' constitutional right to "a healthy and balanced environment fit for human development in order that production activities shall meet present needs but without endangering those of future generations" (article 41 of the Argentine Constitution). The Supreme Court required the three entities (the federal government, the government of the city of Buenos Aires, and the government of the province of Buenos Aires) to prepare and present an integrated plan that would include an environmental plan for the region and would ensure state control over industrial activities as well as require that environmental impact assessments be performed by the companies. The federal government enacted a decree, based on an agreement with the governments of the province of Buenos Aires, the city of Buenos Aires, and the municipalities, creating the Autoridad de la Cuenca Matanza-Riachuelo (Authority of the Matanza-Riachuelo Basin — ACUMAR). This agency is chaired by the federal environmental secretary, and its board is formed by three representatives from the provincial government, two from the government of the city of Buenos Aires, and two from the whole group of municipalities.

Overall, therefore, in the case of fairly concentrated populations living in metropolitan areas — such as Córdoba, Rosario, and Buenos Aires — central cities have a key economic, social, and political role at the metropolitan level. Their governments have a higher management capacity because of their financial resources as well as the availability of trained staff, equipment, and technology. Therefore, these local governments have material resources sufficient to exert a certain level of regional leadership given their metropolitan centrality. But the lesson is that these governments need to take the lead in proposing metropolitan policies — as was the case in Rosario (municipality), which initiated the development of the Metropolitan Strategic Plan discussed earlier. But even in Rosario's case, only once the politics were aligned with the Socialist Party in both the municipal and the provincial palaces (and the governor was the previous mayor) was this accomplishment possible. In Córdoba the attempts failed to come to fruition, however, largely because of competition between the capital city local government and the provincial government. In the case of Mendoza, the central capital municipality did not play a leading role since it was not the largest entity. And as we shall observe below, nor was it the case in Buenos Aires, where the central ACBA government—although powerful—had to confront powerful interests from the government of the province of Buenos Aires, which was resistant to any encroachment on its authority over metropolitan municipalities.

ALTERNATIVES TO METROPOLITAN FRAGMENTATION

Metropolitan fragmentation has become a challenge both institutionally and politically. But it can be addressed in one of two ways: by higher-level government intervention ("jurisdictional centralization") or by territorial agreements between municipal governments ("municipal association"). Higher-level government intervention is based upon constitutional or legal norms that are beyond the remit of municipalities. It is a principle that intermunicipal matters correspond to the provincial government, while interprovincial matters correspond to the federal government. This jurisdictional centralization usually implies some level of "imposition" upon, and "subordination" of local governments, and invariably is weak in terms of political legitimacy, even though it may have functional legitimacy. In the Argentine context such weak political legitimacy is a real problem, as we have observed above, since politics and political rationality tend to trump technical considerations. Thus the regulation and control of public transport and the supply of infrastructure and other types of services at the metropolitan level may be functionally empowered, though there is little political will to ensure effective implementation.

An important if singular exception is the case of the BAMA. On the one hand, by virtue of federal government intervention (over the province), the creation of genuine metropolitan governmental organizations has been facilitated; yet on the other hand those very organizations also often appear to lack political legitimacy. Taking the case of CEAMSE, which was created by a joint decision of the governments of the city of Buenos Aires City and the province of Buenos Aires, under provincial law metropolitan area municipalities are expected to undertake final waste disposal for which they must pay a fee. Having had no voice in this decision, these municipalities are required to pay for a service that previously was a source of economic and social capital for them, regardless of the environmental inadequacy of the system. At the same time CEAMSE benefits Buenos Aires City in particular, since it is the largest solid waste producer in the area and also lacks free land to dump the waste. Thus the lack of participation of municipalities and the inequities among the participating jurisdictions are two problems that have created a negative view of the institution. Today CEAMSE seems to be heading toward a new crisis, since metropolitan municipalities refuse to authorize new dump sites. Currently the three sites in the metropolitan municipalities of San Martín, La Matanza, and Ensenada are almost completely filled.

CEAMSE's dilemma of being functionally responsible but politically weak stems from its having been forcibly created during authoritarian (military) rule. Since the time that democratic and federal relations have been restored, CEAMSE has been a source of resentment, and there have been attempts to eliminate it. But because of the nature of the metropolitan problem—in this case how and where to dispose of solid waste across a multijurisdictional area—and because it is something that no one jurisdiction (province, Autonomous City, or municipality) wishes to handle the anachronistic CEAMSE continues to exist.

The metropolitan role of the provincial government is most clearly evident in relation to municipalities within the BAMA, since it is here that the provincial government has constitutional paramountcy. Here, too, however, important pressures work against the municipalities in the metropolitan area. One is their relatively low representation in the provincial legislature.[23] Moreover, the provincial government cut back on the public spending that each municipality may allocate to its representative institution—the city council—while at the same time increasing the resources of the provincial congresspeople, in many cases for discretionary use. In the 1990s, following a decision taken by the provincial executive, important resources for investment and social programs were channeled into the so-called Conurbated Area Historic Restoration Fund (Danani, Chiara, and Filc 1997) with hardly any municipal involvement and under the direct control of the governor.[24] Similarly, the "discretionary transfers" of the provincial government to the municipalities clearly most benefit those areas ruled by the governor's party. This underscores the electoral and political nature of urban governance and the importance of the calculus of political patronage by major power holders, especially around election time (Badía et al. 2004).

The federal government has a very pronounced (and increasing) political presence, since the territory is "interprovincial," made up of Buenos Aires Province and the ACBA. This presence was demonstrated during the economic policies of the 1990s and the crises of 2001–2,[25] which led to considerable impoverishment similar to that experienced when the economic welfare plans were designed, financed, and driven by the federal government. After the 2001 political crisis, both throughout the country and particularly in the BAMA, these plans were key to ensuring not only the social reproduction of the city population but also a recasting of political relations. The role of the federal government is increasingly recognized by different organizations of the social unemployed, who traditionally were not members of the metropolitan municipalities' client networks. In response to the severity of the crisis, these organizations mobilized, through public demonstrations and road and bridge blockades in the ACBA (the seat of that government), to claim assistance from the federal government.[26] Similarly, the federal government makes basic decisions in relation to metropolitan infrastructure, since it is responsible for the regulation and control of companies that were once state run and later privatized.

So much for opportunities deriving from the centralization of jurisdictional power. The Constitution and provincial laws authorize municipal governments to make agreements and to develop associations that, under various names, deal with communal matters. For example, the Provincial Constitution of Córdoba, which has one of the most autonomous municipal systems, makes provision for these arrangements under section 190 of the Municipal Charter, whereby municipalities can "make agreements among themselves and create intermunicipal entities to render services, do public works, provide technical and financial cooperation, or develop activities of common interest within their capacity."[27] By a ruling of the Córdoba provincial state attorney, intermunicipal entities and arrangements are deemed to have "their own legal capacities different from the municipalities that created them." They have legal status, which allows them to own resources and patrimony, sign contracts, and carry out other legal actions.

In the case of the province of Buenos Aires, two associations of municipalities have been created in the metropolitan area of Buenos Aires (apart from some other regional nonmetropolitan municipal consortia). In 2000, the Región Metropolitana Norte (North Metropolitan Region — NMR) was created with the participation of four municipalities,[28] and by 2001 it represented a population of 1,017,941. These four municipalities have different political histories. Since 1983 the UCR has governed San Isidro and Vicente Lopez, whereas the PJ has governed San Fernando. Until 2007 El Tigre was governed by a local political party, but since then it has been governed by the PJ. The creation of this association was based upon the legal concept of the intermunicipal consortium established by the Constitution of the Province of Buenos Aires and the

Municipal Organic Law (Ley Orgánica Municipal). Even though this legal structure (the intermunicipal consortium) was introduced for very limited purposes, it has allowed promotion of an organization with "the full and equal participation of the four municipalities" aimed at strengthening the role of each. The NMR has an executive board (Consejo Ejecutivo — CE) formed by the mayors of the four municipalities and a technical and planning board (Consejo Técnico y de Planeamiento — CTP) formed by different offices of each municipality. The CE is responsible for enacting internal regulations, setting the agenda, indicating guidelines for action, and representing the consortium. The CTP is responsible for studying and analyzing the issues in the agendas, proposing and recommending common positions and actions, carrying out technical, administrative, or judicial actions on behalf of the CE, and suggesting new issues to the CE. The first projects of the NMR were the creation of an emergency regional center, a traffic master plan, a regional marketing strategy, a strategic master plan, and an information system; the planning of cable and fiber optics installations; the training of municipal human resources personnel; the unification of regulatory systems; and the coordination of public health policies. In effect it is a (mini-) metropolitan governance structure forged through a consortium.

In July 2004, the Consorcio de Municipios del Conurbano Sur (COMCOSUR) was created with the involvement of seven municipalities,[29] which, in 2001, represented a population of 3,044,634 inhabitants. In contrast to the previous case, the seven municipalities have been governed by the PJ, with a few brief exceptions. The COMCOSUR was created with the main objectives of planning, managing, and executing common-interest policies, and while respecting the autonomy of each municipality it was designed to participate in provincial constitutional reform that would promote full municipal autonomy and coordinate national, provincial, and local policies. Given that the provincial legislation on municipal associations is limited, the first task of the COMCOSUR was to reform that legislation, and to that end the consortium jointly worked with members of the government of the province of Buenos Aires and the provincial legislature. The result was the enactment in 2006 of Law 13.580, which recognizes municipal consortia and gives them full legal capacity. The reform allows the associations to have their own budgets, to make contracts, and to be holders of rights and obligations.

After making this legal change in 2007 the consortium agreed on a new statute of organization whereby an administrative board (Consejo de Administración — CA) was formed by the seven municipal mayors, which, as a governmental and administrative body, enacts its own regulations, signs covenants, and carries out all necessary legal acts. A planning board (Consejo de Planificación — CP) was formed, including two representatives from each municipality appointed by the mayor. The CP is subordinate to the CA and coordinates plans, executes projects and programs, and develops their budgets. An advisory board (Consejo Asesor — CA) has been formed including social institutions (grassroots and nongovernmental organizations, universities, etc.) and is appointed by the CA with technical assistance and cooperation functions. Finally, an internal audit (Auditoria Interna — AI) whose members are appointed by the CA is in charge of checking the internal documentation and controlling the consortium organization and functioning. In 2007, the COMCOSUR decided to focus on new arenas of action: environmental legislation, social development, consumer protection, economy, traffic, and enforcement.

The municipal associations in the BAMA have been created to increase the power of municipalities to act in their territories and to strengthen their relations with the provincial and federal governments, as well as with privatized urban service companies. However, inevitably these associations, by their very design and nature, do not have an overall metropolitan perspective: while they do engage in mutual cooperation, they also continue to engender competition with nonconsortia municipalities in the metropolitan area.

ARGENTINA: IS THERE A METROPOLITAN FUTURE?

This discussion offers the opportunity to reflect upon the possibilities within any federal system for the creation of metropolitan institutions of governance — a question raised by the lead authors in the introduction to this book (chapter 1). The dilemma concerns how to create a new level of government within a federal system at a time when the trend is toward decentralization and strengthening of subnational (state and local) governments. One way to accomplish this is through an authoritarian and centralized mandate (alien to federalism) to create metropolitan government institutions.[30] This would lead to the abolition of political inequities that arise from inequitable power accumulation at any one government level, as well as within them, and would do away with clientelistic network relationships. But at the same time such an authoritarian fiat would lack political legitimacy. Two conclusions, therefore, can be drawn. First, while it may seem "easier" to create metropolitan institutions in a centralized and

authoritarian way, paradoxically, if created these are likely to be weak because of their lack of inherent political legitimacy. This approach is less
likely to settle underlying political conflicts than simply to drive them
underground. Second, the challenge would appear to be one of how to
turn competitive relations between units in a metropolitan area into cooperative ones.

The case studies analyzed in this chapter do not offer much optimism
for the consolidation of metropolitan governments and governance in
Argentina. Although Buenos Aires is an important and overarching exception, it is unique in that the populations of other larger metropolitan
areas are mostly concentrated into a single central jurisdiction, making
conurbation-wide amalgamation unnecessary. As in the following chapter on Venezuela in this volume, these municipalities were quite large
in the first place. Whether a metropolitan cross-municipal integration
will be necessary in the future will depend upon growth rates and local
configurations. Certainly these cities would benefit from a city and metropolitan integrative strategy, but amalgamation or cross-municipal cooperation is not de rigueur for effective policy implementation. Among
the case studies discussed here, Mendoza, Buenos Aires, and Rosario are
metropolitan areas that must consider some level of cross-jurisdiction collaboration.

There are also other reasons why metropolitan governance is likely
to be resisted. Politics is the major impediment. Specifically the highly
partisan nature of political decision making and the embedded nature of
political clientelism and the need to deliver electoral support to political
overlords tend to undermine opportunities for collaboration. Paradoxically, authoritarian regimes and the iron fist approach are able to overcome such politicization, but democracy and the need for legitimacy of
governance again make this undesirable. In Argentina, politics is the leit-
motif of metropolitan governance and limits its capacity to develop.

In a similar vein — and also reminiscent of the Venezuelan case — the
role of provincial government is a major force in reducing the possibilities of metropolitan governance, especially (but not exclusively) where
the city is the capital of the province. The classic example here is that of
Rosario: it is a much larger and more important metropolitan area than
that of the provincial capital Santa Fe, yet the latter receives much more
favorable attention from the provincial government.[31] Moreover, under
Argentine law municipalities are firmly placed under provincial control
and are heavily dependent upon the province and the federal govern-

ment for investment resources and intergovernmental transfers. Thus provincial politics trumps municipal politics, and, together with the partisan nature of decision making alluded to above, this results in few incentives for collaboration.

We can identify three types of metropolitan areas, with differing potential for the creation of metropolitan governance: provincial metropolitan areas, interprovincial metropolitan areas, and the BAMA. The BAMA presents the highest level of complexity because of its relative importance at the national scale and because it embraces four jurisdictions often controlled by different political parties. As we have seen, predominance in decision-making processes is based upon the specific power and electoral brokering that takes place in the municipalities, which compete against each other and which are articulated upwards to the government of Buenos Aires Province (Pírez 2004). That is why, regardless of the political nature of the government, cooperation or coordination becomes extremely difficult. The BAMA is also burdened by complexity arising from the very different institutional nature, competence, and resources of the various jurisdictions—Buenos Aires City (autonomous) and municipalities (nonautonomous)—and their very unequal social and economic situations. Poverty and poor living conditions seem to decrease with distance from the city center: that is, the further one moves from the center, the worse conditions become (Pírez 1994, 1998).

As we have seen, the other metropolitan areas in the country are less complex but also have impediments to effective metropolitan governance. An occasional complication arises where a metropolitan area spans two provinces—that is, when its constituent municipalities correspond to two different provincial governments, as in the Neuquén–Río Negro Metropolitan Area. Here one might expect that the opportunities for metropolitan government would be further impeded, notwithstanding the interjurisdictional mandate of the federal government, since yet another player is added, creating imbalances in the political logic and rationality currently in play at the local and provincial levels. In the Neuquén–Río Negro case there is little incentive (or call) for the federal government to get involved. In the BAMA, however, there is such an imperative.

Perhaps the greatest challenge to creating some kind of metropolitan governance that addresses both efficiency and legitimacy is the management of political parties within municipalities that form part of a metropolitan area, as well as in those political parties' relation to the provincial governments (and in some cases to the federal government). The absence of some form of metropolitan governance implies a number of costs for the respective urban areas, ranging from the unequal distribution of resources to (especially) difficulties in addressing environmental issues such as pollution, water management, and flood control, and constraints on limiting urban expansion, especially in the BAMA.

With these impediments in mind, a number of strategies could be expected to improve metropolitan governance, but here it is probably most realistic to focus upon initiatives that would enhance government coordination and cooperation rather than on formal institutional change. In the case of metropolitan areas whose territorial components belong to a single province, one can envisage a sequence of metropolitan governance from (1) particular or specific agreements to jointly address issues (such as solid waste collection and disposal); to (2) the formal constitution of an association or municipal consortium; to (3) the constitution of a metropolitan municipal government for the whole area. Provincial constitutions enable municipalities to make agreements among themselves and to create associations aimed at achieving common goals, so alternatives (1) and (2) are feasible; but their implementation would hinge upon the political processes at the metropolitan and provincial levels. However, a municipal association or consortium is not a government but a technical-administrative mechanism that can advocate on behalf of its members for the rendering of services or the execution of planning activities.

Full-fledged metropolitan governments, although highly unlikely for the reasons outlined above, are actually feasible under provincial constitutions and municipal organic laws that allow for "metropolitan municipalities" to be designated. Each province could design a "metropolitan municipal government" to meet specific needs, but to make it politically feasible, the province would need to acknowledge two government levels: the metropolitan level covering the territory of all municipalities included in the area, which would be in charge of global (metropolitan) matters; and the local level, corresponding to current municipalities, which would be in charge of matters that affect those partial territories. Both levels would have their own authority and resources clearly defined, their own authorities elected, and autonomy in jurisdiction of their own matters. In this manner a decentralized municipality would exist with distribution of power and resources at both levels, but with its authority, autonomy, and coordination procedures clearly identified.

In the more complex case of interprovincial metropolitan areas there are a couple of possibilities. Municipalities included in each of the provinces could be organized as two-level associations. Then they could be coordinated through provincial governments by means, for example, of the constitutional institution of the region, in which the federal government also takes part.

The situation of the BAMA requires unique consideration. Given the current configuration, an agreement between the Buenos Aires province and Buenos Aires city governments could initiate an immediate process of metropolitan organization. To date, however, this has proved impossible because of conflicts between the political parties that go beyond these two jurisdictions. An effective strategy here would need to achieve coordination between both parties' policies and to unify diagnoses, evaluations, and proposals for the area. However, such an agreement between the two "bigger" governments of the area will have little legitimacy if it leaves the municipal governments out of those decisions. A more bottom-up alternative would allow municipalities to "opt in" and designate themselves as associations or "metropolitan municipalities." In the latter a constitutional and legal reform could be enacted on the basis of the principle of municipal autonomy. Naturally it would be desirable that several municipalities opt in.

If the above processes were set in motion, some momentum for change would be achieved at each of the two major government levels as well as in a few "metropolitan municipalities" already engaged in consortium arrangements. Ultimately this momentum might bring the metropolitan components closer together. Thereafter a new aspect of government could begin to emerge encompassing the entire metropolitan area. A "Constitutional Region" might be the most suitable way (FARN 2000) to achieve this with the federal government taking part. This alternative would not imply any institutional modification of Buenos Aires City, which would become part of the metropolitan area as a whole and would include some internal decentralization into the *comunas* (city districts).

In the meantime it is possible — indeed, probably more pragmatic — to think about less formal agreements between the "metropolitan municipalities" and Buenos Aires City. These agreements could be considered once the idea of a provincial metropolitan area had been accepted. However, as long as the full autonomy of Buenos Aires Province municipalities is not acknowledged, undertaking these agreements will continue to be difficult. An additional difficulty lies in the fact that the Buenos Aires City government (a de facto province in power terms) considers the provincial government, not the municipalities, as its counterpart.

Therefore, it would be important for a number of "metropolitan municipalities" to opt in to agreements, so that their power would be more on a par with that of the Autonomous City government. Obviously the support of the provincial government in this scheme would help move the process forward. Nevertheless, because of the intensely interjurisdictional nature of this whole arena, the participation and commitment of the federal government cannot be depended upon.

Finally, some important suggestions and considerations apply in all cases. First, both the provincial and federal governments will have to develop policies enabling municipalities to effectively become stronger and more autonomous. Second, a gradual process should be set in train, starting with small steps such as the creation of a limited interim form of metropolitan collaboration (with little authority and few resources) through agreements, associations, and municipal collaboration. This could later be expanded in scope as it developed momentum and legitimacy and was perceived to be sustainable. Such a process would need to acknowledge the participation of civil society. In the case of nongovernmental forms this could be through agreements and associations that would not require formal intervention or political representation. Once again such involvement is crucial if the idea of metropolitan governance in Argentina is to take root, develop legitimacy, and overcome the frequently intractable political problems discussed in this chapter.

Notes

1. Elected in 1973, Campora resigned so that Perón could be elected president. Perón died in 1974, however, and his widow, who was the vice president, continued the government. The economic crisis and the rising levels of illegal repression promoted by the government increased the instability and insecurity.

2. These data are taken from Lindenboim and Kennedy (2003). In the studies on population and especially urbanization for 2001, the census makes clear that there is a strong undercount, particularly in larger centers. The Buenos Aires City Statistics Directorate estimates an undercount of 7.8 percent for its territory.

3. The Pampa Region is the central area of the country in economic, social, and political terms.

4. In 1960, the BAMA accounted for 33.7 percent of the total population and 44.67 percent of the urban population. Ten years later it made up 36.3 percent of the total population and 44.73 percent of the urban population. Since then, the concentration has decreased, reaching 33.3 percent of the total population and 37.23 percent of the urban population in 2001 (table 6.1).

5. The metropolitan region of Buenos Aires is considerably larger than the metro area. It includes La Plata Metropolitan Area as well as several additional municipalities.

6. The Constitutional Reform of 1994 gave the city of Buenos Aires autonomy to elect its authorities and enact its own constitution. Thus after the first elections in 1996 it became more politically autonomous. Since the reform the main differences between the city of Buenos Aires and the provinces have been that the city does not have full judicial capacities or its own security forces. Furthermore, the federal government regulates and controls infrastructure and public transportation services, both of which are provided by private companies.

7. One of the unique aspects of the Buenos Aires City government is its financial situation. It has the third largest budget in the country (after the federal government and Buenos Aires Province) and has zero financial dependence, since it is able to rely on 90 percent of its own resources.

8. On this topic but for intermediate towns and municipalities, see Pírez (1991); for the BAMA case, see Pírez (2004).

9. While the rest of urban agglomerates are towns, the city of Córdoba is a single municipality within the capital county of the province. This means that its territory is much bigger than that of the other municipalities or localities.

10. Oficina Técnica Rosario, "Plan Estrategico Metropolitano," internal document, 2003.

11. Because the plan extends beyond the metropolitan area and includes many municipalities, it is in effect more a regional plan than a strictly metropolitan one.

12. It provided a mechanism for local governments to channel specific requests and demands for public work to the provincial governments but did not allocate the resources, nor did it have the political will to create and strengthen regional organization, since, in the end, the power still lay in the traditional venues: that of the governor and that of the capital city.

13. In the province of Mendoza, the territories of the municipal governments are aligned with the departments.

14. Its groundwater is replenished by meltwater from the nearby Andes.

15. "Provincial Plan for Solid Urban Waste," cited in Levatino (2009).

16. The DEM has a board made up of the six mayors and funded by municipal resources.

17. In those elections the PJ replaced the UCR.

18. For further discussion, see also Pírez (1994, 1998).

19. Córdoba and Rosario (the second- and third-largest towns) each have 10 percent of the BAMA population, and, as we have seen earlier, a large proportion of their populations is in a single jurisdiction.

20. These services were originally privatized, but they are still regulated and controlled by the federal government. In the first months of 2006 the company supplying water and sewage services was renationalized.

21. Although the subway transport units belong to the Buenos Aires City government, the federal government has privatized them and regulates and controls them.

22. Such is the case of an interjurisdictional service provided by the federal government.

23. In the first and third electoral districts where metropolitan area municipalities are located, a provincial congressman represents 285,353 and 251,302 inhabitants, whereas a provincial senator represents 535,036 and 502,604 inhabitants respectively. Compared with other electoral sections, a congressman never represents more than 100,000 inhabitants, or a senator more than 220,000 (Badía et al. 2004).

24. In the mid-1990s they were up to six hundred million pesos annually and were over four hundred million in 1999 (approximately the same dollar amounts) respectively (Badía et al. 2004).

25. For example, in 2001 in the BAMA, 43 percent of the population was below the poverty line, while in the ACBA it was 12.66 percent; and in the rest of the metropolitan area it was 52.4 percent.

26. These groups have been called *piqueteros* (pickets) because of their blockades and occupations of roads.

27. The principal towns have institutional autonomy: that is, they write their own local constitution under the Municipal Charter. This autonomy limits the intervention of any authority over the municipality.

28. Vicente López, San Isidro, San Fernando, and Tigre.

29. Almirante Brown, Avellaneda, Berazategui, Florencio Varela, Lanas, Lomas de Zamora, and Quilmes.

30. One such arrangement is the Greater Rosario Prefecture, which was created in 1969 by provincial law (during a military government that considered planning a key matter), with the aim of drawing up and supervising the implementation of a development plan. Adoption of the decision was compulsory for the local governments of the area. In 1976, another military government withdrew the plan.

31. Over one million people live in this area. It has several ports from which most of the country's agricultural production is exported, and around it are concentrated a group of tertiary and secondary activities.

Chapter 7

Venezuela

Politics, Urban Reform, and the Challenges of
Metropolitan Governance amid the Struggle for Democracy

DAVID J. MYERS

THE POLITICAL BACKDROP OF VENEZUELAN URBANIZATION

Elites describing themselves as democrats have struggled to control Venezuela since the breakup of Gran Colombia in 1823.[1] Following periods
of dictatorship, they finally gained and held power for four decades from
1959 under a political regime known as Punto Fijo, a compromise negotiated between previously warring elites. Punto Fijo elites normalized their
political regime during the 1970s, but even then there were important
disagreements among them regarding how to modify the regime's political institutions so that they would be more participatory, economically
just, and efficient. As the Punto Fijo regime unraveled during the 1980s
and 1990s, disagreement over how best to save the political regime intensified (McCoy and Myers 2005), and these disagreements became
shriller after the inauguration of Hugo Chávez Frías as president on February 2, 1999. One important component of the debate that surrounded
these disagreements involved decentralization. It is within this context
that the issue of crafting metropolitan institutions of governance reso-
nates in contemporary Venezuelan politics.

Conflict between centralizers based in the capital of Caracas and provincial elites has been a defining characteristic of Venezuelan national life since the 1830s. Violent clashes between these groups led to the deaths of hundreds of thousands in the nineteenth century. Andean warlords conquered Caracas in 1899 and became Venezuela's new ruling elite. Their reign continued unbroken until 1945. Cipriano Castro presided over the first nine years of the Gómez Andean rule, but the dominant Andean political figure of the period was Juan Vicente Gómez, who ruled between 1908 and 1935. Governments presided over by two of his lieutenants (Eleazar López Contreras, 1935–40, and Isias Medina Angarita, 1940–45) closed out the era (Rangel 1966).

Once Castro and the Andeans took control of Caracas, they undermined the capability of rival elites to rebel and challenge their authority. Some of their policies to consolidate power were economic: allies in the provinces were allowed to participate in the lucrative cattle trade. Other policies were militaristic: Gómez strengthened the army, disarmed the regional militias, and built an extensive network of roads to facilitate the rapid movement of military forces into the most remote provinces. Finally, the Andeans reorganized Venezuela's national territory. A centerpiece of this reorganization was the *distrito,* a territorial unit in some ways more analogous to the county in the United States than to the municipalities described elsewhere in this volume. Venezuelan *distritos* were subdivisions of the regions (sometimes called states). They encompassed cities, towns, and rural areas. The president of the republic appointed the chief executive of each *distrito,* and this individual was the president's eyes and ears at the local level.

An alliance of young professional and junior military officers overthrew the ruling Andeans and Caraqueños (residents of Caracas) on October 18, 1945. In the three years that followed, the new governing coalition used their control of the central government to transform the provinces. *Distrito* executives played a pivotal role in ushering in the new order. Caracas-based leaders of the dominant Democratic Action political party (Acción Democrática — AD) instructed *distrito* political authorities to assist in crafting local organizations of the AD political party. These efforts were so successful that in the 1948 municipal elections the AD received more than 70 percent of the vote and gained control of all but a few of the *distrito* governments. The magnitude of this victory confirmed suspicions prevalent among other party leaders — and the Andeans and Caraqueños who lost power in 1945 — that the AD was using its control over the national government to create an unbeatable political machine.

However, some of the junior military officers who had joined with political party leaders in the 1945 revolution feared that the hierarchical political infrastructure that the AD had created challenged military authority. Many of those officers also opposed the leftist policies that the AD initiated between 1945 and 1948. On November 24, 1948, with the backing of Caraqueños, Andeans, the Roman Catholic hierarchy, and some opposition party leaders, a military coup removed the government of President Rómulo Gallegos (AD). The purge of AD leaders, however, was far from complete. In the *distritos* the military allowed many authorities who belonged to the AD party to remain in office. Indeed, these local officials played a key role in the defeat suffered by the military candidate General Pérez Jiménez in the 1952 presidential elections. The general refused to concede and used doctored election returns to seize control, and the transparency of this fraud undermined the legitimacy of the government during the five years (1953–58) that he ruled. During this period Pérez Jiménez vested political and policing authority for the *distritos* in the army and in the Seguridad Nacional, the dictatorship's dreaded secret police.

On January 23, 1958, a popular uprising ended the dictatorship. The civilians who came to power included proponents of centralization and decentralization. Article 25 of the 1961 Constitution established local political institutions as a basic governmental unit of the federal republic. Most political party leaders envisioned rapid passage of a "Law of the Municipalities" to replace the 1904 legislation that had made *distritos* the basic territorial unit of local government. However, before such legislation could be introduced, the new post-1958 democracy found itself under attack by leftist insurgents supported by Fidel Castro and the Soviet Union. This insurgency lasted for ten years and occupied the attention of three presidents: Rómulo Betancourt (1959–64), Raúl Leoni (1964–69), and Rafael Caldera (1969–74). Each feared that autonomous local government would interfere with efforts to defeat the insurgency. Like their authoritarian predecessors, they found that the *distrito* form of government facilitated central control over local territory and politics. Betancourt, Leoni, and Caldera put the issue of empowering local government on the back burner. There it remained until the mid-1970s, when the insurgency had finally been defeated.[2]

The emerging class of young professionals in the secondary cities of the interior lobbied hard for increased local government authority once the insurgency faded away. Movement in this direction occurred late in the 1970s when separate elections for the district councils were established. New legislation also mandated a city manager form of government for the *distritos* (Martínez 1986, 388–401). However, economic difficulties in the 1980s led national party leaders to circumvent the reforms and exercise even tighter control over local as well as regional governments. When economic difficulties intensified and led to widespread rioting in February 1989 (the so-called Caracazo), national leaders made a U-turn. They passed legislation that created the office of elected mayor, increased the taxing powers of *distrito* governments (which were now to be called *municipios*), and reduced the ability of central party leaders to choose candidates for local office. These reforms satisfied the demands of local elites for a greater voice in government and increased the efficiency of public services in selected areas such as water and refuse disposal. They also gave local elites new opportunities to secure lucrative service contracts.

The 1989 *municipio* law (considered part of more comprehensive decentralization reforms) entered into force in a decade marked by an unprecedented economic downturn. Empowered municipal governments had fewer resources to allocate than their predecessors, the centrally dominated *distritos*. Not surprisingly, few residents of Venezuela's shantytowns believed that they benefited from the empowerment of local governments. When Hugo Chávez Frías burst onto the scene as the champion of the urban poor, he criticized the 1989 reforms as having strengthened local political party interests and benefited professionals and business groups at the expense of the urban poor. Once in power, Chávez presented recentralization as a policy that would ensure that the "people" would have direct access to a responsive ruler who sympathized with their interests.

In summary, the tension between local interests and the central government in Venezuela has been a defining characteristic of politics since independence. Venezuelan municipal political institutions (*distrito* governments) were crafted to prevent local landowners from assembling resources with which they could challenge ruling elites in Caracas. As the country became more urban, the national political and economic elites found themselves supportive of the *distrito* institutions that enabled them to dominate the provincial cities. Except for a brief period in the early 1990s, central government authorities have resisted efforts to empower local governments, and as a result and with the exception of Caracas, opportunities to take advantage of the benefits of metropolitan forms of governance have been ignored.

Federalism and Urbanization Trends in Venezuela

Venezuelan constitutions have been federal in form but highly centralized in practice, and the present Constitution of 1999 is no exception. It divides the country into twenty-three states, the Capital District, and a collection of offshore islands known as the Federal Dependencies.[3] Below the state level are 339 municipalities.[4] There are enormous disparities among Venezuelan municipalities in terms of population size. In 1992 14 municipalities each had more than 250,000 inhabitants, 76 had populations of between 50,000 and 250,000, and 192 (equivalent to 68 percent of the total) had fewer than 50,000 inhabitants. On January 31, 2007, President Hugo Chávez proposed territorial reorganization as part of his program to make Venezuelan local government more responsive and efficient. These proposals envisioned a much reduced role for local and regional governments, and they empowered newly created communal councils that received funding directly from the central government. This multifaceted reform package challenged the power and influence of powerful interests, many of which were part of the government coalition. It also raised fears that President Chávez intended to eliminate private property and remain in power indefinitely. In the referendum of December 2, 2007, by the narrowest of margins Venezuelans rejected the president's proposals. Had they passed they would have fundamentally modified the 1999 Constitution.

Until 1940 Venezuela was largely rural. General Juan Vicente Gómez — who as indicated earlier ruled between 1908 and 1936 — disliked urban life and distrusted the Caracas-based national elite. After consolidating his power, Gómez moved his residence to newly acquired lands near the provincial town of Maracay, some seventy miles west of Caracas. He exercised power as a traditional *caudillo* (warlord), surviving initially by using patronage based on cattle (Yarrington 2003). Toward the end of his rule, income from petroleum had become more important in shoring up support for his government. The legacy was that when Gómez passed from the scene the total population of Venezuela was 3.4 million, of which only 16 percent resided in the nine urban centers with twenty thousand or more inhabitants (Venezuela, Ministerio de Fomento 1983). Caracas, although relatively small for capital cities at that time with a population of 135,000, was nevertheless a "primate" city. Maracaibo, a city with roughly half the number of inhabitants of Caracas, occupied second place in the urban hierarchy. The number of inhabitants residing in the third- and fourth-largest cities (Barquisimeto and Valencia) did not exceed fifty thousand.

Table 7.1. Growth in Number of Population Centers with More Than 20,000 Inhabitants

Indicators	1936	1941	1950	1961	1971	1981
Number of centers	9	9	20	36	50	65
Population (thousands)	535.3	696.9	1,659.70	3,631.10	6,470.10	10,276.10
Percent in relation to total national population	15.9	18.1	33	48.3	60.3	70.4
Interannual rate of growth (%) of population in centers with more than 20,000 persons	NA	5.4	10.1	7.4	5.9	4.7

Sources: Venezuela, Ministerio de Fomento (1983).

Nevertheless, population was growing, and urbanization had begun to accelerate as the 1930s drew to a close. The extension of medical care to previously isolated groups was a major factor in population growth. The rate of population increase, which was 1.93 percent during the 1920s, rose to 2.74 percent between 1936 and 1941, and to 3.72 percent during the 1950s. The number of Venezuelan urban centers with a population of twenty thousand or more increased significantly after 1941, as shown in table 7.1.

During World War II and the Korean Conflict, Venezuela was a major supplier of petroleum to the United States and its allies. Income from the sale of petroleum, while invested disproportionately in Caracas, was used to improve the quality of services and physical infrastructure in most cities. Improvements in urban living standards attracted peasants from the countryside, and while in 1941 only two Venezuelan cities (Caracas and Maracaibo) boasted populations of more than one hundred thousand, four decades later some twenty-three Venezuelan cities had more than one hundred thousand inhabitants (Fossi 1984, 474), and fewer than 10 percent of the national population lived in settlements of fewer than one thousand. The urban regions of Caracas and Maracaibo remained the largest; the former boasted a population of 4.4 million (14.4 percent of the national total) and the latter 2.2 million. Several secondary cities grew even faster, and three — Valencia, Barquisimeto, and Maracay — boasted more than a million inhabitants each at the beginning of the twenty-first century. One new major urban center, Ciudad Guyana, was deliberately located in an area that was not included in Venezuela's traditional system

Table 7.2. Growth Rates of Selected Venezuelan Urban Agglomerations, 1936–2000 (percent)

Urban Agglomeration	1936–40	1941–50	1951–60	1961–70	1971–80	1981–90	1991–2000
Caracas	6.5	7.76	6.14	5.03	2.8	1.98	1.67
Maracaibo	2.02	7.63	6.22	4.43	4.5	2.74	2.37
Valencia	2.17	9.08	4.98	7.17	7.93	4.25	3.25
Maracay	2.08	8.49	9.48	6.94	6.35	3.99	3.01
Barquisimeto	8.26	9.14	5.87	5.04	4.89	3.3	2.67
Barcelona/ Pt. La Cruz	4.63	17.95	8.12	4.93	5.15	3.13	2.48
Cd. Guyana	—	—	—	15.1	8.1	5.59	4.46
Maturin	7.38	9.92	7.97	8.6	4.56	3.23	2.7
Acaraigua/Araure	4.84	11.75	6.31	8.03	5.65	3.96	3.23
Venezuela	2.74	3.02	3.72	3.61	3.74	2.73	2.28

Sources: Negrón (1991, table 2.3).

of cities, taking advantage of cheap electricity generated by the nearby Guri Dam. This planned city became the country's most important steel- and aluminum-producing center.

Table 7.2 compares the rates of growth experienced by nine of Venezuela's most important population centers between 1936 and 2000. Migrants arriving in these cities appropriated lands held in reserve by local governments or used for agriculture by private landowners. Initially most growth occurred in territory that lay within a single *distrito,* although this sometimes changed in the 1970s as the rate of growth in secondary cities increased. Urban centers such as Valencia, Maracay, Barcelona-Puerto La Cruz, and Acaraigua-Aurare spilled over into adjoining distritos. The communication networks binding these new urban centers together, and the challenges of providing efficient services for residents, encouraged centers to think of themselves as part of a single metropolitan region. *Generally,* though, political and economic rivalries discouraged the creation of political institutions that crossed *distrito* boundaries.

By 1981, Venezuela was overwhelmingly urban. Internal migration had created a system of sixty-five cities with more than twenty thousand inhabitants (table 7.1), housing more than 70 percent of the total national population. Almost all significant social, political, and economic activity took place in the urban regions of these cities. Metropolitan

Caracas continued to grow, but at a slower rate than such surging secondary cities as Valencia, Barquisimeto, and Maracay (table 7.2), and this was in large part due to incentives offered by the central government to private sector enterprises to relocate outside metropolitan Caracas. The central government followed a similar policy in regard to its investment in public corporations (De la Cruz 2005), reflecting the lower cost of providing infrastructure and services in the secondary cities, as well as the widespread desire within Venezuela to reduce the dominance of the capital city. Caracas, the historic primate city, was no longer the only urban center in which one could reside and enjoy the amenities of life in the developed countries. Indeed, in the first decade of the twenty-first century the quality of life in five and possibly ten urban centers of Venezuela is for most residents at least as high as — and possibly higher than — in Caracas. Venezuela's national population increased dramatically between 1936 and 2000, from four million to twenty-four million. In 2008 the population passed twenty-seven million.

CONSTRAINED METROPOLITANIZATION IN VENEZUELA

Seven urban agglomerations in Venezuela have populations of a size that might lead us to expect that metropolitan political institutions would emerge to improve the quality of citizen participation and service delivery. First and foremost is the urban region of Caracas, still a primate city with 5.2 million inhabitants, roughly 19 percent of the total national population, and with a long history of struggle to craft effective metropolitan political institutions. In contrast are the other six urban agglomerations, which have populations large enough to make metropolitan governance a possibility to consider but which have not developed such institutions. These cities are Maracaibo at 2.8 million, Valencia at 1.5 million, Barquisimeto at 1.4 million, Maracay at 1.3 million, Ciudad Guyana at 875,000, and Barcelona-Puerto La Cruz at 800,000.

This is the puzzle that the Venezuelan case raises: Why, except for the capital, have Venezuelan urban regions not developed metropolitan institutions? To answer, we first compare, historically, the processes of governance of three of the largest: Barquisimeto, Maracaibo, and Caracas. Barquisimeto is encased in a territorial unit sufficiently large that even given its rapid expansion over the past fifty years its built environment has not spilled over into a neighboring political unit. In contrast, Maracaibo, Venezuela's second most important city, is the core of a petroleum-producing

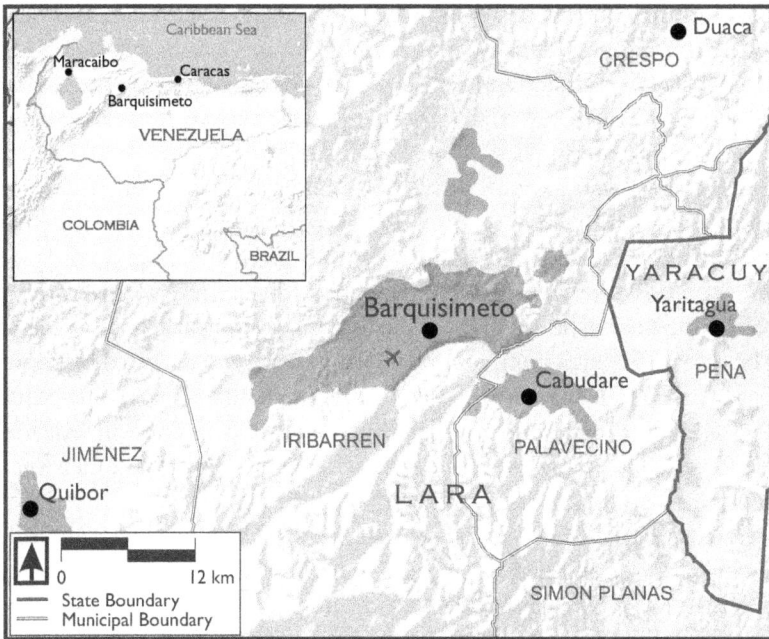

Figure 7.1. Barquisimeto: Encased within the Iribarren Municipio

region and the window to the world of western Venezuela. In 2007 its urban region included seven outlying municipalities, two of which had populations of more than 130,000. Yet as we will see, no serious attention has been given to developing metropolitan political institutions in Greater Maracaibo, and none exist. Finally, Caracas is unlike any other urban area in Venezuela. Here metropolitan political institutions were first imposed by the central government during the 1930s, and the struggle for effective metropolitan institutions has been an ongoing drama.

Barquisimeto: A Case of No Need for Metropolitan Institutions

Barquisimeto, capital of the state of Lara, is located on the Turbio River (figure 7.1). The city dominates Venezuela's west-central axis of communication, industry, and agriculture. It lies halfway between the capital of Caracas and Maracaibo. Founded in 1552 by Don Juan de Vellegas, Barquisimeto occupied several different sites until 1563, when the settlement took root at its present location. As of 2008 Barquisimeto was the fourth-most-populated urban region in Venezuela. The city boasts strong agro-industrial roots, being surrounded by a sugarcane valley and near two of the largest vegetable-producing regions in Venezuela: the Valle de Quíbor (Quíbor Valley) and Sanare. The main economic activities of Barquisimeto are the food industry, plastics, textiles, paper, dairies, farming, and automotive industries.

Barquisimeto's location within one municipality, Iribarren, makes the municipal government the effective local government for the entire metropolitan agglomeration of Barquisimeto (see figure 7.1). In accordance with the 1989 municipal reform legislation, this municipal government has four main functions: executive, legislative, comptroller, and planning. The executive function is managed by the mayor, who is elected by popular vote for a four-year term and who administers the whole municipality. The legislative branch is represented by the municipal council, which is composed of seven councilpersons, also elected by popular vote for a four-year term, and which, like its counterparts throughout the country, deliberates and approves new decrees and local laws. The municipal comptroller supervises local finances, and the municipal planning office oversees development projects and zoning for the municipality (Kelly 1993b).

Between 1959 and 1989, executive power in all Venezuelan municipalities was in the hands of the president of the municipal council (Martínez 1977, 311–12). Over the first decade of this period the AD Party controlled the council and thus the local executive. Subsequently, the Social Christian Party (Partido Social-Cristiano — COPEI) gained strength on the municipal council,[5] and the patronage allocated by the Iribarren Municipality was divided between the AD and the COPEI (according to their relative strength on the council). Sixty percent of total municipal expenditures went to cover the salaries of municipal employees (Martínez 1977, 320). Municipal political institutions in Iribarren at that time provided services (such as street repair, the operation of municipal markets, firefighting, city planning, and a few cultural activities) for metropolitan Barquisimeto. The local tax base was limited, with most funding for these services coming from the constitutional *situado*, this being a percentage of federal revenues that the national government was obliged to transfer to the regional and local governments.[6] Large investments in the physical infrastructure of metropolitan Barquisimeto in areas like public housing, transportation, and sanitary works were made by the national government (González de Pacheco 1993).

The AD and the COPEI dominated politics in the state of Lara and in the Iribarren Municipality between 1959 and 1989. The Lara State secretary general of the AD and the COPEI controlled the nomination of these parties' candidates for municipal council during these years.[7] The secretary generals, in turn, served at the pleasure of the national leaders of their parties. The national party leaders approved their party's candidates for Congress, the state legislature, and municipal councils and also had an important role in the allocation of resources for major infrastructure investments. Despite such hierarchical relations, national party leaders seldom intervened in setting priorities for municipal investments or in dispensing local patronage.

The 1989 municipal reforms increased the size of the Iribarren Municipal Council from seven to twenty-six, as well as establishing the office of elected mayor (Kelly 1993a, 275). The reforms also changed the procedures for electing regional and local leaders in the state of Lara and the Iribarren Municipio. The ability of national party leaders to interfere in the selection of state and municipal officials was reduced, and the taxing powers of the municipality were expanded. However, local politicians hesitated to use their increased powers to tax and continued to rely on the central government transfers (the *situado*), which was now increased to 20 percent of the national budget. Under the (second) government of Carlos Andrés Pérez (1989–93) and that of interim president Ramón Velásquez (1993–94), the mayor and municipal council of Barquisimeto were able to use the funds they received from the central government to allocate resources more or less in accordance with their own priorities. However, the governments of Rafael Caldera (1994–99) and Hugo Chávez Frías (1999–present) regularly refused to transfer the *situado*—at least when the plans for investment of the government of Barquisimeto were different from those of the central government. Also, as in the early years of the Punto Fijo system, large infrastructure investments in the Iribarren Municipio remained under the control of the central government. Thus the single most important upgrade to the Barquisimeto's public transportation system during the Chávez years—the Transbarca trolleybus system—was planned and executed by the Ministry of Infrastructure and was funded by a consortium of the national petroleum company PDVSA (Petróleos de Venezuela), the mayorality of Iribarren, the Ministry of Infrastructure, and the governor's office of the state of Lara.

To summarize, the Iribarren Municipality has functioned as a metropolitan government for greater Barquisimeto for more than a century. At the same time, and with the exception of a brief period in the 1990s, the municipality has enjoyed little autonomy from the central government.

The empowerment of municipal governments envisioned by the 1989 reforms was never fully realized, and the historical tendency toward centralism reasserted itself, first during the presidential administrations of Rafael Caldera and subsequently during the tenure of Hugo Chávez Frías. The current mayor of Barquisimeto, Amalia Sáez (2008–2013), belongs to the United Socialist Party of Venezuela (Partido Socialista Unido de Venezuela — PSUV), President Chávez's political party. Her effectiveness in strengthening the institutions of the Iribarren Municipality will depend on the president's view of her personal loyalty and on the success or failure of efforts by President Chávez to replace the traditional municipal institutions with communal councils.[8] Located within a single municipality, and enjoying strong support from the center (so long as the local politics accord with those of the center), Barquisimeto has never seen the need for a metropolitan government.

Maracaibo: A Story of Unrealized Opportunities

The *municipio* of Maracaibo stretches along the west bank of Lake Maracaibo, just south of the relatively narrow channel opening into the wide lake, which feeds into the Gulf of Venezuela and the Caribbean Sea (figure 7.2). For much of the twentieth century the trajectory of local government in Maracaibo, capital of the state of Zulia, resembled that of Barquisimeto. As the century drew to a close, however, the urban region of Maracaibo expanded beyond its core municipality to encompass petroleum-producing municipalities located along the eastern shore of the lake. Because of Maracaibo's historic isolation from communities on the eastern shore, few Maracuchos (residents of Maracaibo) viewed developments on the eastern shore as having much to do with the governance of their city. Neither did Zulia State officials devote much attention to exploring the advantages of collaboration between the municipalities of the two sides of the lake. Finally, like most of their countrymen during the 1990s, Maracuchos and Zulianos were focusing their political attention on national regime change.

Lake Maracaibo covers an area of thirteen thousand square kilometers and is the twenty-third-largest lake in the world. It is Venezuela's most important lake system and constitutes a highly important waterway for the communities and businesses of westernmost Zulia State. Christopher Columbus passed by the site of Maracaibo on his second voyage to the New World, and the city was founded by the German governor Ambrosio Alfinger in 1529. Pirates who sailed Lake Maracaibo sacked and

MARA

JESÚS ENRIQUE
LOSSADA

MARACAIBO

Maracaibo

La Concepción

Altagracia

FRANCISCO DE MIRANDA

El Canito

✕ SAN FRANCISCO
San Francisco

SANTA RITA

ZULIA   PROVINCE

LA CAÑADA
DE URDANETA

La Concepción

Cabimas

CABIMAS

Patrerite

Lake
Maracaibo

SIMON BOLIVAR

Tía Juana

LAGUNILLAS

Ciudad Ojeda

0   14 km
Municipal Boundary

Figure 7.2. Maracaibo Urban Region

burned the city of Maracaibo on innumerable occasions, and in 1691 Capuchin missionaries settled there and started to bring peace to the region.

In the first half of the twentieth century Maracaibo became the center from which multinational corporations administered their investments in Venezuela's lucrative petroleum industry. The city was somewhat isolated from the rest of the country because of its location on the western bank of the lake. Ferryboats linked the city to settlements on the eastern shore, where the oil fields that made Venezuela one of the world's leading producers of petroleum were located. General Marcos Pérez Jiménez (1952–58) wanted the executives of the multinational petroleum corporations to be where he could keep an eye on them, so he ordered the transfer of their national headquarters to Caracas. Maracaibo, nevertheless, remained the center from which the multinationals managed their daily operational activities in the fields.[9]

The government of General Pérez Jiménez developed plans for a bridge that would connect Maracaibo to the lake's eastern shore, but it fell to the government of Rómulo Betancourt (1959–64) to build the bridge. Urbanists in the Zulia State Planning Office argued that the bridge should include a light rail system that would connect Maracaibo to the eastern shore petroleum-producing cities of Cabimas and Ciudad Ojeda. However, the national Ministry of Public Works controlled policy making for the bridge and decided that it would carry only vehicles, and the resulting General Rafael Urdaneta Bridge was inaugurated on August 24, 1962. Made of concrete and stayed by cables, the bridge spanned 8.7 kilometers. Since its inauguration the General Rafael Urdaneta Bridge has been administered by an autonomous institute of the national government, Servicio Autónomo Puente General Rafael Urdaneta (SAPGRU).

The municipio of Maracaibo encompassed the built-up area of the city of Maracaibo until 1995. In that year, using powers given to subdivisions of the municipalities by the municipal reforms of 1989, the *parroquia* (parish) of San Francisco broke away and became a separate municipality (figure 7.2). Until then, as with Barquisimeto, the president of the municipal council of Maracaibo functioned as the local executive. The 1989 reforms also increased the size of the municipal council of Maracaibo from five to seventeen (Kelly 1993a, 279). However, unlike the municipal Council of Iribarren (Barquisimeto), the Maracaibo Municipal Council was controlled in 1989 by political parties other than the AD and the COPEI, the two partisan institutions that at that time dominated national politics.

Following the construction of the Urdaneta Bridge there was surprisingly little discussion about the idea of treating the eastern side of the lake as part of the Maracaibo urban region. The heritage of isolation limited the attention of most Maracuchos to their own municipality and to local problems on the western shore of the lake. In this context Maracaibo's principal territorial problem was the desire of residents of San Francisco to separate their region from that of the *municipio* of Maracaibo. More than ever after the 1989 decentralization reforms, issues that involved coordinating local services and political participation in Maracaibo, Cabimas, Lagunillas, and Ciudad Ojeda (all eastern shore *municipios*) continued to land in the lap of the governor of the state of Zulia.

Following the two unsuccessful coup attempts of 1992, the little interest that did exist in crafting metropolitan political institutions to link the city of Maracaibo and the communities on the eastern shore of Lake Maracaibo disappeared. Concern with the fate of Punto Fijo democracy and the rise of Hugo Chávez Frías trumped local political concerns, which reached fever pitch when Francisco Arias Cárdenas (a confidant of Hugo Chávez Frías) won the Zulia State governorship in the regional elections of 1994 and was reelected in 1998. However, in 1996 an opponent of Chávez, Manuel Rosales, was elected mayor of Maracaibo and then governor of Zulia in 2000, and was reelected in 2004. But in the concurrent regional and local elections Gian Carlo Di Martino, an ally of now President Chávez, captured the Maracaibo mayoralty. The exigencies of being players in volatile national politics while overseeing the political institutions that already were in place left no time for experimentation with innovations of the magnitude necessary to address local issues of mutual concern to Maracaibo, San Francisco, Cabimas, Lagunillas, and Ciudad Ojeda (figure 7.2).

When President Chávez began experimenting with communal councils in 2004, he directed his centrally controlled "Missions" to assist Mayor Gian Carlo Di Martino in creating progovernment communal councils in the city of Maracaibo. At the same time Governor Manuel Rosales was attempting to establish communal councils favorable to the opposition in the municipalities of San Francisco, Cabimas, Lagunillas, and Ciudad Ojeda. Rivalry between the communal councils created by Rosales and Di Martino ensured that there would be no meaningful cooperation between the communal councils of the Maracaibo urban region.[10] This contrasted with situations in other large urban regions, especially ones controlled by supporters of President Chávez. In those regions, as of late 2007, efforts were under way to create regional councils of the communal councils that approximated embryonic metropolitan institutions.

Caracas: The Politics of Dysfunctional Institutions

Modern-day efforts to craft effective governance for the urban region of Venezuela's capital city date from 1936, and between 1936 and 1972 reformers set in place several metropolitan institutions, most notably a multimunicipality local government, a metropolitan planning office, and a regional police force. The first two succumbed to pressures for new kinds of political participation when the 1989 municipal reform law was applied to Caracas. Subsequent efforts to streamline urban governance in the Caracas region culminated in 2000 with the creation of a metropolitan municipality, the Capital District. This district had its own mayoralty and municipal council, but the powers of these institutions overlapped with those of the district's traditional municipalities, which were not abolished, and political authority in metropolitan Caracas became more confused and fragmented than ever. This fueled clashes between supporters and opponents of President Hugo Chávez, with Chavistas favoring a centralized regional government that would be firmly controlled by the president. Opponents advocated a strong metropolitan government headed by an elected superior mayor (alcalde mayor) who would represent the interests of residents and deliver services throughout the metropolitan area. Stalemate ensued. This debate continues today and is linked to the impasse between the Chavistas and their opponents over how to transform national political institutions.

Incipient Metropolitan Government

The early modernizers who came to power in 1936 quickly revised the structure of local government for the Caracas urban region. At that time the capital city's built environment was expanding to the east, out of the Federal District and into that part of the Caracas Valley where political authority was divided among four rural *municipios* in the neighboring state of Miranda. President López Contreras (1936–41) prevailed upon the national congress to pass legislation that combined the four municipalities (Sucre, Baruta, El Hatillo, and Chacao) into a special territorial unit, the Sucre District. This new district had a single municipal council and a president-appointed prefect with districtwide responsibility for policing and other executive functions. This special district also received a uniquely autonomous status in relation to Miranda State, under whose nominal jurisdiction it remained. From 1936 until the municipal reforms of 1989, the Sucre District was one of the two territorial units with municipal authority over the Caracas Valley.

The Federal District, more populous than the Sucre District, was the other territorial unit that had municipal authority in the Caracas Valley, and historically the Federal District was divided into two semiautonomous subunits: the Libertador Department and the Vargas Department (figure 7.3). A presidential appointee, the Federal District governor presided over the entire district, while Libertador and Vargas each had a prefect named by the Federal District governor. The prefect was respon-

Figure 7.3. Greater Caracas

sible for public security and law enforcement, although during times of political unrest the governor (and sometimes the president) involved himself in Federal District law enforcement. Thus the governor supervised a single district bureaucracy with responsibility for providing services in each of the two departments. Until 1986 legislative power rested with a single Federal District municipal council that was weaker than its counterparts elsewhere, and in 1986 the national government gave the Vargas Department its own municipal council.

Vargas, the less populated northern coastal zone of the historic Federal District, has always been physically and psychologically removed from Libertador, which encompasses the western half of the Caracas Valley. Libertador is the heart of historic Caracas, and fifteen miles of rugged terrain separates it from the port city of La Guaira, which is also the administrative center of the Vargas Department. Moreover, Vargas's urban built environment stretches along the winding coast but is confined to a narrow plain whose width seldom exceeds two miles. It is fifty miles, as the crow flies, from the Vargas Department's westernmost population center (Chichiriviche de la Costa) to its eastern anchor, at the resort of Los Caracas.

The southern boundary of Vargas is a mountain wall that soars to seven thousand feet. First footpaths, then winding mountain roads, and after 1954 a modern freeway linked historic Caracas and La Guaira.[11]

If the physical geography was not conducive to effective integration and collaboration, then neither were the politics: indeed, tensions between the political leaders of Vargas and Libertador predate independence. In 1998 residents of Vargas prevailed upon the national congress to make Vargas the twenty-third state, so that planning and service delivery for Vargas subsequently evolved along lines quite distinct from what occurred in Libertador. The terrain suitable for urban development in the Caracas Valley lies between 2,500 and 3,000 feet above sea level. Until the 1920s the city's built environment lay within the western half of the Caracas Valley and within the boundaries of the Federal District (Morales Tucker 1992, 101–4; Troconis de Veracoechea 1993, ch. 6). This zone contained the locations from which Venezuela's central government controlled the nation. The government's centers of power included the presidential office (Miraflores), the ministries, Congress, the Supreme Court, and the military's base for command and control (Fuerte Tiuna). Early in the twentieth century most Caracas elites resided in the opulent El Paraíso neighborhood, also located in Libertador.

As of 1936, sugar and coffee plantations covered most of Miranda State's Sucre District. A few upper-class Caraqueños (residents of Libertador) maintained weekend retreats among these plantations, but the zone was bucolic. After the death of Juan Vicente Gómez, congestion in the historic core of Caracas increased, and residents from El Paraíso and other affluent neighborhoods looked eastwards. Planned residential subdivisions that catered to the elite appeared in the Sucre District, and modern commercial centers and luxurious recreational facilities sprang up close to the new subdivisions. By the end of World War II eastern Caracas neighborhoods such as the Country Club and Altamira housed most of Venezuela's upper class. Middle-class neighborhoods also developed in the Sucre District, and soon the remaining desirable parcels of vacant land were confined to the southern foothills.

Affluent neighborhoods took shape in the southeastern foothills during the 1950s.[12] Most new residents of this zone were beneficiaries of the economic boom occasioned by General Marcos Pérez Jiménez (1952–58). With the right connections it was possible for "friends of the general" to obtain desirable properties at below-market prices. After the general fled the country, economic recession and conflicting claims to the parcels under development in the southeastern foothills halted urban development in that direction, and it did not resume until the 1970s, when high oil prices created an economic boom that gave rise to a new elite of wealth and power.

The eastern terminus of the Caracas Valley experienced urbanization in a different way than other zones of the Sucre District. Until the 1960s the eastern terminus was most noteworthy as the location of Petare, a colonial village that served as the Sucre District's seat of government. After the overthrow of General Marcos Pérez Jiménez, Petare became a magnet attracting tens of thousands of migrants from the impoverished East, a region dominated by the then ruling AD Party. Soon the foothills surrounding Petare were home to one of the largest swathes of squatter settlements in Caracas. Middle- and upper-class residents to the west of Petare became uneasy as the number of *barrios* and *ranchos* increased. In the 1970s they lobbied successfully to have the national government extend the Eastern Freeway (Autopista del Este) along a path that created a barrier shielding them from the shantytowns.

The Sucre District's financial solvency depended upon taxes paid by the more affluent *municipios,* like Chacao and Baruta. When economic recession in the 1980s led the 1936 Sucre District Municipal Council to raise taxes, community leaders in Chacao protested. They pointed out that only 10 percent of the funds collected in their *municipio* found their way back to Chacao. Businessmen who chafed at the high municipal taxes on commercial establishments and all the major political parties in Chacao agitated for separation from the Sucre District (Ellner and Myers 2002). In 1989 advocates of separation took advantage of the new powers given to regional and local governments by the recently passed decentralization reforms, successfully lobbying the regional (state) government of Miranda to replace the special Sucre District with four municipalities: Chacao, El Hatillo, Baruta, and Sucre (Vallmitjana 1993, 66–67).

Dysfunctional Metropolitan Government Constructions since 1989
The political institutions of the Caracas region were more fragmented in 1999 than they had been in 1959, at the beginning of Punto Fijo democracy (figure 7.4). Part of the cause lay in the population growth of the outer six *municipios* and their functional integration within Greater Caracas.[13] Equally important were pressures to create smaller territorial units that would give control of selected local governments to middle-class residents. In addition, there were preferences based on ideology. Many reformers believed that smaller local government units would lead to greater citizen participation. In any case, in the wake of the 1989

municipal reform legislation, political authority in metropolitan Caracas was divided among the national president and his Federal District governor, two state governors, and, depending on which municipalities are included, as many as thirteen territorial units of local government.

Elimination of the dysfunctional metropolitan government in Caracas was a goal to which most delegates to the 1999 Constituent Assembly paid lip service. But the same balance of conflicting interests that increased fragmentation following the 1989 decentralization reforms impeded the Constituent Assembly from agreeing on new political institutions. The assembly mandated that the first legislation to be passed before the session adjourned, should the new constitution be approved in the upcoming December referendum, would create a metropolitan government for the Caracas region. The resulting legislation, passed in March 2000, led to even more fragmentation. It created a Capital District with a popularly elected "superior mayor" (*alcalde mayor*) and a district council composed of thirteen members. As figure 7.4 shows, the Capital District subsumed the Libertador *municipio* of the old Federal District and the four *municipios* that had comprised the 1936 Sucre District, forming the metropolitan district of Caracas. Each of these component *municipios* had an elected mayor and a municipal council. The powers of the component *municipios* were virtually identical to those of the Capital District regional government. In addition, the four *municipios* of the 1936 Sucre District remained part of Miranda State and were therefore subject to the authority of its governor.

In the elections of July 30, 2000, Alfredo Peña, who had initially been a supporter of the Bolivarian Revolution, won the election for *alcalde mayor*.[14] The mayors of the two most populous *municipios* of the Capital District (Libertador and Sucre) supported President Chávez throughout their terms in office, but Mayor Peña's later move to the opposition led to political conflicts and jurisdictional disputes with his two mayoral counterparts. These became more intense during the events leading up to the April 11, 2002, coup that temporarily removed President Chávez from power. Those disputes continued in 2003 and 2004 when hundreds of thousands of middle-class demonstrators opposed to the government were protected by the metropolitan police force, which had been placed under the jurisdiction of the *alcaldía mayor*. This led President Chávez to take control of the metropolitan police force, demobilize the force, and place Capital District law enforcement in the hands of the National Guard.

Opponents challenged his interference with local government in the Capital District. They petitioned the Supreme Court to delineate responsibilities between the *alcaldía mayor* of the Capital District, its component

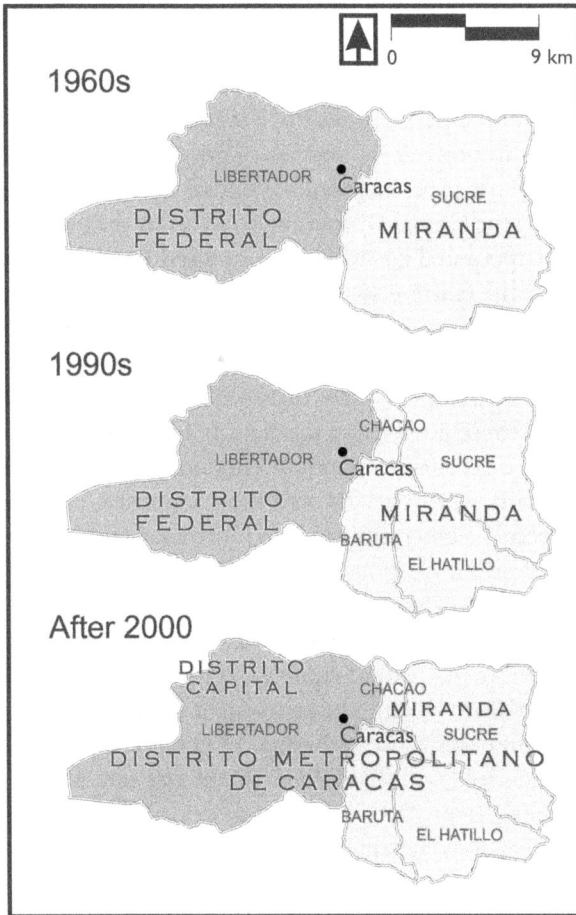

Figure 7.4. Evolution of Caracas Metropolitan Area

municipios, the Miranda regional government, and the national government. The Court, which was controlled by supporters of the president, refused to take the case. In their refusal, the justices stated that what they were being asked to do was political rather than legal. However, they did rule that the national government must return control of the metropolitan police force to the *alcaldía mayor.* President Chávez complied but confiscated the force's most powerful weapons and continued to use the National Guard to police the Capital District. He also ignored the confusing legislation that gave overlapping powers to the potpourri of political institutions present in metropolitan Caracas. The allocation of resources to Caracas was centralized in the presidential Missions and the national ministries. Institutions controlled by supporters of the Bolivarian Revolution received funds and technical assistance. Others did not.

The December 2, 2007, defeat of President Chávez's plans to revise the 1999 Constitution left the process of governance in Caracas as confused as ever. Those plans included a proposal to repeal the March 2000 law establishing the Capital District and to resurrect the traditional system of a president-appointed governor for a restored Federal District (which would include the entire Capital District). Some of President Chávez's hard-line supporters, such as National Assembly president Cecilia Flores, advised the president to use the extraordinary powers he had received under the January 31, 2007, grant of "Enablement" (Ley Habilitante) to impose the system of governance for metropolitan Caracas that had been envisioned in the defeated referendum. Moderates in the Chavista movement argued otherwise. They favored the nomination of Aristóbulo Istúriz, the respected former mayor of the Libertador District, for the office of *alcalde mayor* in the elections for mayors and governors scheduled for November 23, 2008. The moderates believed that with a loyal and competent *alcalde mayor* President Chávez could introduce legislation into the National Assembly that would eliminate duplication between the functions of the *alcaldía mayor* and the component municipalities of the Capital District (Libertador, Chacao, Baruta, El Hatillo, and Petare). Moderates, however, agreed with hard-liners that it was time to end what the urbanist Andrew Nixon (1995, 95) had described as the most politically fragmented urban government in all of Latin America.

EXPLAINING THE METROPOLITAN PUZZLE AND THE LACK OF METROPOLITAN GOVERNANCE

Our comparison of political institutions in the urban agglomerations of Barquisimeto, Maracaibo, and Caracas provides several clues as to why there is only one urban region in Venezuela in which metropolitan political institutions have developed: Greater Caracas. The experience of Barquisimeto is typical of urban *municipios* with populations of between fifty thousand and five hundred thousand, even though in this particular case the city is much larger (over one million), and has no ostensible need for a metropolitan tier of government given that the urban areas, while often large, are contained within a single municipality. The situation of Maracaibo's urban region is more indicative of the barriers that have often prevented the development of metropolitan institutions in places like Barcelona-Puerto La Cruz and Valencia, urban agglomerations, with populations of between nine hundred thousand and two million, where partisan political shenanigans have distracted from any serious attempts to foster intermunicipal collaboration or metropolitan governance. Caracas, of course is unique, but ironically some of the conditions that prevented metropolitan governance in the interior have in fact facilitated its emergence in the capital city's urban region, albeit a rather roller-coaster and intensively politically driven process.

There are at least five reasons why metropolitan political institutions have not developed in Venezuelan urban regions outside Caracas. First, until 1980 few urban built environments outside Caracas extended beyond the territorial boundaries of the large geographical units of local government *(distritos)* created by the Andeans in 1904. Second, the centralist tradition in Venezuelan political culture led political leaders to rely primarily on the national government to resolve problems involving the provision of diverse services (water, education, and electricity) and to take primary responsibility for developing important urban infrastructure. Local governments received the larger part of their budgets from the national government and concerned themselves with secondary services: operating public markets, repairing streets, fighting fires, and collecting garbage. In cases where urban growth made it difficult for local governments to provide secondary services, state governments often stepped in and facilitated the delivery of secondary services.

The Venezuelan government's petroleum income is the third reason why metropolitan governments did not emerge in Venezuela. National bureaucracies received the lion's share of this income, allowing them to allocate resources in ways that gave their local offices the capability to act as de facto metropolitan institutions in any urban agglomeration that extended over multiple *municipios.* Only in times when petroleum income declined did central government bureaucrats express interest in decentralizing powers that would allow *municipio* officials to explore the desirability of crafting metropolitan political institutions, Fourth, in the 1990s, following decentralization reforms in 1989 and 1990, *municipio* governments and politicians devoted much of their energy toward pressuring the central government to hand over in practice the powers that it was required by law to relinquish. The issue of thinking about and creating metropolitan-wide institutions remained on the back burner. Fifth, the Bolivarian Revolution was hierarchical at its core. President Chávez began to recentralize before the newly empowered local governments (the fruit of the decentralization reforms) experienced the frustrations that often accompany the spillover of urban built environments outside the territorial unit within which a city originated.

In an unusual twist of fate, some of the factors that hindered the growth of metropolitan political institutions in secondary cities actively supported their advancement in Caracas. Most important was the desire to maintain central control. Following the death of General Juan Vicente Gómez, once the built environment of Caracas began to spill out beyond the Federal District, the national executive adjusted territorial units in the Caracas region in ways that would ensure continued control by the president. As we have observed, this included creating a special unified *distrito* in eastern Caracas (the Sucre District), giving the metropolitan police force (controlled by the Federal District governor) authority within Sucre District, and by creating a national bureaucracy (the Simon Bolivar Center) to control urban renewal. The breakup of the expanded Sucre District and elimination of the metropolitan planning office were unanticipated consequences of the 1989 decentralization reforms, but the fragmentation also led to the 1999 law that created the Capital District with a popularly elected *alcalde mayor* and metropolitan council.[15] The 1999 law, however, failed to delineate responsibilities between institutions in the Capital District and its component municipalities; thus confused and overlapping institutional responsibility made effective government in the Caracas region all but impossible and further complicated the national government's capacity to control the capital city. This is an important explanation for why President Chávez has often ignored or unilaterally interpreted the law when exercising power in the Capital District.

THE POLITICS OF VENEZUELAN FEDERALISM

Reforms in Venezuelan local government have taken place in the aftermath of major changes in national politics, and only by contextualizing those politics can one begin to understand local government reform in Venezuela. In this section we will look at how the dominant elites in each period have viewed the shaping of local government as an essential part of their reconstituting of the national political order and, as a result, how local government reform has been the cannon fodder of politics and political conflict in Venezuela. For more than a century Venezuelans have shown interest in decentralization, experimented with territorial reorganization, and tinkered with municipal political institutions. Local interests sought increased autonomy and in the process battled Caracas-based elites who were determined to retain control over cities located in the interior. These conflicts gave rise to important municipal reforms on no fewer than four occasions: the first, following the seizure of power by the Andeans in 1899, ending in 1904 when President Cipriano Castro created the *distritos;* the second, after the overthrow of General Pérez Jiménez in 1958 and the consolidation of the regime under the Punto Fijo in the 1970s; the third, during the decentralization reforms nine months after the urban rioting that rocked ten cities during late February 1989; and most recently, during the wave of national political changes that altered city governments in 1999, after President Chávez convinced voters to approve the constitution that established the so-called Fifth Republic.

Dependent Institutions as a Means to National and Regional Control

In colonial Venezuela there was a tradition of limited local autonomy and participation that carried over into the postindependence period. Before long, however, civil strife between regional and local elites ushered in decades of chaos. Early in the twentieth century Andean chieftains gained national power and institutionalized their dominance in the Constitution of 1902. Territorial reorganization legislation, passed in 1904, created the "district" *(distrito)* as the basic geopolitical unit of local government. Districts functioned as administrative subdivisions of the central government.

Abandonment of the more traditional term *municipality (municipio)* reflected the Andeans' resolve to end the tradition of local notables rebelling against central authority. The *distritos* were geographically extensive, similar to counties in the United States of America. They often subsumed one or more urban settlements and the surrounding countryside. Their boundaries could be modified only by the central government. Not until the 1989 Organic Law of Municipal Reforms entered into force were the 1904 boundaries of local territorial units changed. During this period Venezuela had become overwhelmingly urban. The population mushroomed from 2.7 million to 20 million,[16] and military dictatorships gave way to representative democracy.

The Constitutions of 1947, 1953, and 1961 contained language that suggested some interest in increasing the autonomy of local governments. In each a chapter enumerated the powers of local governments and bestowed an autonomous juridical personality on local territorial units. However, the governments that operated under the Constitutions of 1948 and 1953 failed to draft legislation that reorganized district governments. Under the Constitution of 1961 the first halting efforts to reform local government were postponed until 1978. This was because of the precarious hold on power by recently installed democratic elites and the lack of a consensus on how local government should be reformed and territorial boundaries redrawn. Some post-1961 leaders hoped to empower local government, while others favored retaining local governments as administrative dependencies of the national executive (Carrasquero and Hanes de Acevedo 1993, 7).

The Slow March to Misguided Reform

Political conspiracies by rightists, as well as the insurgency mounted by leftists, threatened Punto Fijo democracy during the first fifteen years that the Constitution of 1961 was in force. The perception of being under siege led newly ensconced liberal democratic elites to delay plans for empowering local governments. Leaders of the then-dominant AD and COPEI political parties feared that empowered local officials, if they belonged to the disloyal opposition, would use municipal offices to derail the consolidation of the Punto Fijo regime. However, in the presidential election of 1972 almost 90 percent of voters opted for the presidential candidates of the two establishment political parties. Within the next two years all significant insurgent groups laid down their arms and agreed to seek power through peaceful means. This convinced Punto Fijo elites that their political regime was secure enough to consider empowering local governments (Myers 2005, 20–24).

In 1978 Congress passed the first comprehensive municipal reform legislation since 1904 (Carrasquero and Hanes de Acevedo 1993, 6–7) and provided for separate municipal elections. Until then *distrito* council members had been elected on the same party list as senators, congresspeople, and state legislators. The 1978 reforms also increased local government responsibilities and created the nonpartisan office of city manager. Advocates of the city manager approach hoped that these reforms would reduce partisan politics, increase local participation in municipal government, and embed professionalism in service delivery policy. In practice, neither the AD nor the COPEI surrendered its central control over local government. Caracas-based party leaders continued to dispense patronage in the districts and marginalized the nonpartisan city manager (Martínez 1986, 388–400). This overriding of the spirit and letter of the

1978 municipal reforms stoked the fires of discontent with centralization and party control.

President Jaime Lusinchi (1984–89) concentrated power in the national executive to a greater extent than any government since the transitional Betancourt administration (1959–64). This policy derived from a decline in petroleum revenue that decreased the national executive's willingness to share resource allocation decision making with regional and local leaders. Lusinchi appointed the local secretary generals of his AD Party as governors in most of the states. Party and government control, working in tandem from Caracas, made it even easier to marginalize the theoretically empowered city managers. Still, national government revenue was insufficient to operate quality public services or maintain the physical infrastructure. President Lusinchi was forced to use the rainy day fund (established during the earlier petro-bonanza) to prevent a recession during the 1988 presidential election campaign.

Urban Violence: A Trigger for Meaningful Reform

In the December 1988 presidential election, the AD's Carlos Andrés Pérez (1989–93) defeated Eduardo Fernández of the COPEI and Teodoro Petkoff of the Movement toward Socialism Party (MAS). During the election campaign Pérez and Fernández promised to undo the dysfunctional local government reforms of 1978 and carry out meaningful decentralization. Both believed that by transferring responsibilities to the *distritos* (as well as to the regional governments) they could defuse the anger toward the central government that had intensified under President Lusinchi. President-elect Pérez considered that new taxes were inevitable if public services such as transportation, water, and hospitals were to be updated.[17] He also believed that empowered local governments would be in a stronger position to impose those taxes than the national government, and Eduardo Fernández concurred. Thus the preferences of the two major presidential contenders in the 1988 election coincided with those of the middle-class reformers who believed that strengthening the *distritos* would deepen democracy.

The newly inaugurated president was confronted with declining government revenue from petroleum, minimal foreign exchange reserves, and an exhausted rainy day fund. He attempted to deal with the financial crisis by borrowing from the International Monetary Fund and pricing public services, especially transportation, at their real cost. Increased bus fares and gasoline prices led to the previously noted urban rioting on

February 28, 1989. President Pérez responded by rescinding the increases and experimenting with a different strategy: privatization. The riots also provided leverage for advocates of decentralization to force Congress to pass meaningful decentralization legislation, including municipal empowerment (De la Cruz 2005, 181–82).

The 1989 Organic Law of the Municipal Regime (Ley Orgánica de Régimen Municipal) sought to empower local politicians rather than replace them with nonpartisan professional managers, as had been the case in 1978.[18] The 1989 reforms established the office of a popularly elected mayor and created elected municipal councils of between five and sixteen members (depending upon the population of the *municipio*). It also broadened the tax base for raising municipal revenues and increased the influence of neighborhood legislative bodies, known as *juntas parroquiales* (parish councils). Reformers hoped that the empowered *juntas parroquiales* would deepen citizen participation in the neighborhoods and increase the responsiveness of municipal institutions. The 1989 reforms also changed the term *district (distrito)* to *municipality (municipio)* and transferred the power to change *municipio* boundaries from the central government to the states. Reformers believed that the 1989 "Organic Law of Municipalities" would arrest declining support for Punto Fijo democracy.

Important elements inside the AD and the COPEI opposed political decentralization. They feared that the strengthening of local and regional governments would weaken the political parties and make effective governance more difficult. The leaders of party factions opposed to decentralization maneuvered to circumvent the 1989 Organic Law of Municipalities from the moment it entered into force. Events in 1992 and 1993 (two unsuccessful military coups, President Pérez's removal from office, and the unseating of Eduardo Fernández in the COPEI) reduced the power and influence of those supporting municipal empowerment. With the election of Rafael Caldera to a second presidency (1994–99), the forces favoring centralism regained much of the ground that had been lost during the government of Carlos Andrés Pérez and the interim presidency of Ramón Velásquez (May 1993–February 1994).[19] President Caldera allocated resources in the urban municipalities through the local offices of his national ministries, often ignoring provisions of the 1989 decentralization legislation (Gil Yepes 2004, 238–39). Few of his supporters controlled big-city mayoralties or municipal councils, and he had no intention of building up his opponents. At the end of the Punto Fijo period (in February 1999), mayors and municipal councils enjoyed more power and influence than at the beginning (1959), but their gains were less than the reformers intended.

The Fifth Republic: The Politics of Frustrated Urban Reform

Like Rafael Caldera, President Hugo Chávez Frías believed that empowering the *municipios* had been a mistake and ignored important provisions of the 1989 reforms. Chávez's control of the legislative and judicial branches of government ensured that challenges to his resource allocation policy from *municipio* governments would fall on deaf ears. Elections in 2000 gave control of the National Assembly to Chávez's supporters by a narrow margin. Five years later, after a string of electoral defeats, opponents of President Chávez claimed that he had so tilted the electoral playing field as to make fair elections impossible. Thus opposition political parties boycotted the elections for National Assembly that took place on December 4, 2005. President Chavez's Fifth Republic Movement (Movimiento Quinto República — MVR) and its allies won all 167 seats. During the lead-up to the National Assembly elections, the Assembly passed reforms intended to reorganize local governments so that they could relate better to the *Misiones* and Bolivarian Circles, the latter being the highly organized cells of Chávez supporters in the barrios and shantytowns. However, even as the National Assembly debated municipal reform President Chávez was already imposing a new kind of local government institution, the communal council (Maigon 2007; U. Castro 2007). He envisioned these councils as gradually replacing traditional urban government institutions: the mayoralties, municipal councils, and *juntas parroqiales* (neighborhood councils). Between 2004 and 2007 the government established thirty thousand communal councils, and in some urban regions councils of communal councils began evolving into proto-metropolitan governments (Radio Nacional de Venezuela 2007).

The option of communal councils did not enter the debates of the Constituent Assembly that drafted the 1999 Constitution. That constitution left the 1989 Organic Law of the Municipalities in place. Elections for mayors and municipal councils were held in 2000, 2004, and 2005.[20] The megaelections of July 31, 2000, the first under the 1999 Constitution, gave President Chávez's supporters control over roughly 40 percent of the municipalities, including the newly created metropolitan district of Caracas.[21] Even then President Chávez was undermining local and neighborhood political institutions controlled by the opposition. Between 1999 and 2002 he used local military commanders to allocate funds for many public services, which under the 1989 Organic Law of the Municipalities should have been the province of *municipio* governments. In the shantytowns *(ranchos)* of the large cities, as noted earlier, supporters of President Chávez organized Bolivarian Circles—*Círculos Bolivarianos* (Hawkins and Hansen 2006). The Bolivarian Circles received funding from the central government and provided social services and job training. Circle administrators also kept records on the political attitudes of their neighbors.

After the unsuccessful military coup of April 11–13, 2002, President Chávez's trust in the military plummeted. He began to establish a variety of centrally controlled "Missions" that allocated resources in urban neighborhoods (Penfold Becerra 2007). Each Mission focused on a specific service, such as education, health care, nutrition, or housing. These Missions appeared in the midst of an intensive campaign by middle-class opponents of President Chávez to remove him from office, first through massive demonstrations and subsequently by means of a recall referendum. The Missions allowed the president to dispense patronage directly, rather than through established municipal governments, the majority of which at that time were in opposition hands.

To increase voter participation, the central government established Misión Identidad (Mission Identity), which coordinated with the newly created Ayacucho Command (Comando Ayacucho), itself a pivotal institution of the Chavista political party (MVR) for opposing the recall of President Chávez. In early 2004 the Comando Ayacucho failed to defeat opposition efforts to collect enough signatures to hold the recall election, and Chávez replaced it with the Maisanta Command (Comando Maisanta), which was tied directly to the president and was coordinated more effectively with the Missions than had the Ayacucho Command. The cumulative impact of dispensing patronage through the Missions and mobilizing the president's supporters through the Maisanta Command goes a long way to explain President Chávez's victory in the August 2004 recall referendum.

On October 31, 2004, local and regional elections placed 80 percent of the mayoralties in the hands of government supporters. Six months later, as we have seen, the National Assembly passed a new Organic Law of Municipal Power that, the deputies intended, would streamline linkages between the *municipios*, the national ministries, and the presidential Missions. The 2005 Organic Law of Municipal Powers also envisioned the creation of metropolitan districts at locations where elected officials in neighboring *municipios* decided that metropolitanization would increase the efficiency of service delivery and citizen participation. This law represented the thinking on municipal reform of the National Assembly's Chavista majority. However, no metropolitan governments were established, and implementation of the Organic Law of Municipal Powers itself was delayed. After December 4, 2005, when the president's allies won all of the seats in the National Assembly, his interest in local political reform moved in a new direction — the expansion and empowerment of the communal councils.

The presidential election campaign of 2006 became a vehicle for communal council empowerment. President Chávez expected to win the December 3 elections by a substantial majority, and he used campaign propaganda to prepare Venezuelans for the transformation to the twenty-first-century socialism that he was planning, in which communal councils were to play an important role. Thus, on March 2, 2006, the Chavista-dominated National Assembly passed the Ley de los Consejos Comunales (Law of Communal Councils) which described communal councils as the institutions that would facilitate participation in local governance. They were to replace the *juntas parroquiales* (created by the 1989 municipal reforms) but not the mayors or the municipal councils. Over time, however, the communal councils were expected to assume many responsibilities of local government, thereby rendering mayors and municipal councils irrelevant.[22] After all, *consejos comunales* already existed in the *ranchos* of Caracas, Maracaibo, and the other million-plus cities. Additional councils appeared in middle-class neighborhoods, and by the second half of 2006 the *consejos comunales* had absorbed most of the Bolivarian Circles.

There has been a great deal of trial and error in crafting the role that *consejos comunales* will play in local government (Ellner 2009). By law they are tasked to monitor and coordinate projects that deal with health, education, sports, housing, security, food, and other similar matters. Each council also has a section for security and defense (*mesa de seguridad y la defensa*) that interacts with the national military reserve forces.[23] The Chavistas claim that in each neighborhood individuals interested in participating in local policy making have come forward voluntarily to organize *consejos comunales*. It is common knowledge, however, that the National Ministry of Communes has played an important role in this process. In the few *municipios* not controlled by the government, such as Chacao and Baruta in the Capital District, the mayor's office has organized *consejos comunales,* and not surprisingly, perhaps, these councils have experienced difficulties in obtaining resources for their projects from the presidential

Missions and the National Ministry of Communes. Also, in many neighborhoods where opposition-dominated councils exist the Chavistas have organized rival councils that are under their control;[24] these subsequently tend to enjoy greater success in having their projects funded by the presidential *Misiones*.

Prioritizing the imposition of communal councils did not blind President Chávez to the importance of centralizing control over Caracas. In his January 31, 2007, speech discussing the changes he intended to make under the "Enabling Law" (Ley Habilitante), he mentioned the Capital District of Caracas, constitutionally mandated but never created, and described the political infrastructure of the metropolitan district of Caracas as confusing and in need of change.[25] Deliberations among Chavistas over what political institutions would be most appropriate for the new socialist state's capital region, as indicated earlier, proceeded behind closed doors, although on occasion differences became public. President Chávez eventually sided with moderates in the PSUV who favored nominating Aristóbulo Istúriz as their candidate for *alcalde mayor*. They believed that Istúriz would be elected and would open the doors to crafting a strong and loyal *alcaldía mayor* (metropolitan municipal government) that could facilitate political participation and administer the five *municipios* of metropolitan Caracas. It came as a shock when another former mayor of the Libertador *municipio*, Antonio Ledezma, defeated Istúriz by a comfortable margin. In addition, the opposition captured mayoralties in four of the five *municipios* of the Capital District. The exception, Libertador (also known as the Capital District), was the largest and most important. Voters chose Jorge Rodríguez, one the president's closest collaborators, to be mayor of Libertador.

President Chávez was not about to repeat the conditions of 2000 and 2004 when Alcalde Mayor Alfredo Peña's hostility to the national government allowed demonstrators to create conditions that led to the *golpe del estado* of April 11–13, 2002, that briefly ousted the president. Chávez refused to transfer effective control of the metropolitan Caracas *alcaldía* to Antonio Ledezma. The outgoing *alcalde mayor*, Juan Barreto (2004–8), a Chavista, left the building (El Palacio Metropolitano) from which he governed in disarray. On December 29, 2008, armed groups appeared in front of El Palacio Metropolitano, occupied the building, and refused entrance to Ledezma and his appointees. The newly elected *alcalde mayor* attempted to govern from improvised offices but lacked funds and records. In the meantime supporters of President Chávez took over other buildings from which other activities of the *alcaldía mayor* had been conducted. Paralysis and confusion lasted for four months.

On April 7, 2009, the National Assembly passed the Organic Law of the Capital District, submitted by President Chávez. This legislation essentially restored local government as it had existed in the Federal District prior to 1999 and reassigned the Palicio Metropolitano from the *alcaldía mayor* to the newly created Capital District government. This government would be presided over by a presidentially appointed "head of state," who would be the central government authority in the Capital District (Libertador Department). President Chávez named as head of state of the Capital District Jacqueline Faría, a vice president of the PSUV and president of Movilnet (the cell phone division of the national telephone and communications company CANTV). The organic law limited Faría's authority in the Capital District, but in practice President Chávez has extended it to other activities that previously fell within the province of the *alcaldía mayoria,* such as firefighting and sanitation. Municipal schools were transferred by presidential decree to the national Ministry of Education. Reorganization of local government in metropolitan Caracas remains a work in progress. It is unclear which activities will continue to reside with the municipal governments of Libertador, Chacao, Baruta, El Hatillo, and Petare, and which ones President Chávez will transfer to the government of the Capital District. In the meantime, Superior Mayor Antonio Ledezma remains as the chief executive of a metropolitan area government with no physical location from which to conduct business, no clearly defined responsibilities, and almost no budget.[26] The Organic Law of Metropolitan Caracas requires its component *municipios* to transfer 10 percent of their budgets to the *alcaldía mayor.*

Metropolitan Governance in Venezuela: Status and Prospects

Venezuelan politics appeared to have passed a tipping point in the first half of 2009. President Chávez's success in having term limits removed through referendum (on February 15) increased the probability that he would rule Venezuela for the foreseeable future. This enhancement led the president to quicken the pace of transformation into "twenty-first-century socialism." In June and July of 2009, he increased his control over the military and submitted bills to the National Assembly that would reduce the autonomy of regional governments, regulate freedom of the press, and embed central government officials in schools and universities to ensure that students received a favorable view of the Bolivarian political regime and its ideology. Also, for the past four years, acting under authority granted to him by the Ley Habilitante of January 31, 2007, President Chávez began to augment the powers of the communal councils and the *Missiones* at the expense of mayors and municipal councils. The ability of Venezuelan governments to implement changes of this magnitude has long depended on the stream of revenue provided by the sale of petroleum on the international market. This stream declined by almost half in 2009. However, even if the global recession responsible for this lower level of income persists and threatens the central government's capability to implement policy, President Chávez can draw upon international reserves of more than $31 billion. This suggests that financial constraints will not slow his efforts to reshape local political authority and increase control from Caracas.

In terms of Venezuela's prospects for metropolitan governance, the situation in early 2008 was bleaker than it had been in 1999, at the beginning of the Chávez era. There was almost no likelihood that in the near future political elites would create metropolitan institutions, except possibly in the case of Caracas. The built environments of Barquisimeto and most cities of between one hundred thousand and seven hundred thousand were encased in a single *municipio,* and for them metropolitan governance offered no obvious advantage. Greater Maracaibo and other large urban agglomerations (Valencia, Maracay, and Barcelona-Puerto La Cruz) had spilled over into several surrounding *municipios,* but on the basis of past experience they could be expected to make do within existing municipal political institutions. There appeared to be little incentive to increase the capabilities of *municipio* governments, especially since there was a significant possibility that these would be replaced by communal councils or councils of communal councils with authority that would spill beyond the boundaries of existing *municipios.*

The process of institutionalizing communal councils does seem to be paving the way for councils of communal councils. Organizational meetings of councils of communal councils have been reported in the metropolitan regions of Caracas, Valencia, and Barcelona-Puerto La Cruz. As of mid-2012 they have not given rise to permanent political institutions. Nevertheless, the councils of communal councils have the potential to become institutions that coordinate political participation and service delivery within Venezuela's conurban regions, especially those that revolve about the million-plus cities. If this occurs they will attract interest as a new form of metropolitan government.

Finally, in Caracas there is a strong possibility that the confusing mix of political institutions will be modified to further increase control by the national government. Opponents and supporters of President Chávez agree that the mix of local governments with overlapping powers that the 2000 Organic Law of the Metropolitan District of Caracas and 2009 Organic Law of the Capital District created is both confusing and inefficient. These laws have not increased political participation or improved service delivery. In 2009 President Chávez made progress toward his goal of consolidating central government control over metropolitan Caracas. This illustrates that the fate of local government in the Caracas region, and for that matter in all of Venezuela, is tied closely to national politics. Over the past three years President Chávez has continued to undermine proponents of decentralization and the empowerment of local government. He has expanded the centrally controlled *Missiones,* increased the number of communal councils, and experimented with institutions that blur the boundaries between *municipios* and regional political institutions (the Venezuelan states). These policies have intensified in the run-up to the October 2012 presidential elections, although the fate of the entire Chávez experiment has become uncertain because of the president's battle with an aggressive cancer that may incapacitate him or end his life. Should this take place, the subnational institutions likely will regain much of their power, and the growth of Venezuelan cities may resurrect interest in metropolitan government. On the other hand, if President Chavez's health returns or if he is succeeded by a militantly socialist leader, the prospects for metropolitan government in Venezuela, at least as it is known in other countries of the Americas, are dim indeed.

NOTES

1. Gran Colombia, the former colonial viceroyalty of Nueva Granada, gained its independence from Spain in 1823. Regional rivalries led to the breakup of Gran Colombia, which evolved into the countries of Ecuador, Colombia, and Venezuela.

2. During the Punto Fijo period (1959–99), until the decentralization reforms of 1989, the federal republic of Venezuela was organized into twenty states, a federal district, two territories, and seventy-two islands. The most important critical unit of territorial organization within each state was the *distrito.* There were 185 distritos, between eight and twelve in each state.

3. The Capital District or Distrito Capital encompasses western Caracas, what was once known as the Libertador Department of the Federal District, and the *municipios* (Chacao, Sucre, Baruta, and El Hatillo) of the 1936 expanded Sucre District.

4. Over the past decade several municipalities have been divided to create new units of local government. For example, in 1992, there were only 282 municipalities.

5. The acronym COPEI stands for Comité de Organización Política Electoral Independiente.

6. The 1961 Constitution mandated the channeling of 15 percent of the national budget into grants in aid for subnational units, the *situado*. The *situado* was distributed as follows: 30 percent in equal amounts among the states and 70 percent in proportion to each state's population. The states, in turn, distributed the *situado* amount to the municipal councils of the *distritos*.

7. Miguel Romero, interview by author, July 18, 1978. Romero was the AD governor of the state of Lara during the government of President Raul Leoni (1965–69).

8. The efforts to establish communal councils are discussed later in this chapter.

9. George Hall, Creole Petroleum executive, interview by author, February 17, 1968.

10. Jose Molina, Professor Emeritus of Political Science, University of Zulia, interview by author, May 11, 2007.

11. Violich (1987, 134) claims that the principal road connecting Caracas to La Guaira until the early 1950s contains 365 curves—one for each day of the year.

12. The southeastern zone of metropolitan Caracas is hilly, but there is a great deal of tableland suitable for housing and other construction. Morris (1978, 308) reports that by 1950 the area of reasonably flat land in the Caracas Valley was entirely occupied.

13. After 1981 the "outer six" *municipios* surrounding the Capital District grew rapidly. As of 2006 they boasted a population of one million and functionally have become part of greater Caracas. Members of all classes inhabit these six *municipios,* and they even retain pockets where peasant settlements predominate. More than residents in Baruta, Chacao, El Hatillo, and Sucre, those of Carrizal, Los Salias, Plaza, Zamora, Cristóbal Rojas, and Guaicaipuro look to the state government of Miranda for services. Urbanization throughout this periphery occurred so rapidly and recently that the zone's six local governments have been stretched beyond their administrative and economic capabilities. Overall, less is known about the exercise of power and influence in the outer six *municipios* than about other territorial units in the Capital Region.

14. The sequence of events is complicated. Initially Peña ran as a supporter of President Chávez, but within a year he had become one of the president's

most intractable opponents. For a more complete discussion, see Ellner and Myers (2002, 122–25).

15. At the Constituent Assembly in August 1999, former Caracas mayor (Libertador Department) Aristóbulo Istúriz presented the president's plan. Istúriz called for unification of the most densely populated core of the capital region (the municipalities of Libertador, Chacao, Baruta, Sucre, and El Hatillo) within a metropolitan district of the city of Caracas. He also proposed the creation of an elected superior mayor *(alcalde mayor)* and legislative council for the district. This meant abolishing the office of Federal District governor, a presidential appointment. The dependencies of the governor's office were to be transferred to the *alcaldía mayor.* President Chávez intervened personally in the debate when he stated that Caracas residents should vote in a referendum on this plan and that no individual *municipio* should have a veto in the matter.

16. The official *Handbook of Venezuela* for 1904 estimated the population for the preceding year at 2,663,671.

17. Carlos Andrés Pérez, interview by author, January 31, 1989.

18. Organic Laws have greater force and are more difficult to modify than normal laws. They stand midway between ordinary legislation and constitutional provisions.

19. Ramón Velásquez served as interim president between the impeachment of Carlos Andrés Pérez and the inauguration of Rafael Caldera. Under the powers that he was granted, Velásquez decreed a number of decentralization reforms that had been proposed by Pérez but were held up in Congress by the acrimony that accompanied his removal from office.

20. The elections for mayors were included in the July 31, 2000, megaelections. Elections for municipal councils and *juntas parroquiales* occurred on December 5, 2000.

21. The special law on the regime of the Capital District, envisioned in article 18 of the 1999 Constitution, was intended to provide unified metropolitan government for Caracas. Clashes over the territorial integrity of Miranda State so inflamed the Constituent Assembly that this legislation was never approved. Instead, on May 8, 2000, the National Constituent Assembly issued a special law on the regime of the metropolitan district of Caracas.

22. *El Nacional* reported on February 4, 2007, that the *consejo comunal* of the "El Amparo de Catia" neighborhood in Caracas's Capital District formally questioned the need for the office of metropolitan mayor *(alcaldía metropolitana).*

23. *El Universal,* May 18, 2007.

24. Leopoldo López Gil, mayor of Chacao, interview by author, May 25, 2007.

25. *El Universal,* February 1, 2007.

26. During the administration of Juan Barreto (2004–8) the central government transferred most of the *situado constitucional* (funds mandated by the Constitution for allocation to regional governments) intended for the population

of the metropolitan district of Caracas to the *alcaldía mayor.* After passage of the Organic Law of the Capital District these funds were allocated to the government of the Capital District. Thus the only funds available to Alcaldía Mayor Antonio Ledisma came from *municipios* of Metropolitan Caracas. The Organic Law of Metropolitan Caracas requires its component *municipios* to transfer 10 percent of their budgets to the *alcaldía mayor,* but this accounted for less than 8 percent of the *alcaldía*'s budget during the administration of Juan Barreto.

Chapter 8

Directions and Dynamics of Change, and the Prospects for Metropolitan Governance in the Americas

PETER M. WARD, ROBERT H. WILSON,
AND PETER K. SPINK

Our study has investigated metropolitan governance in federalist countries in the Americas. To put it simply, we find that while the policy issues of metropolitan areas are a common concern in all the six countries and engage considerable academic, technical, and political discussion, the overarching challenge to construct effective governance mechanisms for collective action is far from being resolved. The evidence from our case studies suggests that, in general, creating a new architecture of metropolitan government and governance to address these issues is, unfortunately, not a high priority either for those with the reach to bring it about or for those who may be able to bring the necessary pressure to bear.

The central question of this study has been to determine whether current and emerging initiatives and structures of governance can meet the challenges of collective life in large and complex metropolitan areas. In the absence of any significant attempts to create an overarching architecture of metropolitan governance and structure, we do observe some important midlevel metropolitan practice across, and within, the six federalist countries analyzed in the preceding chapters. In most cases we would characterize these practices as disjointed, fragmented, and largely unconnected experiments. Nevertheless, we did find variation in the frequency of initiatives across the countries and by policy area (discussed further below) and even regional variation of metropolitan initiatives within a single country. We also found that many of the factors outlined a priori in chapter 1—constitutional and governmental structures; jurisdictional geographies; technical and organizational characteristics of service delivery systems; political systems and the practice of politics; and demographic and civic pressures—appear to help explain the types of variation observed across our case studies. When the powers of local government are weak in terms of constitutionally defined authority, administrative capacity, or political legitimacy, then metropolitan collaboration is not likely to emerge. But the exercise of constitutionally defined powers of state or provincial governments in some countries was found to have a quite positive effect on the emergence of metropolitan forms—a point to which we return below. In contrast, subnational political systems tend to retard the emergence of metropolitan initiatives in all countries.

Progress toward reform and the forging of new and more effective structures of metropolitan governance is hindered for many reasons. We find lack of interest on the part of politicians and political parties; power plays and personal agendas of national leaders; low incentives for technical staff whose careers are often linked to existing state, county, or municipal jurisdictions; inadequate financing and fiscal structures that would provide for greater redistribution of resources across the metropolitan space; and the important fact that most people appear to prefer their governments to be smaller, not larger. To the extent that the latter is true, the principal challenge is one of successfully scaling up or down people's identification with and participation in both the local and the metropolitan levels.

Here we return to the specific research questions that we identified in chapter 1, namely: (1) What are the key characteristics of the institutional and organizational forms and the policy issues addressed by these metropolitan initiatives? (2) What factors shape the emergence and dynamics of these metropolitan-based systems? and (3) Are these initiatives offering genuine opportunities for democratic governance, creating and ensuring the necessary incentives for citizens to participate, and thereby acquiring political legitimacy? Later in this concluding chapter we will evaluate these findings to identify other important—but largely unanswered—questions and to develop a research agenda for future work. But we also wish to speak to policy communities and to share expectations developed by this project on how the practice of metropolitan governance might evolve. As we have consistently pointed out, the importance of metropolitan governance for national development is considerable, as is the moral requirement to urgently improve and sustain the quality of life of many metropolitan citizens. We incorporate the lessons learned from our studies to define a set of possible pathways for the emergence of metropolitan initiatives. If our study were to be allowed only one conclusion, it would be that of the urgency of placing metropolitan governance on the wider national agenda of the day. As we argue, we hope these possible pathways can contribute to policy conversations about the metropolitan question in coming decades.

Answering the Research Questions

We adopted a comparative case study methodology in which countries rather than individual cities were the units of analysis. Before we turn to the specific research questions, several observations arise in the comparison of the country experiences that help to remind us of national differences, while also allowing for a preliminary grouping of the different countries and their experiences. First, in terms of policy foci and outcomes, we see significant variation in the frequency of occurrence of metropolitan initiatives across the principal policy areas in which we found activity and across the countries (see table 8.1). The concept of subsidiarity put forward in European discussions about multilevel governance is not used in policy discussions in the Americas, but the frequent use of metropolitan initiatives for major infrastructure systems indicated in table 8.1, such as public transportation and water and wastewater systems, reflects the subsidiarity principle: that is, assignment of functions to levels of government should follow the unique production and service requirements of each service, a topic that will be discussed in more detail below.

We find a continuum across countries, Canada and the United States being at one end with strong local governments and the most extensive experience with metropolitan initiatives (see table 8.1). In the midrange we find Brazil and, to a lesser degree, Mexico, where local governments are developing capacity and authority. At the other end of the continuum, municipal governments in Argentina and Venezuela are relatively weak and, in the case of Venezuela, are even being weakened as a process of centralization is under way. There is very limited experience with metropolitan initiatives in either of these two countries.

Table 8.1. Frequencies of Metropolitan Initiatives by Policy Focus and by Country

	Argentina	Brazil	Canada	Mexico	Venezuela	USA
Public transportation		■	■	■	■	▪
Highways and streets		■				■
Water and wastewater systems	▪	▪	■	■	■	▪
Solid waste management	■	▪	▪	▪		▪
Land use and regional planning	■	▪	■	▪	▪	▪
Environmental protection/ growth management	▪	▪	▪		▪	▪
Emergency services (fire and medical)						■
Public security				▪	▪ᵃ	
Employment and job training						■
Health		▪			▪ᵃ	■
Education						■
Social welfare and services						■
Housing		■				

Key: ■ Important and frequently found policy arena organized at the metropolitan level.

▪ Occasional policy arena organized at the metropolitan level.

a. Caracas in 2008.

In the undertaking of metropolitan initiatives, the roles played by state and provincial governments reflect distinct variations in federalist practices across the six countries. State-driven government and governance construction lead to unitary-type structures within states and provinces, such as those that sometimes occur in Canada (through annexation and consolidation), or to the multiple, raftlike arrangements of local governments that we see in the United States. In all other countries, the federal government has a greater role in defining authority and resources in municipal government, albeit loosely and without any apparent plan for where it expects metropolitan government to lead. In Venezuela the overarching federalist project is one of political control, especially in the capital city, while in Brazil there has been an initial federal and a later state-mandated blueprint for metropolitan regions, but beyond that the practice of intergovernmental relations and collaboration remains in doubt. In Mexico and Argentina, we observe state and provincial governments exerting their authority in the federalist pact, to the detriment, or neglect, of the constituent municipal governments.

As we provide a summary overview of the individual chapters (see table 8.2), we recall that in Canada significant experiences of metropolitan initiatives vary in presence and form across provinces and are in part, at least, a result of variations in political culture. In the United States many metropolitan initiatives are mainly created on an ad hoc basis in which technical and nonpolitical collaboration is most common. In part this is due to a political culture that affirms local control, making geographically broader and more systematic arrangements difficult to achieve. As in Canada, core-suburban conflicts impede metropolitan initiatives in the United States, particularly in the area of redistributive policies.

Brazil has numerous important initiatives in which intermunicipal consortia are increasingly present. Constitutional powers have strengthened local government, but municipalities are still in part dependent on state and federal transfers. So far, though, state governments tend to be the weak partners in metropolitan initiatives. In Mexico metropolitan initiatives are relatively uncommon but are on the increase, and the strengthening of municipal governments remains an incomplete project. Jurisdictional geography seems to play an important role in explaining the infrequency of initiatives, but also political competition between and among parties creates pressures for local leaders to demonstrate policy and institutional effectiveness, and this usually works against collaboration.

In Argentina, municipalities are weak in terms of authority and resources, and there are relatively few initiatives. Provincial governments and political party competition appear to constrain municipal discretionality in moving forward. In Venezuela there are also very few initiatives, and municipal governments have been weakened in recent years as a result of the recentralization of political authority and resources.

These initial observations offer an overview of metropolitan governance in the federalist Americas. In short, each country has its own unique approach to metropolitan initiatives and there is no broad cross-country model. Three countries show only limited initiatives toward creating metropolitan arrangements (Argentina, Mexico, and Venezuela), while the other three demonstrate important examples of metropolitan possibilities, even if these are not generalized within each country. In the remainder of this chapter we examine these scenarios in greater detail.

Table 8.2. Metropolitan Initiatives, Institutions, and Country Context

	Argentina	Brazil	Canada	Mexico	Venezuela	USA
Frequency of Initiatives	Few	Few but increasing	Frequent	Few, moderately increasing	Rare	Frequent
Strength of municipalities/local governments	Weak	Increasing strength	Strong	Modest increase	Weak and weakening	Strong and highly fragmented
State/provincial government authority over local governments	Significant	Limited	Paramount	Significant	Marginal	Paramount
Functional areas of state/provincial in local government interactions	Regulation of some intermunicipal services	Manages some service systems, e.g., public transportation	Establishes powers of local government	Regulation of some intermunicipal services and finances	NA	Establishes powers of local government fiscal equalization for public education
Political systems at local level	Local political parties dependent on state parties	Local political competition; timid efforts with metropolitan legislative-like bodies	Competitive local politics; regional variation in political culture	Increasing competition in local politics, undermining effective metro-level government	National party tending to dominate local governments	Vast range of local political processes; regional variation in political culture
Other significant factors	High urban inequality	High urban inequality	Core-suburban conflicts	High urban inequality	High urban inequality	Core-suburban conflicts

Table 8.3. Frequencies of Metropolitan Initiatives by Type and by Country

	Collaborational	*Organizational*	*Institutional*
Argentina	■	■	□
Brazil	■	■	■
Canada	■	■	■
Mexico	■	■	□
USA	■	■	■
Venezuela	■[a]	■	■[a]

Key: ■ Frequent; ■ Infrequent; □ Absent.

a. But only Caracas.

The Patterns of Metropolitan Government and Governance

Our first research question sought to identify the overarching characteristics of the forms that metropolitan-based governance systems take. Above we utilized frequency of initiatives among traditional government functions, public transportation and the like, as a means to identify patterns. But we also wished to examine the nature of initiatives according to intergovernmental or interorganizational characteristics, recognizing the vast range of specific forms in these six countries. We inductively established three types: (1) collaborative initiatives, (2) organizational initiatives, and (3) institutional initiatives (see table 8.3). Although the source of motivation for establishing a particular initiative — that is, the specific reason for human agency and the form of working relations between government units — varies substantially, the frequency of initiative utilization across these three groups reflects varying degrees of difficulty and political commitment.

Collaborative initiatives are those forms of working relations between government units that depend critically on the willingness and disposition of governments to enter into collaboration; they are essentially questions of decision making and of interpersonal skills by local officials and leaders. Collaborations can be purely voluntary, but higher levels of government may also induce collaboration by enabling legislation, offering financial incentives, brokering, or exercising political pressure. Often key are the leadership and actions of midrange political and social actors, such as mayors, other public officials, associations of associations, and civic leaders, all of whom are capable of articulating connections and building networks across different organizations and policy communities. Indeed, networks of organizations are themselves collaborative activities. In numerical terms collaborative initiatives are the most common in our six countries (see table 8.3). To the extent that these are voluntary, their emergence represents important responses to very real policy challenges, a point on which we elaborate below. In addition, these are the easiest type of metropolitan initiative to create, as we observed in the figures and discussion in chapter 1.

The second type of initiative — organizational — comprises initiatives that change the competencies of existing governmental units by developing their resource base or authority or by redefining operational jurisdictions. They do not depend on voluntary decisions or willingness, as do the collaborative initiatives, but they require concrete action to create or alter, in a formal and binding sense, the architecture of organizational forms and procedures. As an exercise in government reform, leadership here is also important, but it often needs to be of a more managerial nature, linked to skills of getting things done; it can also require persuading citizens to ratify reform. Organizational initiatives are also found in each country, partly because of efforts to enhance the powers of local governments. Decentralization processes, as embedded in the Brazilian Constitution of 1988, have frequently strengthened the municipalities. But in other countries, especially Canada and the United States, state and provincial governments can facilitate the empowering of local governments to address metropolitan challenges. In Argentina organizational initiatives appear most likely to occur when the federal government becomes involved — as it does when city government crosses two provincial territories (the cases of Buenos Aires and Rosario Metropolitan Areas). Reorganization of activities on the basis of subsidiarity principles, as found in Europe, would be characterized as organizational, although no such initiatives were found in the six countries examined here.

The final type of initiative — institutional — consists of new spaces and practices of governance both governmental and public, including councils and governmental authorities. These initiatives do not rise to the level of a newly formed government. As mentioned earlier, no new tiers of governments for metropolitan areas have been formed in our six countries. Rather, the institutional initiatives denote new organizations or associations, but without formal governmental authority. The metropolitan planning organizations in metropolitan areas of the United States reflect the opportunities for higher-level governments to encourage or induce the formation of organizations or associations addressing metropolitan-wide issues. One form of institutional initiatives, the creation of a multipurpose metropolitan authority like Metro Vancouver or Metro Minneapolis–St. Paul, is relatively rare in our six countries. This result is disappointing, since we believed when we began our research project that this sort of structure could have considerable potential to eventually fulfill the ideal of democratic governance across a large metropolitan area. The United States is a partial exception to this conclusion, but even here such governance is achieved through the proliferation of single-purpose governments across the metropolitan areas and not through multipurpose governmental entities, which remain rare.

In practice, the three types of initiatives — collaborative, organizational, and institutional — do not necessarily create mutually exclusive categories, given that a single initiative may have characteristics of more than one type and that initiatives may change over time (for example, a collaborative initiative may become institutionalized), but we find that grouping initiatives in this fashion aids our discussion of identifying significant differences and patterns in a vast range of initiatives.

The significant presence of collaborative initiatives, those that depend on decisions and willingness of local actors, suggests that the current metropolitan governance arena is something of a double-edged sword. On the one hand, it suggests that there is scope for action if those involved are interested in doing so, but it also confirms our initial suspicions that a change in circumstances, such as change in local political leadership, could just as easily undo or undermine metropolitan initiatives.

In a later section we identify pathways to metropolitan governance that build on these primary findings summarized here. Metropolitan-wide issues exist, as evidenced by the frequent use of the limited-purpose collaborative initiative for certain types of services and functions. But these face potential shortcomings, including limited public accountability and neglect of those public services with a redistributive or poverty alleviation element, points we elaborate below. Organizational and institutional initiatives, both of which involve some reassignment of governmental functions and improvement of governmental capacity, have favorable characteristics on several governance principles, especially in terms of citizen engagement. But these are more difficult to achieve and are less frequently encountered.

The Dynamics of Change

The second research question postulated five sets of factors that might explain, at least partially, the emergence and dynamics of metropolitan-based initiatives:

1. The constitutional and/or state-attributed powers of local government, including fiscal capacity
2. Jurisdictional geography of local government
3. Technical and organizational characteristics of service delivery systems
4. Political systems and the practice of politics
5. Demographic and civic pressures

We observe that all five sets of factors are present in different ways across our case studies and that these may help or hinder effective metropolitan governance. But it is also important to recognize that as these factors intersect, so the resulting push-pull forces are likely to create quite distinctive results.

First, *constitutional provisions and powers and authorities attributed by state governments to local government* affect the structuring of government in metropolitan areas. Decentralization and state reform have been on the agenda in the six countries in recent decades. Although these efforts did not address metropolitan affairs, they led to stronger local governments, especially in Brazil and Mexico, and to a much lesser extent in Argentina and Venezuela. Similarly, the historically decentralized federalist structures in the United States and Canada are crucial in determining how metropolitan governance initiatives unfold and explain the significant variation found among states and provinces. In general we have found that when the powers of local government are weak, in terms of constitutionally defined authority, administrative capacity, or political legitimacy, then metropolitan collaboration is less likely to emerge. Put another way, strong local governments are a necessary, but not a sufficient, condition for effective metropolitan governance to emerge.

Changing the Constitution, for purposes of metropolitan governance or otherwise, is a formidable undertaking in all political systems and is generally eschewed. Among the six countries examined here, only in Brazil and, to a much lesser extent, Mexico is there some form of constitutional designation. Consequently, introducing a new tier of government or a new kind of purpose-related government by constitutional means seems unlikely. An important exception is that of single-purpose districts, a practice created by actions of state governments under the dual-sovereignty provision authorized by the U.S. Constitution. However, we find that through the exercise of constitutionally defined powers, state or provincial governments can have a profound effect on the emergence of metropolitan forms — a point to which we return below. In general, also, local governments are limited by their constitutions in their flexibility to improve or significantly change their fiscal capacity by creating new dimensions of revenue collection, by altering the rates of taxation that can be levied (with the exception of property taxes), or by recasting the terms of revenue sharing with higher levels of government to their own advantage.

Another feature of metropolitan areas in all six countries is that of disparities in the levels of economic development across municipalities. In general, the core urban municipalities have much higher levels of per capita income than surrounding municipalities. The U.S. and Canadian cases both have examples of wealthy suburban jurisdictions, but in all countries income disparities across metropolitan areas are the rule. This leads to substantial disparities of fiscal capacity across local governmental jurisdictions, exacerbating the relatively limited authority that local governments have to modify revenue systems and to enhance their own source revenue. Further complicating this problem is that often the less wealthy municipalities have the higher needs for public services in such areas as education and health. The result is a significant mismatch between fiscal capacity of metropolitan municipalities and demand for social services. This mismatch between the tax base and the local government capacity can, in worst-case scenarios, lead to a "beggar thy neighbor strategy" whereby one municipality engages in fiscal games such as offering unfair incentives that poach business and other forms of fiscal rent seeking (e.g., offering lower car license registration fees) from its neighbor(s).

Moreover, as our case study examples have shown, there are few incentives to promote metropolitan redistribution of resources in favor of particularly disadvantaged local governments. The very few attempts at metrowide redistribution or the creation of common funds for selected aspects of metropolitan development have generally foundered on mistrust and a breakdown in collaboration between the constituent players — as the case of Guadalajara amply demonstrated. One exception that proves the rule is Minneapolis–St. Paul, where the Twin Cities share industrial tax-based revenues across the metropolitan area. But even here the shared tax revenues apply only to a single arena, that of the industrial tax base.

Second, the *jurisdictional geography of local government,* referred to earlier as the spatial patchwork of local government, can both facilitate and complicate metropolitan initiatives. Here it is useful to distinguish several types of spatial configurations of local governments in metropolitan areas: large single jurisdictions; polynucleated jurisdictions, in which there are many municipalities with not dissimilar sizes; those featuring a dominant core municipality with adjacent smaller if not dependent municipalities; those featuring a dominant core but also adjacent secondary core municipalities; and those that comprise or contain federal districts (see table 8.4).

Large, single urban jurisdictions are less common and are found in only four of our countries, as in Calgary, Ciudad Juárez, Barquisimeto, and Houston (through annexation), and Miami (through city-county consolidation). Here a single unified public sector usually exists, with its departments and agencies, tax base, and electoral system, although in some contexts it is highly dependent upon support from the state or provincial government. The single urban jurisdiction provides a clearer organizational field from which to address the challenges presented by large urban populations, and public accountability systems in the form of elections for local government are well established.

More common, however, are the more complicated multijurisdictional geographies where the built-up urban area extends into multiple municipalities, adjacent states, and even adjacent nations, forming a much more complex interorganizational and polycentric field, or, to use Abbott's (1993) expression, a *complex metropolitan region*. In all countries, the density of local government activities across these large urban conurbations necessitates collective governmental coordination, echoing the observation of Ostrom, Tiebout, and Warren made decades ago (1961), though difficult to achieve in practice. In such densely populated jurisdictions, the likelihood of metropolitan initiatives can vary according to local circumstances and along a spectrum.

At one end of the spectrum a dominant municipality may have highly dependent municipalities surrounding it with vast disparities in resources, leading to a greater, perhaps resigned, disposition of the dependent municipalities to collaborate; examples here include Salvador (Brazil), Córdoba (Argentina), Edmonton (Canada), and Maracaibo (Venezuela). But this is not always the case, and historically in the United States and, more recently, in Canada (Toronto), the adjacent suburban communities may not find themselves dependent on the core city and may be disinclined to collaborate because of differing policy priorities resulting from their significantly higher socioeconomic status. At the other end of the spectrum are the polynucleated metropolitan areas, where a more evenly balanced distribution of resources and population across municipalities, as in Mendoza (Argentina), Toluca (Mexico), or the Santos coastline in Brazil, may provide greater opportunities for coordination, since potential partners are in similar situations. In the Brazil case, even though there are currently relatively few initiatives, these have tended to take place at this end of the spectrum. In the middle are those scenarios in which a

Table 8.4. Jurisdictional Geography of Metropolitan Areas by Country

	Argentina	Brazil	Canada	Mexico	Venezuela	USA
Large, single jurisdiction			Calgary Ottawa Quebec	Ciudad Juárez	Barquisimeto	Honolulu, El Paso Miami-Dade County[a]
Polynucleated municipalities	Mendoza	Porto Alegre Santos Vitoria	Vancouver	Toluca		Raleigh-Portland Portland, St. Louis
Dominant core with small adjacent municipalities	Cordoba Rosario	Natal Salvador	Edmonton Montreal Winnipeg		Maracaibo	Houston, San Antonio San Diego
Dominant core with adjacent secondary core municipalities	Buenos Aires	Belo Horizonte Campinas Recife Rio de Janeiro São Paulo	Toronto	Monterrey Guadalajara	Caracas	New York City Dallas–Fort Worth Minneapolis–St. Paul
Federal Districts	Buenos Aires	Brasilia	Ottawa	Mexico City	Caracas	Washington, DC

a. Two tiers.

primary municipality containing a significant share of the metropolitan population exists alongside other substantially populated municipalities, as in the case of São Paulo (Brazil), Monterrey and Guadalajara (Mexico), Toronto (Canada), or New York City and Dallas–Fort Worth (United States). Here coordination can occur, in some instances to great effect, as in the cases of the Toronto Metropolitan Council (albeit now defunct), the New York Port Authority, and the Dallas–Fort Worth Airport. However, it remains difficult to achieve and may encounter challenges from actors vying for leadership or from those seeking to forge a separate future for their constituents. Federal districts are a special case of jurisdictional geography. They can offer an alternative model for an intermediary or special tier of government (neither state nor municipality), but as part of metropolitan areas (as in the case of all but the Brazilian Federal District) they can bring a very different dimension to interlocal politics, investments, and resources, although rarely do they appear to do so in a positive way. Despite the potential for preferential access to federal government resources, conflicts between federal districts themselves and adjacent jurisdictions prevent collaboration, as we saw in Buenos Aires and Mexico City. Here we would also highlight an important companion volume by Myers and Dietz (2002) on capital city politics in Latin America.

Third, *the technical and organizational characteristics of service delivery systems* affect the frequency of occurrence of metropolitan initiatives. As anticipated, we find that certain policy areas are more likely to generate collaboration or scaling up of service provision and planning than others. As is apparent in the different country case studies (summarized in table 8.1), the large majority of experiences and existing initiatives address infrastructure systems, such as transportation, transit, water, solid waste, land use, and some types of environmental regulation. As anticipated, public services with very large fixed costs and/or involving territorially extensive systems (environmental or service delivery systems) are most commonly provided through metropolitan initiatives. Their public finance implications and clear benefits from collective action appear to make them good candidates for coordinated action on a metropolitan-wide basis. Similarly, where one or two jurisdictions are expected to incur the costs of an undesirable service for the entire metropolitan region—the management of solid waste disposal, for example—these, too, may be organized at the metropolitan level so that the receiving areas of the "bad" (negative externality) are compensated appropriately.

However, in marked contrast to the relative high frequency of initiatives in the infrastructure-related policy areas is their almost complete absence in initiatives involving redistributive policies. Social services, education, health, and housing are rarely the focus of metropolitan initiatives, though these services are often key concerns in municipal government. Even in instances where institutional incentives might suggest a metropolitan-wide system, delivery systems remain municipality-oriented. In the case of the municipally based unified health service system in Brazil, where states have the capacity and role to create and support synergies through substate regional coordination, the São Paulo Metropolitan Region remains firmly focused on municipal rather than demographic lines, at the same time that other parts of the state have shown considerable advances, as in the area of health consortia between small municipalities. It seems that even more than economy-of-scale considerations, fiscal topography intervenes most here: as noted above, better-off jurisdictions are loath to subsidize others (directly or indirectly) within the metropolitan area, and few political leaders are willing to broach redistribution outside their own jurisdictional limits. The lack of significant metropolitan initiatives for policing (despite the historical role of the police in shaping metropolitan meanings) can be mostly explained by a strong preference of local government to maintain control of policing and public security within its own jurisdiction, in part to guarantee replies to accountability claims.

The high frequency of nonredistributive policies among metropolitan initiatives confirms that political interests can indeed influence the metropolitan agenda, only here the influence is negative: policies that require redistribution of resources are not on the metropolitan agenda. At the same time service managers and technical staff often share the concerns of many academics and other research professionals about ensuring that services are provided adequately and equitably. Increasingly in a number of our countries, adequacy and quality of service provision are becoming the subject of public debate in terms of both citizen participation and at times co-management. Equity, for example, has figured largely in the public health arenas of Latin America, where discussion about service integration and delivery on a demographic-need basis is also present. Without being overly optimistic, we believe that perhaps in this type of context the torch of "metro-thinking" is being kept alight.

Fourth, we found that *political systems and the practice of politics* affect metropolitan initiatives in a variety of ways but that in general their effect is to dampen the prospects for organizational and institutional initiatives.

Historically, very few rising political leaders have embraced metropolitan initiatives as part of their agenda, since most careers arise out of already established local, regional, and national paths. Using a "metropolitan" base as a springboard for political advancement is, in general, a low-reward stratagem. Significant results are unlikely to accrue in the short term. Exceptions that prove the rule are the metropolitan initiatives of President Chávez in Caracas, who appears to have a strong interest in constructing a metropolitan governance structure, albeit one firmly anchored in his Bolivarian Circles. However, when earlier in his career the metropolitan structure was opposed to his political project, he successfully sought to undo it. Similarly, in the case of Monterrey Metropolitan Area, Mexico, the fact that 85 percent of the state population lives in what is the single dynamic national center of manufacturing and commerce makes it imperative that the state governor control the body politic of the metropolitan area, as is done through state executive agencies rather than a new metropolitan institutional architecture.

For similar reasons political parties rarely stake their colors to the mast by advocating for metropolitan governance. Even in Mexico, where a national party (the PRI) had hegemonic control for several decades of the twentieth century and thus was unlikely to be threatened by opposition parties or by constraints in passing constitutional changes, institutional arrangements of multiple subnational and local governments remained tied to patronage and career management. It was imagined that full-fledged regional governments would only create imbalances and instability. In Brazil during the period of military developmentalism in which planning was the religion of the day, there was almost no attempt to use the newly devised metropolitan regions as the lever for intermediate coordination. Where we find activities organized on a metropolitan-wide scale, executive appointees and not elected officials invariably run them, thereby avoiding independent power bases that might carry popular legitimacy and support. In the United States some single-purpose authorities have elected leaders while others have appointed leaders. In Canada, even the progressive Greater Vancouver Regional District has resisted the call for direct elections of its board members; instead, elected council members from the various local jurisdictions are appointed to the board. Direct elections — seen as an integral element of transparent and accountable governance — still remain largely off the agenda.

In the chapter 1 review of the related literature the territorial basis of political parties was observed to affect the prospects for decentralization in Latin American countries (Stepan, in Gibson 2004). We now observe that political parties, even those with a strong territorial dimension, do not engage in metropolitan questions. In fact, the case of the United States, with each party galvanized around different geographies of metropolitan space (the Democratic Party in core cities and the Republican Party in suburban jurisdictions), suggests that consensus among parties on federal policy addressing metropolitan issues is very unlikely and may even constrain the prospects for metropolitan initiatives in some state governments.

Nor does it appear that single-party control or dominance across metropolitan jurisdictions will lead to institutionalization of metropolitan governance. Elected politicians, even under the same party banner, have more to lose than gain from formal institutionalization of government, and this may help explain why, where collaboration occurs, it is voluntary and largely ad hoc. Thus it is probably not surprising that during the recent third-wave democratization that we have seen in Brazil, Mexico, and Argentina political leaders and parties have in general avoided investing a great deal of energy in the creation of new metropolitan arrangements and when they do their interest is often hard to sustain.

The existence of nonpartisan local elections and the figure of city manager are adaptations undertaken to reduce conflicts between the practice of local politics and efficient government. To displace the contentious politics of ward-based systems, the municipal reform movement in the United States argued for at-large, nonpartisan elections. The city manager, a nonpolitical official, was hired to run the city bureaucracy, a practice that was later but unsuccessfully adopted in Caracas.

So what are the politics that explain those relatively rare cases where a metropolitan authority does evolve — for example, the counterfactual cases of Vancouver, Portland, Oregon, and Minneapolis–St. Paul? It is hard, to be sure, but we suspect that the explanations hinge on history and/or the existence of a regional political culture that facilitates metropolitan collaboration. The latter would appear to explain why Vancouver created its regional authority arrangement, and the single-district amalgamations of Montreal and Quebec would also be consistent with this view, in these cases tied to a project of development within francophone language and cultural traditions.

Fifth, the *dynamics of demographic and civic pressures* are an important contextual feature of metropolitan initiatives. While some metropolitan areas continue to grow rapidly, reinforced by decentralization, other metropolitan areas—especially the larger and more established ones—are slow growing and undergoing urban regeneration and redevelopment. Moreover, they are often home to new populations—immigrants from other countries. Montreal, for example, attracts immigrants from francophone countries into its rapidly expanding commercial and service sectors. Many metropolitan areas in the United States are immigration gateways, with increasing proportions of minorities that are sometimes minority-majority (Hispanic especially). Within Latin America there is also considerable transhumance into metropolitan areas from countries like Bolivia, Colombia, and Peru. This increased diversity will pose further challenges to political life and democratic governance.

In those countries with a primate city that also overlaps with the special-district status associated with its being the national capital—Mexico City, Buenos Aires, and Caracas—there may be relatively little opportunity for adaptation: the primate city is simply too large relative to the wider urban structure. In contrast, rapidly growing second-tier cities may offer greater scope for adaptability, observed in Monterrey (Mexico), Campinas (Brazil), Córdoba (Argentina), Portland, Oregon (United States), and Edmonton (Canada), since they develop around new resource opportunities and often have less entrenched political interests.

Perhaps one of the most positive pressures for change comes from democratization itself and the thickening of the civic culture that one observes in terms of public participation and a rising sense of citizenship (Wilson et al. 2008). The level of debate among urban residents has increased dramatically, often led by NGOs and the media, and may stimulate wider metropolitan discussion. Telecommunications are also changing the connectivity that citizens have with the city in terms of access and ability to mobilize information through the media, editorials, debates, blogs, and chat rooms and to provide greater awareness of the efficiency of governmental service providers through public sector websites. This, too, may spill over to a wider metropolitan arena.

However, moving from public debate to more formal structures and opportunities for direct election and citizen participation in policy making seems to present major dilemmas for metropolitan governance. As already observed, citizen representatives and politicians tend to prefer the small and local to the large and metropolitan, so the challenge becomes that of how to foster a sense of identity at both levels: thickening the middle ground of metro affairs without thinning the local ground of municipal life. Indeed, getting away from the idea that metropolitan governance is some kind of zero-sum game for state and municipal jurisdictions may well be part of the challenge.

Democratic Governance and Equitable Development

The third and final research question asks whether the metropolitan initiatives are creating opportunities and incentives for democratic governance and are thereby gaining political legitimacy. Certainly in the four Latin American countries, the democratic openings of the last several decades provide an important contextual element for assessing the success of metropolitan governance. Factors such as structures of government, electoral integration, and opportunities for citizen participation are crucial for establishing legitimacy. In general, however, we find that political legitimacy of the initiatives has rarely been established and that on the more narrowly drawn initiatives, such as infrastructure or service provision, it has not even been raised by citizens. Here we offer lessons on establishing political legitimacy at three different moments: (1) at the moment governmental structures are formed or initiatives launched; (2) around the selection of leadership of the initiatives; and (3) around the formation of public perceptions on the effectiveness of initiatives.

The creation of new metropolitan governance structures occurs in complex institutional and organizational environments. In most countries examined here, state governments play key roles in defining this environment and thus in establishing the intergovernmental framework in which political legitimacy of metropolitan initiatives must be developed. Therefore, the finding that political legitimacy has rarely been established should be understood in the relatively circumscribed intergovernmental and political framework created by state and, occasionally, federal governments. It tends to suggest that metropolitan matters are still seen within an economical and technical rather than social and political perspective, and with a focus on multilevel service management rather than multilevel governance, as in the case of the EU, mentioned in chapter 1.

In two countries, Canada and the United States, citizens are often called upon to vote in referenda to create certain forms of new government structures, thus providing an explicit means for assessing citizen support. Elections to consolidate governmental structures in the United States usually fail because of the dramatically different political interests of central-city voters and suburban voters. In Toronto, citizens in the outer ring defeated the proposal to further consolidate a metropolitan government. In these two countries income and tax base disparities among local municipalities forestall the treatment of redistributive policies being addressed on a metropolitan basis. These outcomes reveal the difficulties in identifying common interests, and thereby political legitimacy, on metropolitan-wide issues.

In contrast to direct elections to approve new structures, a step entirely consistent with the norms of democratic governance, the imposition of metropolitan agencies by the military dictatorship in Brazil may have created a significant political barrier to metropolitan initiatives after the return to democracy. That is to say, asking for citizen endorsement may be consistent with democratic practice despite the possibility of voter rejection, but imposition of metropolitan structures from above undermines legitimacy.

The method of choosing leadership of metropolitan initiatives is another crucial factor in establishing legitimacy. Leadership can be elected, either directly or indirectly, or appointed. Very rarely are direct elections held for metropolitan leadership positions (as in Portland, Oregon). As noted in the U.S. case, the transition from district- or ward-based to at-large election systems, adopted in many cities early in the twentieth century, encouraged political leaders to focus on citywide issues rather than local issues. In addition, the lack of elections for metropolitan-wide offices leads to very limited interest from political parties, whose engagement in metropolitan political processes might bring greater legitimacy to metropolitan institutions. In fact, we observed that under existing governmental structures partisan activities have actually undermined metropolitan collaboration (as discussed for Argentina and Venezuela). Given the exceedingly few instances of elections for metropolitan-wide offices, this potential avenue for establishing political legitimacy of metropolitan initiatives is severely underutilized.

More common are the indirect methods for establishing metropolitan leadership, in which elected officials, representing municipalities or other governmental jurisdictions in the metropolitan area, and, occasionally, representatives of executive branch agencies of technical relevance, assume membership on metropolitan-level governing bodies. In these systems, achieving appropriate spatial representation to allow effective policy debate and deliberation on metropolitan issues is complicated. Even in successful intermunicipal consortia, such as ABC in São Paulo, Brazil, or in several Canadian cases, elected leaders, including mayors, are likely to be most concerned about the interests of their municipal constituencies rather than consortium-wide matters. Consortia often have rules for rotating leadership on short, yearly, cycles, another factor that stands in the way of longer-term dedication. Individual citizens participating in existing election systems that produce indirect representation in metropolitan governance systems will rarely consider metropolitan issues. And given the spatial distribution of constituencies of leaders in the indirect systems, the effectiveness of deliberative forums on metropolitan-wide issues almost invariably depends on the level of resources over which the forums have control.

Citizen perceptions on the performance of metropolitan initiatives also affect the legitimacy of the initiatives. Are these initiatives and related activities visible and accessible to citizens? Does the institutional design of these initiatives create incentives for citizens to engage in them? Many of the initiatives discussed are at a scale or are in areas that do not capture public attention. Frequently, however, the resources or authority can lead to activities that have a modest impact, sometimes directed to small enclaves of metropolitan populations, and may well have quite significant local benefits, such as the restoration of riverfronts and water quality of rivers. However, these may not be apparent or important to the broader metropolitan community. Even in cases of widely used metropolitan infrastructure, such as public transportation or highway systems, deliberations, resolution of conflicts, and consensus building often get buried in planning processes and have a very narrow participation of nongovernmental actors, as was noted in Canada. In addition, interlocal agreements tend to be quite technical and are rarely visible to most citizens or, when they are, as in the introduction of intermodal and inter-jurisdictional travel passes, quickly become taken for granted. The balance between technical efficiency and citizen engagement often favors the former and reduces the opportunity for generating political legitimacy. Participatory municipal budgeting in Brazil, where high levels of citizen engagement and legitimacy have been achieved, requires extraordinary commitment by citizens in order to deliberate on complex urban service delivery systems across the span of a single jurisdiction, but the question remains about whether these can be harnessed at an intermunicipal level (i.e., across several municipalities).

In general, the lack of significant resources or authority in play in metropolitan initiatives reduces the possibilities for developing political legitimacy. But we do find initiatives that began with quite narrow mandates (Portland, Oregon; Vancouver, Canada) later expanding authority over a much wider area, what has been described in the Brazil case (Azevedo and Mares Guia 2004) as incremental institutionalization. In these cases, modest early success mobilized support from elected leaders and citizens for more ambitious efforts. However, incremental institutionalization requires a range of smaller issues on which to build up confidence and competence, and these are very different from the significant majority of metropolitan initiatives, which address major infrastructure provision.

But to conclude on a more upbeat note, one of the most positive pressures for change in governance systems in many of the countries is democratization itself and the thickening of the civic culture that one observes in terms of public participation and a rising sense of citizenship, albeit not yet in metropolitan forums (Wilson et al. 2008). Certainly political debate on urban affairs has increased dramatically in recent decades and is reflected in the structure of national government cabinets and budget provisions. However, moving from the more general public debate to specific structures and opportunities for direct election and citizen participation in policy making at the more intermediate level presents major dilemmas for metropolitan governance. As observed, people tend to prefer the small and local or the really large (state and national) to the intermediary and metropolitan, a preference that largely excludes redistributive policies and equity considerations from metropolitan agendas. The challenge, therefore, is how to foster a more complex sense of identity.

One of our more optimistic initial goals was to try to assess how and whether metropolitan governmental arrangements were working well, meeting the development challenges that they faced. Inter alia, these included efficient and sustainable urban development, the provision of basic services, improvement of equity, enhanced amenities and environmental living conditions, opening of the spaces for public participation, and so on. To the extent that we are able to make such an assessment, our prima facie conclusion is that performance has been mixed. In particular, improving the quality of services to low-income populations has largely been ignored, as has the need to reconcile redistributive policies from richer to poorer municipalities, and this may ultimately seriously undermine political legitimacy. It may well be that any action toward redistributive policies will require reinforcement from regional and federal governments.

The highly local and multigovernmental structures that exist in the United States offer the most dispersed approach to democratic governance, precisely because it is so local and disaggregated, often single purpose, with high demands for democratic participation and citizen oversight. But even here the results on equity are low. Perhaps optimistically we expected to find a more varied set of solid advances from which to look for comparisons, whereas we found far less progress, and as a result a demand for much more precise data sets that would ultimately be conducive to more subtle performance evaluation and equity analysis.

As it appears from the case studies, changes are taking place and progress is being made, though in a heterogeneous manner. This, as we have commented before, is an important finding: metropolitan governance is not going to be solved through a "best practices" template approach. On the other hand, we do not suggest that guidelines are irrelevant or that it should all be left to laissez-faire. Incremental institutionalization from the top may have an important role to play, and however attractive bottom-up muddling through may appear, it does not seem to be helping those in need. Comparative studies have the advantage of pointing out how what may seem singular in one setting can generate counterpart policies and programs elsewhere, thus suggesting possible lines of advance (as appears to have been the case in the integrated rapid transit system of Transmilenio in Bogotá, or the ban on car circulation according to final-digit license plate numbers). However, these too may be constrained by jurisdiction. But as we believe our study has shown, blending the countrywide comparative approach with the specific cases helps to sort out possible scenarios of metropolitan governance. Here, moving toward the discussion of a research agenda for the future, it seems helpful to point to two important and interlinked arenas of action: one concerning public administration and service provision, and the other more to do with politics and civil society.

Within the arena of public administration and service provision, state government intervention appears to assume the more substantial and territorially differentiated role, with the federal government playing a lesser role, usually through primarily nonterritorially based incentives, while also eschewing changes that might require formal constitutional amendment. That said, we also have little doubt that to enhance the powers of local government, federal government leadership and incentives are invariably necessary, a point to which we return below. Progress toward metropolitan initiatives appears to take place within isolated parts of the public administration sector, and interconnections to the civics and political arena remain largely incipient. Thus, in terms of our central research question, we conclude that current and emerging initiatives and structures of governance are still largely incapable of meeting the challenge of collective life in large and complex metropolitan areas. Nor do the dynamics of change appear to be especially conducive at the end of the first decade of the twenty-first century.

On the politics and civil society side, making the metropolitan agenda much more visible and palpable to citizens could create the necessary incentives for greater civil society engagement and would also require more effective mechanisms for democratic governance (including elections), thereby enhancing legitimacy and creating further opportunities for improved metropolitan governance. In a similar vein, strengthening a metropolitan policy agenda (for example, through planning or environmentalism) is likely to stimulate greater discussion about the hierarchical ordering of government functions (including upward and downward subsidiarity). This would also open up questions of fiscal reform (e.g., redefining taxes) and possibly urban reform (e.g., redefining spatial boundaries), both of which also play an important part in increasing the effectiveness of metropolitan-wide activities and help make the metropolitan policy agenda more visible.

A Research Agenda for the Future

While we have been able to advance the metropolitan research agenda in a number of areas, inevitably much more remains to be done. First, it is important to have more detailed studies of the processes involved in ratcheting up metropolitan collaboration and subsequently institutionalizing it. What or who are the "triggers" that help explain the coming together of Minneapolis–St. Paul or Miami–Dade County, United States, or ABC in São Paulo? Does it come down to the interpersonal skills of key actors, or is it something to do with the nature of particular public goods? Is it easier to achieve in more homogeneous populations with more equitable income distribution? How do such processes of collaboration evolve? Case studies of collaboration (successful and unsuccessful) would help answer these and other questions and, like so many of the areas of future research required here, would take us to the heart of bureaucratic politics.

A related question is the role of national and supranational economic processes that could stimulate the emergence of metropolitan agencies. Metropolitan areas throughout the world are experiencing major changes in the dynamics and composition of their labor markets as manufacturing work opportunities decline and are replaced by services (both formal and informal). In this context, business associations may well become important advocates for alternative policies, as demonstrated by Ciudad Juárez and Monterrey in Mexico and the New Regionalism movement in the

United States. Those involved with economic development are likely, it is hypothesized, to be leaders in reframing metropolitan-wide development interests. We note the past cases of the New York Port Authority and of the Dallas–Fort Worth Airport, and more recently the Brazilian ABC region and the state of Nuevo Leon in Mexico, which sought to develop an interstate and intermetropolitan corridor from Saltillo in the neighboring state of Coahuila northwards up the NAFTA Highway to Austin and Dallas in Texas.

In the Americas and elsewhere, natural disasters — such as the 1985 earthquakes in Mexico City, gas explosions in Guadalajara, or the devastation wrought by Hurricane Katrina in New Orleans — and external vulnerabilities can have particularly deleterious effects in metropolitan areas and stimulate demands for change. Crises in global competitiveness or those arising from economic instability, as in Argentina in 1999–2001, can have particularly strong effects in metropolitan economies. These types of crises are found in virtually all regions of the world with increasing frequency and place politicians and decision-making authorities under enormous pressure to come up with short-term solutions and longer-term fixes. They can also be accompanied by major social unrest and public protest, stimulating overarching social movements. More recently still, the social media mobilizations in the Middle East appear likely to precipitate constitutional reforms, and to the extent that the mobilizations began in the large urban and metropolitan areas they offer examples of the potential for recasting governance structures that better encompass representation and participation.

It is also important for further research to extend our understanding about how people and citizen's groups in metropolitan areas prioritize their engagement with governance processes; their views of the city and the conurbation; and their attitudes toward sustainability, the environment, service provision, the location of essential facilities, and the extent of their concerns for equity. There are many different visions and constructions of the moral and political imperatives for new governance structures, and these have already affected municipal agendas during the period of more open (democratic) local government. In short, how can metropolitan governance systems help entrain participation and engagement in civics, and how does involvement vary at each level? People appear to have an affinity with their city or parts of it, but we know relatively little about how that sense of identity is constructed, or of the meanings that are ascribed to self-identification.

We also need to better understand the delivery of services in metro areas. This requires the development of better metrics to assess the effectiveness of metropolitan programs and practices in the context of complex delivery settings systems. Those metrics should be applied across a range of government programs, some of which lend themselves to macro metropolitan organization (transportation, for example), and others that require a more subtle "nesting" of activities at different spatial levels, such as health care. It is here that the reframing of subsidiarity, as discussed in chapter 1, may merit further investigation, not just in terms of service logistics but in terms of intermediary multilevel governance, involving not only nesting but also horizontal redistribution and thematic leadership.

Our rationale for this study sought to control for federalist constitutions, and along the way we have often wondered how and why metropolitan systems of governance emerge more frequently in unitary governments. Multiple research questions arise here, such as whether federal structure is overly rigid in assigning responsibilities between levels of government or whether federalism seeks to devolve government and privilege subnational levels. It would appear to be both of these things, but systematic comparisons of the two would, we believe, merit serious analysis. Later in this chapter we will propose that constructing a new tier of metropolitan governance may be easier in unitary systems, but at the same time we suggest that in some federal systems states and provinces can—to a large extent—operate as if they were unitary governments, with authority over other units under their jurisdiction. But much of our argument falls in the realm of hypothesis and proposition and requires more rigorous testing, including a more careful analysis of certain highly progressive and equity-oriented experiences in the unitary framework, such as the Inner London Education Authority of the United Kingdom. We also recognize the importance of extending this type of research into countries outside the Americas.

We have argued that metropolitan governance is important because these systems will affect the competitiveness and growth prospects of metropolitan economies. There is little empirical evidence in support of this argument, largely because of the difficulty in constructing variables and indicators of metropolitan governance. Nevertheless, significant progress has been made in establishing metrics of governance at the level of the nation, and this should provide a foundation for defining and measuring governance at the metropolitan level, which would be an important step for assessing the effectiveness of different types of metropolitan governance structures.

Although we have discussed the context of metropolitan governance in relation to capitals, we have had little to say about the cases of state capitals. In the case of the Monterrey (Mexico), state government, led by the governor, took direct interest in and had a positive effect on metropolitan issues. Yet in other countries, especially in Argentina, state government officials have seemed to limit efforts of local officials. A more systematic and comparative study of those state, or provincial, capitals that fall within metropolitan areas, especially in terms of the use made of their authority and resources, would certainly be worthwhile.

THE FUTURE PROSPECTS FOR METROPOLITAN GOVERNANCE

When we began this study, each of us imagined that the future probably lay in the recognition that some tier of metropolitan government (building off existing institutional arrangements) would be the solution to providing the planning and vision necessary for integrated and equitable development of large multijurisdictional conurbations and cities. This was certainly embedded in earlier writings of one of us (Ward 1998, 1999a), and it appeared also in planning and technical literature about governance. No one assumed that getting "there" would be easy or straightforward, and in chapter 1 we started with a discussion of the spectrum of actions of intergovernmental cooperation that moved from the relatively easy to the extremely difficult.

To some extent we had always been hostages to one of the visions and imaginaries of the "metropolitan" that we outlined in the first few pages of this volume: namely, that metropolitan meanings made for large-scale and somewhat centralized levels of organization around a core area, even though we advocated for giving preference to the local over the regional level. Our case studies have shown us that when this approach has been adopted, with metropolitan structures being the result of top-down state and provincial actions expressing constitutional authority or de facto power relations over municipalities (as the cases of Argentina, Brazil, Canada, and the United States illustrate), then the conduct of metropolitan affairs is generally not positive, is largely ineffective, and lacks the dimensions of equity and social and economic inclusion. Our initial perspective overlooked the possibility that metropolitan governance might (and should) be best constructed from the bottom up or the middle out, rather than deriving from an umbrella architecture that was inserted over the existing political and socioeconomic realities from the top down.

It would now seem possible to argue on the basis of the case studies that only where a measure of municipal autonomy is assured and genuine is there scope for a more collaborative construction of metropolitan governance structures, building from the bottom up and transferring to metropolitan-wide institutions but also often too with the sanction and support of higher-order government—usually that of the state. This might help to explain why metropolitan governance gets so little traction in Venezuela and Argentina, where municipal authorities are weak and dependent upon higher-level power holders and political influence. Such partisan politics is also an important feature in Brazil and Mexico, but the principle of municipal autonomy, empowered as it is by some independent access to local resource generation, allows those municipalities that wish to do so to explore cross-jurisdictional agreements of one sort or another. These can take the form of intermunicipal consortia, as in the case of Brazil, sometimes ratcheting up, with state-level support, into broader development organizations and agencies such as that of the ABC region of São Paulo. In Mexico, cooperation may emerge between neighboring municipalities and/or may be constructed by supralocal actors such as the governor or the mayor of the largest central-city municipality. But in all cases partisanship and political networks can make such collaboration a nonstarter if a zero-sum game mentality prevails. Municipal autonomy can both facilitate and negate collaborative initiatives.

The Pathways to Metropolitan Governance

Finally, we would like to offer a perspective on the various collaborative, organizational, and institutional pathways to metropolitan governance that we infer from our studies, not as theoretical blueprints, but as possibilities. They draw upon previous studies mentioned that have also mapped out possibilities (Rojas et al. 2008; Gouveâ 2005) but they extend these by specifically referring to federal polities. Quite deliberately we do not present them in any order of relative ease of achievement, since our experience suggests that there are multiple ways of moving forward (and backwards). They are presented as pathways, but they are not necessarily discrete, and one could certainly incorporate aspects of the others. Equally, we would not wish to create the impression that there is a linear progression through the various levels or phases of metropolitan governance and government construction, even though some are undoubtedly more feasible to attain than others, especially when viewed against the opportunities of interorganizational cooperation and coordination (see chapter 1, figures 1.1 and 1.2). As we have learned from the cases, certain factors, such as jurisdictional geography or specific federalist options, may help or hinder, but countries are not likely to change their established institutional models simply on the promise that the change may make metropolitan governance easier.

A first pathway would be the *creation of a new tier of metropolitan government*—either directly or indirectly elected—to lay down normative guidelines for metropolitan governance. Whether this type of body also takes on executive functions will hinge upon whether (1) it is adequately resourced and (2) there is a high degree of consensus among the affected constituencies. The Vancouver case in Canada is a good example of where this has worked well, while the metropolitan council in Mexico's Guadalajara has been a failure. Such arrangements need to give serious consideration to the basis of tax revenue sharing and the creation of effective and substantial metropolitan funds for metropolitan management.

Linked to this first pathway could be the creation of some sort of *wider consultative council and/or "watchdog" body* of civic representatives. Its role would be primarily to supervise the control of such funds but also to ensure some level of public participation and accountability and to enhance the sense of metropolitan identity. Such a body would help to offset the dangers of the metropolitan government becoming overly technocratic and ignoring citizen input (Rolnik and Somekh 2004). In Brazil, the Natal Common Parliament was a potential starter along these lines that then faltered.

A third path starts with the recognition that in many cities full-fledged metropolitan governance remains a distant or even an impossible goal but that in the meantime it is feasible to move ahead by *creating intermunicipal agreements for cooperation*. Falling short of consortia, such arrangements can be as simple as operational agreements between service agencies and in certain circumstances, incrementally, may later lead to the emergence of much more full-fledged institutional structures: witness the cases of Vancouver in Canada, Miami–Dade County and Minneapolis–St. Paul in the United States, and the Greater ABC Chamber in São Paulo. Azevedo and Mares Guia (2004) have used the expression *incremental institutionalization* to refer to this process of gradual consolidation of metro governance between adjoining municipalities and state-level agencies that become formalized through cooperation agreements and the creation of councils. However, we admit to not yet being clear about the circumstances that foster such incremental institutionalization. Interestingly, in the case of Portland the starting point was the creation of a zoo! Starting with issue arenas that are not contentious or urgent may be indeed a reasonable conclusion for those interested in this pathway. The type of leadership we discussed earlier under the collaborative approach to interagency relations also seems to be key.

A variant of the collaborative agreement approach is the *voluntary and explicit transfer of responsibility and control over certain activities* (for example, water, sewage, transportation, health, education) from the individual metropolitan municipalities to either (1) the state, or (2) an intermunicipal consortium, or (3) a single-purpose authority, or (4) one of the municipalities through a process of horizontal contracts. All these follow in different ways the organizational principle of subsidiarity by recognizing the increased complexity of certain conurbation-wide issues and limits of municipal competence despite the municipality's autonomy (and sometimes responsibility) to address those issues. This approach differs from the previous pathway in that the agreement tends to involve substantial obligations for funding, policy formation, and implementation and staff.

Privatization is another form of transfer, and in the 1980s a number of national and state governments began to roll back responsibility from the public to the private sector. The key here is the provenance of operational and investment resources, as well as considerations of efficiency, and sometimes the divestment of political responsibility. But unless adequate incentives exist, few higher-order agencies are likely to want to take over what could be seen as something of a "poisoned chalice." And if the resources were guaranteed (by federal or regional government, for example), then transference upwards might well also be difficult, since in these circumstances many municipalities would probably not wish to relinquish control. However, as we have observed in this volume, municipal agreements — whether single or multipurpose — provide an effective way forward in large part because they are flexible: they do not imply permanence and can be revoked or amended as different political actors come and go or as circumstances change. For that reason alone, perhaps, they represent pragmatically the most viable path to metropolitan collaboration.

A fifth pathway to regional or metropolitan governance is through *federal construction*, but this may apply in only a handful of cases: those of federal district entities such as Ottawa, Gatineau, and Caracas, where the federal government has taken a strong role in shaping the city government structure, as well as in those urban areas that cross more than one state or provincial jurisdiction. Argentina is a case in point, especially in

Buenos Aires, where the federal government plays an important mediating (and sometimes a veto) role in metropolitan governance relations between the provincial and the capital city governments. In the United States, the federal government also plays an important role in creating or fostering certain types of single-purpose entities (river authorities, air control districts, or major transit arrangements). Also in the United States, metropolitan planning organizations date from the 1960s. The federal government now requires that these be set up for federal funding, and they are especially common for major transportation projects. Another example of federal intervention in municipal affairs occurs in Rosario, Argentina, where the federal government has intervened because of the city's preeminence as a port.

In a sixth pathway, metropolitan government may be achieved through *annexation* — incorporating surrounding cities or municipalities or parts thereof. In the United States annexation is quite common, although unfortunately it often entails "cherry picking" of those suburbs or sections of suburbs that the aggrandizing city or municipality wishes to incorporate. However, such metropolitan consolidation paths are likely to occur only where there is consensus from the area about to be incorporated (and then only after a referendum, as in the United States), and/or where consolidation forms part of the provincially mandated expansion process of large single municipalities — as in Calgary and Edmonton (Alberta, Canada). And even here it is less straightforward if the suburbs mobilize resistance.

Elsewhere and in Latin America such incursions and gobbling up of surrounding municipalities are frowned upon. Indeed, in Brazil the opposite is more likely to occur, with parts of municipalities claiming "emancipation" from their parent municipality, and, after a vote and legislative analysis and approval, being spun off as a new independent municipality. Large suburbs or settlements in the United States may self-incorporate as independent cities, and in the past this was one way of trying to ensure control over residential ordinances, education, services, and local policing, increasing the raft of local governments that we described in chapter 3.

A seventh pathway in the same vein yet from a different direction is the proposition that existing *amalgams of municipalities* that form a metropolitan area should be allowed to constitute themselves as a *new, smaller state*. In Brazil in 1960, the transitional arrangements to create the new federal capital of Brasilia allowed the former federal district of Rio de Janeiro to become the new state of Guanabara, which existed until 1975, when the state was disbanded and the city of Rio rejoined the state of Rio de Janeiro to become its capital. In Mexico in the 1980s and 1990s there were long-standing arguments to convert the Mexico City metropolitan area — approximately half of which lies in the Federal District and half in the surrounding state of Mexico — into the thirty-second state of "Anahuac." Those claims lost traction once direct elections were allowed in the Federal District (from 1997) and provided it with an elected (quasi-) governor and an elected assembly (and quasi-state legislature). In Mexico such a thirty-second state would have created a "superstate" of over twenty million people, with various negative consequences and imbalances for the tax base of the surrounding state of Mexico. Nevertheless, such forms of *retrofitting*, using existing institutional forms in new ways, can provide a way forward in settings where greater consistency is required yet there is little scope for creating a new tier of government. Interesting here to note is the use of "metropolitan counties" in some unitary nations, as in the case of Quito, Ecuador.

As a demographic variant on these last two pathways, occasionally all or the lion's share of very large cities or metropolitan areas occupies a single municipality and constitutes a sufficiently large critical mass to create almost a de facto metropolitan municipality. One such example discussed in this book is that of Ciudad Juárez, Mexico, a million-plus city in a single municipality on the United States-Mexico border with El Paso, Texas. In Canada, the central-city municipalities of Calgary and Edmonton contain 95 percent and over 70 percent respectively of the total metropolitan population, making metropolitan amalgamation irrelevant. In the United States it is fairly uncommon for the population of the metropolitan area to dominate a single jurisdiction (Houston and Albuquerque are among the exceptions). Barquisimeto (Venezuela) has all of its population within the municipality, while the major industrial center of Cordoba (Argentina) has 94 percent. In Brazil the central municipality of the metropolitan areas of Salvador and Maceió contains over 80 percent of the population. In all these cases the dominance of one jurisdiction could lead to a more consolidated metropolitan governance structure and for a greater sense of metropolitan identity, providing that surrounding municipalities accepted the redrawing of boundaries.

Toward a Conclusion

An important single feature that emerges from five of the six country cases is that a new architecture of metropolitan governance requires competent and willing municipal, county, or town authorities, each with sufficient incentives to cooperate. But it also requires the serious organizational and fiscal action of state or provincial governments to support, lead, or leverage those initiatives. Both are necessary; neither is sufficient in and of itself. National or federal blueprints seem far less important as causes for change, even though they may provide the institutional space in which change may take place. This is for two fundamental reasons: first, as our country case studies and many other city-based studies have shown, metropolitan mechanisms of governance are, by nature, regional, nested in cultures, economies, and geographies, and should therefore be crafted by, and be responsible and accountable to, the people of the region or state in which they are anchored. This very likely means that tailor-made heterogeneity rather than homogeneity within any country is more likely to be the norm. Second, and here the U.S. case is especially instructive, the federalist design creates in effect a "dual" federalism, to a greater or lesser extent giving control to the states to manage development within their entities. This is clearly the case in the United States and Canada, but it also applies in Argentina, Venezuela, Mexico, and to a lesser extent Brazil, where municipalities are constitutionally defined as autonomous self-regulating entities within the federalist pact.

But the important point here is that, once constructed as part of the federalist design, states can, in varying degrees, act as though they were unitary governments. As we pointed out in chapter 1, unitary governments have the distinct advantage of being able to create, as well as to disestablish, governmental arrangements, and this gives them greater effective flexibility. Thus, while constitutional federal reform to create a new tier of functioning metropolitan governments is unlikely, we argue that there may well be sufficient political space for state or provincial governments to create governance structures—as we saw clearly in Canada and the United States, also in Mexico, and to a limited extent in Argentina, where state governors have created metropolitan-wide arrangements through their control of single- or multipurpose agencies. The key here is the flexibility accorded states to act in a unitary government fashion within their borders.

On the negative side, we need to recognize that the tragedy of the commons lurks always in the background of many of our large conurbations, with their ever more tightly packed and interconnected work and living patterns increasingly vulnerable to climate change or, more simply, the breakdown of logistics and services. Lost opportunities also abound and are triggered by deteriorating urban conditions to which politicians in cities like Mexico City, Buenos Aires, São Paulo, and Caracas have failed to respond. However, history teaches us that politicians usually manage to muddle through and adapt, and some — like Chávez in Caracas — are adept at turning crisis into opportunity. International pressure for a more integrated level of urban development in those metropolitan areas that span national borders, such as Ciudad Juárez and El Paso, Tijuana and San Diego, and Vancouver and Seattle, or that share an important corridor, such as that between Monterrey and Dallas, could encourage each side to adjust and accommodate the dynamics of their neighbors as partners.

The creation of significant streams of new resources for metropolitan governance structures with designated functions is, we suspect, an important incentive. Guadalajara's metropolitan council, through its metropolitan fund, was able to generate some positive outcomes (although largely the outcome of road building), but it foundered on a lack of adequate resources and mistrust between the municipal components: there were few incentives for the municipalities to participate aggressively and collaboratively. The federal government is unlikely to be a primary source of systematic funding, but states and — often — municipalities, counties, or towns do have their own independent tax base (and capacity) that creates regional and local sources of income.

We have found very few examples of effective fiscal incentives or structures (such as metropolitan tax bases) to "think metropolitan." Certainly, doing more than "talking metropolitan" requires moving from the arena of negotiated project finance and "off budget" investment and toward both a more significant and constant budget and a more institutional and transparent basis for spending. The idea of a metropolitan tax that would be levied upon residents of entire metropolitan regions (according to some equitable measure of relative population and socioeconomic profile of the municipalities) linked to matching funds from state and federal agencies, with a joint result large enough to provide adequate incentive for the component jurisdictions to participate and to ensure that benefits flowed back to the constituent parts, is possibly the key that would turn the lock. It could help overcome the difficulties of redistributive policies by funding only projects considered to benefit the metropolitan commonwealth (Selznick 1992), where even those richer municipalities that did not benefit quite so much directly would enjoy the indirect effects of better transportation systems, pollution controls, water procurement, solid waste disposal, greenbelt maintenance, emergency services, and so on. Obviously much would need to be configured locally, but so long as the fund was sustainable it could go a considerable way to offering the sort of incentives that "common funds" achieved in the earlier iterations of the European Community (now Union). Here the experience of the matching-contributions fund of the Brazilian Baixada Santista region shows that this is possible, at least on a smaller scale.

And what of those situations where a single regional government does not have unitary control, as is the case for capital cities or cross-state metropolitan areas? Here, too, the state participants could have primary control, but the additional actor would be the federal government, as in Buenos Aires, which, as well as being the capital city, has two "provincial" governments involved, the Autonomous City of Buenos Aires and the Province of Buenos Aires. But the reality of these cases is that there is often a significant political content in play as well. Once again, significant resources flowing into a metropolitan fund could be important in encouraging good-faith participation of the parts.

While the discussion of fiscal questions is already making itself felt in the academic literature and technical arenas, and while issues of planning are a constant feature of the different professional metropolitan movements, we remain deeply concerned at the lack of practical density in the civics-politics realm. Here some examples of practice in local state-civil society interaction may be relevant for metropolitan initiatives, and in many places the basis for electoral legitimacy of regional (metropolitan) governments already exists and is overseen by state/provincial assemblies (which may have oversight over the municipalities). Thus metropolitan councils or boards could be constructed so as to combine participation of elected mayors, appointees, and so on, without necessarily having to think about direct elections to the metropolitan council (although this might be highly desirable). Certainly the Americas have collectively a wide variety of experiences in extending the basic electoral model through different forms of participation, and there is much to be drawn on in a practical way (Wilson et al. 2008). Moreover, as recent international events show, social media and communications are a major new influence on the ways people do civics, and the municipalities of the metropolitan areas tend to concentrate a fair proportion of computer and smart phone users. Networking social media, "e-government" (electronic government), and "i-government" (information government) are new avenues of civic engagement that can have profound impacts upon government and governance.

In short, our case study experiences have suggested that the way forward is not to wait upon federal leadership and constitutional amendments, or simply to hope that people will muddle through, but rather to support and stimulate the growth of broader metropolitan governance on the basis of interlocal confederations, as we discussed in the chapter on the United States. This finding is not restricted to federal arrangements, of course, but also has wider application in unitary governments where these have some level of state or regional administrative jurisdictions. All but one of our country case studies highlights the role that state governments can and often do play. The exception is Venezuela, not because states are incapable of providing the necessary platform for the development of metropolitan governance, but primarily because the political process and politics run in the opposite direction — namely toward a centralization of control under President Hugo Chávez — with little prospect of change in the medium term.

The politics elsewhere appear to be much more open and potentially conducive to the consideration of new arrangements of metropolitan governance, but we argue that the impetus and momentum will need to emerge from state, provincial, and local governance arrangements rather than federal ones. Local collaborations between municipalities will continue to be important, but these are only ever likely to be partial side agreements and will not, of themselves, provide the necessary momentum toward wider metropolitan changes. We hope that the conversation started in this book, focusing as it has upon the evidence and experiences of a number of metropolitan cases, will encourage a greater awareness of the need for the kind of political consensus that could lead to a new generation of genuine metropolitan governance structures conducive to democratic participation and equitable development in the twenty-first century.

BIBLIOGRAPHY

Abbott, Carl. 1993. *The Metropolitan Frontier: Cities in the Modern American West.* Tucson: University of Arizona Press.

Abrucio, Fernando Luiz, José Mario Brasiliense Carneiro, and Marco Antonio Teixeira, eds. 2000. *O impasse metropolitano: São Paulo em busca de novos caminhos.* São Paulo: CEDEC / Fundação Konrad Adenauer.

Abrucio, Fernando Luiz, and Marcia Miranda Soares. 2001. *Redes federativas no Brasil: Cooperação intermunicipal no Grande ABC.* Série Pesquisas 24. São Paulo: Fundação Konrad Adenauer.

Afonso, António, Ludger Schuknecht, and Vito Tanzi. 2003. "Public Sector Efficiency: An International Comparison." *Public Choice* 123 (June): 321–47.

Aguilar, Adrián G., and Peter Ward. 2003. "Globalization, Regional Development, and Mega-City Expansion in Latin America: Analyzing Mexico City's Peri-Urban Hinterland." *Cities* 20 (1): 3–21.

Aguilar Barajas, Ismael. 2004. "El proceso de urbanización del Área Metropolitana de Monterrey: Algunas reflexiones de la experiencia reciente." In *Procesos metropolitanos y grandes ciudades: Dinámicas recientes en México y otros países,* edited by Adrián Guillermo Aguilar, 219–62. Mexico D. F.: UNAM and Miguel Angel Porrúa.

Almond, Gabriel G., G. Bingham Powell, Kaare Storm, and Russell J. Dalton. 2007. *Comparative Politics Today: A World View.* 2nd ed. New York: Longman.

Altshuler, Alan, William Morrill, Harold Wolman, and Faith Mitchell, eds. 1999. *Governance and Opportunity in Metropolitan America.* Washington, DC: National Academy Press.

Alvarez, Ana Amelia, and Gladys Ruiz de Lima. 2001. "Gran Mendoza, un área metropolitana en expansión, entre los efectos de la globalización y la fragmentación urbana." In *Actas del VI Seminario de la Red Iberoamericana de Investigadores en Globalización y Territorio.* Rosario: Universidad del Rosario.

Araújo Filho, V. F. 1996. "Antecedentes político-institucionais da questão metropolitano no Brasil." In *Gestão metropolitana: Experiências e novas perspectivas,* edited by E. D. Cardoso and V. Z. Zueibil. Rio de Janeiro: Instituto Brasileiro de Administração Municipal.

Auyero, Javier. 2001. *La política de los pobres: Las practicas clientelistas del Peronismo.* Buenos Aires: Manantial.

Azevedo, Sergio de, and Virginia R. Mares Guia. 2000. "Reforma do estado e federalismo: Os desafios da governança metropolitana." In *O futuro das metrópoles: Desigualdades e governabilidade,* edited by Luiz Cesar de Queiroz Ribeiro. Rio de Janeiro: FASE.

———. 2004. "Os dilemas institucionais da gestão metropolitana no Brasil." In *Metrópoles: Entre a coesão e a fragmentação, a cooperação e o conflito,* edited by Luiz Cesar de Queiroz Ribeiro. São Paulo: Editora Fundação Perseu Abramo.

Azevedo, Sergio de, Virginia R. Mares Guia, and Gustavo Machado. 2008. "A Prefeitura de Belo horizonte e a questão metropolitana." In *Democracia participativa: A experiência de Belo Horizonte,* edited by Sergio de Azevedo and Ana Luiza Nabuco. Belo Horizonte: Editora Leitura / Prefeitura de Belo Horizonte.

Bache, Ian, and Matthew Flinders, eds. 2004. *Multi-Level Governance.* Oxford: Oxford University Press.

Badía, G., E. Pereyra, A. Lupis, and P. Fagúndez. 2004. "Aproximándonos a la Región Metropolitana de Buenos Aires como sistema político." In *Aportes a la cuestión del gobierno en la Región Metropolitana del Gran Buenos Aires,* edited by G. Badía and E. Pereyra. Buenos Aires: Ediciones Al Margen, Universidad Nacional de General Sarmiento.

Barbosa, María Cristina, and María Eugenia Salinas. 2000. "Cooperación intermunicipal para la integración y el desarrollo del área metropolitana del Gran Mendoza." Paper presented at V Congreso Internacional del CLAD sobre la reforma del estado y de la administración pública, Santo Domingo, República Dominicana, October 24–27.

Barboza, Hélio Batista, and Francine Lemos Arouca. 2002. "Consórcio Intermunicipal de Produção e Abastecimento—Cinpra." In *20 experiências de gestão pública e cidadania,* edited by Helio Batista Barboza and Peter Spink. São Paulo: Programa Gestão Pública e Cidadania.

Basolo, Victoria, and Dorian Hastings. 2001. "Obstacles to Regional Housing Solutions: A Comparison of Four Metropolitan Areas." *Journal of Urban Affairs* 25 (4): 449–72.

Benjamin, Gerald, and Richard Nathan. 2001. *Regionalism and Realism: A Study of Governments in the New York Metropolitan Area.* Washington, DC: Brookings Institution Press.

Best, Nina Juliette. 2011. "Cooperação e *Multi-level Governance*: O caso do Grande Recife Consórcio de Transporte Metropolitano." MA thesis, Escola de Administração de Empresas de São Paulo, Fundação Getulio Vargas.

Bevir, Mark. 2010. *Democratic Governance.* Princeton: Princeton University Press.

Bevir, Mark, and Frank Trentmann. 2007. *Governance, Consumers and Citizens: Agency and Resistance in Contemporary Politics.* New York: Palgrave Macmillan.

Bish, Robert L., and Eric G. Clemens. 1999. *Local Government in British Columbia.* 3rd ed. Richmond, BC: Union of British Columbia Municipalities.

Booza, Jason, Jackie Cutsinger, and George Galster. 2006. *Where Did They Go? The Decline of Middle-Income Neighborhoods in Metropolitan America.* Washington, DC: Brookings Institution.

Bowman, Ann O'Meara. 2002. "American Federalism on the Horizon." *Publius* 32 (2): 3–22.

Bremaeker, François de. 2001. *Os consórcios na administração municipal.* Serie Estudos Especiais. Rio de Janeiro: Instituto Brasileiro de Administração Municipal.

Brenner, Neil. 2003. "Metropolitan Institutional Reform and the Rescaling of State Space in Contemporary Western Europe." *European Urban and Regional Studies* 10:297–325.

———. 2004. *New State Spaces: Urban Governance and the Rescaling of Statehood.* Oxford: Oxford University Press.

Brierly, Allen B. 2004. "Interlocal Agreements as an Alternative to Consolidation." In *City-County Consolidation and its Alternatives: Reshaping the Local Government Landscape,* edited by Jered Carr and Richard Feiock. New York: M. E. Sharpe.

Brownstone, Meyer, and T. J. Plunkett. 1983. *Metropolitan Winnipeg: Politics and Reform of Local Government.* Berkeley: University of California Press.

Burns, Nancy. 1994. *The Formation of American Local Governments.* New York: Oxford University Press.

Cabrero Mendoza, Enrique. 1995. *La nueva gestión municipal en México: Análisis de experiencias innovadoras en gobiernos locales.* Mexico D. F.: Miguel Angel Porrua.

———, ed. 1996. *Los dilemas de la modernización municipal: Estudios sobre la gestión hacendaria en municipios urbanos de México.* Mexico D. F.: Miguel Angel Porrua.

Camp, Roderic A. 2006. *Politics in Mexico: The Democratic Consolidation.* Oxford: Oxford University Press.

———. 2010. *The Metamorphosis of Leadership in a Democratic Mexico.* Oxford: Oxford University Press.

Campbell, Tim. 2003. *The Quiet Revolution: Decentralization and the Rise of Political Participation in Latin American Cities.* Pittsburgh: University of Pittsburgh Press.

Capital Region Board, Alberta. 2008. "Capital Region Board." http://capital regionboard.ab.ca/ (accessed November 12, 2008).

Carr, Jered. 2004. "Whose Game Do We Play? Local Government Boundary Change and Metropolitan Governance." In *Metropolitan Governance: Conflict, Competition, and Cooperation,* edited by Richard C. Feiock. Washington, DC: Georgetown University Press.

Carr, Jered, and Richard Feiock, eds. 2004. *City-County Consolidation and Its Alternatives: Reshaping the Local Government Landscape.* New York: M. E. Sharpe.

Carrasquero, Otto, and Rexene Hanes de Acevedo. 1993. "El régimen jurídico del municipal venezolano." In *Gerencia municipal,* edited by Janet Kelly, 3–20. Caracas: Ediciones IESA.

Cashaback, David. 2001. *Regional District Governance in British Columbia: A Case Study of Aggregation.* Ottawa: Institute on Governance. http://iog.ca/sites/iog/files/RegionalDistrict.pdf.

Castro, Erika de, and Maciej John Wojciechowski, eds. 2010. *Inclusão, colaboração e governança urbana: Perspectivas Brasileiras.* Vancouver: University of British Columbia; Rio de Janeiro: Observatório das Metrópoles Belo Horizonte: Editora PUC-Minas.

Castro, Ulises. 2007. "La revolución se llama pueblo, potencia rebelde." In *Debate por Venezuela,* edited by Gregorio Castro. Caracas: Editorial Alfa.

Christensen, Terry. 1995. *Local Politics: Governing at the Grass Roots.* Belmont, CA: Wadsworth.

Christoffersen, Henrik, Martin Paldam, and Allan H. Würtz. 2007. "Public versus Private Production and Economies of Scale." *Public Choice* 130 (March): 311–28.

Cieslik, Thomas. 2007. "¿Como gobernar las zonas metropolitanas de México en 2020?" Mexico D. F.: Friedrich-Naumann-Stiftung, Regional Office in Latin America.

City of Calgary. 2005. "Annexation: Frequently Asked Questions." www.calgary.ca/cweb/gateway/gateway.asp?GID=395&CID=0&URL=http%3A%2F%2Fcontent%2Ecalgary%2Eca%2FCCA%2FCity%2BLiving%2FCommunities%2FDevelopment%2BPlans%2Band%2BProjects%2FAnnexation%2BInformation%2FAnnexation%2BFAQ%2Ehtm#3 (accessed October 5, 2005).

Clemente, Roberta. 1999. "Camara do Grande ABC." In *20 experiencias de gestão pública e cidadania,* edited by Luis Mario Fujiwara, Nelson Alessio, and Marta Farah. São Paulo: Fundação Getulio Vargas.

Clementino, Maria do Livramento M. 2003. "A região metropolitana e o Parliamento Comun: A carta dos vereadores da Grande Natal." *Metrópole* 10 (July–December): 27–54.

Collin, Jean-Pierre, and Mariona Tomás. 2004. "Metropolitan Governance in Canada or the Persistence of Institutional Reforms." *Revista de Economía Pública Urbana / Urban Public Economic Review* 2:13–39.

Comisión Nacional para el Área Metropolitana. 1988. *Proyecto 90: Área Metropolitana de Buenos Aires.* Buenos Aires: CONAMBA.

CONAMBA. See Comisión Nacional para el Área Metropolitana.

Crooks, James B. 2004. *Jacksonville: The Consolidation Story, from Civil Rights to the Jaguars.* Gainesville: University Press of Florida.

Cruz, Maria do Carmo. 2002. "Consórcios intermunicipais: Uma alternativa de integração regional ascendente." In *Novos contornos da gestão local: Conceitos em construção,* edited by Peter Spink, Silvio Caccia Bava, and Veronika Paulics. São Paulo: Instituto Polis / Programa Gestão Pública e Cidadania.

Cunha, Rosani Evangelista da. 2004. "Federalismo e relações intergovernamentais: Os consórcios públicos como instrumento de cooperação federativa." *Revista do Serviço Público* 55 (3): 5–36.

Dahl, Robert Alan. 1971. *Polyarchy: Participation and Opposition.* New Haven: Yale University Press.

Danani, Claudia, Magdalena Chiara, and Judith Filc. 1997. *El papel del Fondo de Reparación Histórica del Conurbano Bonaerense: Una aproximación macroinstitucional.* San Miguel: Universidad Nacional de General Sarmiento.

Davidovich, Fany. 2004. A "volta da metrópole" no Brasil: Referências para a gestão territorial. In *Metrópoles: Entre a coesão e a fragmentação, a cooperação e o conflito,* edited by Luiz Cesar de Queiroz Ribeiro. São Paulo: Editora Fundação Perseu Abramo.

De la Cruz, Rafael. 2005. "Decentralization: Key to Understanding a Changing Nation." In *The Unraveling of Representative Democracy in Venezuela,* edited by Jennifer L. McCoy and David Myers. Baltimore: Johns Hopkins University Press.

Demmers, Jolle, Alex E. Fernandez Jilberto, and Barbara Hogenboom, eds. 2004. *Good Governance in the Era of Global Neoliberalism: Conflict and Depolitization in Latin America, Eastern Europe, Asia, and Africa.* New York: Routledge.

Devas, Nick. 2005. "Metropolitan Governance and Urban Poverty." *Public Administration and Development* 25 (4): 351–61.

Diaz-Cayeros, Alberto. 2006. *Federalism, Fiscal Authority, and Centralization in Latin America.* New York: Cambridge University Press.

Dirección de Análisis de Gasto Público y Programas Sociales. 2011. "Gasto Publico Consolidado (1980–2009)." www.mecon.gov.ar/peconomica/basehome/series_gasto.html.

Dodge, William. 1996. *Regional Excellence: Governing Together to Compete Globally and Flourish Locally.* Washington, DC: National League of Cities.

Domínguez, Jorge I., and Michael Shifter, eds. 2003. *Constructing Democratic Governance in Latin America.* 2nd ed. Baltimore: Johns Hopkins University Press.

Duhau, Emilio. 2003. División social del espacio metropolitano y movilidad residencial. *Papeles de Población* 9 (April–June): 161–210. http://redalyc.uaemex .mx/redalyc/src/inicio/ArtPdfRed.jsp?iCve=11203608.

Durand, Luciano. 2006. "La planificación estratégica como herramienta para el desarrollo local: El caso Rosario." MA thesis, Universidad Nacional de San Martín, Universidad Autónoma de Madrid, Buenos Aires.

Eaton, Kent. 2004. *Politics beyond the Capital: The Design of Subnational Institutions in South America.* Stanford: Stanford University Press, 2004.

———. 2006. "Decentralization's Nondemocratic Roots: Authoritarianism and Subnational Reform in Latin America." *Latin American Politics and Society* 48 (1): 1–26.

Elazar, Daniel J. 1987. *Building Cities in America: Urbanization and Suburbanization in a Frontier Society*. Lanham, MD: Hamilton Press.

Ellner, Steve. 2009. "A New Model with Rough Edges: Venezuela's Community Councils." *NACLA Report on the Americas* 42:11–14.

Ellner, Steve, and David Myers. 2002. "Caracas: Incomplete Empowerment amid Geopolitical Federalism." In *Capital City Politics in Latin America*, edited by David J. Myers and Henry Dietz. Boulder, CO: Lynne Rienner.

EMPLASA. See Empresa Paulista de Planejamento Metropolitano.

Empresa Paulista de Planejamento Metropolitano. 2011. "Forum Nacional de Entidades Metropolitanas." www.emplasa.sp.gov.br/fnem/legislacao.asp.

Escolar, Marcelo, and Pedro Pírez. 2004. "La cabeza de Goliat? Región metropolitana y organización federal en Argentina." In *Aportes a la cuestión del gobierno en la Región Metropolitana del Gran Buenos Aires*, edited by Gustavo Badía and Elsa Pereyra. Buenos Aires: Ediciones Al Margen, Universidad Nacional de General Sarmiento.

Estado de São Paulo. 2006. "Metrópole vira 'baleia encalhada' e atrasa o crescimento do país." *Economia e Negócios*, June 25, E1.

Falleti, Tulia G. 2005. "A Sequential Theory of Decentralization: Latin American Cases in Comparative Perspective." *American Political Science Review* 99 (August): 327–46.

———. 2010. *Decentralization and Subnational Politics in Latin America*. New York: Cambridge University Press.

FARN. See Fundación Ambiente y Recursos Naturales.

Fay, Marianne, ed. 2005. *The Urban Poor in Latin America*. Washington, DC: World Bank.

Feiock, Richard C., ed. 2004. *Metropolitan Governance: Conflict, Competition, and Cooperation*. Washington, DC: Georgetown University Press.

Fernandes, Antonio Sergio. 2004. "Gestão municipal versus gestão metropolitana: O caso da Cidade de Salvador." *Cadernos Metrópole* (São Paulo) 11:1–72.

Fernandes, Edésio. 2005. "Apresentação." In *A questão metropolitana no Brasil*, edited by Ronaldo G. Gouvêa. Rio de Janeiro: Editora FGV.

Finfacts Ireland. 2011. "Global/World Income per Capita: From World Bank Development Indicators, 2010." www.finfacts.ie/biz10/globalworldincomepercapita.htm.

Fischer, Mary J. 2003. "The Relative Importance of Income and Race in Determining Residential Outcomes in U.S. Urban Areas, 1970–2000." *Urban Affairs Review* 38 (May): 669–96.

Fisher, William A. 1999. "Does the American Way of Zoning Cause the Suburbs of Metropolitan Areas to Be Too Spread Out?" In *Governance and Opportunity in Metropolitan America,* edited by Alan Altshuler, William Morrill, Harold Wolman, and Faith Mitchell. Washington, DC: National Academy Press.

Fossi, Víctor. 1984. "Desarrollo urbano y vivienda: La desordenada evolución hacia un pais de metrópolis." In *El caso Venezuela: Una ilusión de armonía,* edited by Naim Moisés and Ramon Piñango. Caracas: Ediciones IESA.

Foster, Kathryn. 1997. *The Political Economy of Special Purpose Government.* Washington, DC: Georgetown University Press.

Frederickson, H. George, Gary A. Johnson, and Curtis H. Wood. 2004. *The Adapted City: Institutional Dynamics and Structural Change.* Armonk, NY: M. E. Sharpe.

Frey, William, Jill Wilson, Alan Berube, and Audrey Singer. 2004. *Tracking Metropolitan America into the 21st Century: A Field Guide to the New Metropolitan and Micropolitan Definitions.* Washington, DC: Brookings Institution.

Friedmann, John. 1995. "Where We Stand: A Decade of World City Research." In *World Cities in a World System,* edited by Paul L. Knox and Peter J. Taylor. Cambridge: Cambridge University Press.

Frisken, Frances. 2007. *The Public Metropolis: The Political Dynamics of Urban Expansion in the Toronto Region, 1994–2003.* Toronto: Canadian Scholar's Press.

Frisken, Frances, and Donald F. Norris. 2001. "Regionalism Reconsidered." *Journal of Urban Affairs* 23 (5): 467–78.

Fullerton, Douglas H. 1974. *The Capital of Canada: How Should It Be Governed?* Ottawa: Queen's Printer.

Fundación Ambiente y Recursos Naturales. 2000. "Hacia la construcción de una región metropolitana sustentable." Working paper, Consejo del Plan Urbano Ambiental del Gobierno de la Ciudad de Buenos Aires.

Gainsborough, Juliet F. 2001. "Bridging the City-Suburb Divide: States and the Politics of Regional Cooperation." *Journal of Urban Affairs* 23 (5): 497–512.

Garson, Sol. 2009. *Regiões metropolitanas: Por que não cooperam?* Rio de Janeiro: Letra Capital.

Garson, Sol, L. C. Q. Ribeiro, and J. M. Rodrigues. 2010. "Regiões metropolitanas do Brasil." Observatório das metrópoles. www.observatoriodasmetropoles.net/download/observatorio_RMs2010.pdf.

Garza Villareal, Gustavo, ed. 1996. *Atlas de Monterrey.* Mexico D. F.: El Gobierno de Nuevo León and El Colegio de México.

Germain, Annick, and Damaris Rose. 2000. *Montreal: Quest for a Metropolis.* New York: John Wiley.

Gibson, Edward L., ed. 2004. *Federalism and Democracy in Latin America.* Baltimore: Johns Hopkins University Press.

Giddens, Anthony. 1979. *Central Problems in Social Theory: Action, Structure and Contradiction in Social Analysis.* London: Macmillan.

Gilbert, Alan, ed. 1996. *The Mega-City in Latin America.* New York: United Nations University.

———. 1998. *The Latin American City.* 2nd ed. New York: Monthly Review Press.

Gilbert, Alan, and Peter M. Ward. [1985] 2008. *Housing, the State and the Poor: Policy and Practice in Three Latin American Cities.* Cambridge: Cambridge University Press.

Gil Yepes, José A. 2004. "Public Opinion, Political Socialization and Regime Stabilization." In *The Unraveling of Representative Democracy in Venezuela,* edited by Jennifer L. McCoy and David J. Myers. Baltimore: Johns Hopkins University Press.

Glickman, Norman J., and Robert. H. Wilson. In press. "Urban Policy in the 21st Century: The Legacies of the Great Society." In *Reshaping the Federal Government: The Policy and Management Legacies of the Johnson Years,* edited by Norman J. Glickman, Laurence E. Lynn, and Robert H. Wilson. Austin: University of Texas Press.

González de Pacheco, Rosa Amelia. 1993. "Las finanzas municipales." In *Gerencia municipal,* edited by Janet Kelly. Caracas: Ediciones IESA.

González Parás, Natividad. 2003. *Una nueva visión de la política.* Mexico City: Oceano.

Gottman, Jean. 1961. *Megalopolis: The Urbanized Northeastern Seaboard of the United States.* New York: Twentieth Century Fund.

Gouvêa, Ronaldo G. 2005. *A questão metropolitana no Brasil.* Rio de Janeiro: Editora FGV.

Grodzins, Morton. 1966. *The American System.* Edited by Daniel J. Elazar. Chicago: Rand McNally.

Guimarães, Nathália Arruda. 2004. "Regiões metropolitanas: Aspectos jurídicos." Jus Navigandi. http://jus.com.br/revista/texto/5050/regioes-metropolitanas.

Hagopian, Francis, and Scott Mainwaring. 2005. *The Third Wave of Democratization in Latin America: Advances and Setbacks.* New York: Cambridge University Press.

Hamilton, David K. 2000. "Organizing Government Structure and Governance Functions in Metropolitan Areas." *Journal of Planning Literature* 22 (1): 65–84.

Hardoy, Jorge Enrique. 1972. *Las ciudades en América Latina: Seis ensayos sobre la urbanización contemporánea.* Buenos Aires: Paidós.

Harris, Walter. 1971. *The Growth of Latin American Cities.* Athens: Ohio University Press.

Hawkins, Kirk A., and David Hansen. 2006. "Dependent Civil Society: The Círculos Bolivarianos in Venezuela." *Latin American Research Review* 41 (1): 102–32.

Hirst, Paul. 2000. "Democracy and Governance." In *Debating Governance: Authority, Steering and Democracy,* edited by Jon Pierre. Oxford: Oxford University Press.

Hooghe, Liesbet, and Gary Marks. 2003. "Unravelling the Central State, but How? Types of Multi-Level Governance." *American Political Science Review* 97 (2): 233–43.

Hülsemeyer, Axel. 2000. "Changing 'Political Economies of Scale' and Public Sector Adjustment: Insights from Fiscal Federalism." *Review of International Political Economy* 7 (Spring): 72–100.

Huntington, Samuel P. 1991. *The Third Wave: Democratization in the Late Twentieth Century*. Norman: University of Oklahoma Press.

IBGE. See Instituto Brasileiro de Geografia.

Iceland, John. 2002. "Beyond Black and White: Metropolitan Residential Segregation in Multi-Ethnic America." Paper presented at the annual meeting of the American Sociological Association, Chicago, August 16–19.

Instituto Brasileiro de Geografia e Estatística. 2001. *Tendências demográficas: Uma análise dos resultados da Sinopse Preliminar do Censo Demografico 2000*. Rio de Janeiro: IBGE. www.ibge.gov.br/home/estatistica/populacao/tendencia_demografica/analise_resultados/sinopse_censo2000.pdf.

———. 2009a. "Pesquisa de Informações Básicas Municipais." www.ibge.gov.br/home/estatistica/economia/perfilmunic/2009/munic2009.pdf.

———. 2009b. "Pesquisa Nacional por Amostra de Domicílios—2009." www.ibge.gov.br/home/estatistica/populacao/trabalhoerendimento/pnad2009.

———. 2010. "Censo Demográfico 2010." www.ibge.gov.br/home/estatistica/populacao/censo2010/default.shtm.

Iturburu, Mónica. 2000. *Municipios argentinos: Fortalezas y debilidades de su diseño institucional*. Buenos Aires: INAP.

Jackson, Kenneth T. 1985. *Crabgrass Frontier: The Suburbanization of the United States*. New York: Oxford University Press.

Jacobi, Pedro. 2001. "A experiência da Câmara de Grande ABC." In *Redução da pobreza e dinâmicas locais*, edited by Ilka Camarotti and Peter Spink. Rio de Janeiro: Editora da Fundação Getulio Vargas.

Jacobi, Pedro, and Marco Antonio C. Teixeira. 2000. "Consórcio Quiriri." In *Novas experiencias de gestão pública e cidadania*, edited by Marta Fereira Santos Farah and Hélio Batista Barboza. Rio de Janeiro: Editora Fundação Getulio Vargas.

Johnson, Martin, and Max Neiman. 2004. "Institutional Collective Action: Social Capital and the Formation of Regional Partnerships." In *Metropolitan Governance: Conflict, Competition, and Cooperation*, edited by Richard C. Feiock. Washington, DC: Georgetown University Press.

Jones, Gavin W., and Mike Douglass, eds. 2008. *Mega-Urban Regions in Pacific Asia: Urban Dynamics in a Global Era*. Singapore: NUS Press.

Kanai, J. Miguel. 2009. "In-Between Cities (the Case of Buenos Aires)." Paper presented at the International Sociology Congress, Sao Paulo, Brazil, August 23–25.

Keating, Vallandro, and Ricardo Maranhão. 2008. *Caminhos da conquista: A formação do espaço brasileiro*. São Paulo: Editora Terceiro Nome.

Kellas, Hugh, ed. 2010. *Inclusion, Collaboration and Urban Governance: Brazilian and Canadian Experiences*. Vancouver: University of British Columbia; Rio de Janeiro: Observatório das Metrópoles; Belo Horizonte: Editora PUC-Minas.

Kelleher, Christine, and David Lowery. 2004. "Political Participation and Metropolitan Institutional Contexts." *Urban Affairs Review* 39 (6): 720–57.

Kelly, Janet, ed. 1993a. *Gerencia municipal*. Caracas: Ediciones IESA.

———. 1993b. "El municipio como sistema político." In *Gerencia municipal*, edited by Janet Kelly, 21–40 and appendix. Caracas: Ediciones IESA.

Kemp, Roger, ed. 2003. *Regional Government Innovations*. Jefferson, NC: McFarland.

Klink, Jeroen. 2008. "Recent Perspectives on Metropolitan Organizations, Functions, and Governance." In *Governing the Metropolis: Principles and Cases*, edited by Eduardo Rojas, Juan R. Cuadrado-Roura, and José Miguel Fernandez Guell. Washington, DC: Inter-American Development Bank; Cambridge, MA: Harvard University.

———, ed. 2010. *Governança das metrópoles: Conceitos, experiências e perspectivas*. São Paulo: Editora Annablume.

Knox, Paul L., and Peter J. Taylor, eds. 1995. *World Cities in a World System*. New York: Cambridge University Press.

Lefèvre, Christian. 1998. "Metropolitan Government and Governance in Western Countries: A Critical Review." *International Journal of Urban and Regional Research* 22 (1): 9–25.

Le Galès, Patrick. 2009. "Mega City and Why Size Matters for Urban Governance." Paper presented at the International Sociology Congress, Sao Paulo, Brazil, August 23–25.

Leland, Suzanne, and Kurt Thurmaier. 2004. *Case Studies of City-County Consolidation: Reshaping the Local Government Landscape*. New York: M. E. Sharpe.

———. 2005. "When Efficiency Is Unbelievable: Normative Lessons from 30 Years of City-County Consolidations." *Public Administration Review* 65 (4): 475–89.

Levatino, María Belén. 2009. "La gestión de los residuos urbanos metropolitanos en la provincia de Mendoza." Paper presented at the fifth congress of the Asociación Argentina de Estudios de Administración Pública, San Juan, May 27–29. www.aaeap.org.ar/ponencias/congreso5/index5congreso.html.

Lewis, Paul. 2004. "An Old Debate Confronts New Realities: Large Suburbs and Economic Development in the Metropolis." In *Metropolitan Governance: Conflict, Competition, and Cooperation*, edited by Richard Feiock. Washington, DC: Georgetown University Press.

Lindenboim, Javier, and Damián Kennedy. 2003. "Continuidad y cambios en la dinámica urbana de Argentina." Paper presented at the conference "VII Jornadas de Población" of the Asociación de Estudios de Población de la Argentina, Tafí del Valle, November 5–7.

Lindert, Paul van. 2009. *Decentralized Development in Latin America: Experiences in Local Governance*. New York: Springer.

Linz, Juan, and Alfred Stepan. 1996. *Problems of Democratic Transition and Consolidation*. Baltimore: Johns Hopkins University Press.

Lippi, Mariana Ferreti. 2011. "A Região Metropolitana da Baixada Santista: Uma análise a partir dos fatores que favorecem a capacidade de governança e governabilidade regional." MA thesis, Escola de Administração de Empresas de São Paulo, Fundação Getulio Vargas.

London, Department of the Environment, Transport and the Regions. 1997. *New Leadership for London: The Government's Proposals for a Greater London Authority. A Consultation Paper.* London: HMSO.

Lopez-Calva, Luis F., and Nora Lustig, eds. 2010. *Declining Inequality in Latin America: A Decade of Progress?* Washington, DC: Brookings Institution Press.

López Pérez, Roberto. 2003. "Bases conceptuales y técnicas para la delimitación de zonas metropolitanas en México." *Revista de Información y Análisis* 8 (22): 55–63.

Lynn, Laurence, Carolyn J. Heinrich, and Carolyn J. Hill. 2001. *Improving Governance: A New Logic for Empirical Research.* Washington, DC: Georgetown University Press.

Machado, Gustavo Gomes. 2009. *Gestão metropolitana e autonomia municipal: Dilemas das transações federativas.* Belo Horizonte: Editora PUC Minas.

Maigon, Thais. 2007. "Consejos comunales, ciudadanía, estado y poder popular." In *Debate por Venezuela,* edited by Gregorio Castro. Caracas: Editorial Alfa.

Mainwaring, Scott, and Timothy R. Scully. 2008. "Latin America: Eight Lessons for Governance." *Journal of Democracy* 19 (July): 113–27.

———, eds. 2010. *Democratic Governance in Latin America.* Stanford: Stanford University Press.

Marando, Vincent L. 1974. "The Politics of Metropolitan Reform." *Administration and Society* 6 (2): 229–62.

Martínez, Ildemaro Jesús. 1977. "The Performance of Local Government in Democratic Venezuela." In *Venezuela: The Democratic Experience,* edited by John D. Martz and David J. Myers. New York: Praeger.

———. 1986. "Venezuelan Local Government." In *Venezuela: The Democratic Experience,* rev. ed., edited by John D. Martz and David J. Myers, 384–401. New York: Praeger.

Massey, Douglas, and Nancy Denton. 1994. *American Apartheid: Segregation and the Making of the Underclass.* Cambridge, MA: Harvard University Press.

Masson, Jack, and Edward C. LeSage Jr. 1994. *Alberta's Local Governments: Politics and Democracy.* Edmonton: University of Alberta Press.

McCabe, Barbara C. 2004. "Special Districts: An Alternative to Consolidation." In *City-County Consolidation and Its Alternatives: Reshaping the Local Government Landscape,* edited by Jered Carr and Richard Feiock. New York: M. E. Sharpe.

McCoy, Jennifer L., and David J. Myers, eds. 2005. *The Unraveling of Representative Democracy in Venezuela.* Baltimore: Johns Hopkins University Press.

Metcalfe, L. 1994. "International Policy Coordination and Public Management Reform." *International Review of Administrative Sciences* 60 (2): 271–90.

Miller, David. 2002. *The Regional Governing of Metropolitan America.* Boulder, CO: Westview Press.

Mitchell, Jerry, ed. 1992. *Public Authorities and Public Policy: The Business of Government.* New York: Praeger.

Mitchell-Weaver, Clyde, David Miller, and Ron Deal Jr. 2000. "Multilevel Governance and Metropolitan Regionalism in the USA." *Urban Studies* 37 (5–6): 851–76.

Mkandawire, Thankike. 2007. "'Good Governance': The Itinerary of an Idea." *Development in Practice* 17 (August): 679–81.

Mollenkopf, John H. 1983. *The Contested City.* Princeton: Princeton University Press.

Montero, Alfred P., and David J. Samuels, eds. 2004. *Decentralization and Democracy in Latin America.* Notre Dame: University of Notre Dame Press.

Morales Tucker, Alberto. 1992. *Lo urbano como profesión: Lo academico y lo profesional de Alberto Morales Tucker.* Caracas: Autoridades rectorales do la Universidad Simón Bolívar.

Morçöl, Götkuğ, and Ulf Zimmerman. 2006. "Metropolitan Governance and Business Improvement Districts." *International Journal of Public Administration* 29 (1–3): 5–29.

Morris, A. S. 1978. "Urban Growth Patterns in Latin America with Illustrations from Caracas." *Urban Studies* 15 (1): 299–312.

Myers, David J. 2005. "The Normalization of Punto Fijo Democracy." In *The Unraveling of Representative Democracy in Venezuela,* edited by Jennifer L. McCoy and David J. Myers. Baltimore: Johns Hopkins University Press.

Myers, David J., and Henry A. Dietz, eds. 2002. *Capital City Politics in Latin America: Democratization and Empowerment.* Boulder, CO: Lynne Rienner.

Negrón, Marcos. 1991. "El sistema venezolano de ciudades reconsiderado." Mimeo. Facultad de Arquitectura y Urbanismo, Caracas, Universidad Central de Venezuela.

Newman, Peter. 2000. "Changing Patterns of Regional Governance in the EU." *Urban Studies* 37 (5–6): 895–908.

Nixon, Andrew. 1995. *Local Government in Latin America.* Boulder, CO: Lynne Rienner.

Norris, Donald. 2001. "Prospects for Regional Governance under the New Regionalism: Economic Imperatives versus Political Impediments." *Journal of Urban Affairs* 23 (5): 557–71.

Oakerson, Ronald J. 2004. "Game-Theoretic Models of Metropolitan Cooperation." In *Metropolitan Governance: Conflict, Competition, and Cooperation,* edited by Richard C. Feiock. Washington, DC: Georgetown University Press.

O'Donnell, Guillermo. 1993. "On the State, Democratization and Some Conceptual Problems: A Latin American View with Glances at Some Postcommunist Countries." *World Development* 21 (8): 1355–69.

Orfield, Myron. 2002. *American Metropolitics: The New Suburban Reality.* Washington, DC: Brookings Institution Press.

Ostrom, Vincent, Charles Tiebout, and Robert Warren. 1961. "The Organization of Government in Metropolitan Areas." *American Political Science Review* 55 (December): 831–42.

Padilla Delgado, Héctor Antonio. 2005. "Ciudad Juárez: En busca de un plan estratégico." In *Ciudades del siglo XXI: Competitividad o cooperación?*, edited by Carlos Arce, Enrique Cabrero, and Alicia Ziccardi. Mexico D. F.: CIDE/ Miguel Angel Porrua.

Paiva, Antonio. 2003. *Relevance of Metropolitan Government in Latin American Cities.* Utrecht: Eburon Delft.

Parker, Richard. 2005. "A Uni-City at 50 Years." *Plan Canada* 45 (3): 29–31.

Penfold Becerra, Michael. 2007. "Clientelism and Social Funds: Evidence from Chávez's *Misiones.*" *Latin American Politics and Society* 49 (4): 63–84.

Phares, Donald, ed. 2004. *Metropolitan Governance without Metropolitan Government?* Aldershot: Ashgate.

Pigou, Arthur. [1920] 2002. *Economics of Welfare.* New Brunswick, NJ: Transaction.

Pírez, Pedro. 1991. *Municipio, necesidades sociales y política local.* Buenos Aires: Grupo Editor Latinoamericano / IIED-AL.

———. 1994. *Buenos Aires Metropolitana: Política y gestión de la ciudad.* Buenos Aires: Centro Editor de América Latina.

———. 1996. "La ciudad de Buenos Aires: Una cuestión federal." *Revista Mexicana de Sociología* 58 (3): 192–212.

———. 1998. "The Management of Urban Services in the City of Buenos Aires." *Environment and Urbanization* 10 (2): 209–22.

———. 2004. "Instituciones políticas y gestión urbana en el Área Metropolitana de Buenos Aires." *Cuadernos PROLAM/USP* (Sao Paulo) 3 (2): 73–87.

———. 2005. "Descentralización demográfica y centralización económica en la región Metropolitana de Buenos Aires." *Población de Buenos Aires* 2 (2): 29–44. http://redalyc.uaemex.mx/src/inicio/ArtPdfRed.jsp?iCve= 74020202.

Post, Stephanie S. 2004. "Metropolitan Area Governance and Institutional Collective Action." In *Metropolitan Governance: Conflict, Competition, and Cooperation,* edited by Richard Feiock. Washington, DC: Georgetown University Press.

Province of Manitoba, Regional Planning Advisory Committee. 2003. "A Partnership for the Future: Putting the Pieces Together in the Manitoba Capital Region." www.gov.mb.ca/ia/pdf/cap_partner/fulldoc.pdf.

Province of Ontario, Ministry of Municipal Affairs and Housing. 2005. "Greenbelt Protection." www.mah.gov.on.ca/userfiles/HTML/nts_1_16289_1.html (accessed October 5, 2005).

Puentes, Robert, and David Warren. 2006. "One Fifth of America: A Comprehensive Guide to America's First Suburbs." Brookings Institution Survey Series. February. www.brookings.edu/~/media/Files/rc/reports/2006/02metropolitanpolicy_puentes/20060215_FirstSuburbs.pdf.

Radio Nacional de Venezuela. 2007. "Encuentro Regional de Consejos Comunales de Caracas, Vargas y Miranda." March 23. www.aporrea.org/poderpopular/n92337.html.

Rangel, Domingo A. 1966. *Los Andinos en el poder.* Mérida: Talleres Gráficos Universitarios.

Ravanelli, Paula. 2010. "O Comitê de Articulação Federativa e o desafio da governançametropolitana no Brasil." In *Governança das metrópoles: Conceitos, experiências e perspectivas,* ed. Jeroen Klink, 259–89. São Paulo: Editora Annablume.

Reifschneider, Alexandra Petermann. 2006. *Competition in the Provision of Local Public Goods: Single Function Jurisdictions and Individual Choice.* Northampton, MA: Edward Elgar.

Rezende, Fernando, and Sol Garson. 2004. *Financing Metropolitan Areas in Brazil: Political, Institutional, and Legal Obstacles and Emergence of New Proposals for Improving Coordination.* Ottawa: Forum of Federations.

———. 2006. "Financing Metropolitan Areas in Brazil: Political, Institutional and Legal Obstacles and Emergence of New Proposals for Improving Coordination." *Revista de Economia Contemporânea* 10 (1): 5–34.

Ribeiro, Luiz Cesar de Queiroz, ed. 2000. *O futuro das metrópoles: Desigualdades e governabilidade.* Rio de Janeiro: FASE.

———. 2004a. "As metrópoles e a sociedade brasileira: Futuro comprometido?" In *Metrópoles: Entre a coesão e a fragmentação, a cooperação e o conflito,* edited by Luiz Cesar de Queiroz Ribeiro. São Paulo: Editora Fundação Perseu Abramo.

———, ed. 2004b. *Metrópoles: Entre a coesão e a fragmentação, a cooperação e o conflito.* São Paulo: Editora Fundação Perseu Abramo.

———. 2004c. "Segregação residencial e políticas públicas: Análise do espaço social da cidade na gestão do território." In *Metrópoles: Entre a coesão e a fragmentação, a cooperação e o conflito,* edited by Luiz Cesar de Queiroz Ribeiro. São Paulo: Editora Fundação Perseu Abramo.

———. 2010. "Os desafios da reforma urbana nas metrópoles brasileiras." In *Governança das metrópoles: Conceitos,experiências e perspectivas,* ed. Jeroen Klink, 75–98. São Paulo: Editora Annablume.

Ribeiro, Luiz Cesar de Queiroz, and Lucia Bógus. 2009. "Apresentação: Dossier gestão metropolitana." *Cadernos Metropole* 11 (22): 293–96.

Roberts, Bryan, and Robert H. Wilson, eds. 2009. *Urban Segregation and Governance in the Americas.* New York: Palgrave Macmillan.

Robinson, Jennifer. 2006. *Ordinary Cities: Between Modernity and Development.* New York: Routledge.

Rodrigues, Gilberto Marco Antonio. 2006. "Public Consortiums in Brazil: New Law Stimulates Federal Cooperation." *Federations* 5 (2): 9–10.

Rodríguez, Jorge, and Camilo Arriagada. 2004. "Segregación residencial en la ciudad Latinoamericana." *EURE* (Santiago) 30 (May): 5–24.

Rodríguez, Victoria. 1997. *Decentralization in Mexico: From Reforma Municipal to Solidaridad to Nuevo Federalismo*. Boulder, CO: Westview Press.

Rodriguez-Acosta, C. A., and A. Rosenbaum. 2005. "Local Government and the Governance of Metropolitan Areas in Latin America." *Public Administration and Development* 25 (4): 295–306.

Rogers, Pamela. 2006. "Intraurban Mobility, Immigration, and Urban Settlement Patterns: The Case of Texas Gateways." PhD diss., University of Texas at Austin.

Rogers, Pamela, and Peter Ward. 2008. "Routes to Home Ownership: The Experience of Mexican Migrants to the 'New Gateway' Cities of Texas." In *Cómo se hacen las ciencias sociales: Una antología de ejemplos y preceptos en homenaje a Fernando Pozos Ponce,* edited by Fernando Leal. Guadalajara: Universidad de Guadalajara.

Rojas, Eduardo, Juan R. Cuadrado-Roura, and José Miguel Fernandez Guell, eds. 2008. *Governing the Metropolis: Principles and Cases.* Washington, DC: Inter-American Development Bank; Cambridge, MA: Harvard University.

Rolnik, Raquel, and Nadia Somekh. 2004. "Governar as metrópoles: Dilemas da recentralização." In *Metrópoles: Entre a coesão e a fragmentação, a cooperação e o conflito,* edited by Luiz Cesar de Queiroz Ribeiro. São Paulo: Editora Fundação Perseu Abramo.

Rosenblum, Nancy, and Robert Post. 2002. Introduction to *Civil Society and Government,* edited by Nancy Rosenblum and Robert Post, 1–25. Princeton: Princeton University Press.

Rosenn, Keith S. 1994. "Federalism in the Americas in Comparative Perspective." *University of Miami Inter-American Law Review* 26 (Fall): 1–50.

Rusk, David. 1998. *Inside Game / Outside Game: Winning Strategies for Saving Urban America.* Washington, DC: Brookings Institution.

———. 2003. *Cities without Suburbs: A Census 2000 Update.* Washington, DC: Woodrow Wilson International Center for Scholars.

Sabatini, Francisco. 2003. *The Social Spatial Segregation in the Cities of Latin America.* Washington, DC: Inter-American Development Bank.

Sancton, Andrew. 2000. *Merger Mania: The Assault on Local Government.* Montreal: McGill-Queen's University Press.

———. 2001. "Canadian Cities and the New Regionalism." *Journal of Urban Affairs* 23 (5): 543–55.

———. 2008. *The Limits of Boundaries: Why City-Regions Cannot Be Self-Governing.* Montreal: McGill-Queen's University Press.

Schedler, Andreas. 1998. "What Is Democratic Consolidation?" *Journal of Democracy* 9 (2): 91–107.

Schmitter, Philippe C. 2002. "Introduction to a Discussion on the European Union." In *Participatory Governance: Political and Social Implications,* edited by Jürgen Grote and Bernard Gbipki. Opladen: Leske and Budrich.

———. 2008. "Governance Arrangements for Sustainability: A Regional Perspective." Mimeo, European University Institute, www.eui.eu/Documents/ DepartmentsCentres/SPS/Profiles/Schmitter/PCSCERESGovernance EU.pdf.

Scobie, James R. 1974. *Buenos Aires: From Plaza to Suburb, 1870–1910.* New York: Oxford University Press.

Selznick, Philip. 1984. *Leadership in Administration: A Sociological Interpretation.* Berkeley: University of California Press.

———. 1992. *The Moral Commonwealth: Social Theory and the Promise of Community.* Berkeley: University of California Press.

Singer, Audrey. 2004. "The Rise of New Immigrant Gateways." Living Cities Census Series, February, Center on Urban and Metropolitan Policy, Brookings Institution, www.brookings.edu/~/media/Files/rc/reports/2004/02 demographics_singer/20040301_gateways.pdf.

Smith, Patrick J., and Kennedy Stewart. 1998. "Making Local Accountability Work in British Columbia: Report 2, Reforming Municipal Electoral Accountability." In *Making Local Accountability Work in British Columbia.* Vancouver: Institute of Governance Studies, Simon Fraser University.

Smith, Peter C., and Andrew Street. 2005. "Measuring the Efficiency of Public Services: The Limits of Analysis." *Journal of the Royal Statistical Society* 168 (2): 401–17.

Smith, Peter H. 2005. *Democracy in Latin America: Political Change in Comparative Perspective.* New York: Oxford University Press.

Smoke, Paul, Eduardo J. Gomez, and George E. Peterson, eds. 2006. *Decentralization in Asia and Latin America: Towards a Comparative Interdisciplinary Perspective.* Northampton, MA: Edward Elgar.

Sobrino, Jaime. 2003. *Competitividad de las ciudades en México.* Mexico D. F.: El Colegio de México.

Sørensen, Eva, and Jacob Torfing, eds. 2007. *Theories of Democratic Network Governance.* Basingstoke: Palgrave Macmillan.

Souza, Celina. 2001. "Federalismo e descentralização na Constituição de 1988: Processo decisório, conflitos e alianças." *Dados* (Rio de Janeiro) 44 (3): 513–60.

———. 2002. "Brazil: The Prospects of a Center-Constraining Federation in a Fragmented Polity." *Publius: The Global Review of Federalism* 32 (Spring): 23–48.

———. 2003. "Regiões metropolitanas: Condicionantes do regime político." *Lua Nova* 59:137–58.

———. 2005. "Brazilian Metropolitan Regions: Regime Change and Government Vacuum." *Public Administration and Development* 25 (4): 341–50.

Spink, Peter K. 2000. "The Right Approach to Local Public Management: Experiences from Brazil." *Revista de Administração de Empresas* 40 (3): 45–65.

Spink, Peter K., and Nina J. Best. 2009. "Introduction: Local Democratic Governance, Poverty Reduction and Inequality: The Hybrid Character of Public Action. *IDS Bulletin* 40 (6): 1–12.

Statistics Canada. 2003. "2001 Census: Growth Concentrated in Four Large Urban Regions." http://geodepot.statcan.ca/Diss/Highlights/Page9/Page9_e.cfm.

———. 2007. "2006 Census: Census Metropolitan Area (CMA) and Census Agglomeration (CA)." http://www12.statcan.ca/english/census06/reference/dictionary/geo009.cfm.

———. 2008. "Census: 2006 Community Profiles." http://www12.statcan.gc.ca/census-recensement/2006/dp-pd/prof/92-591/Index.cfm?Lang = E.

———. 2012a. "Population and Dwelling Counts, for Canada and Census Subdivisions (Municipalities) with 5,000-Plus Population, 2011 and 2006 Censuses." http://www12.statcan.gc.ca/census-recensement/2011/dp-pd/hlt-fst/pd-pl/Table-Tableau.cfm?LANG = Eng&T = 307&S = 11&O = A&RPP = 699.

———. 2012b. "Population and Dwelling Counts, for Canada, Census Metropolitan Areas, Census Agglomerations and Census Subdivisions (Municipalities), 2011 and 2006 Censuses." http://www12.statcan.gc.ca/census-recensement/2011/dp-pd/hlt-fst/pd-pl/Select-Geo-Choix.cfm?LANG = Eng&T = 203&GK = CMA.

Stepan, Alfred C. 1999. "Federalism and Democracy: Beyond the U.S." *Model Journal of Democracy* 10 (4): 19–34.

Stephens, G. Ross, and Nelson Wikstrom. 2000. *Metropolitan Government and Governance: Theoretical Perspectives, Empirical Analysis, and the Future.* New York: Oxford University Press.

Strelec, Thamara Caroline. 2011. "Desafios da adaptação institucional: Um estudo do impacto da 'Lei de Consórcios Públicos' no Estado de São Paulo." MA thesis, Escola de Administração de Empresas de São Paulo, Fundação Getulio Vargas.

Stren, Richard, and Robert Cameroon, eds. 2005. "Metropolitan Governance." Special issue, *Public Administration and Development* 25.

Swanson, Bert E. 2004. "Jacksonville/Duval County, Florida: Alternative Explanations for the Adoption of City/County Consolidation in Jacksonville/Duval Florida." In *Case Studies of City-County Consolidation: Reshaping the Local Government Landscape,* edited by Suzanne Leland and Kurt Thurmaier. New York: M. E. Sharpe.

Swanstrom, Todd. 2001. "What We Argue about When We Argue about Regionalism." *Journal of Urban Affairs* 23 (5): 479–96.

Swyngedouw, Erik. 2005. "Governance Innovation and the Citizen: The Janus Face of Governance-beyond-the-State." *Urban Studies* 42 (October): 1991–2006.

Tecco, Claudio, and Silvana Fernández. 2005. "Sobre la necesidad de una gestión urbana asociada entre municipios que conforman la Región Metropolitana de Córdoba." In *Región Metropolitana Córdoba (RMC): Un estudio del sistema urbano y su articulación a la red de ciudades del cono sur,* directed by Claudio Tecco. Córdoba: IIFAP-Universidad Nacional de Córdoba.

Telles, Edward E. 1995. "Structural Sources of Socioeconomic Segregation in Brazilian Metropolitan Areas." *American Journal of Sociology* 100 (5): 1199–1223.

Thurmaier, Kurt, and Curtis Wood. 2002. "Interlocal Agreements as Overlapping Social Networks: Picket-Fence Regionalism in Metropolitan Kansas City." *Public Administration Review* 62 (5): 585–98.

Tiebout, Charles M. 1956. "A Pure Theory of Local Expenditures." *Journal of Political Economy* 64 (October): 416–24.

Toronto City Summit Alliance. 2003. "Enough Talk: An Action Plan for the Toronto Region." www.civicaction.ca/enough-talk-action-plan-toronto-region.

Torre, Juan Carlos, and Elisa Pastoriza. 2002. "La democratización del bienestar." In *Los años Peronistas (1943–1955),* edited by Juan C. Torre. Nueva Historia Argentina 7. Buenos Aires: Sudamericana.

Townroe, P. M., and D. Keene. 1984. "Polarization Reversal in the State of São Paulo, Brazil." *Regional Studies* 18:45–54.

Troconis de Veracoechea, Ermilia. 1993. *Caracas.* Caracas: Editorial Gribaljo.

Trotta, Miguel. 2003. *Las metamorfosis del clientelismo político: Contribución para el análisis institucional.* Buenos Aires: Espacio.

Tulchin, Joseph S., and Amelia Brown. 2002. *Democratic Governance and Social Inequality.* Boulder, CO: Lynne Rienner.

Tulchin, Joseph S., and Andrew Selee, eds. 2004. *Decentralization and Democratic Governance in Latin America.* Washington, DC: Woodrow Wilson International Center for Scholars, Latin American Program.

United Cities and Local Governments. 2009. *Decentralization and Local Democracy in the World: First Global Report, 2008.* World Bank and United Cities and Local Governments. www.cities-localgovernments.org/gold/Upload/gold_report/01_introduction_en.pdf.

———. 2010. *Local Government Finance: The Challenges of the 21st Century: Second Global Report on Decentralization and Local Democracy.* Mexico D. F.: World Bank and United Cities and Local Governments.

United Nations Habitat. 2008. *State of the World's Cities, 2008/2009: Harmonious Cities.* London: Earthscan Publications.

———. 2010. *State of the World's Cities, 2010/2011: Cities for All, Bridging the Urban Divide.* Washington, DC: Earthscan Publications.

United Nations Population Division. Department of Economic and Social Affairs. 2006. *World Urbanization Prospects: The 2005 Revision.* October. www.un.org/esa/population/publications/WUP2005/2005WUPHighlights_Final_Report.pdf.

———. 2009. "World Urbanization Prospects: The 2009 Revision Population Database." http://esa.un.org/wup2009/unup/index.asp?panel=1.

Usach, Natalia. 2005. "La gobernanza del área metropolitana de Mendoza, Argentina. Estudio de caso." Paper presented at VII Seminario Nacional de la Red de Centros Academicos para el Estudio de Gobiernos Locales, Buenos Aires, September 15–16. http://biblioteca.municipios.unq.edu.ar/modules/mislibros/archivos/Ponencia%20Natalia_%20Usach.pdf.

U.S. Agency for International Development. 2007. *Latin America and the Caribbean: Selected Economic and Social Data, 2007.* Washington, DC: U.S. AID. http://pdf.usaid.gov/pdf_docs/PNADK100.pdf.

U.S. AID. See U.S. Agency for International Development.

U.S. Census Bureau. 2003. *2002 Census of Governments.* www.census.gov/prod/2003pubs/gc021x1.pdf.

———. 2008. *2007 Census of Governments.* www.census.gov/govs/cog/.

Vallmitjana, Marta, ed. 1993. "Caracas: Nuevos escenarios para el poder local." In *Caracas: Comisión Presidencial para la Reforma del Estado.* Caracas: Editorial Nueva Sociedad.

Venezuela, Ministerio de Fomento, Oficina Central de Estadística e Informática. 1983. *XI Censo General de Población y Vivienda, 20 de Octubre 1981.* Caracas: OCEI.

Violich, Francis. 1987. *Urban Planning for Latin America: The Challenge of Metropolitan Growth.* With Robert Daughters. Boston: Oelgeschlager, Gunn, and Hain in association with the Lincoln Institute for Land Policy.

Walker, David B. 1987. "Snow White and the 17 Dwarfs: From Metro Cooperation to Governance." *National Civic Review* 76 (1): 14–28.

Ward, Peter M. 1996. "Contemporary Issues in the Government and Administration of Latin American Mega-Cities." In *The Mega-City in Latin America,* edited by Alan Gilbert. New York: United Nations University Press.

———. 1998a. "Future Livelihoods in Mexico City: A Glimpse into the New Millennium." *Cities* 15 (2): 63–74.

———. 1998b. *Mexico City.* 2nd ed. New York: John Wiley and Sons.

———. 1999. "Creating a Metropolitan Tier of Government in Federal Systems: Getting 'There' from 'Here' in Mexico City and in Other Latin American Megacities." *South Texas Law Review Journal* 40 (3): 603–23.

———. 2004. *México, Megaciudad: Desarrollo y Política, 1970–2002.* Toluca: Colegio Mexiquense, Miguel Angel Porrúa.

Ward, Peter M., and Victoria E. Rodríguez. 1999. *New Federalism and State Government in Mexico: Bringing the States Back In.* U.S. Mexican Policy Reports Series No. 9. Austin: Lyndon B. Johnson School of Public Affairs, University of Texas at Austin.

Wheeler, Christopher H., and Elizabeth A. La Jeunesse. 2006. "Trends in the Distributions of Income and Human Capital within Metropolitan Areas: 1980–2000." Working Paper 2006-055A, Federal Reserve Bank of St. Louis, http://research.stlouisfed.org/wp/2006/2006-055.pdf.

White, Richard. 2002. *Urban Infrastructure and Urban Growth in the Toronto Region, 1950s to the 1990s.* Toronto: Neptis Foundation.

Wilson, Robert H. 1993. *States and the Economy: Policymaking and Decentralization.* New York: Praeger.

Wilson, Robert H., and Reid Cramer, eds. 1995. *International Workshop on Good Local Government.* Austin: University of Texas, Lyndon B. Johnson School of Public Affairs.

Wilson, Robert H., and Robert Paterson, eds. 2003. *Innovative Initiatives in Growth Management and Open Space Preservation: A National Study.* Policy Research Project No. 145. Austin: Lyndon B. Johnson School of Public Affairs, University of Texas at Austin.

Wilson, Robert H., Peter M. Ward, Peter K. Spink, and Victoria E. Rodríguez. 2008. *Governance in the Americas: Decentralization, Democracy, and Subnational Government in Brazil, Mexico, and the USA.* Notre Dame: University of Notre Dame Press.

Wolfish, Daniel, and Gordon Smith. 2000. "Governance and Policy in a Multicentric World." *Canadian Public Policy / Analyse de Politiques* 26, suppl. (August): S51–S72.

Wood, Charles, and Bryan Roberts, eds. 2004. *Rethinking Development in Latin America.* University Park: Pennsylvania State University Press.

World Bank. 2009. "Data: Countries and Economies." http://data.worldbank .org/country.

Yarrington, Doug. 2003. "Cattle, Corruption, and Venezuelan State Formation during the Regime of Juan Vicente Gómez, 1908–35." *Latin American Research Review* 35 (2): 3–33.

Ziccardi, A., ed. 2003. *Planeación participativa en el especio local: Cinco programas parciales de Desarrollo Urbano en el Distrito Federal.* Mexico D.F.: UNAM.

Zovatto, Daniel G. 2007. "Direct Democracy Institutions." In *Democracies in Development: Politics and Reform in Latin America,* edited by J. Mark Payne, Daniel G. Zovatto, and Mercedes Mateo Diaz. Washington, DC: Inter-American Development Bank.

ROBERTA CLEMENTE is a member of the research staff of the São Paulo State Legislative Assembly and is a collaborator of the Center for Public Administration and Government at the São Paulo School of Business Administration, Getulio Vargas Foundation. She holds a PhD from the Public Administration and Government Program, Getulio Vargas Foundation.

DAVID J. MYERS is an Associate Professor of Political Science at Pennsylvania State University. Among his recent publications are *Capital City Politics in Latin America* (with Henry Dietz; Lynne Rienner, 2002); *The Unraveling of Representative Democracy in Venezuela* (with Jennifer L. McCoy; Johns Hopkins University Press, 2004); and "Venezuela: Delegative Democracy or Electoral Autocracy," in Jorge Domínguez and Michael Shifter's *Constructing Democratic Governance in Latin America*, 3rd ed. (Johns Hopkins University Press, 2008). He has held faculty positions at the United States Military Academy (West Point), the Instituto de Estudios Superiores de Administración (Caracas, Venezuela), and the Central University of Venezuela. He is a Senior Fulbright Scholar. He holds a PhD from the University of California, Los Angeles.

PEDRO PÍREZ is a Sociologist and Researcher at the Consejo Nacional de Investigaciones Científicas y Técnicas (CONICET; National Council for Scientific and Technical Research), Instituto de Estudios de América Latina y el Caribe (Institute for Latin America and the Caribbean Studies), Universidad de Buenos Aires, and a Professor of Political Science at the Universidad de Buenos Aires. He is author of *Buenos Aires Metropolitana: Política y gestión de la ciudad* (CEAL, 1994); *Basura privada, servicio publico: Los residuos en dos ciudades argentinas* (CEAL, 1994); *El sistema urbano-regional de redes de servicios e infraestructuras: Materiales para su estudio* (Universidad de La Plata, 2003); and *Las sombras de la luz: Distribución eléctrica, configuración urbana y pobreza en la Región Metropolitana de Buenos Aires* (EUDEBA, 2009). He formerly was Professor and Researcher at El Colegio de Mexico and at the Universidad Nacional Autonoma de Mexico. He served as Visiting Professor in Brazil, Spain, and Uruguay. He holds a PhD in law and social science from the Universidad Nacional de Córdoba, Argentina.

HÉCTOR ROBLES was Advisor to the Planning Committee of Development of the State of Jalisco and a member of the Zapopan City Council in Guadalajara, Mexico (2006–9). He was Zapopan's Secretary for Social Development (2009–12) and in 2012 was elected mayor of Zapopan. He holds a PhD in public policy from the Lyndon B. Johnson School for Public Affairs, University of Texas at Austin.

ANDREW SANCTON is a Professor of Political Science at the University of Western Ontario in London and was Department Chair from 2000 to 2005. He is the author of *Merger Mania: The Assault on Local Government* (2000) and *The Limits of Boundaries: Why City-Regions Cannot Be Self-Governing* (2008), both published by McGill-Queen's University Press. His most recent book is *Canadian Local Government: An Urban Perspective,* published by Oxford University Press in 2011. From 1998 until 2000 he was the President of the Canadian Association of Programs in Public Administration and a board member of the Institute of Public Administration of Canada. His work on the relationship between municipal amalgamations and cost savings won the 1996 J. E. Hodgetts Award for the best English-language article in the journal *Canadian Public Administration.* He attended Oxford University as a Rhodes Scholar, obtaining a BPhil and a PhD in politics.

PETER K. SPINK is a Professor of Public Administration and Government in the São Paulo School of Business Administration, Getulio Vargas Foundation, where he served as Academic Dean (1991–95) and as head of the Center for Public Administration and Government (1995–2010). He is currently editor of the *Revista de Administração Pública.* Among his publications are *Reforming the State: Managerial Public Administration in Latin America* (with Luiz Carlos Bresser Pereira; Lynne Rienner, 1999); *Redução da pobreza e dinâmicas locais* (with Ilka Camarotti; Editora da Fundação Getulio Vargas, 2001), *Governo local e desigualdades de gênero* (with Ilka Camarotti; Editora Annablume, 2003), and *Governance in the Americas: Decentralization, Democracy, and Subnational Government in Brazil, Mexico and the USA* (with Robert H. Wilson, Peter M. Ward, and Victoria E. Rodríguez, University of Notre Dame Press, 2008). He has been a Visiting Scholar at the Centre of Latin American Studies, University of Cambridge, and Visiting Professor at the Lyndon B. Johnson School of Public Affairs, University of Texas at Austin, and the Social Psychology Department, Universidad Autonoma de Barcelona. He has a PhD in organizational psychology from the University of London.

MARCO ANTONIO C. TEIXEIRA is a Professor in Public Administration at the São Paulo School of Business Administration, Getulio Vargas Foundation, and a founding member of its Center for Public Administration and Government. His work involves questions of participation, social accountability, relations between the executive and legislative branches of government, and the new accountability agencies in Brazil. He is a political scientist with a PhD from the Pontifical Catholic University, São Paulo (PUC-SP).

PETER M. WARD holds the C. B. Smith Sr. Centennial Chair in U.S.-Mexico Relations in the College of Liberal Arts and is a Professor in the Department of Sociology and in the Lyndon B. Johnson School of Public Affairs at the University of Texas at Austin. At the University of Texas he served as Director of the Mexican Center of the Teresa Lozano Long Institute of Latin American Studies (LLILAS; 1993–97 and 2001–5). He has served as Editor-in-Chief of the *Latin American Research Review*, and his publications include *Housing, the State, and the Poor: Policy and Practice in Three Latin American Cities* (with Alan G. Gilbert; Cambridge University Press, 1985), *Welfare Politics in Mexico: Papering Over the Cracks* (Allen and Unwin, 1986), and *Mexico City*, 2nd ed. (John Wiley, 1998) (all published in major Spanish editions), as well as *Colonias and Public Policy in Texas and Mexico: Urbanization by Stealth* (University of Texas Press, 1999). In 2000, the Mexican government awarded him the Ohtli Medal for his services in the advancement of understanding of Mexican culture and society. He received a PhD from the University of Liverpool in 1976.

ROBERT H. WILSON is a Mike Hogg Professor of Urban Policy and Associate Dean for Research of the Lyndon B. Johnson School of Public Affairs at the University of Texas at Austin. Among his publications are *Urban Segregation and Governance in the Americas* (Palgrave Macmillan, 2009), *Governance in the Americas: Decentralization, Democracy, and Subnational Government in Brazil, Mexico, and the USA* (University of Notre Dame Press, 2008), *Public Policy and Community: Activism and Governance in Texas* (University of Texas Press, 1997), *States and the Economy: Policymaking and Decentralization* (Praeger, 1993), and *The Political Economy of Brazil: Public Policies in an Era of Transition* (University of Texas Press, 1990). He served as a Visiting Professor at the Federal University of Pernambuco (Recife, Brazil); held the Visiting International Philips Professorship at the Getulio Vargas Foundation, São Paulo; and was the Fulbright/FLAD (Luso American Development Foundation) Chair in Knowledge Management Policies at the Advanced Technical Institute, Lisbon. He was inducted into the Brazilian National Order of the Southern Cross, rank of Commander. He holds a PhD in urban and regional planning from the University of Pennsylvania.

www.ingramcontent.com/pod-product-compliance
Lightning Source LLC
Chambersburg PA
CBHW030640270326
41929CB00007B/148

www.ingramcontent.com/pod-product-compliance
Lightning Source LLC
Chambersburg PA
CBHW030640270326
41929CB00007B/148